SITTING ON BAYONETS

America's Endless War on Terror and the Paths to Peace

A Brief Guide To
*What's Going On,
What's Going Wrong,
And What Could Go Much Better*

Keith Spicer

Copyright © 2011 Keith Spicer

ISBN-10: 1460994736
ISBN-13: 9781460994733

Extra copies of this book are available at www.amazon.com, www.createspace.com/3578770, www.sittingonbayonets.com

Also by Keith Spicer

A Samaritan State? External Aid in Canada's Foreign Policy, University of Toronto Press, 1966

Cher Péquiste...et néanmoins ami – propos pré-référendaires dans un esprit post-référendaire, Les Éditions La Presse, 1980.

Winging It, Doubleday, 1981

Think on Your Feet, Doubleday, 1986

Life Sentences – Memoirs of an Incorrigible Canadian, McClelland & Stewart, 2005

Paris Passions – Watching the French Being Brilliant and Bizarre, BookSurge, 2009

Three Little Girls in Paris, 2010 (short stories), 2009

Sitting on Bayonets

DEDICATION

For Madrigal, Grace and Anastasia – and all the other little girls who will make a more peaceful world...

You can do anything with bayonets except sit on them – attributed to Napoleon (also ascribed to Talleyrand, Clemenceau and Émile de Girardin).

No idea has ever been defeated by force — not by siege, not by bombardment, not by being flattened with tank treads and not by marine commandos. To defeat an idea, you have to offer a better idea, a more attractive and acceptable one - Amos Oz, *New York Times*, June 1, 2010, after the Israeli attack on the "Free Gaza" Flotilla, killing nine passengers.

Since wars begin in the minds of men, it is in the minds of men that the defences of peace must be constructed
- UNESCO Constitution.

CONTENTS

Preface .... *xv*
Acknowledgments .... *xxi*
Introduction .... *xxiii*

PART I – WHAT'S GOING ON 1

Chapter One / ISLAM 101 3
    One Faith, Many Voices 4
    Political Islam – Remembering Andalusia 6
    'Reformers' and Reactionaries 16
    Turkey: West's Bridge to Islam, or Islam's Bridgehead
        to Europe? 20
    What Makes a Terrorist? 23

Chapter Two / DESERT TSUNAMI – THE ARABS REBEL 31
    Playing Dominos in a Hurricane 32
    Tottering Tyrants 36
    Bewitched, Bothered and Bewildered 39
    Radical Islam Eclipsed? 41
    Scorecard: Be Careful What You Wish For 46

Chapter Three / DUMBING DOWN AMERICA 53
    Media: Is All News, Like Politics, Local? 55
    Schools: What the Kids Don't Know *Will* Hurt Them 79
    Churches: Onward Christian Soldiers! 86
    Entertainment I: Playing 'Nintendo' for Keeps 94
    Entertainment II: Scary Movies for Our Next War. 98
    Universities: The Egghead Wars 111
    Books: Reading More, or Less, on Tablet Toys? 115
    Congress: Its Own Little America 119
    Flying Low Over the Potomac 120
    The World? Where's That? 122
    No Place for Politics – Just Pettifoggery 126
    The World's Greatest Democracy ... Except for Quite
        a Few Others 129
    Money – the Mother's Milk of Politics 133
    Wall Street and the Washington Consensus 136
    Lobbies – Ain't It a Shame? 139
    Cosmopolitanism Doesn't Trickle Down 141

PART II – WHAT'S GOING WRONG 145
Chapter Four / SHOOT FIRST, THINK LATER (MAYBE) 147
    Running the World ... While Sleep-walking 147
    Oh, What a Lovely War! 152
    Love Me, Love My Gun 153
    Post-1945 Hubris Sets the Stage 162
    Iraq: 'Operation Enduring Occupation' 171
    Shock, Awe, and Mercenaries: the New American Way
        of War 173
    The Other Iraq War: "Infoganda" 181
    Boots versus Sandals: the Psychology of
        Asymmetrical War 187
    Drones, Phones and Internet: Asymmetrical Technology ... 190
    Why (Obviously) the Locals Always Win 193
    Debased COINage? 198
    Annoying the Patriots 200
Chapter Five / DRINKING THE SAUDI KOOL-AID 205
    Who's On First? 206
    Oil, Israel and Illusion 212
    Holding Hands in Crawford 214
    OPEC: Fill 'er Up, at Whatever Price We Want 224
    Uneasy Lies the Head that Wears a Crown 225
Chapter Six / EUROPE-AMERICA DISCONNECT 231
    Islam's Early European Rise and Fall 233
    Colonialism's Bitter Fruits 235
    Twin Failures of 'Integration' 238
    U.S. and Islam – Say Little, Think Less 245

PART III – WHAT COULD GO MUCH BETTER 249
Chapter Seven / INDISPENSABLE 'IMPOSSIBILITIES' 251
    Pass the Ammunition... Forever 251
    Clearing the Decks With Obama? 253
    1. Settle Israel-Palestine - 255
    2. Sort Out "AfPak" – Cockpit of Armageddon? 260
    3. Cure U.S. Oil Addiction 265
    4. Tame the Pentagon 269
    5. Avoid a New "Operation Enduring Occupation" ... 275
    6. Entice the Saudis to Join the World 279
    7. Integrate U.S. Muslims 284

Chapter Eight / MAYBE COMMON SENSE AS POLICY?..... 291
    Smarter-than-"Strong" Defense: Resist and Reconcile .. 292
    Education: It's All in the Mind, Heart... and Jobs 294
    Find Peace Through Culture, Not Technology................. 300
    Taking Care of Business: Open Markets, Micro-credit,
        Training.. 303
    Getting the Message: Media To Excite and Reconcile.... 306

Chapter Nine / FREE THE WOMEN, SAVE THE WORLD.... 313
    Open Season on Girls and Women 313
    Educate a Girl: Educate a Family, a Village, a Country...316
    Get a Life, for a Woman.. 321
    Diamonds Are Not a Girl's Best Friend............................. 326
    Burqa-free Radio 331

Chapter Ten / FIGHT CHEAPER AND SMARTER, OR
       FIGHT FOREVER 339
    Two Frightfully Sincere Men of Religion 339
    Einstein's Nightmare ... and Ours....................................... 341
    A Cheaper Date With Destiny 346
    Mission Unaffordable 349
    It's Still About the Economy, Stupid!................................. 352
    Talking With the Muslim World, Not At It 358
    Leading from Behind: (Muslim) Allies With Answers... 362
    Give Peace a Chance: Dilute the Testosterone.................. 370
    American Jihad: Resistance and Reconciliation............... 374
    Three Voices of Reason: restraint, engagement,
        liberation.. 380

Further Reading.. 389

Preface

Why this book? I wanted to explain today's "war-on-terror" world to myself. Like many, I was perplexed by unforeseen forces in the West's contest with jihadist Islam. The sudden 2011 wave of Arab uprisings, shaking both governments and political Islam, caught even experts off-guard. Before that explosion, politics and media cast still-longer shadows, but little light. Unless you bought handy slogans, nobody seemed to offer a coherent overview. Politicians chattered about personalities, alliances, betrayals, combat needs, regional checker-boards, and fig-leaf exits. Journalists, especially on television, counted bombs, corpses and corrupt contractors. Both sources conveyed impressions of wavering hope, lingering despair, and unstoppable violence. But context? History? Hope? Except from rare media commentators, we got – and still mostly get – the whats and wheres and whos, but very few whys and hows.

Why, for example, today's terrifying confrontation with fanatical jihadism? What to think of America's astonishing martial spirit, exploding defense budgets, and unending wars? Looking at where Islamic and American adversaries draw their ideas, I aimed to test how real, how deep, and how inevitable was Samuel P. Huntington's "clash of civilizations." In the end, I conclude that this formula may make seductive shorthand, but it's too divorced from the daily concerns and aspirations of ordinary people, Muslim or not. Beyond culture and religion, most human beings share common hopes: family, love, work, purpose and respect belong to no single faith or people.

The book's specific goals? First, I hoped to tie the various dimensions of today's global terrorist crisis into some meaningful narrative. Second, I wanted to show why and how in recent decades militarism has become an unchallengeable, bankrupting orthodoxy of America's public discourse. Today it virtually defines U.S. foreign policy. It leads Washington to prefer "strong" security allies over strong democrats, "stability" over civil liberties, alliances over justice. One would like to believe that 2011's failed Arab autocrats taught some lessons. But the jury will still be out for some time.

Recall America's confusion in January-February 2011 as pro-democracy crowds in Cairo's Tahrir Square challenged dictator Hosni Mubarak, America's all-too-known devil. America's freedom rhetoric at first sounded (as it too-often has) shaky – like freedom for a few unsavory friends. Happily, President Barack Obama soon found America's voice and its historic ideals. By adroitly retrieving America's honor, he defied Washington's traditionalists, cynics and agents of vested interests, both foreign and domestic. The deeper impact of the domino-like Arab rebellions of early 2011, possibly still spreading, will take years to fully assess. But it's clear that these uprisings have already helped reshape the contest between West and jihadists.

A third, predominant goal: I wanted to identify proven non-military means for defeating the jihadists, long term. Means, often from within Islam, that already build prosperity and peace in certain terror-threatened countries. In this, and without naivety, I wanted to argue in hard-nosed terms that national defense could only be "strong" if it were "smart." It could only defend America and the West by seeing past lobby-serving tactics to people-serving strategies. By winning minds, not pressing for more troops to win unwinnable guerrilla wars.

Hard-won (though still relatively modest) budget discipline in the spring of 2011 may be the start of a slight leveling-off of U.S. expenditure on trillion-dollar wars. Worries about China's rise will surely keep the U.S. military pot boiling. But in the end, controlling defense spending – still anathema to many super-patriots and lobbyists – may result from a greater national-defense danger: nation-paralyzing budget deficits. "The biggest threat to our national security," argued Admiral Michael Mullen, chairman of the Joint Chiefs of Staff on March 11, 2011, "is our national debt." Will the world witness a replay of the Reagan-Gorbachev era when one superpower, this time China, bankrupts the other (America) to win strategic dominance? Unthinkable? How many other unthinkable things have you witnessed in your lifetime? Since last year?

America is still a superpower, though it's starting to look more like tied-down Gulliver than cheerful Gargantua. As a Canadian – a kind of decaffeinated American – I'm writing about friends I like, respect, and admire. Their openness, decency, enterprise and passion for freedom inspire the world. But I regret America's culture of often cocksure, gun-slinging messianism. This stifles debate, turns off allies, and seems to stir up more trouble with Islam than it resolves. This is especially true when U.S. armies – on even the loftiest of pretexts – enter Muslim lands. Not surprisingly, such intrusions tend to look to locals like invasions and occupations.

We live in a world perhaps as dangerous as the Cold War, though in less controlled ways. Religious obscurantism and bigotry flirt with weapons of mass destruction. Just recall Pakistan's "Muslim A-bomb" in the hands of a state with a track record of secret proliferation – a state tottering toward Islamist fanaticism. This book argues that, to secure peace via military means, less is dramatically more. In the Arab Dawn of 2011, U.S. arms and armies changed nothing – the much-denigrated "Arab street" did. U.S. generals could only wheedle behind the scenes for "orderly transfers of power" as ordinary Arabs freed themselves. It was the Arab peoples, not the Americans, who initiated, and died for, the defense of "American ideals."

Writing this book during the year including these events may not produce "instant history." But with luck, it may give a blurry but reasonable view of a fast-changing world ... as observed while jogging on a treadmill. I believe one early conclusion may stand: the gradual eclipse of jihadism in key countries by democratic and economic progress. This is broadly the view of French jihad expert Gilles Kepel, now prophet of a post-Huntington era. Conceivably, over decades, the so-called "war on terror" may become a race between extremist madrassa schools and something like the Turkish *imam-hatep* schools, with their at least sixty percent secular curriculum. For those charged with national defense, such thinking should take us farther toward security than the next three generations of drones.

What, indeed, *is* "national security?" Any cursory reading of the facts – and I offer a few here – will tell you that more education, not more arms, is the surest long-term way to national security. It's largely about job-related education for the hundreds of millions of explosively frustrated young Muslim (and Third World) men now unequipped to find work, a home, or a bride and family. (If strategists can't understand that lethal danger, they should take a course in male physiology and psychology). Education matters even more for Muslim (and Third World) girls and women. As all studies show, women can make that world, and our whole world, more prosperous, stable and peaceful.

I believe that the U.S. – still for some time the "indispensable nation" – can move from self-defeating, hegemonic militarism to successful, world-rebuilding strategies. I believe that its best traditions can still help lead to a more secure and civilized world. America must robustly resist the horrors of radical Islam. But it can and must seek reconciliation with *mainstream* Islam. And this – no doubt confounding macho militarists – it must do partly by supporting massively the critical role of Muslim women as peace-builders.

Such a strategic, long-term effort is the only way to assure the "national defense" of the U.S. and other western countries. To echo the shibboleth of capitalist philanthropists, we can all do well by doing good. Banalities and bromides? Seemingly so. But perhaps ultimate realism lies in lucid idealism.

As this book goes to press, the world learns that U.S. forces finally caught up with the initiator and symbol of today's twisted, *terrorist* idealism, Osama bin Laden. Plainly, this doesn't mean that George W. Bush's so-called "war on terror" is over. The West will still wrestle indefinitely with the terrorist octopus, even as the monster loses its grip.

But combined with the pro-democratic Arab Spring, bin Laden's death marks an end and an opportunity. An end, one hopes, to reactive, post-9/11 reaching for guns. After Iraq and Afghanistan, it's clear that massed, modern armies in resentful Muslim lands do more harm than good. An opportunity?

If Washington finds the courage and adroitness to seize it, its leaders will urgently press for decisive diplomatic and economic solutions to festering, world-destabilizing Palestine and Kashmir.

But the longer-term opportunity for Washington and the West is to engage peacefully, respectfully and constructively with mainstream Islam. The goal: to help redevelop the Muslim world on values both West and Islam can share. There is much hope of succeeding. Extremists, as well as moderate Islamists, are manoeuvring to capture new democratic movements. But the brave Arab youth who faced despots' live bullets in early 2011, and who still drive liberation, didn't shout religious slogans. They didn't praise the born-rich nihilist who urged them to blow themselves up. And unlike bin Laden, they didn't glorify the afterlife. Overwhelmingly, rebellious youth just demanded decent lives here and now: freedom, dignity, work, families.

The West doesn't have answers for all of these desiderata. But it can help betrayed and battered Muslims defy oppressors. It can help them find their own answers.

K.S
May 3, 2011

Website: www.sittingonbayonets.com

Acknowledgments

Many people deserve thanks for their help.

Paddy Sherman, a man who skis serious mountains in his 80s, was my publisher when I was editor of Canada's daily *Ottawa Citizen*. He passed along his passionate interest in offering readers international news with perspective, and in plain English. He took valuable time off the slopes to critique my first drafts with his wide-ranging knowledge, common sense, and rigorous logic. His unerring radar caught obscurities and wobbly logic, but his friendship and support mattered as much.

Azhar Ali Khan, another colleague from that fine newspaper, was my guide on all things Islamic. A devout, courageous Muslim who has often stood up to extremists, Azhar and his equally wise and well-informed wife Nishat read my key sections on Islam, and made invaluable suggestions.

John Owen is Professor of International Journalism in London's City University, and Executive Producer for Programs for the Al Jazeera English Channel. He is Founding Chairman of Frontline Club Forum, and co-author of *International News Reporting: Frontlines and Deadlines*. He brought an unusually experienced eye to the book, notably to the media sections.

Two especially demanding readers read the entire early manuscript and offered many detailed suggestions. Blanca Turcott bravely subjected herself to three full readings – each time coming up with surprises, as well as frank and very helpful criticism. Her Spanish background gave her a welcome close understanding of Muslim Andalusia. Her deep media experience also served.

Vanessa Dylyn contributed a broad international culture, sound judgment and a former English teacher's demand for clarity. She spotted fuzzy reasoning, contradictions and repetitions enough to help a quick first draft become a tolerable second and third one. Her special feel for women in business made the final section much stronger.

Alan King, a richly talented and cultured friend, designed the stunning cover. At a glance, it tells the book's whole story: the limits of guns in foreign policy, and the limitless hopes of girls and women.

Kathleen Mackey, my technical specialist, came cleverly into play at the production phase. With diligence and good humor, she formatted the manuscript for publication.

Warmest gratitude of all goes to my three accomplished offspring for their steadfast support and understanding – any author's most precious asset. I thank Nick, a respected international journalist, for his perceptive reading of passages on the U.S. media; Geneviève, a public-spirited Jill-of-all-media, for her professional advice on girls' literacy; and Dag, polymathic senior curator of a major science-and-technology museum, for his painstaking and astute review of the entire manuscript. Their help made a huge difference.

Respecting the classic formula, I take sole responsibility for all mistakes and interpretations.

Introduction

Who's winning the "war on terror?" Ponder that next time you're surrendering shoes, belt, coins, liquids, dignity, sang-froid and sense of humor in the airport 'security' line. Osama bin Laden's followers are ruining your trip, wherever you're going. And they intend to spoil all your trips, forever. The only place they want you to fly to is Hell – while they plan to land in Heaven to find 72 voluptuous, doe-eyed virgins. They calculate that their pure seventh-century beliefs, turbocharged by 21st-century technology, can capture the world's richest (though no longer all-powerful) Atlantic nations. "Soft power" – the power of compelling ideas, sensibly implemented – is now real power. In the end, the "war on terror" is a contest of ideas for imposing power.

This book argues that over the past two generations, the United States has fallen in love with militarism. Not necessarily with war – but it has embraced a cult of the military, an ethos claiming armed force as the main, or even only, solution to major international conflicts. America has lost sight of the power of soft power – the art and science of winning friends by attraction, co-option, manifest respect, goodwill, and especially practical support for local ideas.

Unfortunately, a virtually unassailable political-military consensus scorns the adjective "soft" as conveying weakness. Pentagon, Congress – even America's media, schools, churches, intellectuals and entertainment industry – have helped entrench today's militarist consensus. Mainstream America, following its thought leaders, now believes this as gospel: U.S. security depends almost exclusively on armed strength. This dogma demands supporting, even glorifying, the "military-industrial complex." That warning phrase, of course, came from old-soldier President Dwight D. Eisenhower in his January 17, 1961 farewell speech.

The current Barack Obama administration – with eager support from Secretary of State Hillary Clinton – is trying to diversify projection of U.S. power to include "smart-power" vehicles.

These include cultural exchanges and especially women's economic, social and political rights. But it's an uphill battle. — the "strong defense" old-guard tends to see such things as frills.

By decrying the "military-industrial complex," Eisenhower cautioned against a mentality and system that not only *responded* to wars. They sometimes *caused* them – or at least threatened them by spurring arms races. Political propaganda has routinely invented or magnified foreign threats. John K. Kennedy's fictitious "missile gap" with Moscow won him the White House. Eisenhower himself cited the "domino effect" in 1954 to warn that Indochinese states might succumb to communist rule like "falling dominos."

New Adversary, Old Militarism

Today, the U.S. and the entire Western world face a lethal, insidious menace: jihadist or "Holy War" Islam. This breaks the mold of Cold War thinking, of blocs, massed armies and intercontinental thermonuclear missiles. The jihadists, fervent fundamentalists of Islam, can hide anywhere – in our cities, our trains, on our bridges, and especially on our airplanes. Their weapons may lurk in a bottle of lotion or a few grams of plastic explosive. Maybe tomorrow in a suitcase-carried A-bomb.

Against the jihadists – likely to be with us for at least the next generation – big weapons systems and the highest of high-tech are often futile. For as Osama bin Laden and his cohorts have warned, jihadists' main battlefield is the battlefield of the mind. Here, they're winning murderous converts the old-fashioned way: one at a time. And to do so – the ultimate irony – they've mastered symbolism, 'hot' words, imagery, simplicity and mass psychology in ways that put Madison Avenue to shame.

The U.S. – obsessed with winning on the *military* battlefield – has almost ceded victory on the battlefield of Muslim minds. Domestic American political agendas, electoral cycles, non-Muslim geopolitical concerns, engrossing cultural trends, even trivial sex or embezzlement distractions, can help explain this. They cannot excuse it. For keeping the West on a militarist treadmill of always more troops, always more weapons, only condemns us to permanent war. If you like that phrase, you will love a convincing new book, likely the first of many, that explains why and how endless war has begun: Andrew J. Bacevich's *Washington Rules*. [1]

How to understand the West-jihadist contest? You can look at it through two prisms, one studying military methods; the other motivations. The first prism shows sophisticated U.S. military units fighting resourceful Islamic guerrillas – in an "asymmetric," likely long, unwinnable war. The other prism reveals two warring, 'divinely-guided' ideologies: "Islamism" or political Islam, promoting an activist, world-embracing community of Muslim believers; and U.S. idealism, promoting liberty, democracy, and free enterprise – all wrapped up as the American Way of Life.

First, battlefield methods. Against religious-nationalist convictions, can a few more brigades or drones help? Only up to a point. West-despising jihadists are fighting with ideas of triumph backed by guns; the U.S. is fighting with guns now increasingly aimed at escaping a morass. Therein lies the West's likely battlefield defeat in Afghanistan. The jihadists are fighting a war of ground-level gains to control populations; the U.S., though trying to "pacify" Afghan towns and roads, is increasingly fighting a sky war of drones and rockets that alienate "collaterally-damaged" civilians. The more Americans succeed, the more they fail. Their very presence in Iraq and Afghanistan today recruits more extremist enemies for the West, more jihadis, than it kills. To local Muslims, Americans' invasions mainly look like... well, invasions.

This book is not a gratuitous attack on America. And it's certainly not a slur on the American people – a nation which, on balance, does the world infinitely more good than harm. It condemns only the obsessive militarist mentality that drives U.S. politicians to contestable, prolonged wars in faraway Muslim lands. Wars leading them to the illusion that just a few more

---

[1] Andrew J. Bacevich, *Washington Rules: America's Path to Permanent War* (American Empire Project), Metropolitan Books, New York, 2010.

troops, just a few more clever new weapons, will finally win Muslim hearts and minds.

Such thinking has made America – and by extension the West – a Great Satan to many Muslims. Just as extremist actions and words from some Muslims have made Islam a nightmare to many Americans and Europeans. In this, do we indeed risk realizing Samuel P. Huntington's *Clash of Civilizations*? Ironically, the open-ended escalation of U.S. militaristic reasoning and actions deeply threatens American security. Not just by creating more enemies and alienating allies. But by weakening America's economy – thus power to defend itself.

Arms Versus Ideas

You can't win a war of ideas without talking with people — both innocent victims and less-than-innocent enemies. Fleeting (and so far fruitless) efforts to rally some "moderate" Afghan Taliban are a possible start. In any event, guns can't kill ideas. They can only sometimes serve tactical goals: killing a few bad guys, or briefly strengthening a bargaining hand. Strategic victory demands eclipsing seductive but dangerous ideas with even more compelling ones. It demands displacing ideas of despair with ideas of hope.

Much of this hope already arises from the success of 'moderate' or 'mature' Muslim nations such as Turkey, Indonesia and Malaysia. It also gained huge momentum from the early 2011 Arab uprisings: for dignity, democracy and freedom. For it to flower and deepen, hope for previously abused peoples must become concrete in the day-to-day lives of millions – in modern education, gainful employment and, for women and girls, not just education but respect and equal opportunity.

In immediate years, of course, the West must meet guerrilla attacks by armed force. Advancing ideas first demands staying alive. But without well-explained ideas about what constitutes civilization, peace, security and happiness, the armed fight has little meaning. And without a parallel set of non-military tools to start building reconciliation, there will never be a lasting peace.

Instead of dealing with *ideas of practical benefit* to peoples, West and Islam are interacting as competing *ideologies* – as "closed" systems of thought. These systems don't seek to engage others' thinking. They seek only to deny it and, if possible, crush it. Islam began as a messianic, conquering ideology. So did Christianity. Centuries of evolution have tamed Christianity's aggressive flamboyance: the hymn *Onward Christian Soldiers* is not as toe-tapping a marching song now as it was in some of our childhood Sunday-schools.

Today's political Islam is no one-off accident. It has many sources. Gilles Kepel argues that, in our time, religion-rooted politics has prospered in all three Abrahamic faiths: Judaism, Christianity and Islam. Reason: the end of the industrial age gradually led religious rationales and rhetoric to replace socio-economic ones – such as Marxism. [2]

American Muslims – whatever their grievances in America and beyond – are usually thankful to America for giving them a new chance at happiness. But they also instinctively reproach America for foreign policy priorities (mainly Israel-Palestine, then Iraq and Afghanistan) that they see as unjust or demeaning for Muslim brothers and sisters abroad. This affinity with fellow Muslims is not dissimilar to American Jews' protectiveness toward Israel. After 9/11, the 2010 Ground Zero mosque episode, and several recent terror incidents on U.S. soil, American Muslims worry about their place. They should take hope in this: that while America began as a Protestant country, gradually it came to accept distrusted Jews and Catholics. A narrow culture slowly became a broader one. With time, custom and intermarriage, America will also consider Islam an American religion.

As for Islam's "fanaticism" or "militancy," most Muslims would insist that only an extreme few live for a worldwide

---

[2] Gilles Kepel, "Beyond the clash of civilizations," *International Herald Tribune*, March 12, 2011. See also, among Kepel's many authoritative books on Islam and the Arab world: *Jihad – The Trail of Political Islam* (2002) and *The War for Muslim Minds: Islam and the West* (2004), both published by Belknap Press of Harvard University Press, Cambridge, Mass.

umma or community of Muslims. Ordinary Muslims everywhere have lives to lead, families to raise, and, with luck, some kind of living to pursue. They would argue that today's sudden emergence of a highly self-aware (though often backward) international Islam derives from Western abuses: colonialism, U.S.-backed or -tolerated Arab dictatorships, America's wars in Iraq and Afghanistan, Operation Desert Storm's stationing of U.S. troops in "Holy-Cities" Saudi Arabia in 1990-91 – and above all, the bleeding sore of Palestinians' "stolen" land and Israeli oppression. Many devout Muslims assail Western lifestyle "impositions:" pornography, gambling, miniskirts and the fermented grape.

These rationales offer no excuse for blatant, homegrown injustices in many Muslim countries. Low investment in education, religious bigotry, continued censorship, torture and state-commanded murder: these have been choices of too many of today's Muslim-culture governments. At least before 2011. As for the subordination, indeed often outright persecution, of women – including the horror of "honor killings" – this certainly did not come from the West. Local imams in many Muslim nations tolerate, even sometimes incite, such crimes. They disgrace Islam.

But the West should look beyond its own self-justifying narrations. It should try honestly to understand the general Muslim narrative. There may be as much truth in it as in the West's trumpeting that it invariably promotes freedom and democracy. The French helped cancel Algeria's 1991 free-election victory of the Islamic Salvation Front (FIS). Israel, with U.S. approval, in effect rendered inoperative the 2006 free-vote victory of Hamas (a movement, by the way, Israel helped create to sabotage the Palestine Liberation Organization). Today the West backs an array of Muslim dictators from the Saudi, Kuwaiti and Emirates' royal families to – well, check the news to see which autocrat today has followed Tunisia's Ben Ali and Egypt's Hosni Mubarak into oblivion. Only the truly naïve forget President Franklin D. Roosevelt's never-denied, refreshing admission about Nicaraguan dictator Anastasio Somoza: "He may be an S.O.B., but he's *our* S.O.B." The West still holds its nose a lot. It still legitimizes plenty of bad apples with favors, fawning and funding.

Today's American messianism, heavily drawing on Christianity, reflects America's exceptionalist, "divinely-inspired" view of itself as the great Shining City on the Hill. In its domestic culture, America nourishes a passionate sense of its own superiority – moral, economic, political, cultural – and military. Drawing on Founding Fathers' dreams, President Woodrow Wilson put forward his scattershot "Fourteen Points" of 1918. These broadly defined the world in America's image, while tidying up some rather large 'details' of the Versailles Peace Conference. Wilson's vision (much of it nuts-and-bolts war aims) clearly implied American superiority, and an American mission to save the world – indeed to make the world "safe for democracy." Every U.S. president since, including hard-nosed Republicans Richard Nixon and Ronald Reagan, right up to Barack Obama, has echoed "Wilsonian idealism." It has become the bedrock of U.S. policy. And of America's triumphant rhetoric.

'Weapons of Mass Construction'

Now comes today's unforeseen danger. A new and lethal change has occurred since 1945: the explosion of America's cult of the military. Before 1939, Washington starved its army. After 1945, it fattened it even while officially disarming. Defense budgets have soared ever since the Soviet spy scares of 1946–47. The marriage of Wilson's ideological certainty to the hubris of all-surpassing military power has proven a guarantee of almost permanent war – and even, in brief peacetime intervals, of a wartime mentality. American militarism is now central to the American identity. It inspires and defines American foreign policy. It engages not only President Eisenhower's "military-industrial complex," but the whole "lock-and-load," two-party American establishment.

It's no exaggeration to say that, mentally, the U.S. establishment – and by ricochet, media and people – have felt under threat for over half a century. The Cold War, with its threat of nuclear annihilation, amply justified this fear a generation ago. But except for a few years of "peace-dividend" savings after the 1989 end of the Cold War, the Pentagon has still won nearly unceasing budget increases. Now the U.S. defense budget – at $718.79-billion in 2011 – may still be larger than the combined military budgets of the rest of the world.[3]

Far from apologizing for this orgy of military spending, the American political, industrial and even media establishments glorify it. Again, it's the ever-revered "national defense consensus." Curiously, a few rabidly nationalistic Tea Party deficit-cutters would include defense among budget items to trim. But they are at odds with their – dare-one-say? – tax-and-spend (on defense) fellow Republicans.

This marriage of "Wilsonian" idealism and escalating militarism makes the America-vs.-Islam ideological contest even more volatile. Since the trauma of 9/11, a frightened 'always-under-attack' America has faced a Muslim world *also* convinced it is 'always under attack.' Muslims point to Afghanistan, Iraq and, with Muslim holy sites adding mythic force (Jerusalem, Hebron), Palestine. Mutual paranoia: a classic precondition of war. And for creating 'historic' or 'perpetual' enemies.

In an ideal, peace-seeking world, lucid protagonists would try to build understandings. But so much of today's two-way misunderstanding is rooted deeply in each side's culture, education system, and religious history. Can common sense and common values overcome common fears? If not, and unless some miraculous peacemaking (on the order of the end of the Cold War) happens, intensifying distrust between Muslims and Americans will probably lead to catastrophe.

In time, there will be more than Pakistan's "Muslim A-bomb." North Korea, Iran, Myanmar. Might even some Pakistani circles linked to now-released scientist-proliferator Abdul Qadeer

---

3 Bruce Berkowitz, *The New Face of War*, 2007, p.4. China's average yearly defense increases of 17 percent make this calculation imprecise, but still plausible.

Khan leak bomb materials to well-paying terrorists? Or might terrorists simply steal them – as they are known to be trying to do? Might existing Pakistani safeguards also disappear in a coup d'état? Pakistan Army generals angrily reject this possibility. But is a coup in this coup-prone land really inconceivable? Coup-leader General Muhammad Zia-ul-Haq took power in 1977, and a year later imposed Islamic law. Pakistan, already fearful of dropping the death penalty for blasphemy, seems to be sliding toward a highly intolerant Islam. In coming years, if we cannot avoid a full-scale tilt of Pakistan to jihadist ideology, we risk reflecting on the world's fate under a mushroom cloud in London, New York or Washington.

The West needs to stop brooding exclusively about *military* fighting. There are times and places for fighting with arms, and the West must deal unflinchingly with today's real and unavoidable threats. But it should do so with no illusion that it is "winning" the so-called "war on terror." It is only, with luck, coping – and sometimes only fleetingly – with lethal immediate threats. Again, to deal *long term* with the Muslim world, the West needs to fight with *ideas in action* – like real jobs for unemployed youth and widespread women's education. It needs to add to military necessities the intellectual and emotional necessities: a global strategy for winning the legendary "hearts and minds." Even Al-Qaeda recognizes this as its "second battlefield." Indeed the *real* one. General David Petraeus recognized this in August 2010, but adding this variant: "It's not about *us* winning hearts and minds, it's about the Afghan government winning hearts and minds." [4]

Here, in essence, is what we should shout and exemplify: While the jihadists seek weapons of mass destruction, we should fling back that we are fighting with 'weapons of mass construction:' freedom, democracy, and respect for the individual. The West has a surpassing story to tell. But we have only half-mouthed the words, and only too-rarely implemented their reality. Now self-freeing Arabs and other people chant the West's principles. Recall Obama's initial caution about

---

[4] Gen. David Petraeus on *Meet the Press*, posted on *Real Clear Politics*, August 15, 2010.

undermining Mubarak. Against many in his own establishment, he pulled America back from *Realpolitik* to its true path, to its own values. He saw that what could bring down autocracy in Tahrir Square was not military at all. It was youth's cry for America's and the West's values.

Confront, But Reconcile...Especially With Muslim Women

What should be the core of a strategy to counter an aggrieved and militant Islam? A two-track policy: short-term and long-term. The short term should consist – as it does – of keeping ruthless pressure on Al-Qaeda and Taliban leaders. We should so so without bleeding Western lives and treasure combating lower-level Taliban on an unwinnable field. Weapons? We should use any acceptable means short of massive numbers of ground troops in Muslim lands – troops who plainly aggravate the West's problems. Drones, special forces and intrusive counter-intelligence can and do threaten terrorist leaders' lives. We need to use much expanded cyberwar to destroy enemy communications, and far smarter propaganda to disorient and embarrass jihadist bosses. We need to get serious about banking controls and coordinating anti-terrorist information. We need to pressure Saudi and Gulf-Arab terrorism financiers to shrink Islamic leaders' livelihoods. A devilishly difficult Afghan political settlement is critical. Dangerous, unpredictable Pakistan must be part of this.

Long term? The West's key strategy with the Muslim world must be to replace *perceived confrontation* with *manifest and genuine reconciliation*. America being America, this could only work if presented as a new and more effective "defense" strategy. Congressional ideologues and other beneficiaries of permanent war will always fight anything smacking of "peace" or "reconciliation." But with plunging budget deficits and blatantly failed military missions, it should be possible to depict these people as hopelessly out-of-touch and spendthrift. Possible even to 'out-defense' them with non-military tools that demonstrably support U.S. security.

As this book's later chapters suggest, a new strategy of reconciliation would play two cards. First, a policy of listening to, and supporting, successful Muslim experiences in economic, social and political development – many of them remarkably original and effective. Second, a deep and sustained investment in girls and women. These create an irreplaceable multiplier effect for economic, social and political reform.

Women a key to stability and enlightenment? Let's "harp on it" again. For it's not some 'politically correct' slogan. It's now common wisdom among all serious economists and peacebuilders, starting with the United Nations and its uniquely experienced Specialized Agencies. All recognize that Third World peace, democracy and prosperity rely on mobilizing women. Intelligent, long-term "defense" strategies must tap into this reality.

Women's rights, education and opportunities for free enterprise are also at the heart of any long-term Muslim renaissance – and reconciliation with the West. Do such goals merely flow from the West's 'insulting' paternalism? Are they alien and offensive to Muslim culture? Certainly they were not in the Salafi-jihadists' seventh-century Mecca: Khadija, the Prophet Muhammad's first and favorite wife, was a literate, highly successful businesswoman. She supported the Prophet morally and tangibly – allowing him to start from his Cave of Hira and listen, over twenty-three years, to the Angel Gabriel as he dictated to him the Holy Koran.

To come to terms with a more positive Islam, we need unblinkingly to appreciate how howling injustice, corruption and land-stealing occupation have turned Muslims against the West. And how, by gorging on oil, we commit the numbing stupidity of enriching the paymasters of terror. While curing injustices and our addiction to oil, we need to shoot less, and think harder about how the world could be with arms and ideas in saner balance. We need to marshal the power of *universal* ideas that West, Muslims and all communities can comfortably share.

These are the realities – and realistic dreams – that could break America's disastrous militaristic impasse. The drums of war beat ceaselessly in Washington. But there is another, more astute way for America to deal with its fear of Islam: enlightened engagement with Muslims. This is not only more consistent with America's deeper values. It is not only far more affordable than flying massed armies to distant lands. It is – maybe one day even for political hawks? – a far more effective "national defense."

Not to mention more comfortable than sitting on Napoleon's bayonets. America needs a gentler seat to contemplate its softer, wiser options.

PART I – WHAT'S GOING ON

Muhammad was not an apparent failure. He was a dazzling success, politically as well as spiritually, and Islam went from strength to strength to strength
- Karen Armstrong, former Catholic nun, author of *A History of God* and other books of comparative religion.

Islam is the only civilization which has put the survival of the West in doubt.... Statesmen can constructively alter reality only if they recognize and understand it - Samuel P. Huntingdon in *The Clash of Civilizations*.

Chapter One/

ISLAM 101

Islam? A faith and a culture. But it has no single, central institution, or even credo, recognized by all 1.6-billion Muslims worldwide. These believers share the idea of Islam as submission to God. They share five pillars of faith: professing one God, with Muhammad as His final Prophet (after Noah, Moses, Abraham and Jesus); five daily prayers; alms-giving; fasting – obligatory (unless when sick or traveling) during the yearly Ramadan month of nearness to God; and a once-in-a-lifetime pilgrimage to Mecca. Finally, they share access to a body of writings including the Holy Koran, its different formal and informal interpretations, learned commentaries, and biographies. Sects, schools of thought, and recognized or self-declared authorities often disagree on admissible details.

In all that, Islam shares some of the complexities, as well as basic values, of other religions. Certainly, that's the case of its fellow Abraham-rooted faiths of Judaism and Christianity – of which Islam sees itself as a perfected development. Key commonalities: a merciful God, a definitive Holy Scripture, Judgment Day, justice, kindness, respect for life and parents, morality in thought and action. But no Pope, no Archbishop of Canterbury, no Patriarch of Moscow, no Chief Rabbi of Israel unites all Muslims. As a Muslim, you're largely on our own. First, with the Koran. Then, for many believers, with a trusted imam, mullah or famous authority. Only minority Shia Islam translates this priest-like custom into a divinely-inspired hierarchy.

Restating Islam's broadly agreed core beliefs may be as close as we can get to its "unity." But in our all-too-real world, what about its disunity?

One Faith, Many Voices

As with those other two religions born in the dust and sands of the Middle East, you can identify scores of 'Islams.' In a few unstable societies (such as Pakistan) some of them are literally at war with each other. Those who believe too hastily in a "clash of civilizations" should remember this: it's not Christians or Jews who are blowing up mosques in countries such as Pakistan and Iraq. It's other Muslims. Happily, that's an extreme situation, not typical of Islam worldwide. But it underlines that Islam, whatever its grievances with non-Muslim "infidels," still has much to do to put its own many-chambered house in order.

A basic divide among Muslims is mystical versus legalistic. For example, mystical (and ascetic) Sufism includes the famous Turkish "Whirling Dervishes." Some Muslims consider Sufism as pre-Islamic, others as non-Islamic. In contrast to Sufism stands, for example, the strict "desert Islam" of Wahhabism, Saudi Arabia's ultra-strict rules-based version of Islam. The 'Salafi' current that Wahabbism (or "Unitarianism") belongs to insists on codes imagined to describe the Islamic way of life of the Prophet's own time and entourage. Dangerously for the West – indeed the world – is Saudi Arabia's use of its massive oil wealth to fund mosques and schools (*madrassas*) to spread Wahhabi/Salafi distrust (bordering on hate) of the West. More on that later.

A key divide pits "mainstream" Sunni Islam against Shiite Islam – the latter a minority strain, though (as Iran and parts of Iraq show) a passionate one. The well-known Sunni-Shiite divide resulted from an eighth-century political argument between heirs of Muhammad. Sunni ("tradition-following") Muslims believed that the Prophet's personal companions should elect his successor as Muslim leader. A dissident Shia group wanted Muhammad's cousin and son-in-law Ali to succeed him. For over a thousand years, this split has often pitted these 'separated brethren' (as Christian ecumenists would call them) against each other. Often bloodily.

If you enjoy splitting theological hairs, you might look into the many varieties of both Sunni and Shia Islam. To discourage you, let's just mention some of the main Shia strains: 'Twelvers' (the 85 percent of Shias who believe in twelve historic Imams and the return of the *Mahdi* as twelfth); Ismailis (divine revelation ending with Muhammad); and Alawites (four groups, mainly in Syria). To westerners, these distinctions don't matter much – but they do hugely to many sectarian believers. Even the ecstatic, drumming-and-dancing Sufis split into at least three groups whose names you don't need to memorize.

The above are mainly mental distinctions. But these all draw shape and practice from countless differences of history, geography, economics, climate, personalities, and local culture worldwide. Some Muslims may hope to impose a specific set of practices on their society. But they can't easily escape their environments. Such adaptation includes the architecture of mosques: Switzerland now bans new minarets, French mayors resist new mosques. Clothing too is a point of conflict: French and Belgian parliaments ban face-covering "burqas." First-generation Muslim immigrants to western societies often tend to dress in their homeland's traditional garb. But their daughters, more often than not, reject this cover-all approach. A very few daughters decide to "rediscover" Islam and flaunt, as a statement, what they imagine is an "Islamic" head-to-toe black robe. But for most Muslim youth, accommodation with local custom – including dating – draws them into the new country's mainstream.

The great majority of Muslims make lifestyle changes to fit into western societies. Looking out at the world through the Saudi-style eye-slit *niqab* appeals to barely a tiny minority – many of whom, "more Muslim than Muhammad" – seem to be recent Western converts married to insecure and domineering traditional men. A famous 2010 case in France's city of Nantes found one enterprising Algerian-born Muslim man drawing social benefits for four fully-covered European-background French "wives" and their 12 children. This led to the government's ban on all such face-covering in public – a ban now echoed in Belgium and other European countries.

Both Africa and Asia largely escape from Wahhabi face-covering. Almost everywhere, local traditions prove stronger than such imagined Islamic practices as the *niqab* or *burqa*. The strongest example of a moderate local culture defeating what Canadian Muslim "refusenik" Irshad Manji (like some other anti-Wahhabi critics) calls "desert Islam" is probably the world's largest Muslim nation: Indonesia. That nation's police pursue the small terrorist cells that blew up Bali night-clubs. Violence-inciting Indonesian *fatwas* are rare, and often punished. And there's a visible Indonesian difference from female "cover-up" countries: the overwhelming majority of Indonesian women dress for local weather and fairly free-wheeling historical custom. Miss Indonesia Universe 2006 publicly wore a bikini. She didn't win the beauty contest, but did, alas, win death threats.

All the above underlines the complexity of Islam. However, for our purpose – assessing the Islamic challenge to the West – the key distinction separates religious and political Islam. Even to cite such a distinction risks offending many Muslim believers. They argue that Islam should govern every aspect of life. But a religion that purports to guide all aspects of living is hardly revolutionary. And not necessarily dangerous. Nearly all religions make some all-embracing claim. For religion, by definition, tries to make sense of life and the world to perplexed, often frightened, human beings. It may mislead or dupe. But it can also console, give hope, and at least give the illusion of explaining the unexplainable.

Political Islam – Remembering Andalusia

Political Islam is another kettle of *cous-cous* (or curry). It rests on anger and resentment at a world that seems to assault cherished Muslim beliefs and lifestyles – both from *outside* Muslim lands and *within* them. The militant version of political Islam, the sort the West fears, seeks more than heavenly reward. It seeks earthly power – how aggressively, and with what exact intentions, remains the classic "Muslim Brotherhood" question. Founded in 1928 by Egyptian schoolteacher Hassan al-Banna, and present in all Arab and most Muslim countries, the Brotherhood is impressively organized. Do the Brothers, with their many national and ideological variations, really plan to rule all life in society? This basic idea derives from a broad Muslim belief that "mosque and state" are ethically one. At least as an ideal, it insists that religion not only invade, but rule, all life. Hence, Muslim Sharia law is both a civil and criminal guide.

Today's Brotherhood is opposed to violence, except in "extreme" cases. Fanaticized Brothers assassinated President Anwar Sadat in 1981... years after the mainstream Brotherhood had publicly renounced violence. Banned in Egypt until 2011 (and in some other nations), the Brotherhood has spun off extreme groups that preach and practice violence. Osama bin Laden started as a fan of Brotherhood fantasies of a restored Muslim empire. But later, he denounced the group as hopelessly off-course for its non-violence and willingness to face elections.

The Brotherhood professes some noble goals: fighting poverty and corruption, and accepting democracy consistent with Islamic law. It runs commendable social programs, including clinics and family-counseling services. But believing the Koran preaches a perfect way of life, it ideally hopes to see all Islamic governments united in a worldwide Caliphate "from Andalusia to Indonesia." Its everyday cultural stance – for example, opposing daring dress and dancing – would not shock old-school Presbyterians. But the final part of the Brotherhood's credo, considered rather tame by the spun-off groups, is fair warning in any contest of arms or ideas: "God is our purpose, the Prophet our leader, the Qur'an our constitution, Jihad our way, and dying for God's cause our supreme objective."

Dying to defend a homeland, or dying to conquer infidels? For most Muslims, it's more likely the former. But whatever its motivation, the Brotherhood is not the World Federalists making a dreamy pitch for all nations to share a loose, light-handed supra-government. Even less is it a plea for an economy-rooted Muslim version of the European Union. It's the passionate imagining of a spiritual community, ideally with political impact.[5]

Most powerfully, political Islam resents humiliation from outside the *umma*, or worldwide Muslim community. A deep nostalgia: the historic fall of Muslim empires. First, the final defeat of Muslim Spain (*al-Andalus*) in 1492. British and Dutch imperialism in Asia later tamed or crushed Muslim rule, even while propping up "native" figure-head leaders. Nineteenth-century French colonialism in North Africa (Algeria, Tunisia, Morocco) followed suit. In the twentieth century, the infamous 1916 Anglo-French Sykes-Picot agreement carved up the Ottoman Empire's western Asia into zones of influence for Britain, France and Russia. In an *Al Jazeera* broadcast of Oct. 7, 2001, Osama bin Laden referred to the 'outrage' of Sykes-Picot: "What America is tasting now [in the Sept. 11, 2001 attacks] is something insignificant compared to what we have tasted for scores of years. Our nation [the Islamic world] has been tasting this humiliation and this degradation for more than 80 years." [Translation: Associated Press].

The fall of the seven-hundred-year Muslim empire in Andalusia uniquely grates. The West's Dark Ages were Islam's 500-year Golden Age. Translating into Arabic Greek and Roman Antiquity's highest philosophical and scientific texts, mid-8th to mid-13h-century Islam had opened Europe's Renaissance. It also added many of its own contributions, notably in chemistry, geography and meteorology. In mathematics: algebra, algorithms, spherical trigonometry, decimals and, of course, Arabic

---

5 Two authoritative new books on the Brotherhood appeared in 2010: Lorenzo Vidino's rather alarmist *The New Muslim Brotherhood in the West*, Columbia University Press, 326 pp; and Alison Pargeter's more serene *The Muslim Brotherhood: The Burden of Tradition*, Saqi, 248 pp. As an *Economist* joint review suggested, the question about the Brotherhood is basically: "Wolves or sheep?"

numerals. Ibn Sina (Avicenna) helped found modern medicine. Ibn Rushd (Averroes) developed Plato's and Aristotle's thought. In every field of the arts, literature, science, technology, and even agriculture, Muslims fed and led Western thinking for centuries. In 976, the main library of Córdoba alone allegedly employed 500 librarians – some claim it may have held more books than the rest of Europe. Perhaps a little wishful thinking has massaged the numbers. But the basic point is true: While many Europeans were running around in animal-skins, a Muslim elite in Spain – and in Baghdad – was inventing the modern world, their Arabic works translated into several languages, including Latin and Hebrew.

In that same broadcast, bin Laden bemoaned a loss tied to the sixty-year humiliation of Muslims in today's Palestine: "Let the whole world know that we shall never accept that the tragedy of Andalusia would be repeated in Palestine. We cannot accept that Palestine will become Jewish... Neither America nor the people who live in it will dream of security before we live it in Palestine, and not before all the infidel armies leave the land of Muhammad." [The latter referred to bin Laden's original complaint: the 1990-91 stationing of U.S. troops in Saudi Arabia – land of Holy Mecca and Medina – to liberate Iraqi-occupied Kuwait].

But humiliation – thus anger – comes also from *within* Islam. With rare exceptions (Turkey, Indonesia, Malaysia, Bangladesh), nearly all Muslim-majority countries suffer vile dictatorships or dysfunctional states. Muslims in mainly Hindu India may face discrimination, but they benefit amply from the country's democracy. In too many Muslim-majority countries, corruption is rampant, free speech denied, torture common, poverty endemic, education stunted. But beware: do these evils emerge from Islam, or from today's Arab or African local cultures? The question is tricky. For Islam began in Arab lands, its Holy Places are still there, and Arabic remains the Holy Koran's sacred language. Moreover, by far the most populous Muslim countries are not Arab: Indonesia, India (partly Muslim), Pakistan, Iran, Turkey.

Largely because of the Israel-Palestine struggle, most Western, especially U.S., commentaries on 'Islam' are colored by political and cultural affinities with Israel. Far fewer have ties to the worldwide Muslim community. This phenomenon is understandably true of many writers close to Israel. Eminent scholar Bernard Lewis writes on the Middle East and Islam. He cites both religion and culture as factors of "Middle Eastern" decline. In his classic September 1990 essay "The Roots of Muslim Rage" in *The Atlantic* magazine, he vividly sums up how Muslim resentment rose in tandem with Europe's (and now America's) rise to supremacy:

"The Muslim has suffered successive stages of defeat. The first was his loss of domination in the world, to the advancing power of Russia and the West. The second was the undermining of his authority in his own country, through an invasion of foreign ideas and laws and ways of life and sometimes even foreign rulers or settlers, and the enfranchisement of native non-Muslim elements. The third – the last straw – was the challenge to his mastery in his own house, from emancipated women and rebellious children. It was too much to endure, and the outbreak of rage against these alien, infidel, and incomprehensible forces that had subverted his dominance, disrupted his society, and finally violated the sanctuary of his home was inevitable."[6]

With today's hindsight, this analysis seems incomplete, even rather condescending. But it offers a point of departure, a framework, to think further about Muslim unhappiness. A major Lewis omission is the 'self-inflicted' Muslim wound of local autocracy. The 2011 Arab uprisings made it clear that massive assaults on citizens' dignity by their own Muslim rulers was a core cause of felt "defeat."

Fewer scholars study broadly successful Muslim democracies such as Turkey, Indonesia, Bangladesh, and partly Muslim India. Deeper 'Muslim' sources of embarrassment – though usually stifled publicly – are precisely the areas where the first five United Nations *Arab* Human Development Reports (2002–2009) identified underdevelopment: knowledge (creation

---

6 Bernard Lewis, "The Roots of Muslim Rage," *The Atlantic* magazine, September 1990.

and diffusion), women's rights, and freedom. These independent reports, written by eminent Arab scholars and researchers, describe societies mired in stagnation and backwardness – but with a limitless potential.

The first report diagnosed the above three "development deficits." Subsequent reports detailed these, and showed ways to correct them. Almost all problems came back to the lack of diverse and healthy ideas. *New York Times* columnist Thomas L. Friedman linked stifled ideas and opportunities to jihadist recruitment: "Greece alone translated five times more books every year from English to Greek than the entire Arab world translated from English to Arabic; the GDP of Spain was greater than that of all 22 Arab states combined; 65 million Arab adults were illiterate. It was a disturbing picture, bravely produced by Arab academics... Coming out so soon after 9/11, the [2009] report felt like a diagnosis of all the misgovernance bedeviling the Arab world, creating the pools of angry, unemployed youth who become easy prey for extremists."[7]

The 2009 report regretted a tragic lack of progress from earlier urgings. Staggeringly rich oil kingdoms and emirates still lacked the elementary pan-Arab – and Islamic – solidarity to fund massive improvements in health, education, nutrition and human security throughout the Arab lands. And foreign occupation tightened over the Palestinian territories.

Citing the 2009 report, Friedman noted that many Arab citizens still lack "human security — the kind of material and moral foundation that secures lives, livelihoods and an acceptable quality of life for the majority." "A sense of personal security — economic, political and social," he argued, "is a prerequisite for human development, and its widespread absence in Arab countries has held back their progress."

Some Muslim countries – invariably 'moderate' in theological and lifestyle terms – defy such gloom. Indonesia, has an average adult literacy rate of over 90 percent. Turkey has a rate of 88.7 percent. Even Saddam Hussein built Iraq's literacy to nearly 75 percent. These countries are now also closest to any reasonable

---

[7] Thomas L. Friedman, "Green Shoots in Palestine," *New York Times*, August 4, 2009.

definition of democracy – another dividing line within Islam. Egypt clocks in at over 71 percent. The "people power" that literacy and education generated plainly armed the revolutionary Facebook-Twitter youth in 2011's Tahrir Square. Weeks before, it did the same in Ben Ali's Tunisia. Pakistan – like India, scandalously squandering billions on weapons in the dead-end Kashmir conflict – barely makes 50 percent literacy, male and female combined. Next-door Afghanistan claims barely 28 percent. In all cases, especially in religiously 'fundamentalist' countries, women's literacy limps far behind the male rate. And the general quality of education for girls and boys is appalling: in Pakistan and Afghanistan, extremist Wahhabi *madrassa* schools teach mainly rote learning of the Koran and selected, reactionary religious texts.

The early 2011 Arab uprisings in Tunisia, Yemen. Jordan, Algeria – and especially in Egypt – cast a dramatic new light on the Muslim Brotherhood. As Egyptian masses demanded President Hosni Mubarak's resignation in Cairo's Tahrir Square, Western governments and media displayed near-paranoia about "radical Islamists." Would they win future free elections? Israeli prime minister Binyamin Netanyahu warned of "another Iran" if the Brothers won an Egyptian election. President Barack Obama and secretary of state Hillary Clinton, plus many members of Congress, echoed this fear. Both Israel and the U.S. worried that influence might one day lead to breaking the 1979 Israeli-Egyptian peace treaty. This pact both stabilized the region and gave Israel a freer hand in 'containing' the Palestinians.

In France, home to Europe's largest Muslim population (about six million), shoot-from-the-lip, media-star "intellectuals" ran for cover when the uprisings started. Terrified by "Islamism" of any kind, and conditioned by French colonialism to reject the very idea of a genuine Arab democracy, they did what they never do: they shut up. No doubt sheer ignorance also explained this: "What can you expect," sneered their bad-boy colleague Régis Debray, "from people who spend their holidays in their luxury villas in Marrakesh or in palaces in Tunisia or Egypt."[8]

Even level-headed *Le Point* magazine editor Claude Imbert sounded the alarm, linking the Brotherhood's re-emergence in Tunisia and Egypt to the whole, even riskier, Middle East: Syria-Iran's Hezbollah now dominated Lebanon, and Hamas (another Syrian-Iranian client) remained all-powerful in Gaza. But more authoritatively, respected intellectual Tariq Ramadan, grandson of the Brotherhood's founder, Hassan Al-Banna, argued a more nuanced view in the same *Le Point* issue. "It's legitimate to worry about [the Brothers] ... their literature today is not always very clear... [But they] have stayed constant on one undeniable point: they reject violence. Ayman el-Zawahiri, bin Laden's spokesman, left them for this reason, accusing them of collaborating with established governments... There are of course debates among [the Brothers] on how to apply *sharia*, But the future of democracy in Muslim countries requires integrating such movements into the [electoral] debate."[9] Summing up the "terrorist" risk: the Brotherhood and al-Qaeda despise each other cordially. Their views on violence and democracy are diametrically opposed. One struggles to imagine bin Laden running for anything except his life – which he did until U.S. commandos met him for late-night tea on May 2, 2011.

A thought-provoking point often cited: "Al-Banna's youngest brother, 85-year-old liberal reformer Gamal al-Banna, believes it was the torture the Muslim Brothers endured in [President Gamal Abdel] Nasser's dungeons that drove many of them toward the extremist ideology of one of their fellow prisoners, Sayyid Qutb."[10] This was allegedly the case for al-Qaeda's no. 2 man, and key ideologist: Ayman el-Zawahiri.

A last word on the Brothers from two of France's leading specialists on political Islam. Gilles Kepel has long analyzed

---

8   Thomas Wieder, "À Paris, l'intelligentsia du silence," *Le Monde*, February 6-7, 2003.
9   Tariq Ramadan, "Les Frères musulmans sont un mouvement nonviolent, légaliste et qui a une vraie légitimité populaire, *Le Point*, Febuary 3, 2011.
10 Peter Kenyon (interview), "Egypt's Muslim Brotherhood Celebrates Founder," *National Public Radio*, January 2, 2007.

the deep ambiguities within the movement. He has particularly well delineated the internal oppositions between visions of Islam in human life and society. Some 'reformers,' he notes, try to compartmentalize the worlds of society, culture, politics and religion. But traditionalists insist on integrating these worlds. Kepel cites the Brotherhood's many adaptations to changing realities, and its ability to learn from its mistakes. He believes that this adaptability may assure the movement's future in some form. But its very diversity and internal contradictions may sap its energy and focus over coming decades. Predicting that it may last is not the same, he says, as predicting that it will triumph – or "that Islamism, for better or worse, is a necessary outcome for the Muslim world."[11]

Olivier Roy is one of the world's most informed and astute guides to the labyrinth of Islam's currents and personalities. He has tracked the many interactions between religion, culture and globalization. Today's Islam dissects the different paths followed in various established Muslim societies. But he also tracks the diverging cultures and mentalities between 'majority-Muslims' and those in the Muslim diaspora. The latter live increasingly tense, complicated lives as minorities in Western societies. In the West, Muslim identity has many faces, but it mainly expresses itself as a choice between clinging defensively to Muslim values, and seeking a *modus vivendi* with ambient secularism.

To illustrate how this divides Western Muslims, ponder with Roy the diverging paths of Hani and Tariq Ramadan, the two grandsons of Hassan al-Banna, the Brotherhood's founder: "Born in Switzerland and citizens of that country, they express the two faces of modern Salafism: Hani is a neofundamentalist [thus looking more inward to Muslim beliefs and standards] and Tariq seeks some sort of accommodation between a 'Muslim community' (defined by its culture and values) and a secular Western environment."[12] The Brotherhood, like

---

11   Gilles Kepel, *Jihad –The Trail of Political Islam*, The Belknap Press of the Harvard University Press, Cambridge, Massachusetts, 2002, pp. 27–30.
12   Olivier *Roy, Globalized Islam – The Search For a New Ummah*, Columbia University Press, New York, 2004, p. 252.

many other manifestations of Islam, knows well such divisions. And its very diversity of approaches to the West earns it incomprehension — and the distrust accorded a supposed strategic chameleon.

When Western audiences think of political Islam, they tend to hear and see only the obscene architects of chaos who claim a God-ordered mission to terrorize the world – al-Qaeda and its ilk. There are indeed far too many shocking and repugnant aspects of extreme Islam – "honor killings" of sisters and daughters, *fatwa* assassinations, bombings of buildings, aircraft, schools and churches are just a few.

Muslim reformers must speak louder, and organize to purge their religion of its murderous, Islam-twisting exploiters and hijackers. Increasingly, Western-based Muslim leaders are denouncing the killers. This declaration of the Canadian Council of Imams, for example, makes a strong, unambiguous stand: "We believe in peaceful coexistence, dialogue, bridge-building, and cooperation among all faiths and people for the common good of humanity. Islam does not permit the killing of innocent people, regardless of their creed, ethnicity, race, or nationality. The sanctity of human life overrides the sanctity of religious laws."[13] This type of declaration is no doubt natural, indeed "politically correct," in a society like Canada's where respect for diversity is an officially-sanctioned aspect of national identity.

In Muslim homelands, such denunciations of violence are far more muted. They often even convey "understanding" (i.e. subtle approval) of brutality against women, indeed of some terrorist acts. Pakistan today goes even further: murderers of pro-tolerance advocates have recently become popular heroes. With atomic weapons perhaps not impossible to obtain, the world is literally in danger of an inferno if Islam does not modernize, and become more tolerant. Given the sprawling networks of fanatics now at work, or being trained in Saudi-funded Wahhabi *madrassas*, the task is breath-taking.

---

13   See website of Canadian Council of Imams.

'Reformers' and Reactionaries

Who will speak up against the wild-eyed killers? Fortunately, a few daring Muslims have begun to do so. Even Saudi Arabia's arch-conservative, oil-rich monarchy, long in league with the Wahhabis, fears destabilization and is thus rethinking its support for extremists – support that the oil-craving West has simply turned a blind eye to. Now leaning on its clerical elite, the royal family (or key parts of it) has begun to tame radical preachers. And it is trying to re-educate its home-grown terrorists (15 of the 19 Sept. 11 murder gang were Saudis). Alas, Ryadh continues to fund, wherever it can, thousands of mind-twisting *madrassas* and hundreds of radical mosques. We shall look at a counter to this later.

There are also serious Muslim scholars seeking theological renovation. French Islam specialist Olivier Roy cites several major "modern Muslim thinkers:" Muhammad Arkoun, Khaled Abou, El Fadl, Abdolkarim Soroush and others. But, says Roy, they "do not appeal to born-again Muslims, who prefer gurus to teachers ...and seek a ready-made and easily accessible set of norms" to live by and define themselves. As with other religious revivalist movements of our time, Roy notes, believers are not looking for theological refinements. They want an emotional experience. "Charismatic Christian movements, as well as the Jewish Lubavitch, explicitly propose [such] an alternative to an intellectualized faith." [14]

Soroush may be the Muslim world's most brilliant and influential intellectual reformer. One Middle Eastern analyst claims that, in his efforts to show how faith can thrive in an open society, Soroush "may be the most important Muslim thinker since the 11th-century theologian Al-Ghazali."[15] An Iranian philosopher of religion and science, and admirer of liberal democracy, Soroush insists on distinguishing "religion" (divinely inspired, eternal and unknowable) from "religious knowledge"

---

[14] Olivier Roy, *Globalized Islam: the Search for a New Ummah*, Columbia University Press, New York, 2004, 349 pp.
[15] Reuel Marc Gerecht, "Iran's Revolution: Year 2," *New York Times*, June 14, 2010.

(knowable through socio-historical factors, and by sincere, fallible study). Therein simmers the bedrock faith-versus-reason debate that splits all communities of revealed religion – notably Christianity.

But apart from these scholarly 'loyal dissidents' are brave new Muslim voices that speak plainly to the Muslim masses of a peaceful, civilized Islam. More accessible than the scholars, these more popular, straight-talking critics naturally get into hot water within broader Islam.

Consider three immensely brave young women and – of all things – an equally brave imam in Germany from the fundamentalist Salafi (seventh-century-admiring) faction. All four are of course under repeated death threats – sure evidence that they pose a challenge to the blood-thirsty reactionaries who fill our news bulletins.

The *New York Times* called Irshad Manji, a brilliant and controversial Canadian critic of unreformed Islam, "Osama bin Laden's worst nightmare." Others, a little *ad feminam*, term her glib, off-puttingly provocative, and self-aggrandizing (almost a checklist for success these days). Her landmark book *What's Wrong With Islam* has come out in over thirty languages. The Arabic edition has been downloaded over 300,000 times.[16] She also wrote and hosted a PBS documentary called "Faith Without Fear." A clear-eyed "loyal Muslim" who happens to be a media-star lesbian, Ms. Manji knows the Koran very well for a journalist with a few good axes to grind. With traditional scholars, she might not be able to argue theology *surah* and *ayah* (chapter and verse), or even *hadith* (sayings or deeds of Muhammad) for *hadith*. But in broad outline, she knows Muslim history, culture and customs. She claims no wish to destroy Islam. She insists she wants to remain a Muslim – but within a tolerant, modern Islam for our times, not the Prophet's times.

"What I want is an Islamic Reformation," she said in a 2004 interview. "Christianity did it in the sixteenth century. Now we are long overdue. If there was ever a moment for our Reformation, it's now, when Muslim countries are in poverty

---

16   Manji, Irshad, *The Trouble With Islam*, St. Martin's Press, New York, 2003.

and despair. For the love of God, what are we doing about it? ... At this stage, reform isn't about telling ordinary Muslims what not to think. It's about giving them permission to think." [17]

Ms. Manji argues clearly and pungently. Her basic idea: mainstream Muslims need to find the moral courage to question anything in traditional Islam that seems untrue, morally wrong, or seriously irrelevant to modern societies. She attacks abuse of women's rights, superstition, anti-Semitism, the rejection of learning, and the acceptance of violence (including suicide) to advance Islam. If the media too readily present Islam as almost a form of terrorism, she insists, it's because moderate Muslims allow extremists to say or do almost whatever they want. As moderates slink away from confrontation, she concludes, their silence is complicity.

Manji has drawn bitter criticism even from mainstream Muslims. Mohammend Z. Iqbal, writing on the *Muslim America* website on November 22, 2008, accuses Manji of "[continuing] to use the flawed ideas put forth in her book to spawn new efforts in an attempt to undermine the Islamic faith... While addressing topics as complex as religious laws and history, Manji's effort is superficial, simplistic and devoid of useful arguments." Other critics are ruder, calling Manji "batty" and a shameless grandstander – surely compliments for dedicated reformers – and in any case, tags stuck on lots of people whose ideas find big audiences.

Two other well-known critics of Islam are also women: Somali-born Dutch intellectual Ayaan Hirsi Ali and Bangladeshi writer Taslima Nasrin.[18] Both make some criticisms of Islam resembling Manji's – especially in appealing for women's rights. But both have left Islam, giving up on reform. What they and Manji really have in common is an endless stream of death threats – Ali and Nasrin are both living abroad in protective custody. Many others, less known, cower in the shadows – the only answer to their arguments, it seems, is death.

---

17 Johann Hari, "Islam's Marked Woman," *GQ Magazine*, July 2004.
18 Ayaan Hirsi Ali, *Infidel*, Free Press, New York, 2007. Taslima Nasrin, *Shame*, Prometheus Books, 1997.

Another fascinating opponent of radical Islam – though hardly a mainstream Muslim himself – is a Munich imam of the strictest Salafist tendency. His name: Hesham Shashaa. Physically and in dress a dead-ringer for Osama bin Laden himself, Shashaa condemns suicide missions and terrorist acts as anti-Islamic. Traveling from mosque to *madrassa* throughout Europe, the Middle East and Pakistan, he discourages youth from joining violent jihadism. And he attacks their violent elders for poisoning their minds. He does this not to change Islam, but to interpret it in what he considers its original meaning: "We cannot just sit down and let other people hijack our religion."

Naturally, for his trouble – though as traditional as it gets – he also gets the classic jihadists' answer for disagreeing with them: death threats. He accepts these with astonishing good humor. He greets German passersby with "God's wishes" (*Grüss Gott*) in his Bavarian accent, and sometimes wears a sign saying: "I am not bin Laden…" [19]

Whether scholarly or popular, attempts to "reform" Islam or make it more "moderate" run into plenty of resistance – and not just from reactionaries. Mainstream Ottawa critic Abid Ullah Jan warns that any talk of reforming Islam can lead to heresy or hide political motives: "One does not come to the fold of Islam to enlighten and reform it… Considering the main schools of thought with reference to jurisprudence in Islam as various attempts at reformation is a delusion of those who are on a mission of 'rebuilding' Islam [outside] of the prescribed limits in the Qur'an and Sunnah… The resultant mixture can be anything but Islam." [20]

Don't even try to improve Islam, so to speak, or you may end up going too far. A familiar story to Martin Luther, Jan Hus and a congregation of Protestant reformers. Just mentioning these brave men points to this reality: Most Muslims killed today are victims of other Muslims. Both victims and killers commit the unpardonable in fanatics' eyes: they belong to sects that are so

---

[19] Souad Mekhennet, "Munich Imam Tries to Dull Lure of Radical Islam," *New York Times*, May 15, 2010.
[20] Abid Ullah Jan, *Al Jazeera*, April 22, 2004.

awful, so heretical, that their members deserve to die. Christians used to kill each other centuries ago. Their primitive days saw a flowering of angels-on-a-pinhead "heresies," anathemas, schisms and all-round mutual nastiness. Christians gleefully spilled each others' blood well into the 18th-century. The disputatious Irish managed to keep mutual Catholic-Protestant killing going into the 21st-century. But they are an aberration more political, cultural and economic than confessional. Blended Irish whiskey may also play a role.

Now discrimination among Christians has faded – although the Vatican's claim that it can still excommunicate believers smacks a bit of the Inquisition's notorious lack of modesty. In reality, Christians have nothing better to argue about today than priests (women, gay or pedophile), the dubious legalism of the Apostolic Succession, the true nature of Transubstantiation, sharing Communion, and how many candles might make a congenial altar. Happily, the stakes in Christianity are so small these days that Christians can usually laugh about their differences – while thumbing their noses at their own pastors.

Can Islam finally find peace – literally "Islam" – within its own family? As with earlier Christianity, don't Muslims who betray Muhammad's message of peace and fraternity disgrace themselves and their religion? Thoughtful Muslims, horrified by their religion's sectarian violence, raise these questions. They are right to do so.

Turkey: West's Bridge to Islam, or Islam's Bridgehead to Europe?

The case of Turkey is fascinating, indeed momentous. A Muslim nation of ninety million people, it has a tradition of tolerance for Christians and Jews resting on the Ottoman Empire's four hundred years of domination of the Middle East. Occasionally violent acts shatter this live-and-let-live religious tradition, but it remains basically solid. Tensions with Kurds and Armenians are not essentially confessional; they primarily reflect historical and territorial disputes.

Today's Turkey represents a cultural anomaly. Its big cities, such as Istanbul and Ankara, are full of mosques. But the mosques are far from full. Islamic dress covers only a minority. Otherwise, Turkey looks and functions in many ways as a modern West European country. Burqas and bikinis coexist comfortably. But the deep Anatolian countryside is conservative in belief, practice and dress.

This cultural split gives Turkey its intriguing potential. A predominant secular thread grows from the 1923 revolution by Father of the Nation Mustafa Kemal Atatürk. From harem to fez to state ritual, he tried to remove all trace of religion in public life and even private customs. For decades and until very recently, the pro-secular army pulled political strings behind the scenes, backing several coups d'État. Now a moderate Islamic party, the Justice and Development Party (AKP) led by Recep Tayyip Erdoğan, rules on a program mixing mild Islamic customs (e.g. headscarves) with a persevering attempt to join to European Union. The EU – unofficially seeing itself as a "Christian Club" – has welcomed Turkey's bid to join it with all the enthusiasm of a garden-party hostess holding at bay a persistent rug salesman. At the same time, the U.S., starting with Turkey's 2003 refusal to let American troops pass through to invade Iraq, has become alarmed about "losing" Turkey. Like "losing" China in 1950 and "losing" Indochina in 1975.

Alas for both Europeans and Americans, staunch NATO ally Turkey doesn't feel "lost" – because it never felt that anybody but Turks had "found" it. The AKP's 'moderate' Islam clearly helps underpin a resurgent Turkish nationalism. Erdoğan's January 2009 Davos spat with Israeli President Shimon Peres ("When it comes to killing, you know well how to kill!") signaled a cooling of Turkey's pragmatic friendship with Israel. And Israel's May 2010 high-seas killing of nine Turks (one of them also American) on the Gaza-bound "Freedom Flotilla" broke a final western-oriented link. Now the political issue seems to be: Will Turkey "turn East" to Iraq, Iran and the Muslim world, and give up its hopes of anchoring itself in the EU? The religious issue: To what extent do Turkey's Islamic affinities outweigh its wish to continue Atatürk's historic modernizing? Will Turkey grow more Islamic, or more Western? Now cited as an example of happy integration of Islam and democracy, a model of cultural compromise, Turkey is a big hope, but also a big questionmark, for all sides.

Western optimists (which include well-meaning but not excessively-informed Americans) see Turkey as a perfect bridge between East and West. Pessimists – including France and Germany, both with large Muslim populations – fear Turkey-in-Europe means a bridgehead for Islam. A bridgehead to avenge its expulsion from Europe at Poitiers in 723 (defeat of the Umayyad Caliphate)? At Vienna in 1683 (Ottoman defeat)? It all depends on where you studied history...

The likeliest key to the bridge-bridgehead conundrum may not be Islam as such, or at all, but Turkey's national pride. Following Turkey's post-Ottoman eclipse after 1918 and its clinging to America's Cold War umbrella for half a century, it now intends, regionally and beyond, to "punch at its real weight" as a large, prosperous country. The Middle East already feels this. Turkey is a regional superpower, admired by all – especially the Arabs, who praise its standing up for Palestinians against Israel. Even America feels it: an independent May-June 2010 Turkey-Brazil diplomatic initiative muddied the waters for U.S.-led anti-A-bomb sanctions on Iran, rattling Washington teacups. The gesture even started Americans muttering about curtailing sophisticated arms sales to Turkey.

A good bet: Turkey will hold firm, happily keeping a foot in both Western and Eastern camps. Turkey's power is its balance of power. To achieve this, it has every advantage in playing its moderate Muslim card – to please the East, and to scare (but not too much) the West. Meanwhile, Turkey gives the West ample reason not to fling the term "terrorist" at everybody who (sort of) looks Muslim. Instead of looking at people's outsides, Turks would argue, why not look within? What do jihadist Muslims really *think*, and how do they come to hate the West?

What Makes a Terrorist?

A peaceful man like Munich's imam Hesham Shashaa raises this crucial question of the terrorist mentality. What makes a terrorist? Where do they come from and with what mindsets and motivations? Since "assassin" is a medieval Arab word (from a sect murdering enemy leaders), does that suggest that Islam is intrinsically violent? Of course not.

The terrorist mentality can arise from several sources – including illusions of grandeur, fantasies of rewarding martyrdom, anger at occupation of Muslim lands, a need for passionate commitment, or just inbred bigotry. Or indeed state-incited religious fanaticism. In May 2010, Pakistani Islamists of the self-described Punjab Al-Qaeda murdered over 93 Ahmadi Muslims in a Lahore mosque. The Supreme Court of Pakistan – instead of condemning this type of crime – had earlier practically incited such horrors in a landmark 1993 judgment: "How can anyone blame a Muslim," the Court asked rhetorically, "if he loses control of himself on hearing, reading or seeing such blasphemous material as has been produced (by the Ahmadis)." [21]

Psychologists have found many factors that can lead a person to terrorism. Mental unbalance, paranoia, a lack of meaning in life, immaturity, suggestibility, a lack of emotional and/or spiritual anchors, an absence of values-based education, a brutal childhood, a narrow-minded or fanatical upbringing. Or the exact opposite of all the above. For when it comes to personal background and socio-economic status, the creation of a terrorist remains an inexact science. And a given terrorist's outlook can vary dramatically with time, acquaintances, influences and context. In many ways, and notwithstanding various types and styles, each terrorist presents a unique mystery. [22]

Nevertheless, most terrorists share one triggering motivation: a deep sense of personal and/or collective grievance. This

---

[21] Cited in several publications, including *The Daily Times*, Lahore, April 28, 2007.

[22] Rex A. Hudson, "The Sociology and Psychology of Terrorism: Who Becomes a Terrorist and Why?" *Report by the Federal Research Division*, Library of Congress, 1999.

includes dispossession and deep offence, and often forms of culture shock: imposed values, customs, symbols, language and patterns of thinking.

George Washington University Professor Jerrold M. Post founded and ran for twenty-one years the CIA's Center for the Analysis of Personality and Political Behavior. He is among the West's leading experts on terrorist mentalities. He studied many real-life cases to trace paths to terrorism. The most obvious path – the one that studies show animate nearly all Palestinians who resist the Occupation – is a deeply implanted sense of injustice. This Post calls terrorism "when hatred is bred in the bone."

After sixty years of dispossession, countless Palestinians could respond to that description. Post cites a study of Israeli-jailed Palestinian radicals interviewed between the two *intifadas* (1993-2000). "A major finding was that painful early background experiences shaped identity and steered Palestinian children and youth onto the path of terrorism. Over 80 percent of the secular [i.e. non-Islamic] group members reported growing up in communities that were radically involved." [23]

One would think this evidence a little sobering even to hard-line Israelis. Others have drawn a thought-provoking conclusion. Journalist Yossi Sarid, writing in the left-of-center *Haaretz* daily on May 28, 2010, recalled a 10-year-old answer by Israeli defense minister Ehud Barak. "*Haaretz* journalist Gideon Levy had asked him then, as a candidate for prime minister, what he would do had he been born Palestinian and Barak replied frankly: "I would join a terror organization." [24]

Interviews with Post's Palestinian prisoners spelled out this motivation, even comparing it with Zionist feelings: "Enlistment for me was the natural and done thing...in a way, it can be com-

---

[23] Cited in Jerrold M.Post, *The Mind of the Terrorist*, Palgrave Macmillan, London, 2007, p. 27.
[24] This is scarcely a novelty for Israeli (or even many Asian and African) leaders, most of whom passed for "terrorists" in their time. Prime ministers Menachem Begin, Yitzak Shamir and Ariel Sharon all earned the title before Israel's independence. A "freedom-fighter," might say a cynic (or realist), is a terrorist who got to be one of his country's leaders. The same of course, is true of Ghana's Kwame N'Krumah and India's Jawaharlal Nehru and many others. Success is the best PR.

pared to a young Israeli from a nationalist Zionist family who wants to fulfill himself through army service."

But real-life narratives illustrate more vividly the itinerary from suffering to despair to fury. Post cites the famous Leila Khaled, born in Haifa in 1944. In 1969-70 she joined a revolutionary group and participated in two airline hijackings, though killed no one. Her path to militancy? As a small girl, Khaled was twice uprooted from her home, the first time at age four. She remembered life in the UN-supported refugee camps:

"I saw the maimed, the diseased, the broken-hearted. I saw bare-footed children with swollen stomachs, fathers with heads bowed, pale mothers with sickly children, grandparents in despair. I saw the meaning of poverty and hunger and felt the despair of deprivation in my bones..." [She grieved for the loss of her] "homeland, for the loss of a whole people, the pain of my entire nation. Pain truly affects my soul, so does the persecution of my people. It is from pain that I derive the power to resist and to defend the persecuted." [25]

An almost identical story of childhood uprooting and misery is that of Omar Rezag. Born in a Jordan refugee camp of a mother chased from Jaffa, he grew into a remorseless killer, shooting two Israeli women and three Americans in a hijacked airplane. As insensitive to others' pain as a robot, Rezag, says Post, exemplified perfectly how "developmental experiences shaped... attraction to the path of terrorism." He was "a classic case of nationalist-separatist terrorism, carrying on the family cause, seeking revenge for damage done to parents and grandparents, the generational transmission of hatred."

Other cases of childhood trauma created full-blown psychopaths. Abu Nidal founded and long ran of one of the most murderous groups of the 1970s and 1980s. Ruthlessly he murdered hundreds of innocents, including passengers waiting at Rome and Vienna airline counters. Born in Jaffa in a rich family, he hated Israel for ending his comfortable life. Adding to this fury was humiliation within his family. He was mocked as a "son of the maid" – his mother was his father's eighth wife, and originally a maid.

Another monster (who delighted in beheading hostages) was Abu Musab al-Zarqawi. A Jordanian, his main motivations

---

25 Post, pp. 25–26.

were religious and nationalist. Palestine's occupation enraged him mainly as an "invasion" of "Muslim land" by Jews, supported by Christian "Crusaders" (mainly Americans).

Zarqawi was so violent and cruel that he began to worry his loudly-proclaimed mentor, Osama bin Laden – a case of Hitler making Genghis Khan look benign? Bin Laden's number-two man and chief ideologue, Egyptian doctor Ayman al-Zawahiri actually wrote to Zarqawi asking him to stop upsetting Iraqi Sunnis by acting so brutally. Zawahiri himself, coming from a well-off professional family, seems to have become radicalized by a mixture of religion, the Israeli occupation, humiliating torture in Egyptian prison, Soviet (then American) control of Afghanistan, and "infidel" American influence over Middle East oil states.

Apart from Zawahiri's experience of torture, these motivations parallel broadly the accepted motivations of the terrorist superstar himself, Osama bin Laden. Coming from a Yemeni and Saudi background, bin Laden inherited millions of dollars from his construction-engineer father. Coming under the influence of radical university professors, he became the ultimate ideological terrorist. No personal dispossession here – just a rich son's apparent instinct to make his mark. Militant Islam – both religious and political – became his all-consuming mission. His mystical faith, eloquence, engineering know-how and fortune made him the formidable opponent we know. Versatile above all else, bin Laden, with Zawahiri's strategic and organizational skills, created a self-regenerating octopus of hate. Unless the West can kill or starve the beast, it faces decades of danger, disruption and fear.

This Islamic war has gone through several phases: its leaders' indoctrination, isolated early attacks (Sudan, Lebanon, Saudi Arabia, the 1993 New York North Tower bombing, the 1996 and 2004 Khobar violence), more concerted political ones (U.S. embassies in Kenya and Tanzania, 1998), the 2000 USS Cole bombing, and finally September 11, 2001's spectacular massacre of almost 3,000 people in New York, Washington and Pennsylvania. At this stage, bin Laden's Al-Qaeda ("the

Base") organization was a disciplined, centrally-directed network. After the U.S. crippled its Afghanistan headquarters, Al-Qaeda in following years became more of an ideology to inspire freelance terrorists. Having trained thousands of fighters in its camps and infected a new generation with its hate of the West, Al-Qaeda is now less an organization than an idea. It spreads like a cancer wherever the soil of Muslim grievance proves fertile.

A leading French analyst, Jean-Pierre Filiu, writing in June 2010, nevertheless identifies four centers of Al-Qaeda "implantation:" Pakistan's northwest tribal region; Iraq (a much weakened presence, with Shias dominant, but more inclusive); Yemen (an historic breeding-ground, with recruit-fishing in Somalia and the Horn of Africa, and training camps for European-type jihadists); and North Africa (growing but scattered).[26] Filiu sees Al-Qaeda as still able to inspire or even order "distant" events (the U.S. Fort Hood army psychiatrist rampage, the 2009 Christmas Day near-airliner crash and the May 2010 Times Square fiasco. But the Christmas airplane and Times Square events showed operational amateurism. And the Muslim army psychiatrist's case suggested an individual's sudden rage – only heightened, it seems, by urgings from a Yemeni imam born and trained in the U.S., Anwar al-Awlaki. Al-Awlaki reminds us of a fourth "implantation," floating everywhere, but in a way nowhere: Islamist hate-sites. Western counter-terrorist services view these as both a threat and a valuable information source. Like e-mail and other electronic channels, websites give terrorists vital channels of communication. But like a double-edged scimitar (if that could exist), using such channels helps lead their Western trackers directly to the terrorists. Two of countless examples of web-jihadists: The first is that U.S.-born (and Yemeni-raised) jihadist preacher Anwar al-Awlaki. Speaking unaccented American English, al-Awlaki is particularly dangerous for English-speaking countries where he can influence restless, gullible young Muslims. Often these are recent converts who look European and can more easily evade security checks.

---

26 Jean-Pierre Filiu, "M. Obama face au spectre Al-Qaida," *Le Monde*, June 15, 2010.

Seen by Western services as arguably the world's most widely-heard advocate of jihad, he has 1900 videos on YouTube, and turns up on numerous other sites. His many acolytes include the London Tube bombers, the Fort Hood assassin and the "Toronto 18."

The second dispenser of web-based jihadist fury is a woman, Belgian-Moroccan Malika El Aroud. Often termed "the mother of al-Qaeda in Europe," she has used websites to urge young Muslims to fight in Iraq and Afghanistan. Arrested several times, in 2010 she earned an eight-year jail sentence (under appeal) in a Belgian court. She and other women have tried – even though often belittled by male jihadists – to create a kind of *niqab* ladies' auxiliary of al-Qaeda.

The journal *Perspectives on Terrorism* cites three factors in al-Qaeda's popularity among disaffected young Muslims worldwide: "*simple message, powerful image* and *global character.*" [27] Not a word about weapons – just ideas. Al-Qaeda's "global character," by most Muslim accounts, includes this key factor in terrorist recruitment: Israel's nightly-televised crushing of "Palestinian brothers." America, as Israel's unconditional financial, diplomatic and weapons backer, inevitably appears to Muslims as complicit in Israel's behavior.

Unfortunately, the West still fights Islamist ideas essentially with arms – not better, well-thought-out, well-articulated ideas. Not even ideas as elementary as curing violence-funding oil-addiction. Or as building thousands of academically sound schools to rival Pakistan's tens of thousands of mind-numbing, West-reviling *madrassa*s. Or as using radio, TV and the Internet to offer useful education and training. When such ideas emerge in Western media, they appear as either one-shot panaceas, piecemeal improvisations, or token, feel-good fluff – almost never as a serious, integrated strategy.

Washington tends to believe that the best way to deal with political Islam is with guns and soldiers. The very word "Islam" makes Americans edgy – a not entirely irrational reaction after 9/11 and continuing "homeland security" threats. It might be

---

[27] Vol. II, issue 8, 2008.

unfair to suggest that some U.S. politicians, with regard to Islam, echo the famous line (attributed to Goering) in Hanns Johst's 1933 play *Schlageter*: "When I hear the word culture, I reach for my pistol!" But there lingers an ambient whiff of U.S. paranoia. And there are indeed U.S. politicians who think and talk like that. (e.g. Pete Hoekstra, Trent Franks, Michele Bachmann, and neo-McCarthyite Islam investigator Peter King – the latter a former Irish Republican Army terrorist sympathizer).

Against this background, can America change its historic obsession with arms? Can it find a more effective balance between changing regimes, and changing minds? Between killing terrorists and killing their worldviews? Can it bring itself to realize that mega-budgets for "national defense" are of diminishing value into today's worldwide contest of ideas?

The persistent militarism and parochialism of U.S. media, education, religion, entertainment, intellectual life and politics – examined in Chapter Three – don't encourage optimism. But first, to measure the dangers of mixing ignorance with aggressiveness, let's look more closely at the astonishing Arab uprisings of early 2011. This will show, among many things, that the militarization of America seems to prove of negligible value in influencing such 'tectonic-plate' events. It may also show why, in dealing with Islam abroad, America tends to be faster on the draw than on drawing sound conclusions.

Mistaking tactics for strategy, tools for goals, arms for ideas, ruinous expenditure for safety, and cheap oil for endless prosperity, the U.S. keeps shooting itself in the foot. Indeed in *both* of its big, bold cowboy-boots. Today's revolutionary young Arabs – mostly Muslim, but more aspiring-democratic than Islamist – may help America resolve its contradictions. And, with luck, help it stumble onto new paths to peace. On these paths, youth and women, often the real revolutionaries, look best able to lead the way.

Freedom is a bless that deserves fighting for it – Twitter message on January 25, 2011 from Wael Ghonim, Internet animator of Egyptian people's uprising in Tahrir Square, Cairo, 17 days before protestors drove President Hosni Mubarak from office.

Libya will turn into a burning hell... Dance, sing ... go and rejoice ... stay up all night ... this is the spirit! – Impromptu speech in Tripoli's Green Square by Muammar Gaddafi on February 25, 2011, as human rights observers estimated the week's civilian deaths at over 2,000 and Gadaffi's security forces continued to fire indiscriminately on unarmed demonstrators.

Chapter Two /

DESERT TSUNAMI – THE ARABS REBEL

December 17, 2010. A sleepy provincial town in Tunisia called Sidi Bouzid. Mohamed Bouazizi, a 26-year-old fruit-cart street-vendor drenched himself in gasoline, lit a match, and set the entire Arab world on fire. Within days, his self-immolation made Arab dictators from North Africa to the Gulf tremble in their palaces. Within weeks, two long-entrenched dictators fell to democratic protestors. Several other autocrats squirmed to save their power: first with brutality, then bribes, then fatherly rhetoric, then violence again. No Arab dictator now seemed safe. Bouazizi's holocaust-nightmare became for them all a lamp to light "the way," like MacBeth's fools, "to dusty [political] death."

Ten days after Mohamed's agonized martyrdom on January 4, 2011, Tunisia's kleptocratic president Zine El Abidine Ben Ali panicked and ran. Humiliatingly for both him and French President Nicolas Sarkozy, previously fawning, fair-weather-friend France refused to let his escape-plane land. Sarkozy forced him to flee to the more congenial Saudi petro-dictatorship: birds of a feather. As Tunis crowds demanded Ben Ali's downfall, "homeland-of-human-rights" France had backed Ben Ali to the last minute: new French foreign minister, Michèle Alliot-Marie ("MAM") had offered tear-gas grenades and

France's crowd-control "expertise." Blushing later, she admitted she had returned from a Tunisian holiday partly funded by Ben Ali cronies. They had also helped her family set up a real estate deal with a Ben Ali pal. An embarrassed Sarkozy quickly forced her to resign. This only highlighted again the spider-web of personal and state interests corrupting Paris's relations with its ex-colonies: free ministerial (and media-star) holidays for political, PR and commercial favors. MAM became the poster-girl for the massive dysfunctioning of French diplomacy – a decadence denounced in *Le Monde* by an anonymous group of senior French diplomats.[28] Shortly after, to signal that the amateur hour was over, "Sarko" blew the whistle. He appointed as foreign minister old-pro Alain Juppé, a former prime minister who had previously held that job with distinction.[29]

Playing Dominos in a Hurricane

We all watched the unfolding pan-Arab drama on television. Some highlights? Before January was out, mass demonstrations in Tunisia, Egypt, Yemen, Jordan, Algeria and Bahrain, all dictatorships, frightened rulers into window-dressing "concessions." In the last week of January, mighty Egypt blew up. In almost three weeks of frenzied but generally peaceful demonstrations, ordinary Egyptians demanded, and finally won, President Hosni Mubarak's departure. Not even a brutal counter-attack mobilizing Mubarak's thugs could stop the pro-democracy crowds of hundreds of thousands.

---

28 Groupe 'Marly,' "La voix de la France a disparu dans le monde," *Le Monde*, February 22, 2011.

29 Alas, as prime minister, Juppé had become entangled in accusations of abuse of public housing for his son Laurent. Then he became the closed-mouth fall-guy for former President Jacques Chirac who, as Paris mayor, was accused of funding his RPR party via fictitious city hall jobs. Juppé got a suspended sentence of 18 months (then 14) months in jail, plus 10 years of electoral ineligibility. A year of laundering as a professor in Quebec brought him back spotless. He took up his old job as mayor of Bordeaux, which he sees no reason to leave as foreign minister. Chirac had once called Juppé "the best of us all." We digress. But Juppé clearly has the credentials to clean up after mismanagement at home – and in North Africa.

His henchmen included released criminals and disguised police with swords, razors and machetes, a few riding horses and camels. The world watched fascinated for almost three weeks as demonstrators in Tahrir (Liberation) Square continued shouting for Mubarak's resignation. Their steadfastness, leaderless discipline. camaraderie and non-violence gradually made them heroes. The Egyptian army refused to fire on the crowds, and after further Mubarak manoeuvres to cling to power, it gently shuffled the 82-year-old *raïs* off to retirement in his villa at Sharm el-Sheikh.

Next to fall? Many talked of the dominos most likely to go first: Yemen's President Ali Abdullah Saleh, Morocco's King Muhammad VI, Algeria's Abdelaziz Bouteflika, Jordan's King Abdullah II, tiny Bahrain's King Hamad bin Isa Al Khalifa, even Syria's President Bashar Al-Assad were early speculations. The kings, noted U.S. diplomats, had a better chance of hanging on, for they could pretend to be somehow above the brutal, corrupted fray. They routinely fired their yes-men cabinets to divert to them blame for their crimes.

After much uncertainty, and a mini-civil war (including many imported regime mercenaries attacking the people), perhaps the most fanatical autocrat, Libya's Muammar al-Gaddafi, faced a bloody civil war bare weeks after Egypt's Hosni Mubarak. Gaddafi, barking mad as he ordered his air force to strafe and bomb his own people, flew in more foreign mercenaries to massacre his countrymen at will. As his ambassadors and senior soldiers peeled away from him, the international community struggled to find courage to stop the killing. It found lots of words, but little effective action – until French President Sarkozy, eager to efface his Tunisian humiliations, briskly organized an authorizing UN vote and an international coalition to impose a Libyan no-fly zone. Officially, this was to block Gaddafi's aircraft from killing civilians around rebel headquarters in Benghazi. Probably, the coalition hoped that a "stray" Tomahawk missile might accidentally kill Gaddafi. Yemen's Saleh, at time of writing, was also trying to drown his people's revolt in blood – even so-called "moderate" Bahraini royals were following suit, with more than a little help from their nervous Saudi and Gulf autocrat-friends.

The most momentous, but most difficult, possibility for revolution remains Saudi Arabia. Yet when King Abdullah returned on February 22 from a medical absence, even he judged necessary to bribe his people with bags of money. Estimates of his sudden largesse reached $37-billion dollars – *Monopoly* money to secure his family's monopoly of power.

While waiting to assess the full impact of the 2011 rebellions, it's worth asking how and why the dignity-and-democracy storm started. Who exactly was Mohamed Bouazzi, the unknown Tunisian who sparked the firestorm?

Working since age 10 to support his mother and siblings, Bouazzi ran constantly into police browbeating and shakedowns over mythical permits. On December 17, 2010, squeezed by officials with demands for bribes, he was publicly humiliated by a 45-year-old female city functionary named F. Hamdi. She spat on him, slapped his face, insulted his dead father, confiscated his weight-scale, overturned his fruit-cart, and helped two colleagues beat him. Mohamed tried to complain to the local governor, but was turned away. Minutes later, shamed, angry and desperate, he lit his match.

Eighteen days later, he died horribly. Over 5,000 people attended his funeral. Marches to honor him drew tear gas from police. But the protests spread from village to village to the capital, Tunis. After huffing and puffing about "security," Ben Ali took flight – he and his wife reportedly taking millions of dollars in gold from the national bank.

Every Arab hearing Bouazizi's story instantly understood his cry against injustice and indignity. Silent, frightened majorities throughout the Arab world related to his despair as though it was their own. As it was, millions of times over, each time they faced brutal, contemptuous police and bureaucrats. After the brave Tunisian crowds drove out their dictator, Egyptian crowds in Cairo's Tahrir Square refined and made famous a new model of peaceful revolt. A model to capture hearts, imaginations and unsuspected courage. After Cairo, everyone saw the dominos: Tunisia, Egypt, then.... Soon, people were saying that nothing would surprise them.

By the end of the "Arab spring," the geopolitical, economic and even cultural map of the Middle East was unrecognizable. So, on the horizon, was the balance of forces between jihadists and the West, Sunnis and Shias, Israelis and Arabs. The old powers-that-be – the U.S., Israel, Egypt, Syria and Saudi Arabia – now had to review assumptions, reassess priorities, and recalibrate strategies. Why did the Arab sandstorm sweep across a whole region, blinding everyone at first, then revealing new opportunities as well as new dangers? The causes were many: tired oppressions, security-and-oil-obsessed Americans and Europeans, hungry, humiliated peoples, a demographic surge of better-educated youth (including veiled and unveiled women), and a dizzying growth in electronic media.

An *Al Jazeera* blog by network host Riz Khan emphasized how women stepped forward as major freedom advocates: "They have often been stereotyped as passive, voiceless, politically apathetic and religiously repressed. But scenes around the Middle East have complicated preconceptions, with women seen as active political players in trade unions, grass roots activism and other political organizations."[30] Well-known activist Naomi Klein made the same point: "[In both Tunisia and Egypt] ... women protesters were nothing like the Western stereotype: They were front and centre, in news clips and on Facebook forums, and even in the leadership. In Cairo's Tahrir Square, women volunteers, some accompanied by children, worked steadily to support the protests – helping with security, communications and shelter. Many commentators credited the great numbers of women and children with the remarkable overall peacefulness of the protesters in the face of grave provocations. [31]

The electronic media included new independent satellite-TV networks willing to criticize foreign Arab rulers. Qatar's Arabic and English *Al Jazeera* became the dictators' *bête noire* – as well as

---

30 "Arab feminism," Riz Khan, *Al Jazeera,* March 2, 2011.
31 Naomi Klein, "The Middle East's feminist revolution," the *Globe and Mail*, Toronto, March 2, 2011.

the suddenly-favored news network for previously suspicious Washington power-brokers. Hosni Mubarak, on a 2001 visit to the Qatar headquarters of *Al Jazeera*, had famously groused: "All that trouble comes from this little matchbox?" Ten years later, during the 2001 Arab uprisings, both Mubarak and a cornered Muammar Gaddafi whined that the "trouble" was even more painful because it came from "Arab brothers." As the dictators saw it, that meant Qatar's emir: Sheikh Hamad bin Khalifa Al Thani.[32] More broadly, revolution emerged from the people-linking, intrinsically subversive combination of satellite TV, cell phones, satellites, GPS, and "social media" such as YouTube, Facebook and its fast-and-furious little brother, Twitter. To all that, in a significant supporting role, you might add the rebellious youth's two common idioms apart from Arabic: Internet jargon and serviceable English. After looking in more detail at causes, we'll ponder the wildly uncertain consequences of the Arabs' democratic explosion.

Tottering Tyrants

Why, more deeply, the "sudden" serial uprisings of quiescent Arab masses? Many reasons came together in a perfect storm. First reason: pent-up, roiling fury at oppression. Simple but explosive feelings of injustice and long-crushed dignity. From Morocco's Rabat to Bahrain's Manama and Yemen's Sana'a, almost half a century of autocrats had trapped most of the 22 Arab League countries' 355-million people in poverty, humiliation and stunted lives. Dictators denied dignity and freedom to ordinary countrymen, reserving wealth and privilege to their own family and cronies. Tangibly, by pocketing state funds and resource profits, "leaders" starved education, with few exceptions (Tunisia) – thus potential job opportunities. Resulting lack of economic futures denied marriage and children to countless young people, crippling happiness of vast populations. In the *Financial Times*, 21-year-old Yemeni student Abdul Rahman

---

[32] "Special Report: Al Jazeera's news revolution," Regan E. Doherty, Reuters, February 17, 2011.

al-Ashari deplored Ali Abdullah Saleh's dictatorship: "The opposition wants to negotiate now for the sake of its own interests – but for years the government and the opposition have treated Yemen like a game of football, where the people just get kicked around." [33]

This pointless contest built rage in frustrated young men and marginalized young women. The power-abusers stole the lives of at least two generations. Their victims became mass crime's rudderless dreamers in a sea of heartbreak.

Moreover, crony capitalism left little capital for small business – a major start-up potential for young people. As everywhere, personal enterprises should have been the great jobs machine. Archaic, too-theoretical (and theological) training left even 'educated' youth unable to find work, meaningful or not. With public wealth stolen to become rulers' private stash, economies and whole societies simply became stagnant, cesspools of despair. Youth lost its youth, and its future.

After youth – but in conjunction with youth – the central tool of rebellion was electronic. Anger and frustration could now be shared by all but the poorest of youth. Satellite television gave them ideas of revolt (Tunisia), a model of courage and intelligence (Egypt) and almost suicidal bravery (Libya, even Bahrain at the start). In the views of both autocrats and Western audiences, Qatar-based *Al Jazeera* (in both Arabic and English) played a starring role. Cell phones allowed protesters to consult each other, and to agree where and when to meet to plan and protest. The phones also took photos and movies of state violence that damned the authorities: nothing could be hidden anymore, anywhere. The Internet offered instant linkage with other youth for astutely-motivated mobilization. It did so by promoting heroes ("We are all Khaled Said," a Facebook page for a young Egyptian who died in police custody), by slogans ("He will leave, we're not going anywhere"), and by propaganda (constant media interviews with protestors).

All this happened with a speed and expertise that caught security forces asleep, confused and out-organized. Age had

---

[33] "Person in the News: the Arab Youth," Rould Khalaf, *Financial Times*, February 25, 2011.

much to do with this: rebels came from the individual-enhancing Internet generation, police and army came from the era of state TV, the dictators' traditional one-way vehicle for dominating public discourse. The fact now was that nobody could monopolize public discourse. It was liberty against the Luddites.

The shorthand version of history here might be "the Internet meets Arab youth-quake." A few distinguished older Egyptians, especially the respected Nobel Laureate Mohamed ElBaradei, had long before urged democracy for Egypt. He and others continued their campaign by backing the youthful rebels. But youth were the front-lines. Roughly 60 percent of the Arab world is less than 25 years old. Overwhelmingly, they are furious at lacking a future. And most of them have a cell phone, plus access to at least a cyber-café.

A few commentators contest the revolutionary role of social media. Clay Shirky, a New Media professor at New York University, argued in the January-February *Foreign Affairs* that social media's real impact is not in bringing down governments. It's in "supporting civil society and the public sphere...over years and decades."[34] Malcolm Gladwell, a *New Yorker* writer, pooh-poohed *any* role for social media. Noting cutely that Mao Tse-tung didn't have a Facebook page, he said: "Please. People protested and brought down governments before Facebook was invented. They did it before the Internet came along. Barely anyone in East Germany in the nineteen-eighties had a *phone* – and they ended up with hundreds of thousands of people in central Leipzig and brought down a regime that we all thought would last another hundred years – and in the French Revolution the crowd in the streets spoke to one another with that strange, today largely unknown instrument known as the human voice."[35]

Fun, but a little facile. For the youthful revolutionaries of Tahrir Square themselves insist that their electronic toys, sites and messages gave them not only unprecedented organiza-

---

[34] "The Political Power of Social Media – Technology, the Public Sphere, and Political Change," Clay Shirky, *Foreign Affairs*, January-February 2001.
[35] "Does Egypt need Twitter?," Malcolm Gladwell, *The New Yorker*, February 2, 2011.

tional and propaganda power; it brought to their rebellion a decisive intimacy and immediacy. It made hundreds and thousands, indeed millions, feel that they were close friends in a common combat – whether students, non-religious professionals, veiled women, or even Muslim Brothers. Not even the East German *Stasi* or the French Revolutionary Jacobins had tools to shut down something as critical to their economies as the Internet. [Mubarak's secret police, then Gaddafi's and some other Arab censors eventually found a way to unplug the Net]. Even Internet-savvy China can't stop its youth from doing constant end-runs on censorship. Beijing's Internet banning of the word "Jasmine" (symbol of the Tunisian revolution) turned into a joke; It betrayed the Communist Party's terror of the example of a bunch of kids over 10,000 kilometers away.

Bewitched, Bothered and Bewildered

If the uprisings terrified sitting potentates, they startled the West. More than startled: they shocked, confused, and, for many governments cozy with the dictators, frightened. For the United States, much of the fear emanated from Israel. Behind its 30-year-old peace treaty with Egypt, Israel enjoyed a much freer hand to control the Palestinians and to stay on their lands. But the West's publics were thrilled. They quickly identified with uprisings that recalled the post-1989 liberation of eastern and central Europe from Soviet domination. The analogy was far was perfect. But it caught on, and put enormous pressure on Western governments to "get on the right side of history." That meant backing the people's *cri du coeur* against the despots.

The U.S., as the predominant outside power, had to react decisively. For one thing, its Likud-led Israeli ally was mobilizing its full panoply of American Congressional and lobbying resources to push Washington to stick with Israel's favorite Arab: Mubarak. That is – by America's own values of freedom and democracy – to stay on the "wrong side of history."

During the three weeks of the mainly-youth rebellion, Washington's public statements sounded anything but decisive.

As perceived power ricocheted between Mubarak and Tahrir Square, the U.S. line wobbled and shifted a little every day. President Barack Obama and Secretary of State Hillary Clinton began by supporting old ally Mubarak – Vice-President Joe Biden 'helped' even by saying that the old Egyptian air force pilot was "not a dictator." Frank Wisner, a special envoy hand-picked by Mrs. Clinton to advise Mubarak to leave, blurted out on TV effusive praise for Mubarak, saying he should stay on to steer the "transition." Amazingly, nobody had checked Wisner's lobbying background: he was on Mubarak's payroll.

Still, as the Tahrir Square crowds grew, and pro-Mubarak goons attacked them, the tide of U.S. public opinion changed. Obama made increasingly stern calls to Mubarak to convince him to accept democratic reforms – code for resigning. Then, crucially, the Egyptian Amy announced it would never fire on the peaceful demonstrators. On February 3, U.S. armed forces chief Admiral Mike Mullen reported that his Egyptian counterpart General Sami Enan had assured him of this – a first indication that the U.S. was using its close military cooperation with Egyptian forces to gradually try to ease out Mubarak.

In fact, during the three weeks of the Egyptian crisis, these military-to-military (or in the lingo, "mil-mil") links were a critical factor in moving matters toward a peaceful transition. Top American generals knew the top Egyptian generals through decades of staff-college training and political-military management of Washington's $1.3-billion yearly military aid to Cairo.[36] Working hand in glove with the White House and the Secretaries of State and Defense, top U.S. generals (and one supremo admiral, Mike Mullen), eventually managed to shepherd the peaceful transition Obama wanted. When it succeeded, even Obama's harshest adversaries praised his adroitness. Republican House Leader John Boehner, without a tear in his normally weepy eye, said Obama had handled "a very difficult situation about as well as it could be handled." [37]

---

36 "The ties that bind," *The Economist*, February 26, 2011.
37 "Boehner: U.S. handled Egypt crisis as best it could," *Huffington Post*, February 13, 2011.

At least America got it right in the end. European and other allies tagged along in dispersed order. Britain spoke, as always, as though it had a "special relationship" with America. France was reeling from its Tunisian gaffes. Germany took its typical wait-and-see attitude. Italy dallied, fearing new waves of unwanted immigrants. At the time, there was only one immigrant that Prime minister Silvio Berlusconi wanted: "Ruby the Heart-stealer," a teenage Moroccan dancer.

By early March 2011, Washington had caught its breath, and so had Europe. They began working carefully – but very discreetly – to help the still-vulnerable Tunisian and Egyptian regimes consolidate. By then, better-organized American efforts were not only monitoring and/or trying to calm half a dozen Arab uprisings risky for U.S. security. Washington worked intimately with NATO allies and the United Nations to try to bring down Gaddafi. The "mad-dog" colonel in his bunker had by then started drenching his end-of-world *Götterdämmerung* in blood. He planned a chaotic exit, and achieved that. But the world's key nations at least began working together to chase him out.

Most observers agreed that all these events would be just a beginning. But already one could see some common features. Maybe these might serve as tentative conclusions. Among them: the eclipse (temporary?) of religion as a motivating factor for most Arabs, especially youth; paradoxically, the re-emergence of long-suppressed Muslim parties (at least tactically 'moderate') from an earlier generation; the emerging role of women; and the likelihood that for years, indeed decades, the only certainty about democracy will be uncertainty – a long, twisting road for all the protest-shaken countries. As well as for their whole region, and for Western strategists.

Radical Islam Eclipsed?

All the threatened Arab dictators shared a survival trick: They agitated the scarecrow of jihadist Islam – allegedly an irresistible attraction to impressionable youth. Dictatorship was, they claimed, the ever-ready – and only – rampart for their West-friendly rule. The rulers' iron fists guaranteed stability and security for America, the West and Israel. The ploy won them not only firm political support. It secured them billions in military funding. Strangely, this always included internal-security training and equipment – both plainly designed to keep down domestic discontent. Aid for spying on, clubbing, and tear-gassing crowds. Not to mention for arresting and torturing protesters – all, by definition, assured the dictators, sworn enemies of Western ideals.

The early 2011 uprisings quickly unmasked all this as a self-serving fiction. In fact, it showed that violence, with brutality and denied rights, *creates* extremism. It fosters secret scheming and organizing, and makes more credible the libels against the liberating power of freedom. It makes fanatical religion a consoling and unifying force for potential terrorists.

What was the religious dimension of the desert tsunami? Not much. Four obvious facts demonstrate that it was not at all Islam that toppled autocracy, but a thirst for dignity and freedom.

First, almost unanimously, the Arab protesters rejected religion as their motivation. The movements began and ended as non-religious rebellions, even though after they started members of the Muslim Brotherhood smoothly joined the festivities, hoping to appear as discreet elder statesmen of dissent.

Second, indeed, when Muslim Brotherhood leaders began trickling back to Tunisia and Egypt, they wisely made a point of declining too-prominent a role. They made clear that politics was not their urgent concern. They wanted first to work with others to anchor democracy – after which they could play a normal role. Cynics may distrust them for being crafty – for patiently waiting to show their true colors. But most Brotherhood interviews gave the impression that they were likely more interested in 'lifestyle' or 'values' Islam, not political Islam. The future may tell another story. For now, the Brothers may deserve the benefit of doubt.

Yet they will bear watching. Exactly two months after the Egyptian uprising started, the Brotherhood seemed to have started politicking: "There is evidence the Brotherhood struck some kind of a deal with the military early on," said Elijah Zarwan, a senior analyst with the International Crisis Group. It makes sense if you are the military — you want stability and people off the street. The Brotherhood is one address where you can go to get 100,000 people off the street." Warned another observer: "We are all worried," said Amr Koura, 55, a television producer, reflecting the opinions of the secular minority. "The young people have no control of the revolution anymore. It was evident in the last few weeks when you saw a lot of bearded people taking charge. The youth are gone." [38] Similar evidence was emerging in Yemen and, to some extent, Tunisia.

A third feature of at least one key uprising: the revolt of tiny Bahrain's oppressed Shia majority against its Sunni masters, the Al Khalifa royal family. Their quarrel was not in itself a classic sectarian dispute. It was, at the outset, a demand by second-class Shia citizens – 70 percent of Bahrain's 738,000 population – for justice and fairness. The king's initial brutal response to mild protest radicalized many Shias, and sharpened the sectarian divide. Bahrain is of course next door, via the King Fahd Causeway, to Saudi Arabia's also oppressed Shias in the oil-rich Saudi Eastern Province. Ryadh clearly fears that Bahraini Shias may 'contaminate' its own democracy-eager Shias. On March 13 and 14, 2011, the Saudis (with some smaller Gulf Cooperation Council petro-states tagging along) sent 1,000 soldiers and heavy armor to Bahrain to back up Manama's fellow-Sunni royals. The resulting enhanced Sunni-Shia tension could only weaken the Islamic world as a whole. It also put new strain on the Saudi-U.S. relationship – already tense since Obama rejected King Abdullah's urging to support Egypt's tottering Mubarak.[39]

---

38   Michael Slackman, "Islamist Group Is Rising Force in a New Egypt," *New York Times*, March 24, 2011.
39   "Bahrain key in Sunni/Shia divide," Caryle Murphy, *Global Post*, February 26, 2011. In mid-March 2011, King Abdullah refused "for health reasons" to see both Defense Secretary Robert Gates and Secretary of State Hillary Clinton. The 88-year-old king was indeed ill, but perhaps anti-Obama pique was an aggravating factor. The start of a graver Saudi-U.S. misunderstanding?

A fourth, and stunning, fact was the oft-proclaimed agenda of Tahrir and other protestors. They praised values that thoroughly rejected those of al-Qaeda and Co. In Tahrir, Coptic Christians and Muslims guarded each other while each group prayed. Muslims even attended a Coptic Mass. The bin Laden version of Islam consists of blowing up the mosques of "deviant" Muslims like Sufis and Ahmadis. For him, all Christians are of course beyond the pale as "Crusaders." The jihadists teach youth intolerance over tolerance, death as "martyrs" over life, fear and nihilism over hope. The protesting Tunisian and Tahrir youth rejected all this. In fact, they never even referred to it. Terrorist Islam was simply absent from their minds and revolutions.

This doesn't mean that jihadists can't regroup. When Ben Ali and Mubarak fell, revolutionaries released many political Islamists from prison. But at very least, al-Qaeda and its affiliates have a lot of non-*halal* egg on their faces. At the height of protestors' victories, the *New York Times*'s Scott Shane analyzed the jihadists' perceived setback as follows:

"For nearly two decades, the leaders of *al-Qaeda* have denounced the Arab world's dictators as heretics and puppets of the West and called for their downfall. Now, people in country after country have risen to topple their leaders — and al-Qaeda has played absolutely no role.

In fact, the motley opposition movements that have appeared so suddenly and proved so powerful have shunned the two central tenets of the Qaeda credo: murderous violence and religious fanaticism. The demonstrators have used force defensively, treated Islam as an afterthought and embraced democracy, **always** anathema to Osama bin Laden and his followers...

...For many specialists on terrorism and the Middle East, though not all, the past few weeks have the makings of an epochal disaster for Al-Qaeda, making the jihadists look like ineffectual bystanders to history while offering young Muslims an appealing alternative to terrorism."[40]

---

40 Scott Shane, "As Regimes Fall in Arab World, Al-Qaeda Sees History Fly By," *New York Times*, February 27, 2011.

As a clincher, Shane went on to cite an expert mocking Al-Qaeda's number two man and chief ideologue, Ayman Al-Zawahri. "Knocking off Mubarak has been Zawahri's goal for more than 20 years, and he was unable to achieve it," said Brian Fishman, a terrorism expert at the New America Foundation. "Now a nonviolent, nonreligious, pro-democracy movement got rid of him in a matter of weeks. It's a major problem for Al-Qaeda."

If that wasn't hard enough on the Qaeda cave-dwellers in North Waziristan (among other possible hospitable hideouts), the news that women – most of them unveiled – prominently helped pull off these volcanic events must have been deeply depressing.

But there are cautions to all this "post-Qaeda" rejoicing. True, al-Qaeda played no visible role in the 2011 people's protests. Like everybody else, it was caught off guard by the rebellions. It made only a few insipid, knee-jerk theological claims that most Arabs ignored. On the other hand, Western observers, perhaps with wishful thinking, may have been too-thrilled by the Western-educated, English-speaking young protesters they saw on TV. Although inspiring, these engaging youth may not entirely represent the Arab-speaking masses. Often overtly secular, they may not be a perfect mirror to mainstream, still devout, Egypt. *Asalaam Aleikum* and *Inch' Allah* are everyday terms throughout the Muslim world, and reverence for, and basic knowledge of, the Koran are close to universal.

Such customs of cultural Islam are no monopoly of al-Qaeda. They just confirm an ambient religiosity which can always evolve one way or another. We have noted that several post-revolutionary regimes – including Tunisia, Egypt and Yemen – have opened the political doors to previously banned Islamic parties. How far do they truly want to take their programs: a theocratic caliphate, or just a few beards-and-burqas cultural reforms? Another evidence of the Islamic acculturation of ordinary Arabs was Gaddafi's March 2011 *in extremis* attempt to fool the masses by switching from al-Qaeda scourge to defender of

Islam: his NATO and Arab no-fly attackers suddenly became "Crusaders"...

Realistically: al-Qaeda has always proven its resourcefulness and ability to adapt. Once it digests the mainly secular protests, it may well bounce back. Its training camps, especially in Yemen, are making it a priority to brainwash impressionable, disaffected Western youth. Why? Because they don't fit today's terrorist profiles: "Their value," noted one Yemeni expert, "is their Australian [for example] passport."[41] The notorious American-born imam, Anwar al-Awlaki, "the bin Laden of the Internet," preaches and orchestrates terrorism of the most cowardly kind – deliberate killing of civilians. He is on the CIA assassination list, and seems hard to find. He may be in Yemen, but his funding, say experts, comes from people living in those sterling America-"friendly" countries of Saudi Arabia and the Gulf states. Don't write off al-Qaeda yet.

Scorecard: Be Careful What You Wish For [42]

The 2011 Arab awakening is plainly a work in progress. It's a fair guess that at least the next decade will see a rocky, zigzagging – and no doubt sometimes violent – road to the protesters' wished-for democracy. As after all revolutions, we can expect dazzling breakthroughs, heart-breaking setbacks, and long periods of quiet, confusion or morass. Even perhaps recurring civil wars. New ideas, new personalities and new structures will emerge. Foreign patrons, rivals and enemies will compete to shape events.

Above all, it will take a generation or two to define and consolidate healthy *cultures* of freedom and democracy. Die-hard autocrats – as Libya's Gaddafi, Yemen's Saleh and Bahrain's Hamad bin Isa Al Khalifa have shown, will not "go gentle into that good night" toward modern, civilized societies. And if, in time, that bizarre, billionaires' kingdom of Saudi Arabia ever

---

41 See "The Pied Piper of Jihad – Yemen," *Al Jazeera* documentary on terrorist training camps in Yemen sponsored by Anwar al-Awlaki

42 See a cautioning article with this title by Georgetown University professor Charles A. Kupchan, *New York Times*, February 25, 2011.

catches the open-society bug, one can expect, well, more 'tectonic' times. Predicting neither instant paradise nor inevitable hell for now, one can only cheerlead for the good guys – and try to help them on their own terms, never intruding or preempting, as they struggle to rebuild their own countries from the people up.

That much said, who, apart from self-liberating populations, is likely to benefit from the rebellions? And who may lose?

On the surface, among apparent winners: Shia Iran, its Hezbollah and Hamas clients, the oil-tending Shias in Saudi Arabia and their cousins in Bahrain. All look stronger in early 2011. One is tempted to add Shia-dominated Iraq. But the chaos visited upon that unhappy country by George W. Bush and his arrogant, know-nothing, neo-conservative ideologues may weaken old Mesopotamia for another decade.

On the ancient Sunni vs. Shia divide, one might risk these predictions: a) the divide will deepen as Shias grow stronger; and b) in time, this perceived Shia rise, combined with the fall of major Sunni dictators, may force the U.S. and Israel to make new strategic calculations – like rethinking Palestine. Maybe even rethinking Iran. The re-legalization of the officially moderate Muslim Brotherhood (present in some form in most Arab countries) could help preserve Sunni influence. The Brotherhood proclaims Sunni doctrine, but sometimes favors Shia political positions, especially against Israel.[43] But in some countries, notably Yemen, local Brothers may seek radical solutions. The Brotherhood's one-size-fits-all motto – "Islam is the Answer" – could allow many different outcomes – including in some places Saudi-style "vice-and-virtue" police? And systematic anti-West policies?

One can argue, as many have, that Washington's hesitant January 2011 search for an Egyptian policy was just another evidence of American "decline." In the sense that America's

---

[43] Olivier Guitta, "Another front on the Sunni-Shia war," *Terrorism Blog*, February 28, 2009. Guitta notes Saudi nervousness about Iranian-backed campaigns to convert its Sunnis to Shiism. Apart from theological issues, this apprehension clearly reflects fears that Shias might eventually gain decisive influence over the Eastern Province oil industry.

policy of backing strongmen seemed to crumble, this is plausible. But in the end, Obama turned around U.S. policy. He finally backed the youth protestors, and played a subtle carrot-and-stick game with Egypt's army. The Cairo generals, like Washington, wanted to end up on the "right side of history." As a result, one could equally well claim that America came out of Egypt, and most other Arab uprisings, as a "winner" – a sign it was "still" a superpower. By the time the world was uniting to bring down Gaddafi, the U.S. looked like a leader again – or at least an inspiring team-player capable of watching where the sheep might run, then leaping ahead to "lead" them.

Ironies. America's relative "success" was in spite of America. For decades, Washington had backed strongmen who systematically undermined its values and ideals. The people who defended these? The very people – freethinking youth – that the U.S. allowed (and sometimes encouraged) the dictators to suppress by waving the Islamist scarecrow. In the end, both radical Islamists and America were absent from Tahrir Square. We saw the first demonstrations in living memory where nobody even mentioned America, much less denounced it. Until President Obama decided to back the protesters, the U.S. was the AWOL superpower.

This was not the case of Israel, although it too was unheard-of in Tahrir. In fact, it may count as the only big loser. Especially if it sticks to its now discredited policy of go-it-alone regional supremacy. "Regionally," argued Professor Fawaz A. Gerges, "Israel is the biggest loser. It has put all its eggs into the basket of Arab dictators and autocrats, like Egypt's deposed Hosni Mubarak. Israel fought tooth and nail to support Mr. Mubarak, who played a key role in tightening the siege of Gaza and the noose around Hamas's neck. Time and again," he went on:

" ...the Israeli political class has proven to be its own worst enemy. Israel lost Iran 40 years ago because it put all its eggs in the Shah's basket. It has just lost Turkey over the killing of nine activists on board a Gaza-bound Turkish aid ship. And now Israel is likely to lose Egypt, a critical and pivotal neighbor whose Camp David peace agreement in the late 1970s consolidated Israel's superiority in the region and undermined the official Arab state system." [44]

Regardless of what governments emerge out of the rubble of political authoritarianism in the Arab world, they will have assertive foreign policies that challenge Israel's hegemony and further colonization of Palestinian lands. Confirmation of such assertiveness – and of new U.S. weakness in the Middle East – came when Saudi Arabia, without informing Washington, its closest ally, decided in mid-March to send 1,000 troops to rescue fellow Sunni monarch, Bahrain's Hamad bin Isa Al-Khalifa. For Rami G. Khouri, respected Lebanese editor-at-large of Beirut's *Daily Star*, "there [was] no better sign of the reality that Washington has become a marginal player in much of the Middle East, largely as a consequence of its own incompetence, inconsistency, bias and weakness in allowing its policies to be shaped by neoconservative fanatics, pro-Israel zealots, anti-Islamic demagogues, Christian fundamentalist extremists, and assorted other folks who trample American principles and generate foreign policies that marginalize the United States abroad." [45]

Roger Cohen, the astute *New York Times* columnist, dreamt of a more hopeful result between Israelis and Palestinians: "A representative Egyptian government — the one whose birth pangs I believe we are witnessing — will talk about Israel one day and may be less pliant to America's will. But it would carry a vital message for Arabs and Jews: Victimhood is self-defeating and paralyzing — and can be overcome." [46] His point about double but mutually blind victimhood may be the essence of the Israel-Palestine impasse.

A few weeks later, Cohen suggested how to break the Israel-Palestine logjam: Send Obama to the Knesset to deliver some tough-love lucidity: "America is Israel's insurance company

---

44 Fawaz A. Gerges, "Arab unrest: Winners and losers," on *BBC World* website. Gerges is director of the London School of Economics Middle East Centre, February 28, 2011.
45 Rami G. Khouri, "Saudi Arabia's inner beast awakens," *Globe and Mail*, Toronto, March 16, 2011.
46 Roger Cohen, "Exit the Israeli alibi," *New York Times*, January 31, 2011.

and right now we need the C.E.O. to come and tell us, "You are not alone," Daniel Ben-Simon, a Knesset member who recently left the Labor Party told me [Cohen]."We especially need that because Israeli policy is not just a tragedy, it's almost criminal."

"That's right on both fronts," went on Cohen. "A great opportunity could be squandered as the Arab Spring unfurls. I find all the Israeli anxiety troubling for moral and strategic reasons. The moral reason is simple: What could be closer to the hearts of Jews than the sight of peoples fighting to throw off oppression and gain their dignity and freedom?"

"...The Middle East's most vibrant democracy is missing the upside of the birth of new ones. First, when Arabs can legally assemble in places other than mosques, radical Islamism is dealt a blow. Second, American double-standards in backing the likes of Mubarak long gave demagogic ammunition to Israel's enemies, chiefly Iran." [47]

As of this writing, Israel could see signs of a potential closer-to-home rebellion. The Palestinian territories were alive with rumors and nascent efforts to explore a possible combined West Bank-Gaza youth uprising. Repression both from Hamas and the Palestinian Authority looked likely – but so did imitation of a Tunisian-Egyptian revolt. Decades of a stagnant "peace process" in lieu of peace itself, and an older generation divorced from youth's hopes, made some kind of explosion seem likely.

More broadly, Georgetown University's Professor Charles A. Kupchan warned that, even sooner than they fear, democracy's celebrants may miss the 'good old' dictator days: "On two key dimensions – the relationship between religion and politics, and the link between nationalism and social cohesion – the Middle East is following a trajectory quite different from the West's. If democracy does take root in the Middle East – and the jury is still out – the regimes that emerge may well be much tougher customers than the autocracies they replace." [48]

Three tentative, blue-sky conclusions: 1.We should expect more of the unexpected, and from many more fixed-in-amber Arab autocracies. What we *think* may happen may not happen

---

47 "Go to Jerusalem," *Idem.*, March 3, 2011.
48 Kupchan, *Ibid.*

at all, or at least not in the form we anticipate. 2. "Happy" Arab countries (i.e. well-adjusted and reasonably prosperous ones), like Tolstoy's families may "look alike" in successfully marrying tradition and modernity. Each "unhappy" one (i.e. unable to marry past and future) will be "unhappy in its own way." And the reason for that will be: 3. Culture, especially political culture. No leader, no program, no party or institution can entrench a healthy democracy if the customs, values and mentalities of people, politicians and press remain trapped in unhealthy habits – like censorship, cronyism, torture and rampant bribery.

Military cultures also matter. Arab armies often have very different traditions. Those of Tunisia, Egypt, Libya and Yemen had little in common except complicity and corruption. They acted differently at critical moments – though Yemeni generals' March 21, 2011 rallying to protesters after a massacre clearly echoed the Egyptian army's smoother switching-of-sides. Tunisia's army made a sudden move on Ben Ali. And Gaddafi's army was divided, unreliable and frightened. Robert H. Pelletreau, former U.S. Assistant Secretary of State for Near Eastern Affairs, reviewed in *Foreign Affairs* the many originalities that shaped early events in Tunisia, Egypt and Bahrain – history, population, regime, economy, culture.[49]

As of this writing, Middle East turbulence continues. Autocracies in Libya, Yemen and even Bahrain have brutally rejected concessions. A March 17, 2011 UN Security Council decision authorized armed international action to stop Colonel Gaddafi from massacring rebels and innocent civilians. A coalition of Western and Arab countries joined forces to neutralize Gaddafi. But he was determined to go down in typical form, drenching defeat with his own people's blood.

But Libya, a tribe-torn, artificial state with its 6.4 million people, was a sideshow. Egypt, the Arabs' mighty heart, was the key to the Arab world. Home to 84 million people and an inspiring history, Egypt could influence all Arabs. Libya could never have seized anyone's attention had Gaddafi not been a bloodthirsty

---

[49] Robert H. Pelletreau, "Transformation in the Middle East," *Foreign Affairs*, January-February 2011.

thug who lucked on to immense oil and gas reserves. The single greatest challenge for Egypt's post-Mubarak regime – and for the West – was, and remains, to create useful employment for Egypt's tens of millions of hopeless youth. It is also the challenge of all Arab regimes, and indeed of the entire developing world.

It would be presumptuous folly to predict the Arabs' future. Or even the rough impact of their rebellions on the world. On fellow Arabs? On Persian Iran? On China? It would be like trying to catch butterflies while traveling on a fast-moving treadmill. But with luck, butterflies – perhaps metaphors of beauty and peace for the kind that flew among the sumptuous gardens of 15th-century Granada – may well appear in the lifetimes of the young demonstrators from the bloodied protest squares. Whatever happens in decades ahead, these brave young rebels will remember their dreams. And, for sure, the first hero of their awakening: Tunisia's fruit-seller from dusty, desolate Sidi Bouzid, Mohamed Bouazizi.

These first two chapters have tried to offer a brief (and very inadequate) sketch of Islam and the 2011 Arab world – each feared by Americans as cockpits of Islamic terrorism. Both Muslim and Arab universes are infinitely more complex. They are far more rich, more dangerous, and more promising, than Americans and Westerners in general imagine. How next, do Americans see the world, and how do they learn about it?

I have a love interest in every one of my films - a gun
– Arnold Schwarzenegger

The fruits of Christianity were religious wars, butcheries, crusades, inquisitions, extermination of the natives of America and the introduction of African slaves in their place – Arthur Schopenhauer

Chapter Three /

DUMBING DOWN AMERICA

Understanding Islam is hard enough. But understanding Americans? Is it true, as wags sneer, that God invented war to teach Americans geography? Most non-Americans know well that glazed-eye look that afflicts many Americans when they hear too much of anything or anybody beyond their blessed land "from sea to shining sea." Why does the rest of the world seem to bore Americans? Same question: where do average Americans get their ideas about the world's problems?

Six main sources: journalists, teachers, preachers, entertainers, intellectuals, and politicians. Few of those equip the "world's only remaining superpower" with the information and perspectives it needs to lead the world. Or indeed to avoid becoming a myopic rogue elephant stumbling from crisis to crisis. The thought-leaders' mission: to convince Americans that their country is right even when it's plainly wrong. "My country, right or wrong?" An old, familiar theory which leads to hypocrisy and, for its victims (as much as its believers), to buckets of blood, sweat and tears. For America's promise to work, it demands the assiduous cultivation of ignorance, myth and illusion. And a gullible, or at least distracted, citizenry.

Saying that should not insult Americans or America. Plenty of other nations – and not just notoriously self-adulatory France – adore their mirrors and see, like the evil queen in *Snow White*, "the fairest of them all." Overall, Americans are probably no more vain than other peoples. It's just that American media, Hollywood, tourism and troops give them bigger loudspeakers. Americans can claim many splendid qualities: imagination, inventiveness, dynamism, practicality, generosity, a passion for enterprise. Backing all that, at least sometimes, are elites of extraordinary talent and vision.

But America's powerful blend of ignorance and arrogance (usually Siamese twins) carries a cost to talent and vision. Fareed Zakaria, a devastatingly lucid Indian-American journalist, pointed in March 2011 to the blinders worn by the exceptionalist American mainstream:

> Any politician who dares suggest that the U.S. can learn from — let alone copy — other countries is likely to be denounced instantly. If someone points out that Europe gets better health care at half the cost, that's dangerously socialist thinking. If a business leader notes that tax rates in much of the industrialized world are lower and that there are far fewer loopholes than in the U.S., he is brushed aside as trying to impoverish American workers. If a commentator says — correctly — that social mobility from one generation to the next is greater in many European nations than in the U.S., he is laughed at...
>
> ...And it's not just politicians and business leaders. It's all of us. Americans simply don't care much, know much or want to learn much about the outside world. We think of America as a globalized society because it has been at the center of the forces of globalization. [50]

This chapter points out the dangerous disconnect between America's brightest and most banal. Between (not to get partisan) the Barack Obamas of America and the George W. Bushes. For in most of the areas of influence we look at in this chapter you find, behind the elites' excellence, often horrifying obscurantism, fantasy and bigotry. You find too many people, usually noisy and dogmatic, who make America look stupid. Like a know-nothing blunderer. America's many admirers take no joy in this.

Hence, the "dumbing down" of America. From Allan Bloom (*The Closing of the American Mind*) to Harold Bloom (*The Western Canon: The Books and School of the Ages*) to the average educated

---

50   Fareed Zakaria, "Are America's Best Days Behind Us?" *TIME*, March 3, 2011.

and alert parent, you will find little argument about this: American standards of mass education, mass media, and mass culture (including taste) long ago went over a cliff.

This chapter tries to show how lethal such mediocrity is for a country harboring America's grand dreams and apparently uncontrollable arsenals. Ignorance plus militarism is risky enough; when tied to the arrogance of empire, it's almost a guarantee of perpetual war. America's obsession with arms often ends up as contempt for ideas about when – and when not – to use arms. Almost everywhere you turn to see how Americans "see" the world, you find the same story: America is becoming the Pentagon.

Media: Is All News, Like Politics, Local?

Osama bin Laden's September 11, 2001 attacks on New York and Washington shocked America awake to international terrorism. Five weeks later, the Washington-based Freedom Forum, originally an offshoot of the Gannett Foundation, decided that this was no time to broaden interest in the world. It decided America needed fewer, not more, means to influence global opinion: it shut down its highly regarded international division. This closed four resource centers (London, Johannesburg, Hong Kong and Buenos Aires) that had promoted free media, trained journalists from 130 countries, and impressively encouraged international media exchanges.

The closings did not directly affect how Americans got international news – they mainly curtailed help to foreign journalists. But they spoke volumes about the *mentality* of U.S. media leaders on world issues. They mirrored, as we shall see, further retrenchment of already shrinking U.S. press coverage of other countries. They said again that the world outside Fortress America – including foreign coverage of America – did not much matter.

Why did the Foundation kill its international centers? To pour *another* $450 million into its already glitzy Washington "Newseum" – a monument to founder Al Neuhart's ego and to navel-gazing American journalism. But at a time when America needed friends throughout the world – especially in the developing and Muslim worlds – such a shift in priorities wasn't just counter-intuitive. It was breathtakingly dumb. For American security and influence in a suddenly more dangerous world, it was almost suicidal.

The contrast between promoting world awareness and rejecting the world stunned observers. Russ Baker, a contributing editor to the *Columbia Journalism Review*, wrote on his January-February 2002 website a blistering critique of the decision called "Cracks in a Foundation: the Freedom Forum Narrows Its Vision."

Foundation chairman and CEO Charles Overby told Baker that moving the Newseum from its Arlington, Virginia, site to Pennsylvania Avenue in downtown Washington, near "museum row," would double attendance. Forum president, Peter Prichard, admitted that "the [Forum's] international programs were great. You're going to countries where journalism's just developing, and people are sitting around talking about how they can avoid being killed, whether they can get enough newsprint, whether they can stay out of jail if they've written an offending article or drawn an offensive cartoon..." But recognizing that there's no business like show business, he gushed about the enlarged Museum: "Kids will surely love the chance to sit in the very chair in which the first woman was electrocuted, a 1928 milestone surreptitiously photographed by the *New York Daily News* photographer who smuggled a camera strapped to his leg into Sing Sing prison." Already, the Arlington Newseum had been a gee-whiz, all-American funhouse. Now it would become *Grand Guignol* – blood and gore all over the floor.

The Freedom Forum disaster killed America's most influential and beneficial institution favoring press freedom, training and security. But the Forum scandal was just a blip compared with the slow collapse of U.S. international coverage after 9/11. For decades, American network TV coverage of the world had shrunk year by year. Networks had cut bureaus and budgets, and reporters knew less history. On-air clips shrunk from two minutes decades ago to a few seconds. In 1968, sound bites averaged 42 seconds; twenty years later, 10 seconds.[51] For presidential debates, Harvard University studies showed that news-bulletin sound bites in candidates' actual voices fell from 42.3 seconds in 1968 to 7.8 seconds in 2000. [52]

Against all logic and common sense, the U.S. mainstream media now deprive the "world's only remaining superpower" (not a phrase heard much anymore) of its eyes, ears and, above all, its critical judgment.

Sixteen days after 9/11, just before the Freedom Forum shocker, the *Los Angeles Times* told how U.S. print and TV media had been cutting U.S. international reporting to the bone:

"Coverage of international news by the U.S. media has declined significantly in recent years in response to corporate demands for larger profits and an increasingly fragmented audience." [53]

Having decided that readers and viewers in post-Cold War America cared more about celebrities, crime, sex scandals and local news, newspaper editors and television news executives have reduced the space and time devoted to foreign coverage by 70 to 80 percent during the past 15 to 20 years.

Several prominent journalists say these cutbacks might have contributed to the uncertainty and confusion among many Americans about why terrorists committed so heinous an assault on Sept. 11. "I think most Americans are clueless when it comes to the politics and ideology and religion in [the Muslim] world and, in that sense, I think we do bear some responsibility," admitted Martin Baron, editor of the *Boston Globe*. [54]

Eight years later, the field of U.S. foreign reporting resembled a war zone – after the war. Once-mighty networks, anchoring world news with "legendary" newsmen often with impressive

---

51 Brewer, p. 231.
52 "The Dumbing of America – Call me a Snob, but Really, We're a Nation of Dunces," The *Washington Post*, February 17, 2008.
53 David Shaw, "Foreign News Shrinks in Era of Globalization," *Los Angeles Times*, August 27, 2001.
54 *Los Angeles Times*, September 27, 2001.

foreign experience (ABC's Peter Jennings being the prototype) shuttered foreign bureaus and laid off hundreds of reporters. Even CNN – by vocation a serious international network – shut down most of its 32 international bureaus, or cut budgets. One excuse: It had to chase ratings with the more provocative, chatty Fox Network and flashy MSNBC. Paris's excellent Jim Bittermann remained a respected CNN analyst, and in March 2010 Christiane Amanpour decamped to an ABC Sunday morning Washington news show. Her job: officially "to send the message that Peter Jennings' legacy endures even as the network is slashing its news staff and scaling back foreign operations."[55] Translation: to weave "more" international news into an essentially Beltway news-and-gossip format called *This Week*.

Amanpour's challenge, said the *Los Angeles Times*, was "to increase the focus on foreign affairs... to strike a balance between international and domestic policy debates while continuing to satisfy an audience that has come to expect large doses of inside-the-Beltway skinny and analysis of U.S. politics." One wishes her well, but the pull of 'parochial' Washington stories will prove formidable – and perhaps overwhelming if her balanced foreign-domestic mix drops the ratings of previous host George Stephanopoulos [who] made his insider's knowledge of Washington the show's hallmark."

Speaking of 'prestige' or 'personality' U.S. anchors, their multi-million-dollar salaries may have helped drain funds from solid field reporting – thus contributing to reduced foreign coverage. Other countries pay anchors well, but not obscenely. And they coddle them less. In Britain, for example, anchors make do with the less grandiose titles of "news presenter" or "news reader."

Roy Gutman, Pulitzer-Prize-winning reporter for *Newsday*, won honorary citizenship of Sarajevo in April 2010. His stories on Serbian ethnic-cleansing were credited with saving at least 5,000 lives. He deplored constant U.S. cutbacks in foreign coverage. Outside of the international-minded *New York Times*, *Washington Post* and *Wall Street Journal*, he found only certain

---

55 *Idem.*, March 19, 2010.

multi-week single-story assignments useful in developing international reporters.[56]

The multi-week fellowships of the Nieman International Reporting Project (IRP) are a well-known stop-gap."While there were plenty of mid-career journalism fellowship programs," wrote John Schidlosvky, authoritative Johns Hopkins University expert and IRP co-founder wrote, "none were designed to encourage more or better international coverage in the U.S. media. With a three-year start-up grant from the Pew Charitable Trusts, we created a specialized journalism fellowship with a mission of "training the next generation of foreign correspondents," as Loren Jenkins, senior foreign editor at NPR... described it." [57]

Online *Global Post* is a welcome effort, Gutman thinks, but its outsourcing of coverage to local reporters is of uneven quality. "Every time I look at Global Post I see quantity, not quality... They assign people because they are at a certain place - they write a few stories that aren't necessarily of news value or investigative aims. I don't see that as a model."

Against such relative shoestring efforts, consider the cost of maintaining an expat-style foreign reporter: at least $250,000 a year. That can at least double if family and security add inevitable costs. [58]

A contributing factor to today's news-bulletin superficiality is the now long-established U.S. view of news as entertainment. To sound-bite shrinkage add intellectual shrinkage – the dumbing-down and dressing-up of news as "fun" to watch: "Infotainment." Politicians succeed not on ideas, but on how they "come across" on TV. "Talking heads" became "talking hairdos." Signature theme-music, dancing corporate logos and dazzling graphics seize the audience's senses and drag them through a carefully programmed story line-up – if possible end-

---

56   Maria Conde, "Pulitzer Prize-winning journalist Roy Gutman reflects on the future of foreign correspondents," *EditorsWeblog.org*, August 22, 2010.
57   John Schidlovsky, "Foreign Reporting: It's Not Like It Used to Be," *Nieman Reports*, Fall 2010.
58   Diana Saluri Russo, " Is the Foreign News Bureau Part of the Past?", *Global Journalist*, January 30, 2011.

ing with a soft lifestyle piece. Or better still, a cute kid or animal story. Neil Postman, in his landmark 1985 book *Amusing Ourselves to Death: Public Discourse in the Age of Show Business,* showed how the written speech of 19th- and early 20th-century political discourse carried ideas – while modern TV sells images. Logic and connection of ideas, streams of thought, and cogent arguments go out the window.[59] The game is now to thrill the emotions: to delight or anger (preferably enrage). This helps a show "grab" the audience – now known as "eyeballs" – by the eyes, and secondarily, by the ears instead of by the mind. U.S. TV news is no longer a serious form of communication. It's a visual alphabet soup without the alphabet.

A hopeful sign for retrieving 'lost' airtime coverage, and for replacing glitz with grit: digital one-man mini-bureaus. Using young, versatile, tech-savvy reporters, these can extend coverage. But unless reporters are just going to comment on dramatic pictures (which much TV news does), such bureaus will still require reporters with a sense of history, culture and context. All too often, they don't have these. As a result, audiences get a relentless diet of bombs and bullets with little in-depth explanation. How many times have you heard a reporter standing amid bomb wreckage and bodies stating only that a bomb-blast had occurred and that X number of people got killed? When did you last hear a probing *explanation* of the deep and/or close background of the blast? And a thoughtful preview of what might follow – why, where, when and to whom?

In danger zones, networks often risk the lives of young freelance "cowboy" journalists to "get great pictures." Editors know that these young reporters are eager to make a name for themselves, whatever the physical dangers. The yearly journalists' death toll tells the story: in 1997, 28 journalists were killed; in 2009, 110 died. Survival courses, flak jackets and a vigilant NGO called the International News Safety Institute have helped.[60] But the numbers of dead keep rising.

---

59   Viking Penguin, New York, 1985.
60   "Put simply," says the Institute, "we aim to help journalists survive the story." It does so through several objectives, to:

For the record: Most journalists targeted and killed are local ones (many of them cameramen), though visiting foreign journalists die too.

Foreign reporters' high-risk lifestyle may dissuade good candidates for this demanding profession. The expansion of war zones – and some combatants' new willingness to murder journalists – also increase risks. In earlier decades, journalists enjoyed non-combatant status. Now, belligerents' recognition that the "media war" is as important as the "battlefield war" has led to unconscionable acts: in November 2001, the U.S., having been given the coordinates of the Kabul *Al Jazeera* bureau to protect its staff, apparently used them to fire a deadly missile into the office.[61] It did exactly the same thing in Baghdad, after *Al Jazeera* had sent to Donald Rumsfeld a letter giving its office's location. The Americans also attacked the Palestine Hotel, especially on floors where non-'embedded' foreign journalists stayed. On various occasions, U.S. forces have shot (always 'accidentally') cameramen representing networks (*Al Jazeera*, Reuters, ABC, Associated Press) whose pictures of mayhem did not serve the White House-Pentagon line.

A few years later, Secretary of State Hillary Clinton shocked U.S. super-patriots by strongly praising *Al Jazeera* – precisely *because* it was thorough and serious. Speaking to the Senate Foreign Relations Committee on March 2, 2011, she said: "Viewership of *Al Jazeera* is going up in the United States because

---

* Support and develop safety programs for all news media workers on a global and local level;
* Encourage agreements on health and safety matters between employers and staff;
* Disseminate information through practical training, advisories and literature;
* Promote industry best practice for training, equipment and field work;
* Investigate, develop and promote safety services including affordable insurance;
* Establish a global network of organizations committed to risk-reduction;
* Sponsor awareness-raising initiatives at media events.

61   *Al Jazeera* managing director Mohammed Jasim al-Ali said: ""This office has been known by everybody, the American airplanes know the location of the office, they know we are broadcasting from there," *BBC World News*, November 13, 2001.

it's real news...You may not agree with it, but you feel like you're getting real news around the clock instead of a million commercials and, you know, arguments between talking heads and the kind of stuff that we do on our news which, you know, is not particularly informative to us, let alone foreigners."[62] (She cited an Afghan general who believed that U.S. TV, featuring *Baywatch* and *World Wrestling Entertainment,* consisted essentially of girls in bikinis and men wrestling.) In the first months of the Arab uprisings, Internet viewership of *Al Jazeera* English soared (by AJE estimate) 2,500 percent. It is virtually banned in most of the U.S. because of anti-Arab lobbies and George W. Bush-era ideological hostility.

All this conveys a harsh outlook for the new breed of independent journalists. Again, the obstacles and risks tend to curtail high-quality international reporting and analysis. They favor superficial, just-count-the bodies, wow-what-an-explosion reporting. They ignore the *reasons* for the bodies, and likely consequences of the deaths.

Another attempt to restore foreign news to the U.S. media comes from the worldwide news service Associated Press. A long-established American not-for-profit news cooperative, it draws news from 300 offices worldwide. John Schidlovsky, the *Baltimore Sun*'s Beijing bureau chief in the late 1980s, is director of the International Reporting Project at Johns Hopkins University in Washington, D.C. He sees AP taking a larger, more important role on the world stage. "I think that's definitely going to be the trend," he says. He has little time for editors who shrug off foreign news by saying that readers can find anything they want on the Internet. "How many general readers actually spend time looking for news about Turkey or Botswana or Peru? Most people don't know how to find it or don't take the time to," he argues. Schidlovsky, whose project promotes reporting from abroad, insists: "The mainstream news organizations

---

62 "Hillary Clinton Calls Al Jazeera 'Real news,' Criticizing U.S. Media," *Huffington Post,* March 3, 2011.

still have an obligation to educate the public about important international news."

A February 2007 story in *Global Journalist*, a publication of the Vienna-based International Press Institute, declared, "The era of the foreign bureau is close to over. Will the foreign correspondent be the next to go?"

A chicken-and-egg question: Have the American media cut foreign coverage because audiences want less foreign news? Or because news editors – often with little knowledge of the world – make parochial decisions? If you attend a conference of American editors, you will find a prevailing mindset (outside of the three or four top 'national' papers) relentlessly favoring local news, sports, entertainment and celebrity gossip. Familiarity with non-U.S. history or even geography is almost non-existent. Virtually the only metaphors in conversation at editors' conferences, even among women editors, pertain to U.S. sports. To note that is not to be snobbish; it merely conveys the limited imagination of most Middle America editors. Legitimately, a fair amount of 'international news" tends to focus on Americans abroad: soldiers in Iraq and Afghanistan, or the attacks on U.S. embassies and the USS Cole. But much of the time, U.S.-centric trivia gets the nod: opening a new McDonald's in Ulan Bator is a classic.

The following report in the December-January 2008 *American Journalism Review* by Sherry Ricchiardi on the Associated Press Managing Editors conference gives the flavor of key editors' Little-America thinking:

> Although the crowd applauded wildly in appreciation of the Baghdad staff during the APME luncheon, many editors in the room that day [had] a meager appetite for international news. Instead, the mantra "local, local, local" resonated throughout the conference as many news managers see community news as their main franchise – and the key to survival.
>
> Scott Angus, editor of Wisconsin's *Janesville Gazette*, circulation 22,000, doesn't see overseas news as a key part of the paper's repertoire. "You have to focus on what you can do better than anyone else. What we can do best is cover Janesville, Wisconsin. Nobody can touch us when it comes to covering our community. It's not even a close call," says Angus, who recently finished a six-year term on the APME board.

He makes no excuses for pulling back on world events. "What we're reducing is something people can get in many other places. They don't need to read the *Janesville Gazette* to get the latest news out of Iraq or Washington... We realize anybody can Google that and get 1,000 stories from 1,000 places..."

Mark Bowden, editor of the 60,000-circulation *Cedar Rapids Gazette*, sees foreign news differently than Angus. He pegs use of international stories to "local relevancy." His community has a sizable Muslim population, a strong foreign business presence and men and women from Iowa's National Guard serving in Iraq.

"Our eyes are always on the horizon looking at international coverage for those key local connections," says Bowden. The editor notes that when Israeli forces and Hezbollah clashed in southern Lebanon in 2006, some Cedar Rapids residents were vacationing and visiting relatives there. "That became an incredibly local story for us," says Bowden, an APME board member. He recalls times at past APME conferences when the AP staff would present a dramatic slide show spotlighting important global coverage. "People from the smaller markets would sit there, scratching their heads and thinking, "That's great and wonderful, but what about the news out of Peoria? [63]

What's left for credible foreign coverage in the U.S? *National Public Radio*, the *New York Times*, the *Washington Post*, the *Wall Street Journal*, and the less affluent *Christian Science Monitor* (daily online, weekly in print) still do splendid work. On TV, a much-stripped-down CNN competes with two foreign-owned networks, Britain's venerable *BBC World* and Qatar's thorough, world-explaining English-language *Al Jazeera*. Both of the latter are available in the U.S. only via satellite or on nonbasic cable. *France 24*, in English, French and Arabic, is a new and increasingly respected news source. For dedicated newshounds, Net-based *LiveStation* offers access to a broad variety of national TVs. *Al Jazeera*, previously sneered at by the second Bush administration, became the superstar satellite network for its coverage of the January-February 2011 Arab uprisings. In addition to Hillary Clinton's fulsome praise, it reportedly won as regular watchers President Obama and senior military and intelligence staff. [64]

---

63 Sherry Ricchiardi, "Covering the World," *American Journalism Review*, December-January 2008.
64 Glynnis MacNicol, "Even President Obama Is Watching *Al Jazeera*," *Business Insider – The Wire*, January 29, 2011.

A useful new international service is the U.S.-based website called *GlobalPost*. It does a fine job of presenting world news fairly and accurately, within a handy, attractive format. Its mission: "... to help fill the enormous void that has grown up in coverage of the world by US news organizations. More than ever before in history, we need knowledge of other countries and of the global forces that are impacting our economy, our environment, and our very security."[65] Unlike *Al Jazeera* English (AJE), *GlobalPost* does not try hard to use mainly home-country reporters. It may be using a number of subsidized stringers, often ex-pats, as well as freelancers. AJE still uses quite a few highly experienced ex-BBC, ex-ITN and ex-CBC reporters on big stories.

For mostly younger fans, social-network sites fill a gap – especially sites such as Facebook and Twitter. They do so in a haphazard, often unverifiable, way where accuracy and fairness give way to immediacy. And often to powerful scoops. On June 20, 2009, heartbreaking photos of dying Iranian music-student Neda Agha-Soltan appeared on *Twitter* and *Facebook* within minutes of her being shot by a sniper. These confirmed the brutal suppression of post-electoral dissent by the Khamenei-Ahmadinejad regime's Basiji militia. *YouTube,* a free-to-upload, free-to-use video site also carried the scene. It carries countless other international newsworthy videos.

Finally – for now, for new site ideas pop up constantly – there is *Wikileaks*. Launched in 2006 and run by crusading Australian founder Julian Assange, it grabbed sudden fame in 2010.[66] First by uploading to *YouTube* a video baptized *Collateral Murder* accusing U.S. forces of wantonly killing 10 Iraqi civilians and two Reuters employees from a helicopter. In August that year, *Wikileaks* enraged the Pentagon by uploading

---

65 From the *GlobalPost* website.
66 As Assange's exploits and fame grew, he paid a heavy price: resignations of key associates, "lost" luggage with laptops, relentless tracking by angry pursuers (one dares to guess U.S. security people), and even allegations of sexual offences. See John F. Burns and Ravi Somaiya, "On the run: the founder of *Wikileaks*," *New York Times*, October 25, 2010.

76,900 confidential field documents on the U.S.-led war in Afghanistan. [67]

The London-based *Frontline* website (within the Frontline Club) champions independent journalism worldwide. It says Wikileaks' online dissemination of confidential information "... is changing journalism and the relationship between public and power." This reflects a growing view that mainstream media – mainly, but not only, in America – have become apologists for governments and corporate interests. Why would you need a *Wikileaks*, argue these critics, if regular media were doing their job? [68] The shock-value of *Wikileaks* future revelations will certainly guarantee that it helps feed interest in world affairs. Even in the U.S. – where its Australian-led editorship and Swedish website-hosting raise eyebrows over 'foreign plots' against the U.S.

In spite of these specialized services, international coverage in the mainstream U.S. press remains a desolate display of American navel-gazing. It brings to mind the devastating judgment on U.S. TV that Federal Communications Commission Chairman Newton N. Minow famously delivered in 1961: "a vast wasteland." Local news is of course a vital necessity. But offering *only* local news of town and state raises questions about lifting – or even meeting – audiences' horizons. Horizons on the world that their children will live in, and on wars they may have to fight. Horizons on national security here and now.

Other dominant priorities – sex, corruption and especially crime – have their place. But they don't deserve *all* the space and *all* the airtime. In local TV news, and indeed in a lot of network news, "If it bleeds, it leads" still elbows analysis aside.

---

67 The alleged source of the leaked documents, intelligence analyst Private First Class Bradley Manning, also paid a heavy price. Awaiting a possible death penalty, he languishes, often naked, in a U.S. Marine Corps brig in Quantico, Virginia. A senior State Department spokesman, P.J. Crowley, had to resign after calling Manning's mistreatment "counterproductive and stupid."

68 See *Frontline* website for reports in *Wikipedia* and an interview with Assange.

Switch on your TV set, and you get a dismal diet: bank robberies, stakeouts and shootouts, car chases, petty crime, sexual or money peccadilloes, and weird "human-interest" stories ending with cute-and-cuddly animal pieces. All this sells TV ads – "commercials" that, unlike in most countries, cut in during the "news" itself. Perhaps the shoot-'em-up stuff boosts gun and tranquilizer sales? Even when U.S. TV goes international, it brings its guns-and-gore priority with it. It still neglects analysis, depth or context by showing us more bombs and destruction that we need to see. Again, this bloody, smoke-filled mayhem does little to help us understand the real forces in play: history, culture, economics, tribalism, religion, ambitions, lobbies.

Shrinking column inches and minutes (or seconds) of international airtime is only part of the problem. Audiences need context and interpretation – in a word, analysis.

Why analysis? Does it matter that citizens don't grasp all the ins and outs of Afghan tribal rivalries? Of the qualities, weaknesses and chances of possible future European or Asian prime ministers? Within reason, and within the citizen's own life, yes it does. Not every citizen is educated, engaged or alert enough to care about an array of issues. But possibly a select few? At least community leaders and thoughtful voters want, one presumes, to grasp the facts and rationales of public policy. Informed, organized and persistent voters can influence elected officials. They can help shape policy. Examples: Vietnam and Iraq. After tuning out these wars for blood-stained years, many aroused Americans finally did their homework, and asked questions. In time, they reversed leaders' conduct, and stopped ill-advised wars.

A 'built-in' limitation for young reporters: the failure of journalism schools ("J-schools") to offer much training, if any, in foreign reporting. In fact, the U.S. media's tendency to hire mainly J-schools graduates means that media are getting recruits with a weaker general culture than in the distant days before J-schools. Until perhaps the 1950s, picking up a general B.A. would certify at least a veneer of literature and culture, albeit mainly American. Now young hires get mega-doses of the mechanics of print or broadcasting, editing, graphics, multimedia, a little ethics, advertising, and lots of newsroom social-engineering: especially promotion of women and "minorities" (meaning blacks and Hispanics, not those "over-achieving" Asians). Of world history and at least one second language, nothing.

In time, this has to lower the standard of foreign analysis. J-schools are not usually mind-broadening educational institutions. Most are (often pretty good) vocational schools. But they don't routinely turn out thoughtful journalists. They produce lovingly cloned news jockeys – the more "local-minded" the better. Helpfully – since quite a few journalists end up in better-paid public relations, many "journalism" courses are buried within "communications" programs.

To be fair, a few U.S. J-schools may make up for the others. Medill, at Northwestern University, is a diamond in a dollar-store of costume-jewelry: It offers a rare, well-fleshed-out program in Global Journalism featuring theory and hands-on training, including overseas residencies. The Annenberg School for Communication & Journalism at the University of Southern California (USC) has "research networks" in Globalization & Communication and in International Communication, a Center for Public Diplomacy, and a world-minded Center for the Digital Future. The venerable Columbia School of Journalism offers two international dual-degree programs: one with *Sciences Po* in Paris, the other with South Africa's University of Witwatersrand.

One special public desperately needs informed daily coverage of world affairs: public officials, elected or not. Sadly, many members of Congress don't seem to do even basic international homework. They display all the depth and sensitivity of – not to be nasty – Sarah Palin, an international 'expert' because she claimed that in her Wasilla, Alaska, house she saw Russia though her kitchen window. Yet even appallingly ignorant members of Congress vote on defense budgets, as well as on major foreign policy issues. Unkind? Or just scary?

It's bad enough that U.S. voters get a thin diet of foreign news, even as their taxes fund wars they have few ways to understand. But the cost of ignorance hits the government tangibly. Cancelled foreign news coverage can actually harm national security. "That," reported *Yahoo News*, "is the verdict delivered by Daniel Butler, an official in the Office of the Director of National Intelligence, and Kevin O'Connell, a former intelligence analyst for the State and Defense Departments. At a National Press Club panel devoted to open source intelligence — i.e., intelligence gathered from news reports and other unclassified outlets — both men said the dramatic cutbacks in expensive foreign reporting by U.S. newspapers have made it *harder for intelligence analysts to understand global trends.*" [69]

Such top officials juggle scores of radically different world issues each day. Of course, they get reports from their own field officers. But these often run late and/or get buried in a mountain of unread cables. The up-to-the-minute immediacy of on-the-go foreign correspondents routinely fills important gaps in key officials' knowledge and understanding.

There's another, often forgotten, dimension to America's imperiled international coverage: the U.S. media's temptation to cheerlead. In most countries, at least to some extent, some of this is inevitable. But in the U.S. – as the days before and after George W. Bush's Iraq war showed – even stars (both print and TV) of the U.S. media just rolled over on their backs and begged Bush to tickle their tummies. With few exceptions, they bought the whole Bush-Cheney farrago of fabrications. And they took to heart the unspoken (but well-understood) message of the Pentagon news managers: "Shut up and salute!"

A 2009 book by Anthony Dimaggio called *When America Goes to War* digs into the media's cheerleading problem. He analyzes how "elite" media, as part of a shared "infoganda" machine, sold the Iraq war to the American people. He shows how the media stuck to the Bush-Cheney party-line through staggering setbacks on the ground. Even as civil war raged after the first year of occupation, the *New York Times* tended to

---

69   [Author's italics], *Yahoo News*, June 18, 2010.

blame incompetent, struggling Iraq leaders for the mess: "That the United States – by dissolving Iraq's army, government, intelligence agencies, and police – might have been responsible for creating the conditions of civil war in Iraq was apparently unfathomable to the editors of the 'paper of record.'" [70] In his 1945 occupation of Japan, General Douglas MacArthur, with all his faults, was astute enough to keep Emperor Hirohito on his throne, and to impose a 'temporary' constitution to allow a new Japan to function. The cohesion, common culture and basically untouched hierarchies, of Japanese society also helped. Japan, even after a nation-crushing defeat with nuclear weapons, quickly became a functioning society. Iraq did not. Because, with enthusiastic U.S. media support, amateur American pro-consuls in Iraq dismantled the country's entire infrastructure.

Serious media critics such as the *Columbia Journalism Review* CJR) attacked media cheerleading in the months before and after the 2003 Iraq invasion. Generally, it blamed the right-wing conservative media, specifically: "FOX News, *The Weekly Standard, National Review, The Washington Times, The Drudge Report, The Washington Examiner, The American Spectator, CNS News, Town Hall, WorldNetDaily, Insight Magazine* are all explicitly ideological. FOX makes the bizarre and palpably untrue claim of ideological neutrality: "We Report, You Decide" – a claim it violates so routinely that no one takes it seriously." It argued that conservative U.S. media were essentially patriotic "opinion" media, and that objective (i.e. "disloyal") reporting came mainly from the leftwing "liberal" press.

This conveniently overlooked the near-unanimous gung-go, pro-war, pro-military reporting that nearly the whole mainstream press displayed at the outset. Even CNN anchors wore U.S. flag pins. This tempest-in-a-teapot popped up every few years, to divided opinion. TV network ABC banned flag pins; the *Washington Post* and *Altanta Journal-Constitution* also argued against pin-wearing. But super-patriots such as Lou Dobbs and Geraldo Rivera, as well as the always-game-to-salute Fox

---

70 Dimaggio, p. 12.

anchors, clung to their pins like frightened children to security blankets. [71]

Noam Chomsky and Edward S. Herman wrote the classic 1988 book on how corporate media help shape and sell conservative political agendas: *Manufacturing Consent: The Political Economy of the Mass Media.* Several credible frontline journalistic assessments documented George W. Bush's mendacious campaign to lead America to invade Iraq. These reports shockingly confirmed how supine the U.S. media had been before the war. A clear-headed ABC-MSBC reporter, Jessica Yellin (now with CNN), described the atmosphere: "...the press corps was under enormous pressure from corporate executives, frankly, to make sure that this was a war that was presented in a way that was consistent with the patriotic fever in the nation and the president's high approval ratings... And my own experience at the White House was that, the higher the president's approval ratings, the more pressure I had from news executives ... to put on positive stories about the president... They would turn down stories that were more critical and try to put on pieces that were more positive, yes. That was my experience." [72]

Another journalist, CBS's anchor-reporter Katie Couric, had this to say about corporate censorship favoring war: "I think it is a very legitimate allegation. I think it's one of the most embarrassing chapters in American journalism. I think there was a sense of pressure from the corporations who own where we work and from the government itself to really squash any kind of dissent or any kind of questioning of it. I think it was extremely subtle but very, very effective." [73]

As subtle as the September 2010 "rebranding" of the Iraq War? No longer did the Pentagon call its Bush-Cheney-Rumsfeld masterstroke "Operation Iraqi Freedom." Henceforth the

---

71   Lou Dobbs, "Our flag belongs to all Americans," *CNN* site, October 10, 2007.
72   Jessica Yellin,"CNN/MSNBC reporter: Corporate executives forced pro-Bush, pro-war narrative," *Salon*, May 29, 2008.
73   Katie Couric, "Pre-Iraq War Coverage: "Pretty Good Job" or "Embarrassing?" *Columbia Journalism Review*, May 29, 2008.

Pentagon would call it the cheerier "Operation New Dawn."[74] The deferential, not noticeably chastened, U.S. press seemed to go along with this happier, almost poetic non-war – which kept in Iraq a trifling 50,000 troops. But at least the new title avoids the once-touted "Operation Iraqi Liberty" – which a last-minute acronym-check reminded planners would spell OIL...

Understandably and legitimately, the mainstream media's immediate post- 9/11 reporting totally backed the government. And as the Iraq conflict was slowly winding down, it supported Bush's (and now Obama's) new priority of Afghanistan. But shortly, doubts about U.S. deaths and ballooning costs turned mainstream media against "staying the course" in Afghanistan. Constant stories about Afghan government corruption and incompetence completed the shift against the war. By 2010 a clear consensus about "unwinnability" (highlighted by the stunning July 2010 dismissal for 'disloyalty' of General Stanley McChrystal) pointed to an eventual fig-leaf exit. At each stage, the mainstream media followed the government's moods and inclinations, almost in lockstep. Hence DiMaggio's theory of a government-military-media establishment.

New financial and technogical models won't change this home-team rooting. As U.S. foreign bureaus close, novel formats and techniques come into play. Order of the day: shoestring operations, often using very young, inexperienced freelance reporters eager to make a name – and to take both physical and financial risks to make that name. Tim Windsor, on the Nieman Journalism Lab website, describes the tough media universe would-be young foreign correspondents must deal with:

...there are now fewer reporters covering fewer stories in foreign countries for American news organizations.

Some of those that do remain are still in the employ of the few remaining deep-pocketed organizations with bureaus. But an increasing number are independent or loosely confederated reporters, chasing stories first and finding buyers for them second.

---

74 "It's the New, Improved Iraq War!," *Center for Media and Democracy*, February 10, 2010.

Organizations such as the recently launched *GlobalPost.com* — a rare news startup with an international focus — features a mix of staff and freelance correspondents who cover the world for American eyes, both directly through the site and through syndication.

It's a lean operation — paying reporters about $1,000 a month, *according to PBS MediaShift*. [75]

There's another well-entrenched media cheerleading game shaping the U.S. public's views. On Israel. One cannot understate the power and omnipresence of pro-Israel voices in the USA. Many reflect a widespread belief that America and Israel share common values of freedom and democracy. Many of them emerge from America's strong Biblical culture, in which Christians study the Old Testament, sometimes as the literal "Word of God." Many Christians come from a born-again Christian lobby backing Israel's occupation of Palestinian territories on Messianic Biblical grounds. Other pro-Israel support arises of course from the American Jewish community which – legitimately and naturally – wants the State of Israel to flourish. Many media voices speak up for Israel on grounds of history, fair play, intellectual conviction, and just plain sympathy for the Middle East's "only democracy" – a claim never entirely true for Israeli Arabs, and now simply unusable as Egypt, Tunisia and several other Arab nations struggle to build democratic regimes.

The result is that there is in the U.S. media an almost universal pro- Israel orthodoxy. With rare exceptions, if Israel acts extremely badly, the news either gets ignored or quickly shuffled off to insignificance. No other nation in the world beside the U.S. – and certainly not Israel's own feisty, argumentative press – almost monolithically supports the government of Israel, whatever it may choose to do.

There's a darker side to this. Any American editor or journalist dealing with Middle Eastern affairs will confirm that (as for members of Congress and even professors) there is a price to be paid for daring to criticize Israel – even factually and fairly. The

---

75   *Nieman Journalism Lab* website, January 29, 2009.

kind of fearless, critical analysis you can read or hear about the Israeli government, army and society in the Israeli media would draw a firestorm of orchestrated Jewish-lobby protest if aired in America. Almost immediately, the offending editor or journalist would attract strident, *ad hominem* attacks and demands for retraction. In Israel, writers such as Amira Hass, Gideon Levy, Amos Oz, David Grossman and Akiva Eldar face right-wing fury for writing about Israel's oppression of Palestinians. But they are not harassed as foreigners are. And they can still get published.

Routinely, non-Jewish American (and other) journalists get tarred with the shockingly bigoted epithet of "anti-Semitic." Jewish offenders of the current (essentially right-wing) Israeli orthodoxy can draw contempt as "self-hating Jews." In March 2011, Israel's Prime Minister Binyamin Netanyahu was too busy to meet Jeremy Ben Ami, founder-president of Washington's moderate pro-Israel lobby J-Street (representing "170,000 pro-Israel, pro-peace" American Jews). Curiously, during Ben Ami's visit, Netanyahu found time to have dinner with a more politically congenial guest: far-right, far-out Sarah Palin. Likudniks wouldn't dare hit Ben Ami with the self-hating tag. But the prime minister's refusal to meet Ben Ami seemed, in political terms, at least to hint unfairly at some kind of 'disloyalty' to Israel. Or at just the impossibility, in some right-wing minds, of being both pro-Israel and pro-peace?

Nasty name-calling – smearing, in a word – is of course disgusting. But it's a highly effective form of intellectual terrorism. Dangerously distorting, it skews ordinary Americans' thinking about the world. For example, it is close to suicidal in U.S. journalism to report that most of the world, Muslim or not, sees the brutal Israeli occupation of Palestine as an aggravating cause of Islamic terrorism throughout the world. Even to mention the phrase "Jewish lobby" drags out accusations that the commentator is paranoid (and of course "anti-Semitic") in pointing out that such a lobby may indeed exist. This, although the American Israel Public Affairs Committee (AIPAC), the chief orchestrator of protest, terms itself "America's Pro-Israel Lobby." As it is, and has every right to be – without shame or apology. [76]

Perhaps the most authoritative confirmation of the lobby's relentless ganging-up on wayward American journalists comes from a former spokesman for the Israeli consulate-general in New York, Menachem Shalev (who, for his part, unblushingly and commendably calls a lobby a lobby): "Of course, a lot of self-censorship goes on. Journalists, editors, and politicians are going to think twice about criticizing Israel if they know they are going to get thousands of angry calls in a matter of hours. The Jewish lobby is good at orchestrating pressure." [77]

The point of all this? It links directly to the militarization of U.S. public discourse. For the U.S.-Israeli relationship includes a huge component of U.S. taxpayers' military aid: at least half of the $106-billion of U.S. aid to Israel has gone to military use. And American military aid for 2013-2018 will amount to an average of $3.15 billion per year. [78] It is exactly this aid for aircraft and other modern weapons that Muslims (and many others) throughout the world see as feeding the fires of *al-Qaeda*-style terrorism. A high percentage of stories about Israel highlight defense issues and activities. Constant speeches about "identical" U.S. and Israeli interests, U.S. arms aid, and "intimate' U.S.-Israel military cooperation present to the world the image of an indissoluble tandem – armed to the teeth, and working

---

76 Shame and apology have sometimes surfaced. Even sober *Wikipedia* cites two cases where AIPAC officials seemed to go way over the line in pressuring Washington. The 1992 "Steiner case" records that AIPAC President David Steiner had to resign for bragging about how he had extracted huge funds for Israel and weighed in on key appointments. In 2005, AIPAC had to fire two senior officials for alleged involvement in espionage. The two officials were "indicted for illegally conspiring to gather and disclose classified national security information to Israel" – but charges were later dropped.
77 Cited in the impressively documented, much-denounced *The Israel Lobby* by Harvard professors John J. Mearsheimer and Stephen M. Walt, Farrar, Straus & Giroux, New York, 2007, p. 172.
78 The $106-billion figure comes from a pro-Israel source. A more balanced source – The *Washington Report on Middle Eastern Affairs* (backed by former ambassadors and Congressmen) estimates that the total of U.S. aid to Israel only until 2008 was $114-billion. See "A Conservative Estimate of Total Direct U.S. Aid to Israel: Almost $114 Billion," website of the *Report*.

hand in glove to occupy and "humiliate" Muslims. The F-16s firing laser-guided missiles that killed hundreds in January 2009 Gaza, Muslims know, didn't come from Liechtenstein.

To ignore the objective – and immensely counter-productive – PR effect of this is simply to deny reality. Angry dismissals of the impact of U.S.-armed Israeli crushing of Palestinians are in great part a calculated diversion. There *is* plainly a cause-and-effect link between gifts of U.S. weapons and their use. And as senior U.S. generals started recognizing publicly in 2010, American soldiers are dying in Afghanistan, as in Iraq, at least partly because of Israeli behavior in Palestine (details later in this chapter). Jihadists everywhere cite faraway Palestine as one of their motivations.

The U.S. media eagerly convey the many "benefits" of U.S.-Israeli cooperation. They sincerely believe that such collaboration is always good news. In intelligence matters, that is undoubtedly true: Israel knows its volatile neighborhood pretty well. But as Israel's decades-old Jonathan Pollard and Ben-Ami Kadish anti-U.S. espionage affairs showed, it also has many ways of knowing America. [79] The American media are right to praise cultural and technology affinities with Israel. But were they imaginative and daring enough to take a more critical view of the heavily military U.S.-Israeli relationship, they might do a service to both countries. And to the rest of the Western world. For Europe, Asia, Africa, Canada and Australasia also indirectly pay, in terrorism, the price of Palestine. The price for Islamic militancy inflamed by the endless, televised drama of Palestinian injustice and suffering.

Is it "anti-Semitic" to say that? Of course it is, to those in the habit of flinging that obscene insult at anybody who disagrees with them. Others may find the observation of Palestinian suffering self-evident. Things being as they are, the U.S. media will not soon find the ambition to report a fairer truth on Israel and Palestine. Or the courage to say it. Meanwhile, many brave and distinguished Israeli journalists are not afraid to say it for them.

---

79 Both men, American citizens, were convicted of passing U.S. secrets to Israel. Pollard went to jail, Kadish, after pleading guilty, was fined and allowed to retire.

The Israeli press, as we noted, is fearlessly free and frank – but largely unquoted in the U.S.

One reason courage is missing in action in mainstream U.S. media – and politics – is the relentlessly xenophobic (but vociferously pro-Israel) trio of *Fox News*, Rush Limbaugh and Glenn Beck. All are daily screamers of Big Lies, far-right version. America-First *Fox News* ludicrously terms itself "fair and balanced" – but that is only within the ever-narrowing U.S. spectrum of the hysterical Right. Limbaugh and Beck are masters of open-mouth radio. Beck is also an uncanny mimic of Jimmy-Swaggart style, low-evangelical weepiness about God and country. American's only visible antidote to this madness is Jon Stewart's *The Daily Show*, a brilliantly wacky left-of-center nightly TV show. In terms of craziness, the big difference between Stewart and the Terrible Trio is that he is *intentionally* funny. Stewart, though denying he's a journalist, works with skilled writers to present coverage often more rigorous than that of the traditional networks' evening news.

The low-road Fox-Beck-Limbaugh brand of news ensures that even mainstream media end up covering fanatics, freaks and xenophobes This can blow up an isolated, eccentric event to hit the national – then international – news. The infamous Florida "pastor" Terry Jones, who wanted to burn copies of the Koran, was a huge hit with newshounds. Unfortunately, their exorbitant coverage gave his ego a gigantic boost and the story went viral on *YouTube*. In the confusing circus of 9/11's ninth anniversary and the "Ground Zero mosque," a frightened Jones disappeared into a virus-free black hole. But his "stunt," as Obama aptly called it, did become a splendid recruiting tool for *al-Qaeda*.

What hopes exist for richer, more diverse, international coverage in the U.S? We won't likely see again the large foreign bureaus of yesteryear. Parochial news executives, technology, the Internet, and of course budgets will ensure that. And today's lean years for young new reporters don't suggest a major flow of money for original, alternative voices and perspectives. One phenomenon to watch: the development of national TV networks seeking international audiences via widely-spoken languages. Apart from the BBC and CNN, there are now, for example, *Al Jazeera* English and Arabic, *France 24* French, English and Arabic, *DW-World (Deutsche Welle)* German and English, *NHK World* Japanese and English, *CCTV* Chinese and English, British *Sky News*, Israeli *Guysen TV* French (in Europe). In most countries, carriage, once approved in principle, depends on the willingness of satellite or cable owners to include new channels. Such inclusion can become the object of pro or con lobbies with either commercial, ethno-cultural or political axes to grind. Or all three.

In addition to large international networks, the Internet offers hundreds of local TV and radio channels free of charge. These normally find only small, committed audiences who have sought them out. But they do diversify the choices of news available. Try "Spanish TV" or "French TV" or even "Romanian TV" on Google, and you will see how the news world is now as local as you choose.

Finally, what about smaller technologies? Each year – if not each week – new technologies seem to open up fresh news potentials. We have seen camera-and-video cell-phones, Facebook and Twitter as spot-news auxiliaries. And highly personal or specialized blogs of unequal value. But these remain for now just quick hits. They can also give a keyhole look at events, often from very biased or ill-informed people. They don't provide the deep background or analysis that allows audiences to form or rethink well-substantiated opinions. One can only shudder to imagine what nano-microphones and cameras might produce in future – beside raging debates on freedom of information, privacy and ethics. Let's at least hope that technology will soon give us something worthwhile: like hi-def, holographic TV of the Bolshoi Ballet, pirouetting through our living-rooms?

Would even that induce Americans to think about international affairs? Maybe, though likely not. To package and interpret such marvels, you would likely still need editors, and even credible news brands. Otherwise, audiences would just float through a kaleidoscope world, unable to make any sense of the blur.

Let's look now at how America's schools make sense of the world. And at where indeed their world might be. It's probably out there somewhere – but never as interesting as Homeland America?

Schools: What the Kids Don't Know *Will* Hurt Them

If, as noted later, the best American universities can dare to brag about being the "best in the world," Most American elementary and secondary schools are lucky to pass for the best in their own minds. They are not Utopia, but Myopia. Alas, it's at these early levels that every child integrates basic, lifelong knowledge. If certain things are not absorbed before age 18, they often never will be. History, and especially geography (both physical and human), are such fields. At least as much as culture, language, literature, math and science, they are the fundamental building blocks for understanding the world. For they tell us who we are, where we are in the world, and how we got here – as well as who our neighbors are, and where and how they live.

Unfortunately, American pre-university schools – in the famous K-12 years (kindergarten to Grade 12) – are at the very heart of American ignorance of the world outside Fortress America. They purvey a parochialism that dangerously shapes attitudes of American supremacy – and, not so subtly, America's military mindset. If all you know is America, and that America is militarily paramount, chances are you will find it normal for the U.S. to run the world. Indeed, can you really understand the U.S. in its world context? Remember Kipling's: "What should they know of England, who only England know?" At very least, you won't ask a lot of questions about why the U.S. maintains military bases around the world. And an economy-draining military establishment at home.

Stroll through an average U.S. classroom – primary or secondary. A big, solitary map of the United States and a huge U.S. flag suggest a place where love of country is a constant priority. You may find a national map in some other countries' classrooms, but usually with a world map too. In France, Germany or the UK, you will almost never see a national flag, and certainly no "Pledge of Allegiance" to the flag. In next-door Canada, you might see a flag, but likely not. And certainly no quasi-religious oath to the flag.

But studying geography and history are the surest measures of how U.S. students see, know and imagine our globe. And of how they react to international news or topics.

In 1980, a study by curriculum researcher Gary Manson revealed that "*less than 20%* [author's italics] of all students will have taken a geography course by the time they graduate from high school. Geography at the high school level is usually an elective. At the elementary level, it is usually integrated into a social studies curriculum. Neglect of geography is an old U.S. story: 1980 statistics from the National Assessment of Education Progress (NAEP) indicated that geographic knowledge of students was "inadequate." [80] Since then, observers have noted a fast slalom downhill.

An aggravating factor: the National Education Association reports that for decades, half of all new U.S. K-12 teachers resign within five years. This attrition – due to low salaries and poor working conditions – not only documents an awesome waste of talent. It helps explain why U.S. primary and secondary education broadly lags in quality behind schools in other advanced countries. Geography and history are a notable part of this backwardness. [81]

In 2006, the *National Geographic*-Roper Public Affairs Geographic Literacy Study [still painted] a dismal picture of the geographic knowledge of recent U.S. graduates. "After more than three years of combat and nearly 2,400 U.S. military deaths in Iraq," noted a *CNN* report on this, "nearly two-thirds of Americans aged 18 to 24 still cannot find Iraq on a map ... these

---

80   Gary Manson, "An Analysis of the Status of Geography in American Schools," Education Resources Information Center, April 13–16, 1980.
81   Lisa Lambert, "Half of teachers Quit in 5 Years," *Washington Post*, (from Reuters), May 9, 2006.

results suggest that young people in the United States ... are unprepared for an increasingly global future... Far too many lack even the most basic skills for navigating the international economy or understanding the relationships among people and places that provide critical context for world events... 88 percent of those questioned could not find Afghanistan on a map of Asia despite widespread coverage of the U.S.-led overthrow of the Taliban in 2001 and the political rebirth of the country... In the Middle East, 63 percent could not find Iraq or Saudi Arabia on a map, and 75 percent could not point out Iran or Israel. Forty-four percent couldn't find any one of those four countries ... Americans scored next to last on overall geographic knowledge, trailing Canada, France, Germany, Great Britain, Italy, Japan and Sweden." [82]

Happily, the *National Geographic* Education Foundation soon after launched a campaign called "My Wonderful World" to improve Americans' geographic knowledge. The long existence (since 1888) of the National Geographic Society, and its main magazine's 6.69-million circulation, have made it a powerful motivating force in U.S. families. Its many other publications, international TV channels and feature documentaries make it the logical leader for geographic reform. Needless to say, a radical improvement in young Americans' geographic knowledge will take time. Meanwhile, still another generation of young graduates is entering public service and private professions where Americans remain at a serious international disadvantage.

U.S. schools struggle with untrained geography teachers and superficial, America-centered textbooks. See this review of a widely-used textbook for Christian-oriented schools called *My America and My World* – Grades 1-8: "This very brief overview of the United States and the world is patriotic and upbeat. It offers tidbits about famous people and places (including the fable about George Washington and the cherry tree). "World" study features a few paragraphs about selected countries." [83]

---

82 "Study: Geography Greek to Young Americans," *CNN*, May 4, 2006.
83 Beka Books, 1999 edition.

Thin gruel for future masters of the universe. A further publisher's explanation:

"This is really a geography/social studies book more than history. It includes church history, and frequently addresses forms of government, particularly communism. Throughout the book, Christianity and the Bible are used as the standard and measure of comparison for all cultures and ideas. One entire chapter is titled: "Christianity: The Greatest Force in History...Historical coverage seems more extensive in studies of ancient civilizations than those that are more modern. For example, more than six pages [go] to Sumer, while France gets about three pages." [84] [Note: The Sumerians only invented writing; the French publish almost 600 unreadable novels every year – most of them seeming to win a prize of some sort].

Surely, textbooks used in public elementary and secondary schools do better? The Thomas B. Fordham Institute – "a non-profit think-tank dedicated to advancing educational excellence" – reviewed a number of mainstream history texts. It found merit in some, but generally judged them completely ill-adapted to classroom learning. It accused most textbooks of being, in effect, paralyzed by political correctness, and terrified of offending or praising anybody – that is, frightened of taking a stand or even making sense of isolated facts and actions. "The result," said the Institute, is:

... fat, dull, boring books that mention everything but explain practically nothing; plenty of information but no sorting, prioritizing, or evaluating; and a collective loss of American memory. World-history texts present similar problems. It's hard to name a culture or era that doesn't turn up somewhere in these sprawling compilations, but no real story is told. There's no thread, no priorities, no winnowing of the important from the trivial, the history-shaping from the incidental. It's as if a car's chrome trim and speaker system were equivalent to its chassis and engine.

Why does this matter? Some successful countries like Japan and Singapore come to mind. They get by fine with slender curriculum guides rather than enormous textbooks. That's because their teachers are subject-matter experts in fields like history and, when supplied with guidance about

---

84   *Cathy Duffy Reviews* – see website of that name. Ms. Duffy is a well-known U.S. curriculum specialist, notably serving the home-schooling market.

what state or national standard-setters deem most important, can easily generate their own lessons and find their own materials. They don't depend on textbooks except as reference works.

That's not true in the United States, where few history teachers ever learned much history themselves. More than half of high school history teachers did not major or even minor in history in college. Instead, most studied education or psychology or sociology, perhaps with a focus on "social studies education." As a result, teachers charged with imparting essential information to young Americans about the history of their country and world must rely heavily on the textbooks available to them...[Textbooks should] tell "the main story" without neglecting lesser stories that form part of an accurate picture of the past. What they must not be is sprawling, drab assemblages of disjointed information in which everything matters equally and nothing is truly important. [85]

An even greater threat to serious teaching about the international community is a surging U.S. conservative trend to a new parochialism, akin to xenophobia. See this *New York Times* report on a Texas Board of Education vote of March 12, 2010. Its significance expands because many states follow Texas textbook standards and choices:

After three days of turbulent meetings, the Texas Board of Education on Friday approved a social studies curriculum that will put a conservative stamp on history and economics textbooks, stressing the superiority of American capitalism, questioning the Founding Fathers' commitment to a purely secular government and presenting Republican political philosophies in a more positive light. The vote was 10 to 5 along party lines, with all the Republicans on the board voting for it.

In recent years, board members have been locked in an ideological battle between a bloc of conservatives who question Darwin's theory of evolution and believe the Founding Fathers were guided by Christian principles, and a handful of Democrats and moderate Republicans who have fought to preserve the teaching of Darwinism and the separation of church and state.

Since January, Republicans on the board have passed more than 100 amendments to the 120-page curriculum standards affecting history, sociology and economics courses from elementary to high school. The standards were proposed by a panel of teachers...

"[The Conservatives] are going overboard, they are not experts, they are not historians," [said board member Mary Helen Berlanga]. "They are rewriting history, not only of Texas but of the United States and the world...

---

85 "A Consumer's Guide to High School History Textbooks," Diane Ravitch, Thomas B. Fordham Institute, February 26, 2004.

"Even the course on world history," went on the *Times* report, "did not escape the board's scalpel:"

> Cynthia Dunbar, a lawyer from Richmond who is a strict constitutionalist and thinks the nation was founded on Christian beliefs, managed to cut Thomas Jefferson from a list of figures whose writings inspired revolutions in the late 18th century and 19th century, replacing him with St. Thomas Aquinas, John Calvin and William Blackstone. (Jefferson is not well-liked among conservatives on the board because he coined the term "separation between church and state.") "The Enlightenment was not the only philosophy on which these revolutions were based," Ms. Dunbar said. [86]

Liberal-conservative culture wars seem likely to rage on in the U.S. education system. Much of this tension clearly has to do with the pervasive role of religiosity and organized religion in American society – a phenomenon unique in advanced, modern nations. It also appears to draw on the teaching of American exceptionalism, including a sense of military-backed U.S. superiority. It echoes the conviction that America is strong enough to do whatever it wants – and that whatever it wants is by definition good, moral, even blessed.

As we shall see again in the next section, God and guns have always made congenial partners in America. Wrapping their alliance in a flag can in some places (like boards of education) simply stop debate. For a "liberal" or "left-wing" backlash to offer children real open-mindedness and curiosity about the world would require taking on America's whole, highly politicized religious establishment. As the March 2010 Texas vote showed, ignorance tied to born-again group-think has won and closed a lot of minds.

With trends like the above, it's no shock to learn that on a 2009 national history test for high-school seniors barely 47 percent achieved "basic" level. A February 2011 Fordham study on the quality of history teaching gave grades of "D" or "F" to 28 states. Thank goodness, political leaders do better. Republican Congresswoman Michele Bachmann, delightfully untroubled by details, once assured that her country's Founding Fathers

---

86 James C. McKinley Jr., "Texas Conservatives Win Curriculum Change," *New York Times*, March 12, 2010.

"worked tirelessly until slavery was no more"... in 1865.[87] With a schedule that long, surely they had a right to doze off once in a while.

In spite of all, good news is on the horizon. On June 7, 2010, the national Common Core Standards Initiative announced almost unanimous agreement on tougher national academic standards. Guided by state governors and chief state education officers, the Initiative published impressive new standards for kindergarten to Grade 12 – K-12. These constitute a considerable improvement. But it will take a generation before its beneficiaries enter professions. The nagging problems of inter-school inequality (rich-poor, black-white) may take even longer to settle. For they are anchored deep in American society.

Although the quality of K-12 education is suffering across the U.S., problems aren't necessarily evenly distributed. Academic standards at public (elementary) schools are so inconsistent that students in one school could be getting an excellent education, while their peers in another school just streets or towns away are left in the dust. These differences don't always follow obvious lines - suburban vs. inner-city, for example. But it's not hard to see that it's low-income children in underfunded and overcrowded schools who lose out. [88]

No big surprise: Two states, Texas and Alaska, refuse the proposed new national standards. They allege these represent 'outside' interference. Unfortunately, as we noted, Texas (in spite of new split-run and print-on-demand technologies) still exerts disproportionate influence on national textbook choices. And we have just seen that the Texas Board of Education plans to build a new Alamo around its children's minds. Alaska, homeland of Sarah Palin, will presumably downplay history and geography to teach more efficient skinning of grizzly bears.

---

87   "Teaching standards – Don't know much about history," *The Economist*. February 19, 2011.
88   "National Academic Standards Program Has Launched," *Education-Portal.com*, June 7, 2010.

Churches: Onward Christian Soldiers!

America's God is an equal-opportunity warmonger. Especially among Christians. Of course historically, a handful of Christian clerics, both Protestant and Roman Catholic, have taken anti-war stands. Jesuit Robert Drinan, an anti-war Jesuit, became a peace-promoting Congressman in 1970 until ordered to resign by Pope John Paul II on pain of excommunication. Over the years, individual Protestant pastors have granted sanctuary in their churches to war resisters. In 1968, Rev. Robert Gardiner of Welksley, Mass., tried to do this – as did hundreds of other ministers – until the FBI arrested a 20-year-old war resister his congregation was harboring.[89]

U.S. rabbis, to their credit, do not seem to have gone out of their way publicly to glorify the U.S. military. The Israeli Defense Force (Israeli Army) understandably attracts their admiration as a rampart of Israeli security and an element of Israel's national identity. A few Canadian rabbis, no doubt in touch with U.S. colleagues since the Vietnam War, tried to help U.S. war resisters find a home in Canada. (In recent years, such efforts have gotten little sympathy from an unusually pro-U.S. Canadian government. One of its arguments: today's war-resisters have signed up to fight – they are not the Vietnam War's conscripts). The rabbis' organization, called Our Way Home, operated from British Columbia. It honored "the courage of those resisting current US militarism by seeking safe haven in Canada... The Our Way Home Reunion will honor the thousands of Canadians who helped them resettle in this country..." [90]

---

[89] "Churches: The Concept of Sanctuary," *TIME* magazine, June 28, 1968. See too the *Our Way Home* website: http://www.ourwayhomereunion.com/home.php. Note: The Conservative Party government of Canada's born-again Christian prime minister Stephen Harper is widely attacked in Canada for changing the longstanding Canadian tradition of welcoming threatened U.S. residents, from slaves to war resisters. His policy is to deport war resisters and send them back to face U.S. military justice. It would be a stretch to consider this as further evidence of Christian-backed militarism. But historically, U.S. and Canadian political and religious history have radically diverged.

[90] [89] *Our Way Home* website.

But overwhelmingly, the U.S. Christian clergy – and most of its believers – accept at face value Washington's word that its wars deserve support. What does that mean in practice? "Supporting the troops," whatever the reasons the politicians come up with for sending them to possible death. Clergymen, more at ease with emotion than analysis, bless soldiers' departures and returning home. They pray a lot and aloud, bless the caskets, visit the wounded, and console grieving families – all noble service.

Other clergymen turn into cheerleaders for war. Their churches display flags that Jesus wouldn't recognize. They pray not only for soldiers in the field and for their families, but for their war-making leaders. Commendably, padres of all major faiths (now including Islam as well as Protestant and Roman Catholic Christianity, and Judaism) offer much-needed emotional support for soldiers in the war zones – often across confessional boundaries.

If there's a caveat here, it concerns the clerics at the top. The Billy Grahams who ostentatiously prayed with a long series of presidents, perhaps to reassure them that God would understand and/or forgive their wars. Graham, however, the most influential of all modern evangelists, did refuse to play the military game, at least overtly. In 1979 he said, in refusing to join Jerry Falwell's Moral Majority: "I'm for morality, but morality goes beyond sex to human freedom and social justice. We as clergy know so very little to speak with authority on the Panama Canal or superiority of armaments." [91]

One fears that Billy's son, Franklin, a chip off the suspicious old Christian-bloc dad, may prefer to feed the flames of Pentagon-benefiting Christian militancy. Suggesting that President Obama carries at least "the seed of Islam," he told CNN that "the teaching of Islam is to hate the Jew, to hate the Christian, to kill them. Their goal is world domination." [92]

---

91 Attributed in "Billy Graham," *Wikipedia*.
92 Cited in Maureen Dowd, "Going Mad in herds: America's national lunacy," *New York Times*, August 23, 2010.

Bracing advice to stiffen the spines of members of Congress voting on the next Pentagon budget.

Prominent clergy also officiate at Congressional Prayer Breakfasts – a phenomenon that leaves most non-American Westerners aghast for an assembly officially devoted to separating church and state. Such divine invocations don't specifically lobby for policy changes or a new piece of defense hardware. But they put organized religion at the heart of an establishment where constantly reinforced national defense is as unquestioned as God Himself.

Clerics of America's three main faiths have, however, amply earned the right to sing the parody "Pass the Lord and Praise the Ammunition." That graced a 1967 poster denouncing the warmongering of New York's notorious Francis Cardinal Spellman. The good cardinal made such a career of blessing guns and hyping the military (as well as egging on politicians) that his many enemies termed Vietnam "Spelly's war." His many visits to the troops made him (echoing the comedian's yearly tour of overseas bases) "the Bob Hope of the clergy." He had urged intervention in Vietnam as early as 1954 to back Roman Catholics in "Christ's War" against North Vietnam and the Vietcong. Recognized by his own, Spellman in 1967 won the prestigious West Point "Sylvanus Thayer Award." The honor, for "outstanding service to the nation," goes yearly to an American best exemplifying the military academy's motto: "Duty, Honor, Country." Today the clergy are more discreet, usually sticking to the pastoral work of consoling troops and their families.

Among high-flying Protestant clergy, Jerry Falwell was a staunch backer of the military. National defense was a key plank in the platform of his lobby group, the Moral Majority. Its agenda, he said, was "pro-family," "pro-life," "pro-defense" and "pro-Israel." Like most fundamentalist preachers, Falwell bought into the Israeli pro-settlement agenda – a theme directly at odds with official U.S. policy against these illegal settlements. He was a staunch "friend of Israel." That meant, in lobbyists' code, that he supported massive military aid for Israel and the closest possible U.S.-Israeli military cooperation.

Pat Robertson – always entertaining for his loose-cannon ad-libs – regularly praised military strength as a rampart of America's beneficent power in the world. He might blame lesbians for September 11, abortion for Hurricane Katrina, and a devil's pact for Haiti's 2010 earthquake. But on defense, he was stodgily Pentagon-orthodox. It's true that sometimes he had ideas that could, by their off-the-wall originality, make him sound like Jack Ruby on a peacenik's mission. On August 22, 2005, he called for the assassination of Venezuelan President Hugo Chavez. A shocking idea, of course – until you realize that, in his mind, Robertson was actually arguing for *preventing* a war. Well, for saving on the defense budget: "We have the ability to take him out, and I think the time has come that we exercise that ability. We don't need another $200-billion war to get rid of one, you know, strong-arm dictator. It's a whole lot easier to have some of the covert operatives do the job and then get it over with." Jesus would surely understand.

Notwithstanding this episode, Robertson has always played the vociferous patriot. He's a foreign policy hawk, and backed both Bushes' Iraq wars, plus the war in Afghanistan. On April 29, 2010, Robertson and ten other prominent Catholic and Protestant "Christian Leaders for a Nuclear-free Iran" wrote to top Congressional leaders. They urged prompt passage of "tough sanctions on Iran intended to prevent the regime from obtaining nuclear weapons." In his interviews and statements, Robertson always made clear that standing up for Christ and America meant "supporting the troops" and the whole defense establishment – from White House to Pentagon to arms industries.

Acting directly to promote George W. Bush's agenda of American militarism and world supremacy is Tim Lahaye. Perhaps the "most influential evangelical you have never heard of," Lahaye is actually extremely well known in born-again

Christian circles. He's a central player at the intersection of military and evangelical Christian activity. Writing with professional author Jerry B. Jenkins, LaHaye has sold over 55 million copies of his apocalyptic *Left Behind* religious books. These are end-of-the-world, Jesus-is-coming books that also preach unquestioning political and military support for today's Israel. A parallel military series glorifies the U.S. military in a series of thrillers about gung-ho Marine Special Forces and U.S. Rangers.[93]

These Bible-and-bullets credentials made LaHaye a natural companion for George W. Bush and his pro-military view of the world. LaHaye helped rally decisive evangelical support for Bush in the 2000 presidential election. He also played a key role in founding the shadowy, Christian right-wing, three-meetings-a-year conclave called the Council for National Policy. Its composition and program: "Our over 600 members include many of our nation's leaders from the fields of government, business, the media, religion, and the professions. Our members are united in their belief in a free enterprise system, a strong national defense, and support for traditional western values." [94]

As a group, U.S. Christian leaders rarely seem to meet a war they don't like. Effusive praise for the military is fine if it aims to console soldiers and their families under stress. But should Christian luminaries be exalting the Pentagon and the defense industries? Such exaltation seeps like the Deepwater Horizon oil gusher through Christian rhetoric about a "strong America."

One senses that a "strong America" means essentially weapons, and always bigger defense budgets. Few religious leaders seem to talk of a "strong culture" or a "strong education system" as ramparts of a strong nation. Ironically, the great majority of current and potential recruits for foreign wars come from low-education, Christian backgrounds. These, as Michael Moore showed, are not the sons and daughters of Congressmen. They are society's drop-outs and ethno-cultural unfortunates. The ones whom recruiting sergeants chase down in strip-malls

---

93 Lahaye's website: https://timlahaye.com/default.asp
94 From the Council's website: http://www.cfnp.org/

of despair. "Only 83 percent of new Army recruits had a high school diploma (or at least 15 college credits), compared with the Department of Defense (DOD) average of 92 percent. The Army even has a special program, called Army Prep School, that allows individuals to enlist who have no high school diploma or GED." [95]

From the elite cadre of clerics such as now-retired Dr. Robert H. Schuller of California's Crystal Cathedral down to the foot-soldiers of weepy evangelism such as unlamented Jimmy and Tammy Bakker and aforementioned Jimmy Swaggart, one sees a promising, gun-affirming future for Christ in America. None of these drum-beaters for the military has yet gone broke – except in possible cases of mismanagement.[96]

Enjoy Schuller's November 21, 2008 "sermon" entitled "I am the American Flag." With a wall of huge U.S. flags behind him, Schuller told of "our crew-cut American soldiers, with pluck, who plowed on through the mud, leaving a trail of their own blood, as they liberated people they never met before and would never see again, and along the way they found time to deliver a baby from a primitive mother and pass out chewing gum to their kids." And... "all they [the soldiers] wanted was to go home... I know no other people [besides Americans] who have... unselfishly borrowed and spent billions of dollars to rescue beleaguered and besieged human people... with skin colors and facial features and languages and foreign religions that seem really odd to the young soldiers from Peoria, Illinois, and Sioux City, Iowa..." [97]

Pentagon budget chiefs, as well as Iraqis and Afghans and other peoples with foreign religions and odd facial features,

---

95 General Educational Development test, certifying marks higher than 60% of each year's nationwide high-school graduating classes. See also "Minimum Required ASVAB Scores and Education Level," Rod Powers, *About.Com* website.

96 After Robert H. Schuller retired in 2006, his son replaced him as leader, then his daughter after the father fired the son. On October 10, 2010, reports Wikipedia, "[she] announced that the Crystal Cathedral was seeking bankruptcy protection." The filing listed 550 creditors owed $48-million.

97 Robert H. Schuller, *Hour of Power*, Crystal Cathedral Ministries, *YouTube*, November 21, 2008.

were surely pleased. So, probably, were primitive mothers. Though perhaps a few parishioners asked why, instead of Bible-based spiritual guidance, they got a commercial for the U.S. Army.

Pioneering U.S. evangelists such as Aimee Semple McPherson and Elmer Gantry may have wanted a little money and sex with their salvations. But not a few of the current crop of Bible-pounders seem curiously concerned with the care and feeding of the Pentagon. Some born-again believers have even become welcome allies of *Israel*'s U.S.-backed military. They believe that the Palestinian lands ("the Biblical lands") really belong to Israel – well, at least until the Messiah comes. The pro-settlement Israeli right smilingly accepts this unusual support here and now – on the assumption that it may be a while before Jesus returns – as the evangelicals believe – to convert the Jews...

An old and contentious question is whether religion foments war. For even a superficial answer, you would have to survey a dozen or more religions over long histories. We can't pursue the countless variations and hypotheses here. What seems certain is that religious belief has often served as a pretext for war. Europe's old Catholic-Protestant wars of religion were often wars of dynasty and class – but also of conscience (Martin Luther, John Calvin) against authoritarian institutions (the Vatican and its international priesthood). In societies that have not yet resolved basic ideological conflicts, both power and faith seem motors of discord. Power meaning a dominant majority versus an aggrieved minority.

Examples: Ulster between Protestants and Catholics; many Muslim nations between Sunnis and Shias (among other so-called "heretical" groups); Sri Lanka between Buddhists and Hindus (with a sprinkling of Muslims and Christians); Thailand between Buddhists and southern Muslims; Ex-Yugoslavia between Orthodox Christians, Roman Catholics and Bosnian-Kosovar Muslims. But rival historic mythologies also drive conflict, notably in the Balkans. And for almost all "religious" conflicts, economic rivalry likely plays a part. Not to mention demagogic leaders. Yet what gives even the economic, ethnic and linguistic-cultural conflicts a really hateful, die-hard punch is God. Who, in passing, would probably prefer to turn down the flattering offer of whispering *Gott Mit Uns* to all sides.

Applying these knotty questions to the American religious scene doesn't really fit. For America's history of religion is unique. The Pilgrim Fathers fled English persecution to continue worshipping in their purer, simpler, priest-despising ways. They "dissented" from the Church of England and resisted state intrusion in their beliefs. They set a tone of passionate independence, emotional faith and strict moral "judgmentalism" that persists to this day. Over time, other variations of Christianity, plus Judaism, have implanted themselves on U.S. soil. Islam too is on its way to Main Street. But if you dig down into the popular American consensus of what constitutes right and wrong, you strike a foundation of Puritan 'morality.' Of sturdy, stubborn, moralizing Protestantism. It can be hypocritical in the extreme, as many fallen televangelists have shown. But it's always there – as Roman Polanski discovered to his dismay when a Californian prosecutor tried to get him extradited from Switzerland for a sexual scrape 33 years before. It was a crime that many Europeans dismissed as an ambiguous escapade, long-ago forgiven by the victim.

A final note on Christianity and U.S. militarism: A new book by Lutheran minister Kelly Denton-Borhaug called *U.S. War Culture, Sacrifice and Redemption* analyzes the overlaps. The author promises that her book "traces the enduring links between U.S. war-culture and the discourse and rituals of sacrifice." She adds in her book's promotional summary:

"The military-industrial complex in the U.S. has grown exponentially in recent decades, and now includes technological, academic, entertainment, scientific, cyber, intelligence, and security facets in addition to the traditional intertwining of the military with corporate and government institutions. Yet the reality of war-culture remains invisible to most Americans.

Sacrificial rhetoric and practices energize and naturalize war-culture's base and operations; sacrifice permeates just-war discourse and tradition; and popular Christian understandings of redemption in the U.S. also rely upon sacrificial formulations. The sacred canopy of war as "a necessary sacrifice" obfuscates the pernicious reality of U.S. war-culture, aided by abusive and manipulative formulations of Christian redemption conflated with militarism." [98]

Now, God willing, let's see how war, preferably mixed with religion, can keep crowds rolling into movie-houses. Or at least keep Hollywood rolling in war-begotten profits.

Entertainment I : Playing 'Nintendo' for Keeps

Far more to our point about dumbing down the U.S. public: The last 20 years' rush to new aggressive wars, especially in Muslim lands, has made cinematic militarism a still more powerful common denominator. These were originally the peace-hoping years after the Berlin Wall fell (November 1989). A prostrate Russia couldn't stop the U.S. from peacefully 'invading' Eastern Europe, or from stringing bases pretty well wherever it wanted. On March 1, 1991, date of the Allied victory versus Iraq in the First Gulf War, President George H.W. Bush exulted about starting a "New World Order" of U.S. hegemony – an unfortunate echo of the Second World War Axis's New World Order of Hitler, Mussolini and Tojo. "By God, we've kicked the Vietnam syndrome once and for all," he back-slapped colleagues, recalling how America's shameful defeat in Vietnam had paralyzed its will to make war since the fall of Saigon in April 1975.

The same day in 1991 Bush almost gleefully noted the potential for manipulating public opinion toward more wars: "No question about it, the country's solid. There isn't any anti-war movement out there. There is pride in these [our armed] forces." [99] And these forces, glowing in their new-found virtue,

---

98 From *Amazon.com* website page. The book will appear in 2010 or 2011.
99 Cited in Roger Stahl, *Militainment, Inc. – War, Media and Popular Culture*, Routledge, New York, 2010.

were to find incredibly powerful new ways of shaping public opinion. This they would do directly and, through supervised, even scripted media, indirectly. Movie producers and directors wanting to use Pentagon arms or facilities would have to submit scripts for approval – oh, and perhaps to hear a few little suggestions. An inevitable tradeoff.

But for new and amazing ways to shape opinion, read on. Roger Stahl, in his book *Militainment Inc. – War, Media and Popular Culture*, examines the U.S. military's systematic efforts to seduce the public to embrace – indeed enjoy – "all-consuming war." High-tech wizardry makes it all seem like an amusement park. As indeed, for recruitment, it is, through *Soldier of Fortune* magazine and mock-killing spectacles at country fairs:

> In the midst of the occupations of Iraq and Afghanistan, an American would only have to travel to Sherman, Texas – alone or with a corporate retreat group – a private "military amusement park" called Tactical Tanks. [Here] one could spend an entire day running "missions" in an actual tank for $8,500. On a budget, one might have caught up with the Army's traveling "Special Operations Adventure Van," a recruiting effort that offers a chance to hop aboard a tank, a helicopter, and a variety of other weapons simulators.
>
> One might take the family to the local fairground to try out the 19,000 square-foot "Army Virtual Experience," located near the tilt-a-whirl, which includes rides in Humvee and helicopter simulators. Such exhibits will likely be a permanent feature at the local mall in the coming years. [100]

Desert Storm General "Stormin' Norman Schwartzkopf cautioned in 1991 that war is "not a Nintendo game." But increasingly Washington sells war as just that to a bemused public – and especially to arcade-game-playing young males of military age.

You don't even have to go to a fairground or mall to try out these toys of RMA – the "Revolution in Military Affairs." Marrying "new operational" concepts to the technology demanding them, RMA now brings to video-games that you can buy or rent virtual "fun" with space-age surveillance, communications, robotics and uncannily accurate remotely-guided bombs and rockets. Carl Boggs and Tom Pollard in their

---

[100] *Ibid.*, pp. 2-3, referring to the "Military-Industrial-Entertainment Network."

book *Hollywood War Machine* note that "the military is now the main designers of war games, developed through a working partnership with the entertainment industry, computer firms and academia." Players can enjoy RMA-quality techno-war on DVDs, or in multiplex movie lobbies or games stores. "Simulated on large, high-resolution screens, the drama of war engulfs the total visual field, imbuing combat with elements of esthetic beauty and playful excitement, what one game producer calls the "dopamine rush." [101]

To appreciate the gleeful horror of this 'insensitivity training,' watch on *YouTube* or the *Wikileaks* website cited earlier as remote army killers order a helicopter crew to "engage" with "individuals" – which means murdering people who could easily be civilians, including children, families or journalists. This April 6, 2010 real-life U.S. Army video on *YouTube* shows the killing of two Reuters journalists (one already wounded) and over 10 other civilians. [102]

The calm, antiseptic voices ordering murder call up before your eyes machine-gun fire that rips up the bodies you see bouncing and writhing on the ground below. Using fuzzy images, the pilot told his controller that the newsmen's cameras were "RPGs" (rocket-launchers) – thus securing permission to blast away at the small crowd. The Army tried to cover up these murders committed from an Apache helicopter – but imprisoned 22-year-old Private Bradley Manning for leaking the incriminating video. [103]

Not a Nintendo game indeed. But such atrocities – these cold-blooded killings – are being taught to teenagers – and younger

---

101 Carl Boggs and Tom Pollard, *The Hollywood War Machine – U.S. Militarism and Popular Culture*, Paradigm Publishers, Boulder CO, 2007.
102 The U.S. Army has 'inadvertently' killed some "foreign" journalists such as Reuters and *Al Jazeera* newsmen – whose cameras they tended (as in Iraq and Afghanistan) to "confuse" with AK-47s. As we saw, it also 'accidentally' (but precisely) targeted the *Al Jazeera* bureaus in Kabul (November 13, 2001) and Baghdad (April 8, 2003).
103 As of October 26, 2010, as noted, Manning was being held – and (as later reported) routinely humiliated at a military prison in Quantico, Virginia. (*CNN* website).

kids – 'playing' those video-games you park them to enjoy in the malls.

In effect, America is mythologizing, distracting and drugging itself into a permanent war frenzy. It is schooling its youth in remorseless murder, always blessed by America's divinely-appointed 'missions' and sense of superpower impunity. Through movies, TV and video games, plus 'messianic' fantasies and NRA gun madness, Americans are now so familiar with the sounds, sights and pace of combat that war no longer shocks or distresses them. It has completely desensitized them to violence. Killing and maiming are becoming just America doing what it does so well: being heroic, and reshaping the world to its model. Militarism isn't in the air. It *is* the air – the very air Americans breathe. It's what Americans have been fooled and brain-washed into believing is "normal." That the rest of the world finds this military obsession as sick as the gun culture its draws on is of no concern. Foreigners are here to watch, learn and admire – not judge or preach.

The above is not the rant of foreigners who hate America. It's the opinion of many thoughtful Americans – including, broadly, several cited in this book and its bibliography. They are still a very small minority. But their fears about militarism are far less dangerous than Pentagon-induced paranoia – a terror designed, if two plus two still make eight (military budget math), to keep Americans eager to increase defense budgets.

Entertainment II : Scary Movies for Our Next War.

American popular culture, needless to say, doesn't go out of its way to educate Americans. And since entertainers, like preachers, want to make their audiences feel good, lifting I.Q. levels, taste or cultural standards is not a cosmic priority. Priorities target profits – and in the much-quoted dictum of H.L. Mencken, "Nobody ever went broke underestimating the intelligence of the American public." Given the public's home-school-and-NRA education in guns, the entertainment industry never recoils from making a buck out of violence. Military mythology offers the ideal feel-good mixture of killing and virtue – in both the Roman root-meaning of manliness and the Pilgrim Fathers' love of goodness.

As in the lower reaches of journalism, good entertainment sometimes gets in the way of facts. Hollywood's goal, an understandable foible, is to fabricate American heroes. The film *Pearl Harbor* (2001) showed U.S. pilots shooting down a significant number of Japanese planes – an utter fantasy in this massive U.S. defeat. Other war movies parachute American "heroes" into movies where they had a modest, or non-existent, historical role. *The Great Escape* (1963) was an essentially British show, but U.S. stars (Steve McQueen, James Garner) predominate. *Dam Busters* (1955) was an all-British affair with UK and Canadian Lancaster bombers – but Warner Brothers slipped a U.S. Air Force Flying Fortress into a crash scene for the U.S. market (an error later removed). *The Longest Day* (1962) was historically a U.S.-UK-Canada affair on the 1944 Normandy invasion. But the movie shows a mainly U.S. operation, suggesting "America freed Europe" – even though the U.S. entered the war well over *two years after* its English-speaking allies stood Hitler at bay. (Reminder: The Soviet Union did more than any country to defeat Nazi Germany).

All harmless, if misleading, stuff. He who holds the camera picks the pix.

How does U.S. pop culture keep war and the military alive in Americans' minds? Music plays a supporting role – both for and against war. In this, patriotic songs have a long history as a natural, fairly innocent expression of emotion. *Tipperary, Over There, and Mademoiselle from Armentières* in the First World War. And in the Second, *Our Sergeant Major* (George Formby), *White Cliffs of Dover, We'll Meet Again* (Vera Lynn) and *Boogie-Woogie Bugle Boy* (Andrews Sisters), not to mention *Lili Marlene* (Marlene Dietrich in German and several other languages), *I had a Comrade* (*Wehrmacht*, the German Army), *A Man of Habit* (Soviet tankmen's song with lots of girls). *YouTube* brings all this and more alive.

Surely there's nothing wrong with these morale-boosting songs? They console, amuse, and encourage frightened human beings. But objectively, they make war more tolerable – and more acceptable. They sweep listeners' feelings along. They induce audiences to think less, and salute more. A very good thing if, as during the London Blitz, you seek hope of survival. Not so good if you're Hitler's Panzer divisions rolling into Poland to the rollicking, victim-mocking *Horst Wessel* Song.

The homeland of John Philip Sousa, with its phenomenal musical creativity, has a genius for capturing the spirit of war. But also, in fairness, the spirit of peace. America's Vietnam War, of course, produced a plethora of anti-war songs. A major anthem – *We Shall Overcome,* made famous by the war's emblematic *Pasionaria* Joan Baez – mobilized crowds. Groups such as Jefferson Airplane and Creedence Clearwater Revival, Crosby, Stills, Nash and Young, plus Pete Seeger, also dominated the anti-war music "market," echoing the anguish of young men open to conscription.

Favorite pro-war songs were official martial music: the Marines' Hymn, the Navy's *Anchors Away, The Army Goes Rolling Along,* the Air Force's (via Sousa) *Off We Go Into The Wild Blue Yonder.* The national anthem and *God Bless America* added poetry and veneration. Other pro-war music consisted of revivals. *She Wore a Yellow Ribbon* was brought to the U.S. centuries before by English settlers. *Tie a Yellow Ribbon Round the Old Oak Tree* became famous during the 1979 Iran hostage crisis. It was used forever after as a "come-home-soon" for overseas troops. [104]

Is singing about war evidence of "dumbing down?" Not directly. But as argue some pesky French philosophers we shall shortly see, putting wars to music may be part of the mind-numbing transformation of war into a variation of showbiz. The spectacle of combat – accompanied by exciting music – may

---

[104] In March 2011, the Marines' Hymn's opening line "From the Halls of Montezuma to the Shores of Tripoli" seemed amazingly prescient. U.S. drones were then helping nail Mexican drug gangs, and the U.S., for Libyan starters, fired 110 Tomahawk missiles at Tripoli. As top American authorities unconvincingly assured, these were not aimed killing Colonel Muammar Gaddafi as he plotted new civilian massacres. They only aimed to spoil his breakfast.

weaken audiences' inclination to analyze the war's causes, contours and consequences.

Several major countries make war movies – like America's, often to 'invent' and sell national heroes. Britain, France, Germany and Russia are perennial producers of such films. Differences with the U.S? American films tend dramatically to highlight violence. And, as a measure of influence, good or bad, they blanket screens throughout the world.

Pro-violence and pro-war messages surge overwhelmingly from U.S. movies and TV. Violence is the mother's milk of Hollywood script-writers and directors. Arthur Penn's *Bonnie and Clyde* (1967), Stanley Kubrick's *A Clockwork Orange* (1971), Sam Peckinpah's *Straw Dogs* (1971), and Michael Mann's *Public Enemies* (2009) make extreme, close-up mayhem as seductive as an erotic poem. Extreme, arguably gratuitous, violence is so omnipresent that it's almost never even seen as controversial. Hollywood – whether for TV series or films – wallows in gun-related and military myths. This started with perennially popular cowboy movies, and their mythology of westward exploration (and barely-cited theft of aboriginal lands, plus massacres of natives). This coincided with the development of famous guns – Remington rifles, Colt handguns and, later in the 19th-century, the murderous Gatling machine-gun.

Cowboy or "western" movies and TV shows keep alive Frontier justice. They're often great fun – unless you're an American Indian. They remind us of childhood good-vs-evil melodramas and days of apparently limitless freedom. Jimmy Stewart, Gary Cooper, John Wayne and Clint Eastwood long owned the genre. Now Antonio Banderas and a vast posse of other cool gunslingers have ridden off in all directions, killing Indians and bad guys, all while taking unerring potshots at incautious rodents. The U.S. Cavalry still gallops in at the last minute before crafty Indians or Mexicans nearly grab their land back. Not to let such a tradition crumble before technology, the U.S. Army keeps going its 3d Armored Cavalry Regiment – though without horses to ride to anybody's aid.

As time cantered on, film and TV diversified their ways of glorifying violence. Countless war movies continue to promote the U.S. armed forces, even when (as in 1917 and 1941) they arrived pretty late at the party. The 2007 book *The Hollywood War Machine* lists 128 war movies since 1915. That's actually not so shocking, since the figure includes two world wars, the Korean War, the Cold War (with its devious spies and threat of nuclear Armageddon), and two Gulf Wars – not to mention other countries' often far more murderous wars (e.g. Rwanda, the Congo).

The list also includes pro-war movies that memorably portray combat. *Top Gun* was the quintessential love-the-Pentagon movie. But the list is much longer than the well-known *Full Metal Jacket, Saving Private Ryan* and the 2001 *Band of Brothers* which later became a 10-part TV mini-series. It includes the heart-tearing 1993 *Schindler's List* (about a 'good' German who saves Jews), people's-war classics such as *Mrs. Miniver* (1942), Stanley Kubrick's 1964 black comedy *Dr. Strangelove*, even (then-) witty James Bond spoofs, manic Robin Williams in *Good Morning, Vietnam* (1987) and the insidiously anti-war movie (leading to a later TV series) *MASH* (1970). In many such movies, Hollywood showed intelligence and sensitivity of a high order.

Is it paranoid to point out that the U.S. military machine actively promotes fear of "foreign" enemies by encouraging movies about "threats" from alien "evil-doers?" "The film industry has a long partnership with the armed forces," notes *The Hollywood War Machine:* "military public-relations offices typically review movie scripts in exchange for access to bases, equipment, stock footage and expert consultation, all needed for 'authenticity.'" Of course, America's right-leaning political and media culture also inclines producers to fearful, flag-waving movies. But with the Pentagon "reviewing" scripts, it's no wonder so many end up on the screen looking like recruitment infomercials.

A fine example of paranoia is the hyper-violent *Rambo* film series, starring sweaty, bare-chested Sylvester Stallone. Famous worldwide, especially in primitive, war-torn societies, the *Rambo* fantasies glorify U.S. weapons and fighters, notably special forces and soldiers-of-fortune types. These brutal, simple-minded movies specialize in impossible rescues. They teach that killing is usually the handiest way to settle an argument or get a job done. Pure comic-book stuff, these movies (and the videogames and cartoons spun off from them) confirm every report ever issued on media violence and children by the American Psychiatric Association, the American Medical Association and the U.S. Surgeon-General. In sum: a relentless diet of extreme violence *desensitizes* children to violence. It accustoms children to thinking of violence as the "best way," if not the "only way," to settle disagreements.

Two French books of the 1960s warned of this numbing of public consciousness through dramatic "shows." The first book *La Société du spectacle* (1967) by Guy Debord, reveals how politicians use images to distract, amuse and "demobilize" the masses. In effect, they dissolve democracy into a blur of intriguing pictures. The second book, *L'Etat-spectacle - sur et contre le star system en politique* (1977) by Roger-Gérard Schwartzenberg, develops this further, focusing on compelling personalities. Translatable as the "Show-biz State," this classic essay demonstrates how "people-ization" (as in today's *People* magazine) and "mediapolitics" substitute famous faces for ideas, distracting citizens from thinking-through policies. The combined effect of symbolic images and seductive faces makes the whole realm of public policy a virtual situation comedy. Lies, cover-ups, scandals and phony fights come to seem normal. Deep down, people see politics – including its intensely political U.S. military extension – as "just a movie." A movie where nobody *really* gets killed, everything is a special effect, and the billions of dollars wasted are just *Monopoly* money.

A third French author – and surely that's quite enough devious, cheese-eating *philosophes* to upset French-distrusting U.S. strategists! – was Jean Baudrillard. This iconoclastic sociologist's most famous book (1991) was *The Iraq War Did Not Take Place* (a wink at Jean Giraudoux's famous 1935 two-act play *The Trojan War Will Not Take Place*). In essence, he denounced the first Gulf War as a media-suckering hoax, a *son-et-lumière* fireworks display. It was, he argued, a jazzed-up narrative of flashing, exploding, real-time, live-action pictures that brought war safely but compellingly into living-rooms. In 2003, the Americans – actually and officially – called their opening-night Baghdad barrage of ground-shaking, sky-lighting missiles "Shock and Awe." NBC reporter Peter Arnett had little time for analysis – he was busy ducking missiles, and could only comment on the "show."[He was later fired for telling Iraqi state TV that the American-British invasion had stalled]. Arnett earned notoriety in 1968 Saigon for quoting a U.S. major musing on flattening a Vietnamese town: "It became necessary to destroy the town to save it." Other U.S. officers seemed to apply this judgment to America's Iraq. Tacitus had of course famously said: "We made a desert, and called it peace." *Plus ça change...*

One way to illustrate the Pentagon's grip on U.S. minds is to look again at a few fairly typical movies. All of these dazzle with techno-frenzy, or merely peddle racist, usually anti-Arab and anti-Muslim, contempt – with other enemies occasionally adding welcome variation. All sublimate thoughtful analysis into dizzying glorifications of the U.S. military. Boggs and Pollard look at scores of such movies in *The Hollywood War Machine*. But in a chapter called "Cinematic Warfare in the New World Order," they analyze four box-office hits: the *Delta Force* series (1986-91), *Rules of Engagement* (2000), *Black Hawk Down* (2001), and *Behind Enemy Lines* (2001).

American Mideast "terrorist" movies began in the early 1980s after the 1972 massacre of Israeli athletes at the Munch Olympic Games. At least five movies dramatized this horror. And for over two decades, Palestinians did practice terrorism to advance their goals of national liberation and recovery of lost lands. But from 1986 to 1991, Israel funded and produced with Hollywood expertise and actors a series of gung-ho adventures – first against Iran, then against Palestinians. Said Boggs and Pollard about America's enemies: "These groups replaced Communists and kindred time-honored demons as larger-than-life screen villains... The terrorist enemy was seen as crude, semi-civilized, shady, violent, beyond redemption, capable of horrendous crimes – traits making them quite suitable for extermination." In *Delta Force 3*, Palestinian terrorists implausibly threaten to nuke Miami.

Even warm and cuddly Roman Polanski made *Frantic* (1988), moving critic Douglas Kellner to note that such racist caricatures of Arabs sometimes recalled the Nazis' sickening portrayal of Jews. [105]

Boggs and Pollard call *Rules of Engagement* "one of the most anti-Arab films ever shot, and that is saying a good deal... [A] crowd of protesters is full of venomous, evil-looking Others intent on making life miserable for innocent, businesslike Americans...Filled with veiled women, screaming and gesturing men, and out-of-control children, the mob appears onscreen as nothing more than a vehicle of hate and destruction....Nowhere do we find any suggestions that these might be human beings with actual *reasons* to protest. Once the firing starts and a marine is hit, Col. Childers decides to respond, screaming 'waste the motherfuckers!'" At least that is franker than the civilian-killing, U.S. *YouTube* helicopter pilot's "engage with the individuals!" But it means exactly the same: a massacre. [106]

This film's murderous fantasy seems to serve no purpose other than to generate fear and contempt of Arabs and Muslims as supposed sub-humans. In a courtroom scene that exonerates those clean-cut American killers in uniform, it seems to say (again) that the U,S. – *whatever* it does – is above morality or law. Its military can do anything it wants to the faceless Muslims and escape punishment. Military supremacy guarantees impunity. Might is right, even to massacres of innocents. It is 'right' even, as in real-life exposés of U.S. behavior in Iraq and Afghanistan, to torture, kill prisoners, and commit civilian atrocities, careless or intentional. [107]

---

105 *Ibid.*, pp. 191–92.
106 *Ibid.*, pp. 184–87.
107 Such behavior continued long after the infamous 2006 Abu Ghraib Prison horrors. In March 2011, Germany's *Der Spiegel* ran photos of Afghan civilians randomly tortured, killed and mutilated by members of the U.S. Army's 5th Stryker Combat Brigade.

This film, by giving blanket blessing to clearly criminal action, accustoms the public to thinking that their "clean-cut" boys – and 'girls' like Lynndie England (of Abu Ghraib "Arab-on-a-chain" fame) – can do no wrong. Because they are Americans. Just happy-go-lucky brothers-in-arms who, at the end, eschew remorse about setting dogs on prisoners, and joke about going fishing together.

Black Hawk Down continues the same "primitive, savage Arabs" narrative by landing about 140 cocky, heavily-armed U.S. Army Rangers, Delta Force soldiers and Special Operations Aviation-Regiment specialists into the middle of a lawless Mogadishu. Their ostensible purpose: to protect United Nations humanitarian food shipments. But quickly, the troops discover to their amazement that they are not welcome. The hungry, frightened Somalis below see coming at them terrifying, big black helicopters, then hulking foreign soldiers with machine-guns pointing at anything that moves, or even just watches. Thousands of Somali militiamen also threaten the town – but they are at least compatriots. The militiamen's leaders whip up street crowds to resist the "foreign invasion" – and public fury explodes against the massively outnumbered U.S. troops.

This hyper-violent movie never seriously looks at local history or culture, or asks what underlying reasons *might* explain the crowds' anger. It seems perplexed at how the ragtag Somalis can even face, much less defeat, Americans presumably superior in weapons, training and intelligence. Once the militiamen shoot down two Black Hawk helicopters, the crowds descend on the hapless downed soldiers – dragging at least one of them naked through the streets as CNN cameras watch. (The mission had begun with CNN landing first, in order to film U.S. troops bravely splashing ashore).

In all, the film fairly praises U.S. courage under fire. But the message throughout is that America faces nasty, murderous Muslims who hate virtuous America for no reason. Its real contribution is to update the public on the latest U.S. weaponry and communications. The unasked questions: Why do so many "alien" peoples hate Americans? And what is there in Islam that makes so many people "crazy" and "vile?"

Both sexy weapons and U.S. victimhood served a purpose: military recruitment. They do so again and again, never really lifting horizons for those potential heroes from low-income, low-education Middle America. Fear, over-confidence, extreme patriotism and contempt for foreigners: these are the central elements in mobilizing a certain U.S.A. And for getting voters to support endlessly ballooning defense budgets. The Pentagon's steady, throbbing message is that there is only one way to think of the world: "the global dialectic of militarism and terrorism." [108]

The movie *Behind Enemy Lines* gives Muslims a bit of a break. The nasties here are Serbs. In fact, Serbs harming Muslims in Kosovo. President Slobodan Milosevic had stirred up hate against Muslims in this historic cradle of Serbian Orthodoxy. He initiated a vicious campaign of ethnic cleansing. To stop a possible genocide of Kosovar Muslims, NATO decided to launch a long bombing campaign against Serbia. A U.S. Navy pilot got shot down and bailed out in Serb-held territory.

The whole story turns on the pilot's miraculous escape. This took place in a heart-pounding chase by thuggish-looking Serbs, and with a daring rescue mission from a nearby U.S. aircraft carrier. Once more, with a thin and implausible plot, the movie highlights U.S. weaponry and superhuman courage in a noble cause.

The point again: this was a classic Manichean cowboys-and-Indians, good-guys-versus-bad-guys scenario – but with the undercurrent that the Serbs were resisting U.S. control of the Balkans. The brilliantly competent and resourceful Yanks outwit the slow-witted, genocidal Serbs. Americans are all heroes, including not just the pilot, but his risk-taking rescuers and a carrier captain who sacrifices his career to save one brave man. Message: Join the armed forces and we'll stick by you. And let you play with the very latest tech-war toys.

---

108 *Ibid.*, p.189.

No one can blame the Pentagon for backing such engaging movies. But movies such as this only get made when Hollywood agrees to tango with the military. A necessary evil? Likely. But with script-approved techno-toys, flag-waving and larger-than-life heroes, we're in still another Pentagon infomercial here. Once again, Hollywood marches lockstep to war with the brass.

Increasingly, technology is buttressing, if not replacing, character. Vastly entertaining *Charlie Wilson's War* tells the true story of how a hard-drinking, skirt-chasing, maverick Congressman single-handedly pressed the Pentagon to put Stinger shoulder-to-air missiles into the hands of Afghan and Arab fighters. These soon brought down Soviet helicopters and kicked the Russians out of Afghanistan. The movie doesn't bore us with this little downer: many of these same *Stingers* stayed in jihadist hands when America lost interest in Afghanistan on Russia's departure in 1989. The CIA had to buy them (*all* of them?) back. The movie stars (beside Tom Hanks)...those erotic Stinger missiles and Julia Roberts's plunging neckline. War is sexy.

In July 2010, *Wikipedia* listed 30 war movies about Iraq alone. One, the excellent *The Hurt Locker* about bomb-disposal experts, won six Academy Awards. Most such movies combine wowie U.S. weapons with soldiers' dramas. By the same date, 11 Afghan-story movies hit movie screens – most of them military. But at least one – low-budget *Osama*, about an Afghan girl disguised as a boy so she could eat – is a shocking, true-to-life drama about the ghastly fate of young Afghan women. Films such as *Brothers* (about Post-Trauma Stress Disorder), and several movies bordering on science fiction and/or horror, still seduce some audiences. The aftershocks of America's Iraq and Afghan wars will undoubtedly keep drawing audiences for several more years.

On television, the nightly news keeps the Afghan and Iraq wars relentlessly on American minds. But the impact is more numbing than attractive – images of several bombs a day news make an unappealing recruiting poster. Already-mentioned

Band of Brothers is, however, a perfectly justifiable paean to the "good war" against Hitler.

Marines and mayhem are not the only shows helping Americans love violence. Detective and crime shows have always been a staple of American TV – as they have been in most other countries. Some series offer more for mind than emotions. *Columbo*, a series about a shuffling but inspired detective, was not very graphically violent at all – neither was *Murder She Wrote*, a charming series about an elderly lady detective in the mold of Agatha Christie's Miss Marple.

But many rougher TV cop shows have run through the decades: from the *FBI Story* to *CSI* (Crime Scene Investigation) to Jack Bauer's *24*. These have accustomed audiences to seeing guns as the ultimate equalizer, peacemaker, tool of justice, and probably secret phallic compensator.

In all, U.S. daytime TV, with its game-shows and Dr. Phil tear-eliciting, still justifies Newton N. Minow's 1961 "vast wasteland" tag. Most evening TV does too, with its vacuous situation comedies. But you can't get through an evening of television without a solid dose of violence – of news items "bleeding, thus leading," gory crime, and terrifying wars in which, with few exceptions, foreign bad guys attack U.S. good guys. The evening may make America consistently terrifying. But paranoia about external enemies is vital to feeding – forgive the cynicism – the war machine.

Anyway, peace hurts ratings, as does too much happiness.

Happiness definitely prevailed in the 1997 black-comedy movie *Wag the Dog*. To distract voters in an imminent election from a presidential sex scandal, crafty spin-doctors cooked up a fake war against Albania. The plot was zany, as was the acting and outcome. But the movie did illustrate the implausible idea of a tiny, faraway country influencing the "world's only remaining superpower."

A great idea for a comedy. But here's an afterthought about tails wagging dogs. Even a cursory study of U.S. movies and TV adventure drama shows that today's equivalents of the Second World War's evil Nazis and murderous, dentallychallenged "Japs" are Muslims. Especially Arabs – and above all, Palestinians. The September 11 trauma and continuing acts of Islamic terror groups explain some of this obsession. But the astonishingly narrow and biased worldview of Hollywood studio chiefs, and even some New York producers, too often veers toward anti-Arab racism and anti-Palestinian distortions. Some movies weave in Palestinian bad guys, even though these characters may have nothing or little to do with the plot. Never, it seems, does any prime-time network film or show suggest that the Palestinians might conceivably have legitimate interests and viewpoints. A pity, and not just for the Palestinians. But for Americans' understanding of the world – and of their own strategic interests.

It's not a libel – just a universally recognized fact – to note that talented Jews founded, and still largely shape, the U.S. film business.[109] In many ways, they passionately defend creative freedom and encourage novel viewpoints. But because of executives' understandable 'family' attachment to Israel, and fears for its security, many have turned a blind eye to elementary Middle East facts and fair play.

As of mid-2010, and especially since the 2011 Arab democracy uprisings, the tectonic plates of U.S. attitudes toward Israel, right or wrong, seemed to be shifting. The new Israel lobby J-Street is presenting a more realistic view of a possible peace. Three very senior U.S. officials – General David Petraeus, Joint Chiefs of Staff Chairman Admiral Michael Mullen and Obama chief political advisor David Axelrod – all linked Israel's Palestinian conflict to risks facing U.S. troops elsewhere.[110] Even Meir Dagan, chief of Israel's *Mossad* spy service, said on

---

[109] See Neal Gabler's book *An Empire of Their Own: How the Jews Invented Hollywood*, Crown Publishers Inc., New York, 1988.

[110] Petraeus said that "enduring hostilities between Israel and some of its neighbors present distinct challenges to our ability to advance our interests..." See "U.S. general: Israel-Palestinian conflict foments anti-U.S. sentiment," *Haaretz Service*, March 17, 2010. These high-level comments – hinting that Israel's treatment of the Palestinians might be endangering U.S. lives elsewhere – were the first crack in the Israeli story-line that Israel's interests were automatically and indissolubly America's too.

June 1, 2010, that "Israel is gradually turning from an asset to the United States to a burden." [111] The U.S.-Israel narrative could stand updating.

Maybe, in time, Hollywood will change its prevailing Middle Eastern orthodoxy. Presenting in cinemas or on TV the moving, multiple-prize-winning film *Budrus* on the Palestinian non-violence movement could open many minds. Through the usual pressures, it seems quarantined in the U.S. festival-art-house circuit. But in March 2011, a more Hollywood-style drama appeared: *Miral*. Made by Zionist-raised Jewish director Julian Schnabel, it follows the story of a teenage Palestinian girl during the late- 1980s first *Intifada*. Based on the life of his Palestinian lady-friend, Rula Jebreal, a Haifa-born Palestinian tortured in an Israeli prison, it opened in New York "to a fusillade of criticism from American Jewish groups that consider it anti-Israeli." Asked if he had portrayed Israel in a negative light, Schnabel replied: "I think it portrays Israel in an accurate way...I think it's very light in the context of things that happened." [112]

Schnabel, needless to say, is a rare exception. Will other movie moguls stop stereotyping Palestinians in ways that would be termed racist and anti-Semitic if applied to Jews? Perhaps, in a miraculous era of Israeli-Palestinian peace, Hollywood will remember that Palestinians and Jews are both Semitic peoples. Then find other foreign villains to caricature. How about those scary Canadians?

Universities: The Egghead Wars

America, it's well known, has some of the world's top universities. In the social sciences – which include history and geography, the fields concerning us here – the 2010 Shanghai

---

111 Dagan, speaking before the Knesset's Foreign Affairs and Defense Committee. See "Mossad chief: Israel gradually becoming burden on U.S," *Haaretz*, June 1, 2010.
112 Deborah Sontag, "Julian Schnabel's Palestinian odyssey," *International Herald Tribune, March 25, 2011.*

international survey ranking foremost universities assigned to U.S. universities 14 of the top 15 places worldwide. [113]

At first glance, this seems testimony to the existence of a dazzling U.S. intellectual elite. Indeed, that is largely true. This "thinking class" has grown from the constantly renewed admixture of foreign talents with native American ones. To oversimplify, it may be the result of highly disciplined, 'international-minded' intellects meeting an ambient American mindset of innovation. Such a joining seems to produce a uniquely American ferment of ideas – look at the long list of foreign-born American Nobel Prize winners in science and medicine, and of Fields Medal winners in mathematics.

These awards, tellingly, are a key criterion in the Shanghai rankings. Never mind that a surprising percentage of these prize-winners were born and first educated outside the U.S. For our purpose, the most misleading impression from the Shanghai and other "publish-or-perish" standards of university excellence is that they judge what *professors know*, not what *students learn*. We are not interested here in a few top professors' prizes – but in *how Americans learn about the world*. In other words, we are talking about the quality of *teaching* in U.S. universities.

Browse the Amazon site or any of the fast-disappearing good U.S. bookstores.[114] Alas, you will find a small, smoldering library of furious American books blowing up the most distinguished ivory towers as teaching institutions: Harvard, Princeton, Stanford, MIT. For example: Marc Scheer's *No Sucker Left Behind: Avoiding the Great College Rip-off*; Craig Brandon's *The Five-Year Party: How Colleges Have Given Up on Educating*

---

113 Academic Ranking of World Universities in Social Sciences, Shanghai Ranking Consultancy, 2010: http://www.arwu.org/FieldSOC2010.jsp
114 Joseph Checkler and Jeffrey A. Trachtenberg, "Bookseller Borders Begins a New Chapter...11," *Wall Street Journal*, February 17, 2011. The mighty Borders chain (which also operates Waldenbooks) announced imminent closing of "about 200" of its 642 remaining stores. "It had already closed hundreds of locations in the past few years. In 2005, it operated 1,329 stores." This does not *necessarily* mean Americans are reading fewer books. On-line Amazon's hard-to-beat prices, and *Kindle*-type e-readers plainly harmed the big generalist chains. There is also evidence that smaller, specialized stores targeting a specific local demographic could still do well.

Your Child and What You Can Do About It. And especially Andrew Hacker's and Claudia Dreifus's *Higher Education?: How Colleges Are Wasting Our Money and Failing Our Kids – and What We Can Do About It*. This last book, published in 2010, elicited lyrical reviews from an Honor Roll of U.S. intellectuals.

What do such books say? They tell tales of 19- and 20-year-old sophomores teaching huge classes for absent tenured profs away on their regular every-three-years sabbaticals; of bloated university bureaucracies; of an obsession with fund-raising and sports. And most corrupting of all, they denounce a nasty implicit tradeoff between gigantic student fees and virtually-guaranteed, absurdly inflated grades. Pay a fortune – now estimated at a quarter of a million dollars for an undergraduate degree – and you can safely expect to get a lot of As. Having taught in two fine U.S. universities, the author can respectfully testify that these stories are legends, but not myths. [115]

In January 2011, an explosive new book documented America's undergraduate disaster. Surveying over 2,300 undergraduates at two dozen universities, authors Richard Arum and Josipa Roksa found that 45 percent of college students showed "no significant gain in critical thinking, analytical reasoning and written communications during the first two years of college." Roughly 32 percent, in a typical semester, did not take "any courses with more than 40 pages of reading a week. Half of these students "did not take a single course in which they wrote more than 20 pages" in a single semester. [116]

The frightening conclusion: Even in many famous institutions, you can get a U.S. arts or social science degree and remain, well, not very well informed about the world – including its many cultures, histories and contrasting values. Let's not even delve into what engineers, scientists, mathematicians and doctors learn in university about the world's cultural textures. More perhaps than in most countries, they pretty well have to study these on their own.

---

115 Fondly biting the hand that used to feed him: these were Dartmouth College and UCLA.
116 Richard Arum and Josipa Roksa, *Academically Adrift – Limited Learning on College Campuses*, University of Chicago Press, 2011.

A generation earlier, two brilliant professors stepped into the cultural breach. They tried to broaden and enrich U.S. on-campus. intellectual life. Allan Bloom and Harold Bloom shared a name and Renaissance-man outlook. In 1987, Allan Bloom published *The Closing of the American Mind*, a broadside against the mediocrity of American universities in the wake of the 1960s student rebellion. The book defends rigorous academic standards, and above all the teaching of a classic liberal-arts curriculum. Handing control of the universities to student demagogues appalled Allan Bloom.

In some ways, the pendulum has since swung back. But, deplored Bloom, the damage of political correctness remains: "I was convinced in the early sixties that what was wanted was a liberal education to give such students the wherewithal to examine their lives and survey their potential. This was the one thing the universities were unequipped and unwilling to offer them. The students' wandering and wayward energies finally found a political outlet. By the mid-sixties the universities were offering them every concession other than education, but appeasement failed and the whole experiment in excellence was washed away, leaving not a trace. [117]

Bloom condemned professors who taught only method and structure, not real ideas. Teachers ignored the source of most of the ideas worth teaching: the great books of Western civilization. Professors, he believed, now neglect these for trendy academic "disciplines" without much discipline or studied foundations. Among the worst offenders: 'identity' academics, who study communities defining themselves by language, ethnicity or religion. For these, only possessing such identity can dictate truth on an 'identity' topic – not honest enquiry and independent judgment. A white American cannot interpret Apache culture; a man of whatever ethnicity certainly can't understand women [quite apart from well-founded common wisdom].

Bloom insisted that "dead white men" had fashioned the world as we know it. The evidence: They often turn up in

---

[117] Allan Bloom, *The Closing of the American Mind*, Simon & Shuster Inc., New York, 1987.

universal literatures in Asia, Africa and Latin America, as well as in Europe and North America. Bloom saw the decay of American intellectual life, especially on campus, as evidence of a kind of new pre-Nazi Weimar Republic. A rejection of Plato's "just society" and the Enlightenment's spirit of enquiry.

Triumphantly joining Allan Bloom in the Great Books camp is Harold Bloom, author of *The Western Canon*. Published in 1994, the *Canon* echoes (in an unforgivable pun) the cannon-shot of *The Closing of the American Mind*. Between them, the Blooms represent a brave, sudden (here we go again!) flowering of a broad, civilized education in the human mind and heart. They are a two-man renaissance, so to speak, of the Renaissance and the best that followed.

The *Canon* masterpiece, among other Harold Bloom masterpieces, suffers from no whiff of the persecution complex that added pain to Allan Bloom's rage. Its subtitle proclaims that the book defends "The Books and School [singular] of the Ages." Taking Shakespeare as – if not quite God, then the world's single 'most universal' author – Bloom runs through all the great names of Europe and North and South America. In these globalized days, when Asian, African and even Caribbean books are finding wider audiences, one could fault Bloom – as many do – for Eurocentrism. His 25 choices for closer treatment justify this criticism. So does his jaw-dropping list of world authors in the appendices: They completely ignore China and Japan.

But basically, Bloom's daring, confident assertion of the superiority of the classics that he does analyze stands up. At least indirectly, his *Canon* remains under attack by both America's extreme left and extreme right. But his lucid and passionate defense of our predominant civilization only underlines the poverty of mainstream U.S. intellectual life. Yesterday's campus culture and today's are sworn enemies. Defenders of the old Renaissance-Enlightenment order of thinking no longer argue that the barbarians are at the gate. They leapt over it 50 years ago. But that's, Enlightenment-style, a matter of opinion...

Coda: A few top universities offer brilliant and comprehensive "area studies" of various countries and cultures. Some of their professors – as in many other fields – produce world-class books. But mainstream American society does not seem to draw much knowledge or understanding of the world from this area expertise. For much more than in Europe, U.S. institutions of higher learning see themselves as separate from society at large. They are true ivory towers. They function as mini-worlds with mini-rules and their own mini-police forces to enforce their own mini-moralities. That may be the most world-stunting problem of all: the invention and fortress-like mentality of the U.S. campus.

Books: Reading More, or Less, on Tablet Toys?

On February 17, 2008, author Susan Jacoby published a thought-provoking overview of American anti-intellectualism in the *Washington Post*. In its most stupidly arrogant form, she argues, anti-intellectualism turns into anti-rationalism. This in turn leads to ignoring the vital importance of information such as basic science or world geography – a priority that ought to be self-evident. Sadly, ignorance can include bragging about *not needing* to know – because one is American, one assumes, a people around whom the whole world revolves. [118]

Jacoby recalls the deep, historical origins and reaffirmations of this "know-nothingism." She starts with Ralph Waldo Emerson's 1837 comment: "The mind of this country, taught to aim at low objects, eats upon itself." Nineteenth-century elementary school tests in the three Rs would seem impossibly difficult to most of today's children. Over the past century "ordinary folks'" contempt for thinkers turned into a recurring trend. Jacoby cites the classic 1963 work by Columbia University historian Richard Hofstadter on populist America's reverse snobbery: *Anti-Intellectualism in American Life*. "Hofstadter," she said, "saw American anti-intellectualism as a basically cyclical

---

[118] Susan Jacoby, "The Dumbing of America – Call me a Snob, but Really, We're a Nation of Dunces," *The Washington Post*, February 17, 2008. See also her books on this topic: *The Age of American Unreason*, Vintage Books, New York, 2009, and *Freethinkers – A History of American Secularism*, Henry Holt and Company, New York, 2004.

phenomenon that often manifested itself as the dark side of the country's democratic impulses in religion and education. But today's brand of anti-intellectualism is less a cycle than a flood. If Hofstadter... had lived long enough to write a modern-day sequel, he would have found that our era of 24/7 infotainment has outstripped his most apocalyptic predictions about the future of American culture."

Other thoughtful observers agreed broadly with Hofstadter. Senator Daniel Patrick Moynihan in the 1970s and 1980s was one. Others, like Canadian media guru Marshall McLuhan, saw video as one of the intellectually sapping forces. Any number of objective studies of TV confirm a lowering of IQ, and of ability to reason or analyze. The victory of video (in all its forms) over print has sucked away the leisurely, actively thinking absorption of ideas. Jacoby notes: "Reading has declined not only among the poorly educated, according to a report last year by the National Endowment for the Arts. In 1982, 82 percent of college graduates read novels or poems for pleasure; two decades later, only 67 percent did. And more than 40 percent of Americans under 44 did not read a single book – fiction or nonfiction – over the course of a year. The proportion of 17-year-olds who read nothing (unless required to do so for school) more than doubled between 1984 and 2004. This time period, of course, encompasses the rise of personal computers, Web surfing and video games."

No doubt Jeff Bezos of Amazon's online bookstore can point to booming sales. His assertion in July 2010 that he had sold more books on his *Kindle* electronic reader than the same book in hardcover misled many to think the game was over for "paper" books. But did he prove that more people are reading more books? He does not often cite the number of bookstores his irresistible online convenience has closed (see our previous section citing the Borders book-chain bankruptcy).

Publishing technology and economics are changing so fast that trying to predict anything is like playing poker in a sandstorm. Still, there are healthy signs for writers, thus readers: Self-publishing has achieved new respectability, bringing many more choices to online book marketing. Cutting out middlemen such as cost-*in*effective distributors allows higher royalties for writers. So does inventory-avoiding Print-on-Demand (POD) – a stunning technology that takes an order for a single book, prints it with full-color cover, and mails it out – all within 24 hours. New "platforms" (ways of displaying words) make reading in different venues easier – though one should perhaps not take a pricey *iPad* to bathroom or beach. An electronic reader can make reading several books at once – a common habit – handier.

Nevertheless, video's victory over print is clear. And it plainly diminishes the depth and sophistication of argument – in favor of quick, often totally misleading, visual impressions. Even the new "electronic-print" reading "tablets" are sneaking into texts little movies to ease video-brainwashed readers into "enriched," "enhanced" or "amplified" online editions. "It's a wide-open world," said Molly Barton, director of business development for Penguin. "You can show readers the world around the books that they're reading." [119] What an idea: picture-books!

Back to the future: Doesn't this sound a lot like the 1980s' trendy dabbling in "multimedia?" Schoolbooks then started coming out as "kits" with fold-out "original" documents, music, interactive games, separately-shown movies, and even scripted "shows" by impresario teachers. Much of that was sound pedagogy. A lot was just show-and-tell fun. But for today's text-lovers, savoring words' unique evocations, combinations and rhythms, such 'enriching' books may seem a distraction, a watering-down of the 'literary' experience. Moreover, if a whole population becomes accustomed to 'surfing on the surface' of issues, instead of digging into them, that's wonderful news for manipulators of every ilk – including agenda-setters in foreign-policy and defense.

Democracy is not 'mobocracy.' The latter – demagogy for crowds – deceives and distorts with reductive slogans, screaming, and flashes of provocative symbols. Democracy, to foster free choice, demands nuance, counter-checks and sober second

---

119 "E-books fly beyond mere text," *New York Times*, July 29, 2010.

thoughts. Only solitary reading of text allows the leisure to pause, reflect, absorb or reject, and move on.

This is not to spoil our fun with those sexy *iPads, Kindles* and their rivals. But will more little videos, instead of more little books, stimulate and enlighten us? Or just amuse us, bore us and confuse us? Or, as the video-age already shows, leave us only a choice between the superficially profound and the profoundly superficial?

The issue is: What have these toys got to do with education? Maybe a lot, maybe not. Meanwhile – apart from their convenient electronic book-reading function – they guarantee that we will become addicted to even more buttons, screens and keyboards, and miss contemplating life as we watch the sun go down. The Luddites were not invariably wrong. A beautiful, elegiac column by Roger Cohen measured how tech-frenzy has stolen our real lives to leave us only virtual ones: "And if back in that century — back when exactly? — in the time before the tremendous technological leap, in the time of mists and drabness and dreams, if back then, without passwords, we managed just the same, even in black and white, and certainly not in hi-def, or even 3-D, how strange to think we had to change everything or we would not be managing at all. [120]

Obviously, the technological changes above are not restricted to America. They instantly sweep the globe. But they contribute to making Americans' view of the world more fleeting and impressionistic at a time when other forces do the same. They make serious reflection on foreign and defense policies (now practically the same) even more unlikely.

Congress: Its Own Little America

Now, speaking of short attention spans, let's look at a final place where Americans get their knowledge of the world: the United States Congress. A vital caveat before dumping on Congress: a rich and dynamic source of ideas feeding into universities, media and Congress is Washington's effervescent

---

120 Roger Cohen, "Change or Perish," *New York Times*, October 4, 2010.

world of think-tanks. Many of these are one-issue lobbies, but many stir the pot on a variety of questions. A recent count shows some 103 public-policy foundations, roughly classifiable as follows: 34 centrist, 20 conservative – broadly backed by 17 more libertarian groups – and 21 groups termed "liberal." Eleven deal specifically with foreign affairs.

In American parlance, of course, "liberal" means left of center. Elsewhere in the world, "liberal" usually means right of center – mainly because rooted in classic "liberal" *economic* theory – capitalism, laissez-faire, free enterprise, free markets. Take your pick, as long as you remember Adam Smith and his market's "Invisible Hand." In the U.S., "liberal" seems to focus heavily – along with big spending – on *social* issues. "Liberal" no doubt also sounds a bit too close to "loose" in a country that began as the land of the Puritans, and whose sinful history perseveres as James A. Morone's *Hellfire Nation*. American "conservatives" (who would be called "liberal" in Europe) seem to think that their social liberals have more fun – hence a sometimes envious edge to their stands on sex.

Many of these think-tanks play a vital role in both U.S. intellectual and political life. A typical, well-known conservative outfit: the Heritage Foundation. With offices near both Senate and House, its staff of 240 (backed by 700,000 fee-paying members) constantly guide legislators: "When a bill is being mooted, Heritage supplies ideas. During drafting, Heritage scholars suggest revisions. And when a vote is near, Heritage gives every lawmaker an easily digestible two-page document explaining what the bill contains, and what its effects might be." [121]

A typical "liberal" foundation could be the Center for American Progress or the Council on Foreign Relations. A centrist-liberal group, the Brookings Institution, is independent but attractive to leading Democrats. It has a yearly budget of $80-million. The Cato Institute promotes limited governments, free markets and individual liberty. Journalists pay heed to key foundations, for they know foundation ideas often creep into legislation and many think-tank scholars are top-notch.

---

121 "Not for sale," *The Economist*, January 22-28, 2011.

These are some of the sources of Big American Ideas. But we're considering here how *ordinary* Americans get their *international* information. Congress's filter of all the above brain-power gives limited cause for joy. For instead of Big Ideas, critics find big egos, big corruption. big gridlock, and very big trouble for America's success in the world.

Flying Low Over the Potomac

After blaming everybody else for American parochialism, let's finally flail away at U.S. politicians – who should be, you'd hope, enlightened leaders with real knowledge of the world. Congress harbors a small platoon of exceptional minds. It also billets brigades of elected "folks" who are unutterably parochial. Even many national politicians manage to look inward without being introspective. Introspective about *anything* – local, national or international.

A few of them (usually the loud mouths) are, like Longfellow's little girl with a little curl on her forehead: "… When she was good, she was very, very good / But when she was bad she was horrid." Most, alas, fly low, and think as little as possible about complex "foreign" issues.

Now, alongside the Tea Party movement, we have a poster-girl for the "horrid little girl" – the wonderful, sexy Sarah Palin. Mrs. Palin, with her nagging sarcasms and head-nodding non-sequiturs, would have shone in the 19th-century Know-Nothing" movement. She flies low indeed on foreign affairs – but high on defense spending. Her rhetoric demands spending cuts on everything, except defense. Mrs. Palin goes to bat for the Pentagon with all the zeal of a snout-in-the-trough, ex-general lobbyist of the military-industrial complex. No cuts on defense, she argues, because defense is sacred. [122] "We must make sure," she intoned on her Facebook page on June 10, 2010… "that we do nothing to undermine the effectiveness of our military. If we lose wars, if we lose the ability to deter adversaries, if we lose

---

122 Jim Galloway, "Using Sarah Palin as a bulwark against defense cuts," *Atlanta Journal-Constitution*, July 8, 2010.

the ability to provide security for ourselves and for our allies, we risk losing all that makes America great!"

Now, as some "Tea Partiers" want to add defense to the deficit-cutting chopping-block, Mrs. Palin may have to choose: how critical is a healthier budget to "strong defense."

A strong (so to speak) Palin rival is fellow-Republican Minnesota Representative and Tea Party stalwart, Michele Bachmann. Mrs. Bachmann, however, allowed in March 2011 that deficit reduction could include up to $15-billion off the defense budget. Unwisely, she was willing to chop $4.5-billion off veterans' benefits – an idea that predictably drew furious opposition: ""No way, no how, will we let this proposal get any traction in Congress," said Richard Eubank, national commander of the Veterans of Foreign Wars... "There are certain things you do not do when our nation is at war, and at the top of that list is not caring for our wounded and disabled servicemen and women when they return home." [123]

Since rumors claim that Bachmann – self-described as "armed and dangerous" – may challenge a possible 2012 Palin presidential bid, America may be seeing lots of flying, politically incorrect, fur. But this U.S. version of Saddam Hussein's "Mother of All Battles," with two very tough mothers, is just entertainment.

The U.S. Congress, especially the Senate, has harbored some admirably wise, international-minded members. One thinks of Arthur H. Vandenberg (bipartisan internationalism, including defending invaded South Korea in 1950); George McGovern (anti-Vietnam war, feeding the Third World); Mike Mansfield (Latin American and Far Eastern affairs); Richard Lugar (nuclear, chemical and biological disarmament); Carl Levin (oversight of defense and collective security); and Joe Biden (bipartisanship on arms control, Europe, NATO). John Kerry, chairman of the Senate Foreign Relations Committee, continues to play a broad, creative role in international affairs, often stepping into crises to help President Obama.

---

123 Rick Maze, "Veterans blast proposed tea party cuts.," *Army Times*, January 28, 2011.

But the list of brilliant internationalists is short – office and accomplishment rest mainly on domestic issues. This is where you have to (re)quote the late House Speaker "Tip" O'Neill's famous dictum: "All politics is local."

But before you get teary-eyed about the Senate – which modestly calls itself the "world's greatest deliberative body" – remember that plenty of close observers consider this fireplace-and-armchairs salon as a self-important club where no shirt is too young to stuff. Once you fund-raise your way in, you've got it made: little work, less accomplishment, and a filibuster-full of silly, paralyzing rules. Timothy Egan wrote in the *New York Times*: "Cobwebbed by senseless rituals, speeches which no one listens to and rules that make it all but impossible to act on the will of the people, the Senate cries for more ridicule, decorum breaches and old-fashioned wit....the default in the Senate, less by design than by institutional arteriosclerosis, is insulated decay." [124]

Egan went on to summarize a superbly detailed August 9, 2010 *New Yorker* article ("The Empty Chamber") by George Packer. Wrote Egan: "In a devastating profile this month of the broken Senate ... Packer... reveals a place that might as well be stuffed with mummies. Senators from opposite parties avoid eye contact, even a few feet apart. The choreography is as well-plotted as an old-style Soviet party congress – everything known in advance. Senators work a three-day week, and spend about 50 percent of their free time raising money for reelection." [125]

The World? Where's That?

Run-of-the-mill Senators, like other members of Congress, are not intrigued by, or even much interested in, international issues. With one exception: They pay extraordinary attention to Israel, whose AIPAC lobby, close to Israel's right-wing Likud Party, keeps their feet to the Middle East fire. In perfect legality,

---

[124] "The mirthless Senate," *New York Times*, August 11, 2010.
[125] Ibid.

AIPAC uses campaign money, media surveillance and participation, constant interaction with members of Congress, and an astonishing cobweb of overlapping American-Jewish organizations to praise or condemn politicians and opinion-makers. It's not 'anti-Semitic' (the lobby's A-bomb slur) to say this. It's simply factual. [126] AIPAC is brilliantly organized. Its only rival for lobbying skills being, by all accounts, the National Rifle Association.

As mentioned, a new pro-Israel lobby – this one oriented to peace and fair-play for Palestinians as well as Israelis – is J-Street. If Congress ever decides to listen more to J-Street, the level of Congressional debate on the Middle East may actually rise above the level of sloganeering. It may set a new standard for "defending Israel" – thoughtfully and creatively, as well as aggressively. AIPAC-J-Street rivalry has some potential to influence the Israeli-Palestinian "peace process" – a game long stressing (for Israel) more postponing process than peace.

In recent years, other strong Jewish-American voices have been speaking up for realism and fair-play in American policy toward Israel.[127] In March 2011, David Remnick, editor of *The New Yorker*, was 53 years old. Peter Beinart, now Associate Professor of Journalism and Political Science at the City University of New York, was 40. Why cite their ages? Because increasingly, it's clear that traditional pro-Israel, anti-Palestinian U.S. supporters tend to be elderly – in their 70s, and especially 80s.

Mainstream Jewish-American youth – except for the intensely religious Orthodox – have long been drifting away from blind support for Israel. Reported Beinart in May 2010 about Republican pollster Frank Luntz's 2003 study of U.S. Jewish college students:

The philanthropists [Luntz's sponsors] wanted to know what Jewish students thought about Israel. Luntz found that they mostly didn't. "Six times we have brought Jewish youth together as a group to talk about their

---

126 See again *The Israel Lobby* by Harvard professors John J. Mearsheimer and Stephen M. Walt, Farrar, Straus & Giroux, New York, 2007.
127 M.J. Rosenberg, Senior Foreign Policy Fellow, *Media Matters Action Network*, "Israel: the eroding consensus," *Al Jazeera* English website, March 28, 2011.

Jewishness and connection to Israel," he reported. "Six times the topic of Israel did not come up until it was prompted. Six times these Jewish youth used the word '*they*' rather than '*us*' to describe the situation.

That Luntz encountered indifference was not surprising. In recent years, several studies have revealed, in the words of Steven Cohen of Hebrew Union College and Ari Kelman of the University of California at Davis, that "non-Orthodox younger Jews, on the whole, feel much less attached to Israel than their elders," with many professing "a near-total absence of positive feelings." In 2008, the student senate at Brandeis, the only nonsectarian Jewish-sponsored university in America, rejected a resolution commemorating the sixtieth anniversary of the Jewish state." [128]

The U.S. Congress – still impressed and/or intimidated by well-organized and –funded AIPAC – has always harbored an eager xenophobic clientele (demonized Palestinians making a perfect target). This is partly because Congress is mesmerized by America's physical isolation from other continents, but also by its historic prophets. Thomas Paine, in his *Common Sense*, harped on the dangers of linking up with foreigners – comical advice, coming from an English girdle-maker who played notable roles in both the American and French Revolutions. George Washington, in his farewell address, warned: "The great rule of conduct for us, in regard to foreign nations, is in extending our commercial relations, to have with them as little political connection as possible." Thomas Jefferson, in his 1801 inaugural address, preached only "honest friendship with all nations, entangling alliances with none." With fear-the-'furriner' icons like this, no wonder American politicians hide under their desks when the world intrudes on debate.

Hammering a decisive nail into the coffin of world-scanning internationalism, President James Monroe (in his 1823 so-called Monroe Doctrine) limited American interests to the New World: "In the wars of the European powers, in matters relating to themselves, we have never taken part, nor does it comport with our policy, so to do. It is only when our rights are invaded, or seriously menaced, that we resent injuries, or make preparations for our defense."

---

128 Peter Beinart, "The Failure of the American Jewish Establishment," *The New York Review of Books*, May 12, 2010.

Shortly after, during the 1840s and 1850s, a "Know-Nothing" movement agued against "dangerous" German and Italian (mainly Catholic) immigration. Before fading into the Republican Party, the Know-Nothings called themselves the Native American Party. They certainly weren't thinking of native-American aboriginals. They were thinking of genuine WASPS – White Anglo-Saxon Protestants. Today's Republican Party still carries the anti-foreigner virus. Quickly assimilated immigrants themselves retransmit this to more recent newcomers. These too, in turn, soon become "Americans with seniority." The extreme Tea Party wing of the Republicans loves guns and God (in that order?), but not foreigners. When Fox-Network and Sarah Palin pal Glenn Beck scribbled his "evil" list on a blackboard to promote his August 2010 Lincoln Memorial show, he circled "International" just after "Left."

These attitudes draw on earlier isolationism. Germany sucked America into the First World War by sinking the *RMS Lusitania* (1915), then stupidly offering several southwestern U.S. states "back" to Mexico (1917). Japan bombed the U.S. into the Second World War (at Pearl Harbor on December 7, 1941. But before then, American legislators ferociously resisted international commitments to freedom.[129] Or to anything else except cash-and-carry profit (from both sides) in the weapons trade. Domestic immigrant lobbies (German and Irish) militated against helping Britain in 1914, and especially in 1940. They helped delay for over two years U.S. participation in the fight against Hitler.

Today the big international issues remain defense, energy security (oil and gas), the hard-to-end Afghan war, the Israeli-Palestinian impasse, and nuclear-risky North Korea and Iran. On all, members of Congress face phalanxes of lobbyists (many

---

129 See the famous January 17, 1917, "Zimmermann telegram." German Foreign Secretary Arthur Zimmermann sent a coded message to the German ambassador in Mexico instructing him to offer Mexico a military alliance if the U.S. seemed likely to enter the war. The payoff: Germany would help Mexico recover Texas, New Mexico and Arizona. Britain broke the German code and, hard pressed by German U-boats, gleefully passed this news to Washington – which declared war on Germany on April 6, 1917.

of them former Congressional colleagues) who descend on them, locust-like, with bags of money and threats of electoral defeat.

No Place for Politics – Just Pettifoggery

"What's wrong with Congress?" Over the years, countless articles and debates have started with that title – before dredging up evidence of hard-to-believe dysfunction, waste, corruption, stupidity, frivolity and scandal.[130] Like Inspector Renault in the movie *Casablanca*, some commentators are even shocked – *shocked!* – that Congress indulges in politics, partisanship, demagoguery, subterfuge, grandstanding, trickery, and systematic opposition. That's a little like finding that hospitals are full of sick people, and dog pounds full of dogs. For at bottom, don't national assemblies and parliaments exist as substitutes for civil war?

Each political system, constitution and legislature brings its own virtues to bear – as well as its own pathologies. In the U.S., these illnesses occupy the attention of thousands of despairing legislators, scheming lobbyists, delighted journalists and thrilled political science professors – not to mention millions of angry and/or appalled voters.

Lacking a monarchy to symbolize national unity, the U.S. Constitution fills a nearly sacred place in American's imagination. Not only jurists, but ordinary citizens, invoke the Constitution as a totem of divine wisdom – or at very least as an example for the world: "The work of many minds," says the National Archives' website *Charters of Freedom*, "the Constitution stands as a model of cooperative statesmanship and the art of compromise." Perhaps when colonial Englishmen wore wigs. But now, as Tea Party true believers shake skyward their abridged U.S. Constitutions, swearing they will only accept laws rooted in a specific clause, they remind one of other

---

[130] See Gregg Easterbrook, "What's wrong with Congress," *Atlantic Monthly*, December, 1984.

tea-drinkers: Mao Tse-tung's Red-Guard Oolong idiots. "It's all in there," claimed the Party's fervent believers about Mao's *Little Red Book*. Always.[131]

The Founding Fathers' dream stands as a monument to 18th-century rationalism. In colliding with today's human reality, the dream doesn't look very practical. In fact, in many ways, the U.S. democratic system is a corrupt, diseased and unworkable mess. Notes a *New York Times* commentator about Congress in July 2010: "The nasty and prolonged brawl over extended unemployment benefits – formerly a popular, consensus issue – and the jettisoning this week of a climate change bill, were just the latest manifestations of the near-paralysis that has infected the Senate despite the Democrats' control of 59 votes... Veteran senators say they have never seen the chamber so bogged down in partisanship. Members are getting whiplash as they watch colleagues come and go, creating an aura of instability. 'It is topsy-turvy but it is also very partisan,' said Senator Max Baucus, the six-term Montana Democrat who has been known in the past to cut deals with Republicans. 'Between those two dynamics, it is just nuts.'" [132]

But let's consider underlying problems of America's complicated democracy. First, for a constitution that wanted to get rid of kings, the presidency gave one man more theoretical and real power than Britain's George III. But it hamstrung the chief executive with an elected assembly that couldn't govern in his place, but could tie him in knots even on urgently needed national policies. Foreign affairs, our concern here, became a dog's breakfast of contradictory policies – not just reflecting partisan interests, but often lobbyists' interests (oil, Israel, Ireland, defense industries) or even personal hobby-horses (unneeded weapons systems). Foreign issues also echoed personal and

---

131 Mao's literary imitator, Libyan dictator Muammar Gaddafi had his iconic *Green Book*, a mish-mash of pretentious nonsense whose first section, revealingly, was entitled: "The Solution of the Problem of Democracy." Some of his compatriots in Benghazi found the solution for him in early 2011.

132 Carl Hulse, "Change Comes Quickly to a Place That Doesn't Care for It," *New York Times*, July 24, 2010.

procedural rivalries among congressional chairmen and their 20 committees, 68 subcommittees and four joint committees.

Routinely, on a politically sexy issue, you may find several committees rushing to out-grandstand the others by "seizing" an issue. Think of the 2010 BP oil spill in the Gulf of Mexico. BP's hapless Tony Hayward faced two Senate committees as well as one House committee. A major foreign affairs issue – especially on defense – may bring into play the Senate's Armed Forces Committee, its Committee on Foreign Relations, and one or more pertinent committees such as Homeland Security. Finance and the 30-Senator Appropriations Committee. The latter must approve any spending from the federal treasury.

At first glance, scrutinizing presidential appointments seems an eminently democratic cause. But Congress's many committees and sub-committees usually assess candidates' ideological purity from a left or right perspective. Their lengthy interrogations often take up inordinate time – grilling nominees just to embarrass the White House. Often they delay or even block appointments. This frustrates voters' will to have a government that governs roughly according to its announced priorities. In some cases, harassed nominees, though highly qualified, have had to withdraw. Senators have blackballed qualified ambassadors, Cabinet Secretaries and even functionaries further down the totem pole. They do this sometimes just to annoy the president, or to secure a trade-off with an unrelated goal.

By the way, the Senate programs itself for quirky, reactionary procedures by making each committee's oldest-serving member its chairman. Chairmen's jobs potentially become lifetime jobs. Senator Robert C. Byrd served three times as chairman of the all-important Appropriations Committee – for a total of 10 years. He facilitated huge defense spending, though he eloquently denounced George W. Bush's 2003 Iraq invasion: "Today I weep for my country," he said on March 19, 2003. "I have watched the events of recent months with a heavy, heavy heart. No more is the image of America one of strong, yet benevolent peacekeeper. The image of America has changed. Around the globe, our friends mistrust us, our word is disputed, our intentions are questioned. Instead of reasoning with those with whom we disagree, we demand obedience or threaten recrimination."[133]

The World's Greatest Democracy ... Except for Quite a Few Others

The constitution's lyrically-praised division of executive, legislative and judicial powers has proven, more often than not, a formula for deadlock and delay. In a "responsible" or parliamentary system such as Britain's, Canada's or Sweden's – where the actual (not ceremonial) executive governs by the legitimacy of its majority in the national legislature – the executive can pass laws reflecting the voters' will. It does so through governing-party solidarity, disciplined not only by threats of demotion or withheld promotions, but by the prime minister's doomsday threat of advising the ceremonial monarch to dissolve the chamber. Parliamentary democracy, however 'indirect' or unwieldy in theory, works fairly easily in practice. If no single party holds a legislative majority, coalitions can form. They can stay in power as long as they command a majority of parliamentary votes. Presidential regimes may delight admirers of Locke's and Montesquieu's division of powers. But in modern states, especially the U.S., this division muddles or frustrates the people's will. It hands enormous power not to governments, but to a scattershot array of lobbyists and preening, paralysis-craving legislators.

In a sensible world, dealing with foreign nations requires one national policy, not several rival policies. The U.S. constitution's requirement of Senate ratification of treaties is cumbersome, costly, time-consuming and dangerous. The Senate's rejection of the 1919 Versailles Treaty weakened the League of Nations at its birth by keeping the U.S. out. The absent U.S. couldn't fully play the valuable role in preventing European and Far Eastern war that it might have.

---

[133] Congressional Record.

If an Administration really wants a war now, it can easily use its "bully puppet" and lots of gall to start one without informed legislative authorization. George W. Bush's regime rigged evidence in 2003 to allege that Iraq had weapons of mass destruction and was in league with al-Qaeda. Lyndon Johnson's White House lied in 1964 to get Congress's authorizing approval to broaden hostilities in Vietnam (the infamous Gulf of Tonkin Resolution). Barack Obama, upsetting some legislators, agreed on his own in March 2011 to participate in (i.e. at least initially run) a no-fly zone over Libya to keep Muammar Gaddafi from continuing to massacre his own civilians.

But in less dramatic circumstances, no nation can negotiate a treaty or even major understanding with Washington knowing for sure that the White House can keep its word. Treaties require a two-thirds majority vote in the Senate. Foreign diplomats have to lobby Congress to back the President's policies. Senators and Representatives routinely tinker and rejig texts – sometimes forcing further international negotiations. And, of course, further "reconciliations" of House and Senate versions. Democracy or Disneyland?

This is a ridiculously awkward (and for foreign partners, insulting) system. It can drag out the conclusion, and application, of a much-needed international agreement by months, even years. Examples among countless others: the 1994 North American Free Trade Agreement purporting to facilitate trade among Canada, the U.S. and Mexico. Or the April 2010 Russian-American Nuclear Arms Reduction Treaty (START).

Two *New York Times* op-ed pieces on November 24, 2010 summed up how Congress routinely weakens national security. Kay King, former deputy assistant secretary of state for legislative affairs, and vice president of Washington Initiatives at the Council on Foreign Relations, warned of Washington's loss of international influence: "...lawmakers exposed the world to a flawed legislative system of backroom deals, outdated rules and procedures, and obsolete committee structures that favored obstruction over deliberation, partisanship over statesmanship, and narrow interests over national objectives. The inability of the U.S. Congress to address tough problems, both domestic and international, has serious national-security consequences. It prompts both allies and adversaries to question whether a world power with a dysfunctional national legislature can continue to lead on the global stage." [134]

James P. Rubin, former assistant undersecretary of state in the Clinton administration, and now teaching at Columbia University's School of International and Public Affairs, dismissed the Senate's typical hold-ups of international treaties as often harmful, and probably outdated: "... the same treaties that are so easily ratified in other countries are, for good or ill, often left to languish in the Senate, where 67 votes are needed for approval. The result is international frustration with American leadership, as many widely shared goals — from children's rights to a ban on nuclear weapons testing — are held hostage by a small group of senators, who often represent a tiny percentage of the American public." [135]

Another nasty little Congressional dysfunction: the custom of Minority legislators of refusing to recognize that the Majority won the last election. During the 1990s, Republicans organized what Hillary Clinton, not inaccurately, called a "vast right-wing conspiracy" against her and her presidential husband. Most of this smear campaign – about old legal fees, too-sweet investments and the infamous Whitewater real estate scandal – was fabricated, or blown up, to feed endless rounds of "investigating" committees. Unfortunately, in the Monica Lewinsky silliness, President Bill Clinton let down his wife, his voters and his party along with his trousers. Soon after President Obama won his office, Republicans began the same nonsense. They tried, and try, to paralyze – and if possible, reverse – his democratically approved agenda – such as his landmark health-care reform. All they offer is much more obstruction. Their unlimited legal right to subpoena White House and other senior officials promises endless distraction from substantive business.

---

[134] "Congress vs. National Security," Kay King, *New York Times*, November 22, 2010.
[135] James P. Rubin, "Farewell to the Age of the Treaty." *New York Times*, November 21, 2010.

That's par for the course for this great parliamentary institution the world is supposed to admire.

That's not all that smells rotten in America's Kingdom of Denmark. Gerrymandering and money-madness also define the discredit of U.S. democracy. Gerrymandering – the redrawing of electoral boundaries to favor incumbents – has long been endemic to Congress. By all accounts, the trend is getting worse. And it's accelerating Congress's ideological polarization and illegitimacy.

In June 2010, two non-resident Brookings Foreign Policy Fellows documented how the U.S. Congress's obsession with rigging (called 'redistricting' or reapportioning) congressional districts to favor incumbents was a major factor in increasing the ideological polarization of American law-making. "Critically," argued Micah Altman and Michael P. McDonald, "decisions are made with little or no public input or accountability... most states gerrymander legislative lines behind closed doors. Figures from both major parties tilt the electoral playing field so much that one party is essentially assured of winning a given district, controlling the state legislature or winning the most seats in the state's congressional delegation. In other words, the democratic process is subverted. In this system, politicians select voters rather than voters electing politicians." [136] As a result, candidates no longer have to play to a moderate center. They pitch to a strengthened hard-core party base by taking extreme positions. The left-right cleavage yawns.

President Barack Obama's health-care legislation demonstrated the depth of resulting fanaticism. After months of Democrats' trying to negotiate a reasonable compromise, Republicans voted against the plan en masse. Various hysterical legislators warned that giving 45 million Americans decent health-care was "an Armageddon," "the end of America as we know it," and "the ruin of our country." So much for the National Archives fantasy of the Constitution as "a model of cooperative statesmanship and the art of compromise." Armageddon, it seems, may mean a slight drop in insurance company profits.

---

136 "Pulling back the curtain on redistricting," *Washington Post*, July 9, 2010.

But even that is unlikely – rather the opposite will happen, with the new obligation for all to obtain coverage.

All of the above is both appalling and perversely entertaining. But none of it can match the core corruption of U.S. democracy that vaulted George W. Bush into the Presidency. You still believe that the U.S. enjoys separation of powers? Think back to Bush's dubious, razor-thin electoral defeat of Democrat Al Gore in 2000. After weeks of figuring out how to count "hanging chads" (surely an inspiration to 'backward' nations like Liberia or Kosovo), and how to fix tricky voting machines, the Republican-majority U.S. Supreme Court awarded the presidential election to Bush by a 5-4 vote – after halting a Florida recount that would almost certainly have handed Gore the White House. In the end, who elected Bush? Not 300 million Americans. But one Republican lawyer, the swing vote on the Supreme Court.

That Americans could tolerate such a sham left foreigners agape. A member of the *appointed* judiciary – not the people, or even its elected Congress – named the chief executive. Why did Americans tolerate this? Fatigue, incomprehension, embarrassment at worldwide ridicule, unattended government business? Yes, but also because of a mystical regard for the American Constitution – and inflated respect for lawyers. It all reduced left-out American citizens to the status of English peasants cowering under William the Conqueror. But at least the Brits got an overlord whose vision started Britain on the road to world power. The Yanks got a president by skullduggery and pettifoggery, and his incompetence put America on a long, slow slide to decline.

Money – the Mother's Milk of Politics

A more pervasive evil of the U.S. democratic system: the omnipresent influence of, and requirement for, money. Not just in "buying" or "renting" Members of Congress to support lobbyists' interests; but in funding the gigantic costs of TV advocacy and "attack ads." Paid TV ads replace a long-dead system of reasoned debate funded by stations as a public interest, in exchange for the privilege of making money from regulated airwaves. Today's pay-or-go-home system clearly favors extremely wealthy candidates: Billionaire Meg Whitman, former president and CEO of eBay, ran for governor of California with a 2010 personal net worth of 1.3-billion dollars. Democratic presidential still-hopeful Senator John Kerry allegedly holds a $231-million nest-egg – for running on a diet heavy on ketchup. [137] New York mayor Michael Bloomberg, though not running (yet) for anything federal, need not run around, Clinton-style, to endless fund-raisers to get elected: his 2010 *Forbes*-listed personal wealth stood at a comforting $18-billion.

Amy Goodman, TV columnist on 450 public stations, nailed American democracy's money-sickness in 2007 (multiply the costs for today):

"Money is now considered the single most important factor in our electoral process. Ideas and issues take a back seat to the bottom line. This prostitution of our electoral process has one key culprit: television advertising.

Political advertising makes or breaks candidates, and it takes a huge amount of money to implement a national advertising strategy. Now more than 20 states are piling onto Feb. 5, 2008, as their primary day, including states like California and New York with large, expensive media markets. The early, deciding role of money and television advertising in determining who gets to run for president is secure.

The costs of running for federal office have been skyrocketing. More than $880 million was raised by the 2004 presidential campaigns. The 2008 election is expected to cost more than $1 billion. Sixty percent will be spent on advertising." [138]

The U.S. Constitution deepens the damage. By specifying U.S. elections every two years (for one-third of the six-year-term 100 Senators, and all of the 435 Representatives), the Congressional electoral cycle makes for a state of virtually permanent elec-

---

[137] He married a Heinz Ketchup heiress. See Brian C. Mooney and Matt Viser, "Senator's wealth was long in coming and not always carried comfortably," *Boston Globe*, July 30, 2010.
[138] Amy Goodman, *truthdig*, April 10, 2007.

tioneering. Hence again, more polarization and new Niagaras of money for TV ads. This means, in effect, that politicians are in almost constant fund-raising mode. This in turn creates more scope for lobbies to, in effect, bribe and blackmail politicians on narrow issues.

The 11,916 U.S. lobbies cited as active in 2010 by the Center for responsible Politics are immensely skilled at this game.[139] They outnumber elected politicians twenty to one. In the last full year studied, lobbyists spent $3.49-billion, mainly to influence Congress. The year 2010 ran higher – the chief sectors throwing money at politicians being the financial (securities, investment, banking), energy and health-care sectors.

Aggravating the money madness is the U.S. tax code. *TIME* magazine's Fareed Zakaria described it in November 2010 as "16,000 pages long and riddled with exemptions and loopholes, specific favors to special interests. As such, it represents the deep, institutionalized corruption at the heart of the American political process, in which it is now considered routine to buy a Member of Congress's support for a particular, narrow provision that will be advantageous for your business." [140] In the World Bank Group's *Paying Taxes 2010* report on relative national "ease of paying taxes" for small- to medium-sized businesses, the U.S. ranks a droopy 61st in the world. Compare this to 'socialist' France at 59th, satirical Borat's Kazakhstan at an almost 'glorious' 52nd, 'bureaucratic' Britain at 16th... and the fast-sinking but head-high Maldives at 1st (i.e. it has the most business-friendly tax-collection in the world – until further global warming puts the whole archipelago under the Indian Ocean). [141]

Paul Krugman, *New York Times* columnist and Nobel Prize economist, points out that the "very, very rich" – and even humble billionaires – are more and more running Congress. Many of their acolytes favor extreme language: Radio-mouth Rush Limbaugh called the President "Imam Hussein Obama;" another

---

139 *Open Secrets.org*, Center for Responsible Politics, as of August 5, 2010.
140 Fareed Zakaria, "Restoring the American Dream," *TIME*, November 1, 2010.
141 Doing Business 2010: Economic Rankings, World Bank, 2010.

compared closing a hedge-fund tax loophole with the Nazi invasion of Poland.[142] Krugman's op-ed page colleague Thomas L. Friedman is even blunter. Friedman deplores a "a country in a state of incremental decline and losing its competitive edge, because our politics has become just another form of sports entertainment, our Congress a forum for legalized bribery and our main law-making institutions divided by toxic partisanship to the point of paralysis."[143] Soon after, Friedman predicted that incurable partisanship could lead to the rise of a serious third party in the 2012 elections. To sum up why, he cited Stanford University political scientist Larry Diamond describing U.S. politics as "two bankrupt parties bankrupting the country." [144]

Wall Street and the Washington Consensus

The most visible culprit causing bankruptcy: Wall Street. After snagging a nearly trillion-dollar bailout from the hated government, plenty of Wall Streeters thought it was time to bite the hand that was no longer feeding them. Their money talks. It screams, bellows, and whines. It makes politicians both talk and walk their greedy, delusional talk. Doing a slow burn, voters (with the Tea Party helping) are extrapolating Friedman's dramatic conclusion about both parties of today's Congress: Throw the bums out. The Tea Partiers, we have already seen, would just as soon skin a too-wobbly Republican grizzly as a Democratic one.

The other culprit – now entrenched in the renowned "Washington Consensus" on ever-larger defense spending – is even more dangerous. For the consensus now seems omnipresent, self-feeding, and unstoppable. It is dedicated to endless increases in "defense" spending to fund endless wars with perplexing rationales and no-visible exit strategies. Rallied round the Pentagon are loyal supporting players in the defense industries, Congress, media, entertainment, and, as we saw, even

---

142 *New York Times*, August 31, 2010.
143 Thomas L. Friedman, "The Tea Kettle Movement," *New York Times*, September 28, 2010.
144 *Ibid.*, October 5, 2010.

churches. Together, with mindless joy and assurance, they sing the same earnest song about a "strong national defense." That mantra is now a coded and incontestable test of real, red-white-and-blue Americanism.

Two questions. First: defense against whom and what? Answer: Anybody, however implausible, that the Pentagon's professional contingency planners and war-gamers can even remotely imagine threatening the U.S. Unstable, terrorist-harboring, nuclear-tipped Pakistan for sure. India – only as a nuclear rival of Pakistan. The crazies in North Korea, and their imitators in Myanmar. Unpredictable and theocratic Iran. China for sure – it's already building up a navy puny in U.S. terms, but able to cause waves around smaller states in the South China Sea. A revived Russia, maybe – it still has thousands of nukes and may yearn somehow to reconstitute the Soviet Union. Brazil is coming up, and may eventually stir Latin America. The Central-Asian Islamic "-stans" (Kazakhstan, etc.). It's routine to plan for almost any threat to the U.S. – probably all the way from Albania to Zimbabwe.

But for realistic planning over the next 20 years, how many of these situations are really unmanageable by peaceful means? Some, but likely not all. Arguing for unquestionable, ever-costlier defense must at some stage face a test of rationality.

Corollary question: In raising a defense budget, need the U.S. expect a cascade of wars all at once? Can you ever have *too much* defense, more than you need by any less-than-fantasy expectation? Is it possible to, in effect, *waste* money on the military that might better 'defend' America by non-military means? Even some top brass hint, at least rhetorically, that enough defense may be enough – and that non-military tools may also serve U.S. security. Admiral Michael Mullen, Chairman, U.S. Joint Chiefs of Staff, avowed to the *New York Times* on March 3, 2010 that "U.S. foreign policy is still too dominated by the military." Later that year he went further, saying: "Our national debt is our biggest national security threat." [145]

---

[145] Laura Bassett, "Adm. Mike Mullen: National Debt Is Our Biggest Security Threat," *Huffington Post*, June 24, 2010.

Andrew J. Bacevich, in his stunning, already-cited 2010 book *Washington Rules – America's Path to Permanent War*, documents the terrifying rise of all-dominating military power in the U.S. One example: He traces the careers of CIA founder Allen Dulles and Strategic Air Command (SAC) boss, General Curtis E. LeMay. (Note: LeMay was thought the inspiration for H-bomb-crazed General Buck Turgidson – played by George C. Scott – in the film *Dr. Strangelove* starring Peter Sellers.) Together, Dulles (brother of Secretary of State John Foster Dulles) and LeMay created a defense establishment capable of thwarting even the White House. For decades, the CIA could easily secure budget increases to fight shadowy wars against the USSR. And the SAC – a state within the Pentagon state – extracted virtually no-ceiling funding for a thermonuclear strike force capable of wiping the *entire Communist world* (USSR, China, Eastern and Central Europe) off the face of the earth – then of bombing the bouncing rubble to make sure.

"Under LeMay's successors at SAC," records Bacevich, "the process continued. By 1963, the war plan included 8,400 [nuclear missile] targets across the communist bloc. By 1970, that number exceeded 10,000... Whether capabilities were driving requirements or vice versa became impossible to discern; the two worked in tandem. This much was indisputable: The war plan devised by SAC provided it with essentially unlimited drawing rights on the U.S. Treasury..." [146]

Today, the Balance of Terror – the perfectly named MAD for Mutual Assured Destruction – lies more or less fallow. And nuclear stocks have radically melted. But military budgets still boom. For current wars, wars that might come, and wars that just exist in the far-out reaches of "contingency" minds. The crux: Would it not make a *stronger defense,* and a far more affordable one, to avert many dangers by astute diplomacy, sound trade policies, investment, and support for peaceful domestic elements in some "threatening" nations? This option is not on any serious Washington "defense" table. It passes for mushy thinking, naïveté and mere boy-scout stuff – silliness

---

146 Andrew J. Bacevich, *Washington Rules*, p.52.

imagined light-years from the Real World that only generals understand.

Curious coincidence: Rejecting more thoughtful, strategic solutions for winning the "hearts and minds" – that even the generals say they seek – has one result: it keeps the money-spigot pouring out the cash for Congressmen, the defense industries, and the Pentagon. When you want a "strong defense," surely money is no object.

Even as the U.S. economy is becoming a disaster zone – facing job-destroying threats from China, India and Brazil, among others – what is official America thinking? The American middle class, squeezed between the job-obsolescence of high-tech and the wage-cutting of globalization, feels whip-sawed and dispossessed. Chances are it will not look for 'reasonable' solutions.

Final question: What *is* "defense" in America' 21st century? Is it military or economic? Educational, scientific, or even cultural? Is anybody asking? So far, certainly not Congress.

Lobbies - Ain't It a Shame?

"Single-issue" lobbies in foreign relations include defense lobbies and pro-Israel lobbies. As mentioned, many observers consider that the two most effective and professional lobbies are the National Rifle Association and the American Israel Public Affairs Committee (AIPAC).

But the biggest and most influential lobbies of all (after finance, health and energy) are linked to defense. Surprisingly, defense lobbying only comes 10th in terms of expenditure. But its presence in every state and its patriotic resonance make it incredibly powerful. The defense industries financially support the great majority of elected representatives. As a result, and at incalculable cost, U.S. taxpayers get stuck with monumental bills for unwanted weapons systems. And for wars and foreign-base networks that the Pentagon favors. Most politicians, swept along by pro-military public opinion and defense-industry money, see weapons systems as jobs and votes at home, as well as fascinating – and possibly even useful. With hand on heart and NRA memberships in pocket, they see little wrong with a country that resembles a garrison. It's a big, bad world beyond America's shores, and the U.S.A. must be "strong." It's all about loving America, and America can never be loved enough, or strong enough.

A dirty little secret: Members of Congress – milking "national security" for electoral gain, routinely tack billions of dollars in "pork" (boondoggles or unneeded projects) on to defense appropriations. For 2005, they added between $8.5-billion and $10-billion to a defense budget of about $500-billion. They took the self-serving pork money out of "operations and maintenance" accounts that give ordinary fighting soldiers a multitude of practical tools affecting their safety: nice things like body-armor, vehicle-armor, night-goggles, and spare parts. [147] But heck, doesn't America need bridges to nowhere too?

On top of a ballooning share of "entitlement" spending (for military pensions and hospitals), defense spending eats up 29 percent of the U.S. federal budget. This, with no Cold War against another superpower. China may loom as a distant threat, but not yet. Meanwhile, the U.S. maintains *eleven* carrier strike groups. The Pentagon argues that these offer invaluable force projection for fighting wars around the world. But to other experts, multi-billion-dollar aircraft carriers look like sitting ducks. Say, for sophisticated cruise missiles?

Thinking more strategically: Haven't such distant "force-projecting wars" in Iraq, Afghanistan and the Horn of Africa simply generated more West-hating Muslim millions for more Huntington-style wars of civilizations? Read the 92,000-document *Afghan War Diary* released by whistle-blowing website *Wikileaks* in July 2010. Or its 391,832-document *Iraq War Logs* exposé in October 2010. Then think hard. Even to many earlier supporters of George W. Bush's nine-year Afghan War, this conflict looks provocative, carelessly brutal, and unwinnable. It's a cauldron cooking up not Iraqi-style "enduring freedom," but enduring hatred.

---

147 See Winslow T. Wheeler, *Wastrels of Defense: How Congress Sabotages U.S. Security*, Naval Institute Press, Annapolis, 2004.

The October 2010 *Wikileaks* report on the Iraq War cited 15,000 additional, U.S. Army-documented Iraqi civilian deaths. Most occurred at Army checkpoints, where nervous soldiers summarily shot civilians (even families with children) that they suspected might be dangerous. One soldier who shot civilians told of this instruction from higher up: when a roadside bomb explodes, fire on anybody "in the area." The 15,000 extra death-list does not include deaths possibly attributable to CIA agents, special forces or contractors such as Blackwater. For the latter (whose unpunished mercenaries killed 17 civilians at Baghdad's Al Nasoor Square on September 17, 2007) and all Americans except U.S. Army soldiers: total impunity for the foreign killers of Iraqis. Washington avoided prosecutions so as "not to demoralize" Americans in Iraq. No word about demoralizing Iraqi citizens waiting seven years to be protected.

The thousands of American, British, Canadian, Dutch and other Allied soldiers fighting the Taliban deserve immense respect for their sacrifices. The politicians and senior military officers sending them to die, or be maimed or traumatized, deserve much less.

Cosmopolitanism Doesn't Trickle Down

We've now looked at the main sources for average Americans' knowledge about the world. Cataloguing so many U.S. inadequacies – even while recognizing unique and undeniable U.S. strengths – may seem unduly harsh. But the examples are factual, and drawn from reputable American sources. They show how opinion-shapers in almost all America's elites have encouraged leaders to pursue military, indeed specifically Pentagon-friendly, solutions to international problems.

At the intellectual top of U.S. foreign-relations thinking, there is substantially more diversification. Authoritative insider journal *Foreign Affairs* of the Council on Foreign Relations can and does plant seeds, even agendas, among the political class. Occasionally, as in George Kennan's legendary July 1947 article urging "containment" of Soviet expansionism, it has directly reshaped policy. The Kennan piece, signed "X," inspired President Harry S. Truman's stand-firm Soviet policy. It also led to the complementary Moscow-thwarting Marshall Plan for European recovery. Later, the journal promoted the ideas and careers of Dwight D. Eisenhower and Henry Kissinger – both also strong-defense advocates. Most of the time *Foreign Affairs* does not deviate radically from the national defense consensus. It amends, kneads and adjusts it. A sea-change is possible, but – as in the Kennan case – the time must be ripe.

Another serious journal is *Foreign Policy*, a glossy, well-informed bimonthly now owned by the *Washington Post* Company. Co-founded by Samuel P. Huntington of "class of civilizations" fame, it's a spirited, close-to-the-news publication always worth a look.

Apart from specialized academic journals on a feast of topics, the U.S. *commentariat* can and does dip into a few foreign sources – mainly British newspapers and magazines available online. Hands-down, the most influential magazine is London's *The Economist*, read worldwide by decision-makers and media observers. Even though this weekly calls itself a newspaper, it's essentially a very high-end interpretation and opinion magazine. Known for its sometimes arcane wit and Gibraltar-like certainties, it's unofficial slogan ought to be: "Often wrong [as on the second Iraq War], but never in doubt." Its global circulation of about 1.4-million in roughly 200 countries includes a hefty 822,000 in the U.S. This American majority has led some old-time readers – and not just the ones harrumphing in plush London clubs – to claim that mere profits have slanted the weekly's coverage to please Americans. Mere profits. Yes, that awful stuff that funds foreign correspondents in Bhutan and Cap Verde.

Little of this sophistication seeps very far down into the U.S. mainstream. Likewise, eloquent national-media critics – such as *New York Times* or *Washington Post* columnists, or writers for *Atlantic* magazine – don't easily reach the mainstream masses. Or get to overturn the national narrative. Events do that more than opinions. The 2006 *Abu Ghraib* torture scandal did more to spread skepticism about George W. Bush's Iraq war than a chattering bag-full of columnists. A rare exception of smart media swaying the masses: Walter Kronkite's famous February 1968 turn against the Vietnam War. This led to President Lyndon Johnson's resignation and subsequent war-ending negotiations.

Elite columnists often pass for dreamers, even 'dissidents,' in a country unaware that there are, on national defense, very fallible orthodoxies. That means agreed truths that 'patriots' can loyally challenge. 'Average' Americans, bathed from childhood in strident patriotism (and its darker twin, militarism), don't seem to worry deeply about this state of affairs. Or about a gun-crazy, violence-accepting national state of mind that frightens even America's friends.

To "foreigners," the Land of the Free – apart from its countless admirable, entertaining and endearing charms – is starting to resemble a tottering empire. An empire, as in Matthew Arnold's poem "Dover Beach," that is retreating in a "melancholy, long withdrawing roar." Articles on America's decline (i.e. waning influence) are an old U.S. tradition. They are now in full masochistic flow, and with both military and economic examples. The obvious futility of Washington's huge armory in most of the early-2011 Arab uprisings led to much hand-wringing. More deeply, China's "rise" in coming years to top economic power dismays many Americans. Mocking "declinism" as merely a perennial intellectual cult doesn't change such realities. [148]

If you focus mainly on popular opinion (i.e. voters), America is an empire at risk from its own ignorance. From its love of brute force. From its immeasurable self-regard. From its blinkered conviction that God gave it a mission to reshape the world in its image.

Maybe He did. But maybe He didn't. The image of a constantly-at-war U.S. doesn't encourage potential imitators. The point of marshalling this chapter's evidence of U.S. ignorance and parochialism is that navel-gazing has taken Americans' eyes and minds off the world. Off a world that America – for its own "national defense" – needs to know and understand far better.

---

[148] Alan Dowd, "Three Centuries of American Declinism," *Real Clear Politics*, August 27, 2007.

PART II – WHAT'S GOING WRONG

... we are in a battle, and... more than half of this battle is taking place in the battlefield of the media... we are in a media battle in a race for the hearts and minds of our Umma [worldwide Muslim community] - Ayman al-Zawahiri, chief ideologist, al-*Qaeda*

This is a global theater in which you can win the hearts and minds of people... You have to deal with the media with the same seriousness that you deal with other theaters of war - Col. Ra'anan Gissin, former foreign media spokesman for Israeli Prime Minister Ariel Sharon, November 12, 2006

Chapter Four/

SHOOT FIRST, THINK LATER (MAYBE)

Even the Dalai Lama admitted that "if someone has a gun and is trying to kill you, it would be reasonable to shoot back with your own gun." [149] The U.S. likes to have guns, planes, ships and personnel pretty well everywhere in the world in case somebody decides to "shoot at it." To be fair, the massive U.S. forces scattered worldwide are not necessarily proof of intended aggression. They are certainly evidence of a) a strong intention to defend and advance American interests everywhere possible; and b) a tendency to see perhaps too many complex international problems as soluble by military means; c) a conviction that America is special, unique, even God-inspired to guide the world. It has a bred-in-the-bone certainty that America is the Exceptional Country, not quite bound to follow rules that everybody else at least pretends to respect.

Running the World ... While Sleep-walking

"It was an Orwellian experience," wrote Ahmed Rashid, an author and journalist widely published in the West, "to visit Washington during [George W.] Bush's first term. Outsiders

---

149 *Seattle Times*, May 15, 2001.

like me found it remarkable that a U.S. president could live in such an unreal world, where the entire military and intelligence establishments were so gullible, the media so complacent, Congress so unquestioning – all of them involved in feeding half-truths to the American public." [150]

He cites a university lecture tour by former CIA official Paul Pillar, after which Pillar deplored that students were "so poorly educated about world history, geography, and politics that they could not make political decisions for themselves about the world outside and left such choices to their leaders. The neocons [fanatical right-ring Bushites] counted on just this ignorance and compliance to conduct their foreign policy...the neocon ideology now focused on keeping the American public in a constant state of fear, with looming exaggerated threats and potential war." [151] As even memoirs from George W. Bush and Donald Rumsfeld now betray, the Iraq war emerged from a vast illusion rooted in ignorance and hubris.

But before taking a further whack at the American Way of War, let's praise the poor guys who have to conduct it at ground level. For sure, there are bad apples – a handful of murderers and torturers – but when caught, they go to jail. Most U.S. combatants are decent, honorable people. And – notwithstanding American hero-inflation and soldiers' as well as contractors' trigger-happy impunity – many really *are* heroes. Every day, in the heat and dust and danger of Afghanistan (and still occasionally in Iraq), the grunts face terror, death, maiming, damaged minds, constant discomfort, filth, and aching hearts for loved-ones abandoned. Ted Adams, when a U.S. officer serving in Afghanistan, conveyed the grit and gore and grief of field-soldiers' life in this e-mail reproduced in the *New York Times:*

IEDs are the bane of my existence.
They drive us all crazy, but I take it personal. It is hard to imagine how much we could get done if we didn't have to put the effort into protecting

---

150 Ahmed Rashid, *Descent Into Chaos: Pakistan, Afghanistan and the Threat to Global Security*, Penguin Group, London & New York, 2009, p. XLIX.
151 *Ibid.*

ourselves from these "improvised explosive devices" and avoiding them. We've been hit by more than 10 IEDs in the last couple of weeks. During my last convoy we hit one on the way, and one on the way back. I don't like those averages...

During the recent convoy, one IED in particular was pretty powerful and ripped through the armor within the wheel-well and floorboards of the truck. This resulted in the most serious injury any of our Marines have suffered to date; an open fracture of the lower leg. We called in a helicopter medevac and continued with the mission...

That Marine will likely make a full recovery. He'll have some extra hardware in his leg that may set off metal detectors, but he'll be there to see his kids grow up. Most of us consider that a happy ending. Day in and day out our Marines climb back into their trucks without a complaint and quietly accomplish the mission... [152]

Not all soldiers survive wounds or get sent home. As of August 2010, American deaths in Afghanistan totaled 1,230, British 338, Canadian 151, with other nationalities suffering proportionally. Most deaths resulted from IEDs or landmines – both invisible, sudden and deadly in impact. In the false security of an armored vehicle which may become your coffin, they're endlessly terrifying.

But our purpose here is not to weep for individual soldiers, however much they deserve our sympathy. Our goal is to judge *official U.S. policy and practice* – the collective illustration of the militarist mindset. Let's start by looking at the spider's web of American presence in the world. Then let's see how in major Muslim contexts (Iraq and Afghanistan, mainly) Washington seems almost cavalierly to decide how to wield its strength. In both countries, Washington developed a self-defeating habit of fighting first, then thinking second. Thinking about its real reasons for war, thinking about its goals, thinking about how to get out of the war, and thinking about what to do with the country it invaded.

Start with the U.S. belief that America, the post-Cold War's "indispensable nation" (Madeleine Albright), is "the world's only remaining superpower" (Condoleezza Rice). Both comments remain largely true. But with China (and later India) rising, for how long? Still being top dog, the U.S. believes it

---

152 Lt-Col. Ted Adams, *New York Times*, Otober 6, 2010.

must be everywhere at once. Result: the U.S. military presence abroad now touches over 150 countries. As of July 2010, the U.S. deployed more than 369,000 of its 1,379,551 active-duty personnel outside the United States and its territories. Some fought wars in large units, (Iraq, Afghanistan); others served in residual Cold War bases; others carried out hush-hush "special ops" work; others performed peacekeeping, humanitarian missions, training missions, or running refueling and supply bases. Bottom line: the U.S. is everywhere. Even Russia allows U.S. over-flights to supply U.S. troops in Afghanistan. So does ex-Soviet Kyrgyzstan and, when not sulking or playing off incipient Russian-U.S. rivalries, Kazakhstan.

In Iraq, Afghanistan, the Persian Gulf and the Horn of Africa, one rarely hears any other Washington proposal than this: How many more soldiers to send, and which kind?. Or how many more drones target-jockeys need in order to assassinate this month's quota of Taliban, or Pakistani or Yemeni terrorists? President Barack Obama's lengthy debate in late 2009 on sending "surge" troops to Afghanistan turned on one issue: whether to send 20,000, 30,000 or 40,000 more troops. Was that "strategy," or political coin-tossing? Obama's bizarre announcement of sending 30,000 troops – only to start bringing them home a year later – looked like a straight saw-off with the Pentagon. And logical nonsense.

Background: In the fall of 2009, General Stanley McChrystal, then riding high as an insurgency-killer, had made known that he wanted for Afghanistan an Iraq-style "surge" of 40,000 troops. Obama, fearing an Afghan quagmire, hoped to keep this new surge to much less. McChrystal, already presaging the insubordination that got him fired in June 2010, lobbied publicly, in a London speech, for 40,000. He also dismissed a leaner drone-heavy approach favored by Vice-President Joe Biden. Obama summoned McChrystal to his plane at the Copenhagen tarmac to chastise him. Eventually – no doubt partly to ward off Republican attacks alleging his 'weakness' on national security – Obama agreed to the 30,000 figure.

On June 23, 2010, Obama fired McChrystal as Afghanistan commander. Cause: offensive remarks the general and his entourage had allegedly made ridiculing the White House security team (including the President) in a *Rolling Stones* magazine article. Hanging out with ink-stained wretches over drinks is a risky business.

At this point, Obama, Biden and Defense Secretary Robert Gates fell into a dance of ambiguity about how long the surge troops would stay. Biden suggested they would move out of Afghanistan en masse in mid-2011; Gates implied all would depend on how the war was going; and Obama insisted that troops would "start" coming home by mid-2011. That left a six-lane highway open as to a date all troops would leave. If ever.

Complicating the decision: Everybody agreed by mid-2010 that the war was unwinnable by either the 45-nation U.S. coalition or the Taliban. Yet the Taliban swore they would not negotiate a peace unless all foreign troops left. To add to Obama's problems, Afghan President Hamid Karzai was tangoing with both sides: praising the Americans and taking their money, but playing footsie with America's adversaries. With the U.S. covering one eye, he ran back-track negotiations with the Taliban and the shadowy Pakistani Inter-Services Intelligence Directorate (ISI), known to be close to some terrorist groups. Minority Tajik, Uzbek and Hazara tribes feared that a Karzai-Pakistan-Taliban deal might put them under the thumb of Karzai's Pashtun tribe. If it did, they said, a new inter-tribal civil war would break out after the foreigners left. All the foreigners were eager to do so. But they worried that a chaotic Afghanistan without them would again become a base for *al-Qaeda* terrorism. Given the Taliban's Afghan-Pashtun loyalties, a not-unlikely eventuality.

In this magnificent fog of tossed-about numbers, ancient rivalries, and panicky liaisons, one seeks in vain for a truly coherent, stable vision of U.S. (and inevitably Western) goals. That is, apart from a hope to get out of the mess without looking too defeated. A classic "fig-leaf exit."

Sometimes, it's true, a wrong-headed "coherent" plan can be worse that winging it. George W. Bush's wildly pretentious, ignorant fantasy of remaking the Middle East met Ariel Sharon's short-term Israeli – and Saudi – security advantage. But it horrendously squandered American blood and treasure, and killed tens of thousands of Iraqis. To what avail? To another form of Iraqi instability – and a strengthening of Israel's (and America's) far more lethal enemy, Shia Iran. How? First, the clumsy and brutal 2003 U.S. invasion of Iraq neutralized that country, Iran's historic enemy. Saddam had no weapons of mass destruction, as Israeli, British and American spies had alleged. Then, interminable U.S. distractions with Iran's Western and Eastern neighbor-rivals (Iraq and Afghanistan) favored Iran even more. They helped produce the populist anti-Israel Mahmoud Ahmadinejad. This deadlier, crazier adversary, with his tactical adroitness in evading nuclear controls, will soon almost certainly have A-bombs to fit to his Shahab-3 Middle-East-covering ballistic missiles. And if not he, then his successor will.

"Stuxnet" malware (that slowed Iran's A-bomb work) and other tricks may delay this. But it's hard to see how the West can really stymie an Iran that it keeps reinforcing by its military-diplomatic policies. Bombing Iran's Bushehr, Natanz and other possibly new-found nuclear facilities is a short-sighted fantasy. It might delay the inevitable for a few years. But meanwhile, it would set off a worldwide firestorm of new accusations that the West was again "attacking the Muslim world."

With its global web of bases and commitments, America is building a ragged, unstable and resentment-stirring empire. It is doing so largely by reacting and improvising. It is doing what Sir Robert Seeley famously said about how the British Empire came to be: "We seem, as it were, to have conquered and peopled half the world in a fit of absence of mind."

Oh, What a Lovely War!

Let's recall again (as seen by many foreigners) how America fell in love with things military. Then we'll ponder how

Americans are fighting Muslims – that is, enemies who just happen to be Muslims.

Like many newborn nations, late 18th-century America delighted in the glory and ultimate success of its soldiers. The Minutemen, a fast-moving elite of militiamen, were the Special Forces of their time. Ready on a "minute's notice," they harried the massed ranks of the rigid British "squares," picking off the red-coats at will. They quickly became a romantic, rag-tag brotherhood of men with guns.

Revolutions are always exciting, especially if you don't get killed. A lot of eloquent Englishmen played key roles in America's 1776 breakaway from Britain (starting with George Washington, a disappointed English colonial officer who led revolutionary forces). The songs and books and legends they helped inspire were memorable. *The Star-Spangled Banner* relives the "the perilous fight," "the ramparts" and "the rocket's red glare, the bombs bursting in air." But it's not in the sanguinary league of *La Marseillaise* with its "bloody standard," "howling of fearsome soldiers," "throat-cutting" and "impure blood [to] water our furrows." Or even in that of peace-loving Danes who still sing that King Christian's sword "was hammering so fast, through Gothic helm and brain it passed." In the anthem *O Canada*, as you might expect, those gentle Canadians don't cracks any skulls (except at hockey games); they just "stand on guard" about fifty times. But between skulking and skull-cracking, the U.S. anthem comes off as a fairly satisfying warlike hymn. Its big problem: It's a waltz – thus impossible to march to, unless you are Viennese or have three legs. Even the Aussies' *Waltzing Matilda* is in splendidly 'marchable' 4/4 time.

But let's not digress.

Love Me, Love My Gun

Another early push to militarism came on December 15, 1791 with adoption of the constitution's Second Amendment: "A well regulated Militia, being necessary to the security of a free State, the right of the people to keep and bear Arms, shall not be infringed." Since then, as everyone knows, this clause – originally conceived as a means to resist tyranny – gradually became a debate-stopping slogan to promote the U.S. gun industry and culture. Never mind "militias." The right to bear arms, argues the gun lobby, extends to individuals. In gun enthusiasts' eyes, if you don't own, indeed revere, your personal gun(s), you're probably not quite a patriotic American. In fact today, if you oppose automatic weapons like machine-guns, many will consider you at least a limp American. No one has yet tested extending the Second Amendment to personally-owned tanks, high-altitude bombers, drones or suitcase-carried atomic bombs. But the National Rifle Association (NRA) will stand vigilant for Americans' rights, however they may expand. And U.S. politicians, bought, rented and/or intimidated on this issue, will bless whatever's next.

As a measure of Congressional support for guns, note the "overwhelming" 2009 backing of 251 Representatives and 58 Senators for arguing that the pro-gun Second Amendment applies to state governments as well as to the federal government. [153] This, plus Supreme Court gun backing, handily overrules pesky local anti-gun initiatives.

It's hard to overstate the legislative influence of the NRA and its vulnerability to satire. Thankfully, Michael Moore made a close-to-definitive hatchet-job on it in his wickedly on-target film *Bowling for Columbine*. It shows a sadly diminished Charlton Heston raving about clinging to his gun with his "cold, dead hands." This, as the gun lobby dismisses one year's over 100,000 Americans shot (including 2010's 31,224 U.S. dead in gun crimes) with its mantra that "guns don't kill people, people do." It's not certain that Stokely Carmichael really invented the phrase "violence is as American as apple-pie." But a January 2011 *TIME* article opined, "guns are as American as covered wagons and the infield-fly rule."[154] The gun lobby tries hard to

---

153 "Bipartisan Majority of U.S. Congress Signs Amicus Brief Supporting NRA's Position in Pivotal Supreme Court Case," website of National Rifle Association-Institute for Legislative Action, November 23, 2009.
154 Michael Grunwald, "Is Gun Control a Dead Issue?," cover-story of shooting of Congresswoman Gabrielle Giffords that left six dead and 14

make that come true. It now backs guns (hidden or displayed) in public restaurants and *bars* – only its latest contribution to insanity. (Well, maybe you need a Colt-44 to protect your Big Mac from all those ravenous, obese kids at McDonalds). Thank goodness, Sarah Palin is the NRA's new poster-girl: a prettier Annie Oakley with Kazuo Kawasaki 704 designer eyeglasses.

You can't blame all the gun madness on the firearms industry – manufacturers, importers, wholesalers, retailers, gun-fair operators, gun-magazine owners and the vast culture of drum-bangers who shout the joys of being armed to the teeth. A gullible, myth-mesmerized people and cowardly or fanatical political elitists surely bear some responsibility too. Even for guns in churches, mosques and synagogues? But why not concealed weapons in churches?, urge gun-lovers. Louisana Governor Bobby Kindal signed into law a July 2010 bill allowing just that. Humorists joked that this might be necessary to give the faithful recourse against boring sermons or a sloppy organist. But lawmakers were not laughing.

Churches may indeed be the perfect venue to ponder guns in America. For guns have long become, in the eyes of the rest of the civilized world, not just a national American illness, but, as it is for millions of Americans, a national U.S. religion. Decades of brainwashing about "sacred" gun rights clearly led to Republican Sharron Angle's amazing comment (from which she later tried to back off) that the public might resort to "Second Amendment remedies" to protect against an elected government that, in her view, might become "tyrannical." Her comment also specifically cited the possible assassination of a Democratic opponent, then Senator Majority Leader Harry Reid. During the radio interview in question, Angle helpfully hinted that she was likely carrying a .44-caliber concealed magnum model 29. [155]

This kind of twisted reasoning obviously played a role in the January 10, 2011 assassination attempt on the life of respected Democratic Representative Gabrielle Giffords in a Tucson,

wounded, *TIME*. January 24, 2011.
155 Sam Stein, "Sharron Angle Floated '2nd Amendment Remedies' As "Cure' For 'The Harry Reid Problems,'" *Huffington Post*, June 16, 2011.

Arizona shopping center. Ferocious, hateful Tea Party and Republican attacks on Representative Giffords for her moderate stances, and her support for health-care reform, drew some gun-happy politicians – including Alaska gun-totin' "Grizzly Mama" Sarah Palin – to play with firearms metaphors. Palin "targeted" Giffords, and her website even ran a gun-sight drawing over Giffords' district. When, on January 10, 2011, a paranoid schizophrenic called Jared Loughner took the advice literally, Palin tried to squirm out of any responsibility, reading a confused and furious text about alleged "blood libel" – showing no understanding of that term's anti-Semitic origins (Mrs. Giffords is Jewish). A Palin assistant feebly tried to argue that the gun-crosshairs were only "surveyor's marks."

As usual after mass shootings – six people died, while Giffords barely survived and over a dozen more were wounded – Americans teared up, grieved exuberantly, wrung their hands, muttered that "something" must be done... as long as it didn't interfere with almost unlimited freedom to carry, hide and eventually use guns of all kinds. That of course includes handguns, whose single purpose is to kill human beings.

Obviously, it would be unpatriotic to reduce the number of guns. Public safety demanded the opposite. So after the attack on their elected representative, many rushed out to buy *more* guns, especially the handy, dandy Glock that Giffords herself, an ardent pro-gun advocate, was proud of packing: "I have a Glock 9 millimeter and I'm a pretty good shot," she boasted in 2011. [156] Once again, the trusty NRA argued that the cause of gun killings was anything except guns. It was crazies, criminals, sloppy handling, unsupervised children, drunkenness, freak accidents. The NRA insisted that a society already awash in people-killing handguns wasn't awash enough. It plainly needed still more guns for good people to kill bad guys.

No argument by anti-gun groups makes a dent in the quasi-religious conviction that guns are God's constitutionally-protected solution for defending "freedom." The excellent Brady

---

[156] Mary Papenfuss, "Giffords Boasted of Her Prowess With a Glock - Startling comment highlights Arizona passion for weapons," *Newser*, January 11, 2011.

Campaign to Prevent Gun Violence, started by Jim and Sarah Brady after Jim took a bullet in the head aimed at President Ronald Reagan, lacks money, members and especially brave members of Congress ready to defy the NRA. As far ahead as one can see, gun madness will rule America, to the amazement and horror of mature, enlightened peoples everywhere.

How dangerous to U.S. democracy is the gun religion? The day after the Giffords shooting, several Arizona Republican officials resigned for fear of being killed...by other Republicans. The level of hate rhetoric between Republican factions – Tea Party and 'mainstream' Republicans – terrified many into leaving politics. Are we in Zimbabwe here? Or maybe Albania? There too, politicians are shot down in public places. There too, candidates and party workers resign for fear of death for themselves and their families. ..."I wasn't going to resign, but decided to quit after what happened Saturday," [Republican District Chairman Anthony] Miller said. "I love the Republican Party but I don't want to take a bullet for anyone." [157]

P.S. on "militias." Although Americans have inflated the right to bear arms wildly beyond the Second Amendment's "well regulated militias," the U.S. is crawling with *un*regulated militias.[158] Many are very scary. All consider the federal government as their enemy, and many militiamen are unhinged by the devil incarnate, President Barack Obama: "a black man with a foreign-sounding name and a Muslim-born father." Experts agree that the idea of a "black man in the White House" is intolerable to many of the resurgent militias. Militiamen, some armed with heavy M-60 machine-guns, prepare to confront jack-booted federal, United Nations, Mexican or even Blackwater "soldiers" – all coming to take away their guns. A 2010 exercise of the "Ohio Defense Force" drilled to defeat a "marauding Islamic army" that an "Islam-sympathizing" Obama wouldn't stop. A wealthy Nazi sympathizer collected radioactive materials for a mass-killing "dirty bomb" until his wife put a timely end to

---

157 "Gabrielle Giffords shooting prompts resignations," Edythe Jensen, *Arizona Republic*, January 11, 2011.
158 Barton Gellman, "The Secret World of Extreme Militias," *TIME* magazine, September 30, 2010.

his plans – and his life. Another elderly racist loner, infected by white-supremacist groups, shot and killed a guard outside Washington's Holocaust Museum.

No other Western country knows America's gun sickness. Or the freaky paranoia of America's gun-obsessed militias. The closest country in the world might be failed-state Somalia. Where did this American craziness come from? Of course from early-Frontier lawlessness and the mystique of stand-tall, fast-on-the-draw gunslingers. From the shameless NRA gun lobby which never met a gun it didn't like. Hollywood's gun-crazy Charlton Heston also promoted contempt for the federal government. But perhaps the real democracy-sapping culprit was Hollywood's sunny, good-guy Ronald Reagan. To play voters against those "meddling, big-spending" Democrats, didn't he say these innocent-sounding but insidiously words: "Government isn't the answer. Government is the problem." Fair comment to an extent – when you consider bureaucracy, profligacy and insensitivity to citizens in a huge country. But to marginals tending to hysteria, this may easily translate into: "The government isn't your friend. It's your enemy."

Extrapolated result: Reagan may have helped eviscerate another Republican's core idea of democracy. Wasn't it Lincoln, not sunny at all, who defined that as "government of the people, by the people, for the people?"

Another rampart of U.S. military thinking is the National Guard. This used to be for weekend and vacation-time soldiers. Now the state-based Guard sends whole components of reservists to Iraq and Afghanistan. This practice reaches deeply into small-town, poor or less educated families, considered vulnerable to flag-waving appeals to duty and the glory of guns. Not even the high proportion of such soldiers – estimated at 20 to 35 percent, returning with Post-Traumatic Stress Disorder (PTSD) – puts this institution in doubt. The Guard is now an intimate part of national admiration for things military. George W. Bush loved it: The Texas Air National Guard kept him out of harm's way in Vietnam, while he protected the Lone Star State against Oklahoma.

Inspired by the Manifest Destiny of the "Anglo-Saxon race," U.S. 19th-century history tells Americans some thrilling tales. Tales of stealing land from Mexicans (Texas, New Mexico, California, Arizona and Nevada). Of bullying Britain into giving up the Alaska Panhandle. Of grabbing bits of the Spanish Empire (Cuba, the Philippines), and of course of wiping out Indians. Revenge for Little Big Horn: Custer remained a mere American icon. But Crazy Horse won worldwide notoriety: Tourists from everywhere now flock to the sexy chorus-girl Paris theater named after him...

The combined total of American deaths in all three battles (Alamo, Little Bighorn, San Juan Hill) was less than epic: well under 1,000. But together, these modest incidents exerted enormous symbolic power. The young American Republic had established that it could not only take over all of its day's American territory; it could even begin to assemble an empire. Although shyly declining to call its empire an empire, the U.S. did a remarkable job of glorifying its anecdotal triumphs in books, myth and, as we saw, movies.

A less violent, though highly militaristic, phenomenon promoting a soldier-like mindset is America's network of "military academies." Sometimes called "boot camps for troubled teens," these schools may be Christian or not. They all try to form young people in a military mold of love-America flag-worship and mildly Spartan discipline. In many cases, they may offer a valuable service in steering lost kids to a life of purpose. Yet the outcome is usually a military career – or at least a deep-seated respect for the military. That's a far-from-familiar sentiment in many other countries, whether pacifist or neo-fascist.

Not counting Christian and other religious boarding-schools where a strict regimen prevails, some twenty-two well-known military academies welcome boys of both elementary and secondary levels. Scores of others welcome both boys and girls, or just girls. In all cases, the goal is to offer a "military education" carrying the following values: "respect, discipline, leadership, solidarity and accountability."[159] Good, solid, unexceptionable values – but within a culture encouraging deep, passionately

---

[159] Military School national website: http://www.military-school.org/

expressed patriotism. And more than a strong hint that joining the armed forces might not be a bad idea.

Underpinning all this is the extraordinary American sense of country-love. Of what Washington now terms the Homeland – in this context a neologism recalling the German *Heimat*, French *Patrie* or Russian *Rodina*. Instilled in childhood and echoed at sports events, churches and schools, pride in America inevitably helps prepare Americans to make or accept war. Other countries express patriotism, some even vociferously. But the daily recital of the U.S. Pledge of Allegiance throughout school years imprints an inerasable sense of civic loyalty and duty, as well as a quasi-religious reverence for "Old Glory," the "Stars and Stripes:" "I pledge allegiance to the flag of the United States of America, and to the republic for which it stands, one nation under God, indivisible, with liberty and justice for all." In schools, as we shall see, all this is surrounded by a presumption of American exceptionalism, indeed superiority. Children learn that America can and should do whatever it wants, because it is good, moral, envied – and often in danger.

Danger implies enemies. Thus resistance, thus frequent wars. Wars where every soldier is a "hero." The abuse of this appellation amazes non-Americans. These usually believe that their soldiers sign up to get shot at. And if some of the poor guys get killed, that's bad luck, not heroism. America fosters fantasies that every dead, wounded or captured soldier is a hero – even if he or she got in trouble through his or her own incompetence, cowardice, stupidity or just rotten luck. Examples of massively hyped "heroes:" useful symbols and soldiers killed by "friendly fire." One hoped-for dream symbol was Jessica Lynch – a U.S. Army private captured in 2003 by Saddam Hussein's forces, then rescued by U.S. special operations forces. Pvt. Lynch later accused the Pentagon of "embellishing" the story as part of its propaganda effort. She told Congress that she had never even fired her jammed M-16 rifle, and had been knocked unconscious when her vehicle crashed.[160]

Unconscious heroism? Well, many real heroes are unaware of their heroism...

---

160 See Jessica Lynch, *Wikipedia*.

Football star Pat Tillman, killed in Iraq in 2004, was a classic case of a soldier accidentally killed by his own comrades, but promoted posthumously and praised as a "hero." Again the Pentagon lied – though Tillman certainly deserved commendation for re-enrolling in the Rangers when his option was a profitable professional football contract. Ironically, although Tillman became a poster-boy for recruitment, he actually harbored anti-war views. Noam Chomsky confirmed that Tillman had even contacted him to express such opinions. Yet at Tillman's funeral, religious as well as military myth-making continued the "hero," theme. The religious echo, universal in military funerals, led his angry younger brother to snap: "Pat isn't with God. He's fucking dead. He wasn't religious. So thank you for your thoughts, but he's fucking dead." [161]

Hero-inflation is too deeply entrenched in U.S. culture to change. It starts with children's sports, and, as we saw, it rolls right on to TV and movies – and no doubt to arm-wrestling, drinking-contests and long-running spelling bees.

In passing, let's not forget patriotic "national" animals, emblems of the nation. Presumably, these incarnate virtues that various peoples see in themselves. Britain and at least four other countries (Sweden, Liberia, Bulgaria, Belgium) feel they roar like a lion; India threatens (Pakistan?) like a King Cobra; Iceland's falcon speeds bank collapses and world-stopping volcanic ash; France crows like a rooster; quiet Canada beavers away anonymously; and Italy, no doubt with gallant Silvio Berlusconi in mind, sees itself as a wolf. The U.S., flying in formation with Russia, Austria, Germany, Armenia and Albania, soars high above the world like an eagle – the perfect symbol of being above it all. If you're going to extend your mandate as a superpower, Americans know, the eagle was a great choice – even the Bald Eagle, though it's often on the edge of 'imperial' extinction.

Those are some of the entrenched reasons, in fact and symbol (and serious or tongue in cheek) why many Americans have come to see international problems as essentially military. After World War II – the Allies' "Good War" against Hitler, Mussolini

---

161 Pat Tillman, *Wikipedia*.

and Tojo – America had cause to believe that armies and democracy could go together. Then came the great Soviet menace over Europe, and later elsewhere. Both pride and fear drove America to re-arm. For over 40 years, the militarization of America in economics, politics, mentalities and popular culture accelerated dramatically. And made Americans feel their oats.

Post-1945 Hubris Sets the Stage

As Germany, then Japan, fell to the Allies on May 8 and September 2, 1945, the U.S. bestrode the world like a Colossus – which it was. It had grown rich from the war, first by selling to both sides, then by pulling itself out of the Depression by massive investments in war industries. Some of these, like vehicle manufacturers, were easy to convert to satisfy pent-up peacetime demand. As in 1918, America believed it had made the world "safe for democracy." Demobilization began immediately, and most Americans believed in rapid, radical disarmament.

Then in succession, five new factors drove a return to America's "under attack" psychology: the August 1945 atomic bombs (leading to soon-justified fears of stolen secrets); the September 1945 Igor Gouzenko spy scandal in Ottawa revealing widespread Soviet penetration of the West; the October 1949 triumph of Mao tse-tung's Chinese Communists; then, a year later, the June 1950 Korean War as North Korea invaded South Korea. Finally, the March 1951 trial for atomic espionage of Julius and Ethel Rosenberg brought home shockingly the reality of Soviet infiltration. In condemning the couple to death, Judge Irving Kaufman said: "I consider your crime worse than murder... who knows but that millions more of innocent people may pay the price of your treason." By declining in 1953 to commute the Rosenbergs' death sentence to life imprisonment, President Dwight D. Eisenhower agreed.

Soon, war began anew –"hot" in Korea, but "cold" and obsessive with Russia. From roughly 1950 to 1954, the U.S. Senate undertook public hearings that raised popular fears of omnipresent "communism" to white heat. A hobby-horse of several politicians – especially the infamous Senator Joseph McCarthy – the unmasking of "traitors" and "un-American" public servants and intellectuals bordered on hysteria.

This was a mood to enchant a hungry defense industry. Its fast gearing-up and expansion presaged Eisenhower's January 17, 1961 farewell-speech denunciation of the "military-industrial complex." Defense budgets boomed again, especially with the 1950-53 Korean War – which, technically, has still never ended. The half-century that followed "Korea" led to a worldwide (but controlled) Cold War. U.S.-Soviet Mutual Assured Destruction, with its cheerfully accurate acronym MAD, made the world live within a radioactive balance of terror. Not today's foot-soldier fear of improvised roadside bombs. But an all-humanity nightmare of universal nuclear incineration. The awful phrase "nuclear winter" – made famous by Jonathan Schell's book *The Fate of the Earth* – theorized that a "thermonuclear exchange" would cause climate chill and toxic soot for months – similar to the effects of asteroids that killed off the dinosaurs.

This atmosphere of distrust and fear lifted when the Berlin Wall fell in November 1989. But building a new Russian-American trust proceeded by starts and stops. Then by STARTS (Strategic Arms Reduction Treaties, signed in 1991 and 2010) and stops. George W. Bush, unlike his Cold War-ending father George H.W. Bush, never seemed much at ease with real détente. Temperamentally, he itched for a fight. He was afflicted, as some authors alleged, with "intractable provincialism, religious zealotry, and the reckless temperament of a gunslinger."[162] Little wonder that his 2002 *National Security Strategy* proposed the permanent pre-eminence of the United States and the authorization of pre-emptive war.

Barack Obama also had few illusions about Russia. But he thought Washington and Moscow could learn to manage their differences. They could make mutual interest override suspicion even as geopolitical rivalries continued. Washington's adroit balancing of interests in the Caucasus, for example, eventually

---

162 Andrew J. Bacevich, *The New American Militarism: How Americans Are Seduced by War*, Oxford University Press, 2005, p.4.

allowed new flexibilities on both sides. The comic-opera spy-swap melodrama of June-July 2010 made professionals on both sides smile or blush, with no harm done.

It's simplistic to blame today's American militarism only on the infamous trio of the untutored George W. Bush, his evil genius Richard Cheney and his cockily incompetent defense secretary Donald Rumsfeld. By the time they clawed their way back to power via the raucously corrupt 2000 presidential election, America was already well primed for an exhilarating war or two. Today, the American military establishment is essentially on eternal stand-by – not actually starting new wars, but maintaining and extending anti-terrorist battlefields. And of course – a normal, legitimate military activity – U.S. generals plan for possible wars. The Pentagon's sprawling network of overseas bases is just part of this.

One of the most authoritative students of longstanding, accelerating U.S. militarism is Andrew J. Bacevich. In his view: "... well before September 11, 2001, and before the younger Bush's ascent to the presidency, a militaristic predisposition was already in place both in official circles and among Americans more generally.... 9/11 deserves to be seen as an event that gave added impetus to already existing tendencies rather than as a turning point. For his part, Bush ought to be seen as a player reciting his lines rather than a playwright drafting an entirely new script." [163]

Robert Kagan, praised by Bacevich, said: "America did not change on September 11. It only became more itself." [164]

A number of other authors have also described the creeping militarization of America. They have illustrated the glorification of U.S. military ideals, genius, discipline and accomplishments. Michael Sherry's *In the Shadow of War* describes how, since the 1930s Depression, the nation has never escaped its obsession with security. War of every kind, real or imagined or metaphorical, has defined an always vulnerable, frightened national personality. Constantly enhanced militarization came to reshape "every realm of American life – politics and foreign policy, eco-

---

163 *Ibid.*, pp. 4–5.
164 *Ibid.*, p. 13.

nomics and technology, culture and social relations..." [165] This universal feeling of being threatened strikes many Americans as merely vigilant patriotism. Many non-Americans see it as a form of mass paranoia. Or at very least, of adolescent fragility requiring reassuring patriotic mantras and totem words – flag, defense, security.

Nick Turse's 2008 *The Complex: How the Military Invades Our Everyday Lives* lists an Orwellian series of intrusions of the military in Americans' daily lives. From Starbucks to golf to the revolving-door, conflict-of-interest colonels, he tells us it's way too late to worry: the Pentagon already owns us. [166]

Chalmers A. Johnson's 2004 *The Sorrows of Empire* offered a doomsday view of the inevitable progression from republic to empire to dictatorship. He drew inspiration from the Roman empire. [167] He insisted that America's world-girdling ring of hundreds of bases exists to create a juggernaut for imposing its real strategic goals: "oil, Israel and... to fulfill our self-perceived destiny as the new Rome." He believed it would take a revolution to wrest political control of America from the Pentagon, back to the people.

Seeming confirmation of Johnson's conspiracy theory was Bush's October 26, 2001 signature on the civil-rights-curtailing Patriot Act. This gave broad new powers to law enforcement and immigration authorities as a then-plausible reaction to the trauma of 9/11. It also authorized domestic snooping, and a huge expansion on the rules on search, privacy and banking secrecy. However useful in intercepting terrorist plots – and these were and are real and active – this radical beefing up of police and eavesdropping inevitably heightened popular paranoia. This in turn predisposed the public even more to supporting the Pentagon, right or wrong. After all, this was the

---

165 Michael Sherry, *In the Shadow of War: the United States Since the 1930s*, Yale University Press, New Haven, 1995.
166 Nick Turse, *The Complex: How the Military Invades Our Everyday Lives*, American Empire Project, Henry Holt and Company, LLC, New York, 2008, pp. 23–28.
167 Chalmers A. Johnson, *The Sorrows of Empire: Militarism, Secrecy, and the End of the Republic,* 2004.

Department of *Defense* – those well-intentioned, patriotic fellows who look after our young soldiers overseas (curiosity: one can still call male soldiers "boys," but not call female soldiers "girls."...).

A watershed accelerator of militarism for many older Americans came in the "anti-war" 1960s. The free-wheeling, free-sex, disrespectful Sixties generation provoked a society-wide parental backlash. Burning flags and bras, rebellious youth also burned their elders, as well as many potential allies with conservative cultural tastes. America's reaction to the hippies and their crowd resembled in some ways the pendulum-swings that shook the Chinese Communist Party in the late 1980s and beyond. Deng Xiaoping rejected both Old-Party thinking (with his pragmatic "It doesn't matter if a cat is black or white, as long as it catches mice") – and New-Party Tiananmen Square youth defiance of Party control.

As Bacevich summed up the post-Sixties' years: "The new American militarism made its appearance in reaction to the 1960s, and especially to Vietnam. It evolved over a period of decades...in full view and with considerable popular approval." He called it the handiwork of several disparate groups that shared little in common – apart from being intent on undoing the purportedly nefarious effects of the 1960s: "...military officers intent on rehabilitating their profession; intellectuals fearing that the loss of confidence at home was paving the way for the triumph of totalitarianism abroad; religious leaders dismayed by the collapse of traditional moral standards; strategists wrestling with the implications of a humiliating defeat that had undermined their credibility; politicians on the make; purveyors of pop culture looking to make a buck: as early as 1980, each saw military power as the apparent answer to any number of problems." [168]

Before reviewing how the Terrible Trio of Brush, Cheney and Rumsfeld plunged America into its new Iraq-Vietnam quagmire, let's look at some deeper background. How and why did Americans – left, right and center – buy into the militarist fantasy over recent decades?

---

[168] Andrew J. Bacevich, *The New American Militarism*, p. 6.

Remember that Bacevich, who explains all this consummately, can scarcely be termed "un-American." A "conservative Catholic" professional army officer who served in Vietnam, he holds impressive credentials. Two of his recent books, *The New American Militarism: How Americans Are Seduced By War* and *Washington Rules: America's Path to Permanent War* are already provocative classics. His January-February 2011 article in *Atlantic* traces the term "national-security state" back to the Eisenhower era. It also credits C. Wright Mills's 1956 canonic book *The Power Elite* with coining the term "military metaphysics." This refers to "the cast of mind that defines international reality as basically military" – a fair short-hand for today's defense-obsessed Washington. [169]

In 2010, *Washington Rules* ruled the militarism debate. A review by the Ruth Group anti-war site summarizes it well: "*Washington Rules* is composed of two elements which are taken as a given, a kind of national wallpaper which we don't notice but is forever present... If the first element of *Washington Rules* is the belief that American values should govern the international order, the second is the means by how this to be done. Bacevich calls this *The Trinity* – three parts to one means. The means is military might — staggeringly greater than is needed for self-defense. *The Trinity* is: Global military presence; global power projection and a policy of global interventionism. Together, credo and trinity – the one defining purpose, the other practice – constitute the essence of the way that Washington has attempted to govern and police the American Century." [170]

Bacevich is amazed at how "political leaders, liberals and conservatives alike, became enamored with military might." One is used to Republicans beating war drums. And to politicians making careers off their military stories. One only wishes that John McCain were as brave now in politics as he was under North Vietnamese torture. Democratic presidential candidates are just as proud of their medals. Said John Kerry in his 2004 campaign: "Keeping our military strong and keeping our troops

---

169 Bacevich, "The Tyranny of Defense Inc.," *Atlantic*, January-February 2011.
170 *The Ruth Group* website, August 19, 2010.

as safe as they can be should be our highest priority." Playing up his Swift Boat exploits was a central image for him – until the dubious Republican "Swift Boat Veterans" sunk his craft.

Every Congressional candidate tries to sound "tough" on defense. Even female candidates seem to drink testosterone cocktails before making foreign policy speeches. Hillary Clinton, whose presidential instincts were rather lively, asked, when joining the Senate, to serve on the Armed Services Committee. No "It takes a village" or warm-and-fuzzy feminist nation-building speeches there; just hard-nosed "It takes a division" – or maybe even an A-bomb, as when, during her Democratic presidential bid, she straightened back and jaw to threaten to "totally obliterate" Iran if Teheran attacked Israel with a nuclear weapon.

There's another, more practical, reason that elected representatives beat the drums of war. Most get financial support from arms suppliers, and are close to being bought (or at least rented) by military contractors. Congressmen support weapons systems almost without question – even if official government reports claim the new weapons are defective or not even needed. Elected officials are knee-jerk backers of military bases. The U.S. has some 969 military bases within the fifty states ("jobs for the folks back home") and 725 outside the U.S. This doesn't include many secret bases. Sworn to secrecy on Congressional military or security committees, politicians rarely question real needs, either within or outside the U.S. Congressmen who break ranks on this will get a sharp reminder when they examine, at the next election, their total election budget or voter support. The U.S. Congress is part and parcel of the national defense establishment – body, mind, soul and pocketbooks.

In August 2010 Congress showed again how dutifully it leaps to defend Pentagon contractors and constituency jobs, even against the Pentagon's ostensible leaders. Defense Secretary Robert Gates announced a plan to trim bloated ranks of generals and contractors, partly to free up cash for front-line soldiers. Within hours, Congress howled its opposition: "At the end of the day, Secretary Gates and his team will have to convince members of this committee that these efforts will not weaken our nation's defense," warned Buck McKeon, the senior Republican on the House Armed Services Committee. Virginia Democratic Senator Mark Warner avowed he could see "no rational basis" for eliminating the Joint Forces Command, based in his state. "In the business world, you sometimes have to spend money in order to save money," he sermonized." [171]

Such protesting alacrity, applied to all 50 states and thousands of defense contractors, shows why cutting U.S. defense spending is close to impossible. It's a self-feeding monster. Example: Once you get new toys and troops, don't you have to devise reasons to use them?

A *New York Times* editorial saw out-of-control lobbies causing grievous security and financial implications: "Defense Secretary Robert Gates has pledged to restrain military spending. Predictably, members of Congress, industry lobbyists and military commanders are all pushing back. This is a battle well worth fighting. If anything, he needs to be even more ambitious. The Pentagon's annual budget has doubled in the last decade to over $700-billion, including $130 billion in 2010 to pay for wars in Iraq and Afghanistan. There is no way to address the nation's deep fiscal crisis or its security threats without a more rational approach to defense procurement and tough choices on personnel policies." [172]

Bacevich's greatest surprise: America's lefty "liberals" or "progressives" who praise the military. They line up, click their heels, and salute the flag. Then-Harvard human-rights professor Michael Ignatieff (a decent man, now less bellicose as Leader of Canada's Loyal parliamentary Opposition), told future U.S. naval officers in 2003 that "empire has become a precondition for democracy" and the U.S. should "use imperial power to strengthen respect for self-determination [and] to give states back to abused, oppressed people who deserve to rule them for

---

[171] Anne Gearan and Anne Flaherty, "Defense secretary vows to shutter Virginia command, slash contractors to save money," *Associated Press*, August 9, 2010.
[172] *New York Times*, August 14, 2010.

themselves." [173] (Ignatieff repented his support for the Iraq invasion in a *New York Times* article of August 5, 2007 However, his urgings for Washington to back oppressed peoples made some sense during the 2011 Arab uprisings).

Another surprising pro-military endorsement came from usually Pentagon-skeptical *New York Times* columnist Thomas L. Friedman. He termed "morally and strategically bankrupt" Americans who, at the 2004 Super Bowl half-time show, did not remember the burden carried by Iraq-serving U.S. soldiers and their families. Friedman's principled point: Americans should feel included in soldiers' sacrifices. Bacevich's final example of a "liberal" gone gung-ho is none other than Chicago philosopher-genius Allan Bloom. The author of the *Closing of the American Mind* opened his enough to propose a "military personage as president... with the American Empire, like the Roman before it, seeking to impose a Roman peace upon the world." [174] Hail Caesar!

Bacevich's final comment on this is to quote writer Max Boot on using force to spread the American Way of Life... imposing the rule of law, property rights and other guarantees, "at gunpoint if need be." [175]

Speaking of "democracy at gunpoint," George W. Bush's 2003 invasion and occupation of Iraq was a textbook example of unprovoked, pre-emptive war. It started with a long campaign of fear, hate and lies against the planned victim, a rallying of potential allies, then a *Blitzkrieg* amid self-righteous protests of defending sacred principles. (In this case, oil and Israel? By the way, does this war-prepping conceivably remind you of 1939 Danzig?) Bush would install "freedom" and "democracy" in Iraq in the hope that a new, national model would sweep the Middle East. The New Middle East would then fit that old American fantasy: to confer on the whole world the American Way of Life.

---

173 Michael Ignatieff, "The Challenges of American Imperial Power," *Naval War College Review* , Spring 2003. (Cited in , p. 25).
174 Bacevich, *The New American Militarism*, p. 32.
175 *Ibid*, p. 33.

Iraq: 'Operation Enduring Occupation'

Alas, the assault on Iraq – code-named "Operation Iraqi Freedom" – did not quite achieve this. Rather, it illustrated exquisitely how, on faraway, unfamiliar ground, America's limitless self-regard, cultural and historical ignorance, plus its military hubris could design a long, lethal quagmire. Eight years later, Americans still struggled to extricate themselves from this self-created horror show.

A spectacular way to measure America's trigger-happiness with Muslims is to recall how Bush Jr. took America (with Britain's Tony Blair tagging along) into this disastrous war. Bush, backed by flimsy 'intelligence' from Blair, blatantly lied about Saddam Hussein's having weapons of mass destruction (WMD). Bush and his team did all they could to dismiss or derail serious examination of this WMD hypothesis by the Hans Blix-Mohamed ElBaradei UN weapons inspection team. Secondly, Bush and his vice-presidential mentor Richard W. Cheney concocted out of rumor a phony plot between Saddam and Osama bin Laden. They based this on a meeting in Prague that never happened.

The only remaining pretexts for war were that Saddam had once tried to assassinate Bush's father, and that Ariel Sharon's Israel – ready to fight to the last American – quietly wanted the U.S. to dispose of one of its main regional adversaries. Coincidentally, given the predominant focus on Israeli security, Saudi Arabia also wanted Saddam destroyed. It had shuddered seeing Saddam's forces come within less than 250 kilometers of Ryadh during the 1990-91 Iraq-Kuwait war. Both Bush and Cheney, notoriously in bed with the Texas oil industry, also saw profits for U.S. oil companies and secure oil supplies for the U.S. forces. In all, the 2003 Iraq invasion pleased the U.S. (for oil security), Israel (for existential security), Saudi Arabia (for security of the Saudi throne) and even Iran – which had recently lost a horrifically murderous war with Iraq (1980-88).

But no one at the top cared to follow Secretary of State Colin Powell's test for starting wars, later called the "Powell Doctrine:"

1. Is a vital national security interest threatened?
2. Do we have a clear, attainable objective?
3. Have the risks and costs been fully and frankly analyzed?
4. Have all other non-violent policy means been fully exhausted?
5. Is there a plausible exit strategy to avoid endless entanglement?
6. Have the consequences of our action been fully considered?
7. Is the action supported by the American people?
8. Do we have genuine broad international support? [176]

U.S. conduct of the war was a comic-book charade of removing Saddam and searching for WMDs. First, pyrotechnical hubris: a massive, opening barrage called "Shock and Awe" (actually von Clausewitz might have approved). But the televised fireworks seemed more to stir warlike passions among taxpayers than really to intimidate the enemy.

How did the "world's only remaining superpower" fight George W. Bush's Iraq war? Ignorantly, arrogantly, ideologically, corruptly, stupidly – and disastrously for both Iraq and the U.S.

To begin, the Bushites planned the war with almost no serious historical knowledge of Middle East history or cultures. The State Department had serious historians at hand, as well as experienced professional diplomats. But Bush assigned both the planned Iraq invasion and subsequent reconstruction to the Department of Defense – run by an abrasive, know-it-all, bureaucratic infighter called Donald Rumsfeld. "Rummy" quickly outflanked courtly Secretary of State Colin Powell. This sidelined State's comparatively thoughtful plans for diplomatic support and reconstruction.

Rumsfeld's main claim to Iraq experience: his trip to Baghdad in 1983 to promise arms – including deadly chemical and bacteriological ones (anthrax and bubonic plague) – to America's then-beloved ally, Saddam Hussein. Saddam used these against both his own people and the Iranians, who never forgot the Rumsfeld missions.

---

176 See Powell Doctrine, *Wikipedia*.

To make matters worse, Bush had made the shamelessly manipulative Vice-president Richard Cheney his de facto "prime minister." Cheney enjoyed virtually limitless real power, wielded in tandem with Rumsfeld. He used – and abused – his office to invent fairy-tales to justify the invasion: On TV he repeatedly flogged the WMD and Prague canards to fool the American people.

The Bush White House was steeped in born-again Christianity, Biblical culture and messianic faith in America's divine "liberty" mission. Playing on these, Likud-sympathizing "neocon" friends – Richard Perle, Paul Wolfowitz and Douglas Feith, among many others – beat the drums for "reordering" the entire Middle East. The themes: once again, oil and Israel. These were watchwords, as even now. The "neocons" demanded removing any force likely to threaten the security of either Israel or the oil-rich Saudis. Saddam had frightened Israel with his Scud rockets on Tel Aviv during the first Gulf War 1990-91); and his financial aid to Palestinian widows of suicide bombers infuriated Israel.

But Bush's mystical "liberty" mission also drove the invasion. If Iraqis couldn't depose their own tyrant and set up a respectable, U.S.-friendly regime, America would force it on them. Iraqis would be "free," whether they liked it or not. Eight years later, they were finally pretty free. But, amid continuing violence, they still struggled to form a government. But daily violence continued. And civil war hovered, a constant nightmare.

Shock, Awe, and Mercenaries: the New American Way of War

How did America fight in Iraq? And how in Afghanistan? For years now, the U.S. has fielded two armies: its official one, and its private-sector 'contractors.' Both depend on the heaviest possible fire-power and a sense of unquestioned impunity. Both display only isolated examples of cultural thoughtfulness – General David Petraeus comes to mind as a model. But mostly, armed Americans tend to be trigger-happy. They care more for "force protection" (meaning self-protection) than about hurting local peoples' bodies, hearts and minds. If both military and contractors have ended up among Iraqis and Afghans looking like insensitive brutes, that's no surprise. It reflects an entrenched American attitude of superiority, of being missionaries of freedom. Americans' intrinsic, 'God-ordained' virtue can do no wrong – even when, manifestly, it does a lot of wrong, such as negligently – or, very occasionally, deliberately – killing civilians.

Persistent reports of U.S. "collateral damage" in both Iraq (in the past) and now Afghanistan, may have created more terrorists than Americans have killed. That is the routine testimony of villagers whose relatives Americans have accidentally, sometimes almost casually, killed. Modern war is infinitely less "surgical" than experts allege. It's just as sloppy, unpredictable and capricious as always. But Americans are fighting an intercultural war. They are making the massive mistake of seeing soldiers and weapons, including more helicopters and drones, as substitutes for winning the parallel propaganda war. That war must be fought through basic security, electricity, schools, the media and economic development – and obvious respect for local people and for their cultural and religious norms. You need soldiers for security. But – from the *beginning* – you have to show results in the softer areas to win friends.

Senior generals understood well this need to rally local populations. Admiral Michael Mullen, Chairman, U.S. Joint Chiefs of Staff, for example, told the *Los Angeles Times* on March 4, 2010, that "the battlefield isn't necessarily a field anymore. It's in the minds of the people." Unfortunately, earlier military actions often defied this wisdom.

When the U.S. Army arrived in Iraq in 2003, it wore bulky body-armor, scary sunglasses, weird helmet-cameras and huge M16 assault rifles. It kicked in doors and frisked horrified Muslim women. In time, it changed these habits, but initially it made irreconcilable enemies. The same happened in Afghanistan at the beginning. American male soldiers scandalized devout, prudish Muslim families where a family's honor depended hugely on defending women's virtue. After countless clumsy examples of invading homes where even women were in a state of undress, U.S. forces began to take more care – but upsetting stories still occasionally arise.

In general, American forces' fighting style is big, heavy and overwhelming. Not light, nimble and versatile. Their extraordinary emphasis on "force protection" weighs down U.S. soldiers so much that they often cannot run as fast as lighter-armed insurgents. Here's a grunt's-eye view from a U.S. Marine in Afghanistan, identified on his anonymous blog only as "K:" "I'm still not sure I agree with the whole idea of replacing the venerable [Russian-Afghan *Kalashnikov* rifle] with the [American] M16 for these [Afghan soldiers that we're training]. Seems I remember reading somewhere that we should train indigenous forces to mirror the enemy, not to mirror us. By giving them armored Humvees and NATO weapons, we're certainly making them look a lot like us, which would be great if the Afghan Army had any hope of supporting an army with such equipment." He went on to suggest that Afghan soldiers forget body-armor and armored vehicles, and scramble up hills to fight the elusive Taliban enemies on equal (i.e. far lighter) terms.[177]

In Iraq as well as Afghanistan, American soldiers and Marines rode around in heavy vehicles such as Humvees and armored personnel carriers (APCs). In the end, these may have killed more soldiers than did snipers. The heavy vehicles became choice targets for mines and for a new weapon invented (and constantly improved) just for them: Improvised Explosive Devices, IEDs – roadside bombs.

For eight years and more, American forces have in some ways programmed their own defeat. Their 18th-century forebears defeated the formal British redcoat "squares" by sniping at them from behind trees. Today's Americans follow a cult of relentless, ill-adapted modernity. Giving troops the *"best"* equipment has come to mean giving them the *heaviest*, least practical weapons, especially for armor and movement. Again,

---

177 Anonymous, "Embedded in Afghanistan," http://bc235.blogspot.com/2009/07/m16.html

the great, unwieldy, money-tainted military-industrial complex blesses the Pentagon with ever-growing budgets – while saddling U.S. soldiers with ever-growing, lethal burdens.

In December 2004, Rumsfeld needed tougher body armor himself to deflect body-armor questions from frightened soldiers headed for Iraq. Reported the *New York Times*: "Specialist Thomas Wilson, a scout with a Tennessee National Guard unit set to roll into Iraq this week, was the first to step forward, saying that soldiers had had to scrounge through landfills here for pieces of rusty scrap metal and bulletproof glass - what they called "hillbilly armor" - to bolt to their trucks. [He asked Rumsfeld]: "Why don't we have those resources readily available to us?"

Rumsfeld replied with no concern or promise to help: "You go to war with the Army you have, not the Army you might want or wish to have at a later time."[178] No doubt very reassuring.

Another characteristic of the "American War of War" is American forces' shockingly expensive and inefficient "tooth-to-tail" ratio. "Tooth" means combat soldiers; "tail" means logistics and communications. In these terms, the U.S. has a very low tooth-to-tail ratio: fewer fighters, but lots of supply sergeants and PX mini-markets with consumer stuff from home. Insurgent enemies have a high ratio, because they focus on guns, bombs, light equipment and fleet-of-foot mobility. Among NATO forces, the U.S. has the worst tooth-to-tail ratio, the Norwegians the best. Obviously, Norway uses pitifully-paid gnomes to staff its 'cheap' supply chain.

America's Defense Advanced Research Projects Agency (DARPA) works constantly on shrinking the Army's "tail" in relation to combat soldiers. Computer graphics, hypertext and ubiquitous computers supply fast info to front-line soldiers. But up-to-the-second technical toys don't always beat the eyes, ears, terrain-familiarity and neighborhood spies that insurgents can use. Bottom-line: America's armies may have the best equipment; but it costs a fortune – and, to put it chastely, it's not very good at winning today's kind of insurgencies.

---

178 Eric Schmitt, "Troops' Queries Leave Rumsfeld on the Defensive," *New York Times*, December 9, 2004.

Still another burden is the out-of-control proliferation of private Pentagon contractors. The Center for Public Integrity reported that "tens of thousands of private contractors" lived and worked in Iraq during the U.S. occupation. Supposedly, to save money, Congress and the Pentagon authorized hiring these firms called Private Military Contractors (PMCs). Over six years in Iraq, Washington spent $300 *billion* on 12 companies via 3,601 contracts. These firms did many jobs: from training, manning checkpoints, guarding installations and VIPS, and basically anything the official forces didn't care to do.

America is the only modern country (not counting thuggish African ones) to subcontract its wars to companies with no real loyalty to either the sponsoring nation (America) or occupied countries. Personnel of these firms obey no military hierarchy, and they are above the law in the country they "work" in. The infamous Blackwater company ended up in so many ultra-violent scandals against local populations that it eventually lost its primary contract in Iraq. It even had to change its name to the unrecognizable Xe.[179] In spite of Blackwater – and evidence that PMCs were funding Congressional campaigns to keep the money flowing – the Pentagon still counts heavily on PMCs. Despite evidence that many cause irreparable damage to local citizens, battlefield success, and America's reputation.

Indeed, wrote the *New York Times* on October 25, 2010 in relation to Iraq: "The military was often outright hostile to contractors, for being amateurish, overpaid, and, often, trigger-happy. Contractors shot with little discrimination – and few if any consequences – at unarmed Iraqi civilians, Iraqi security forces, U.S. troops, and even other contractors, stirring public outrage and undermining much of what the coalition forces were sent to accomplish." [180]

---

179 "Blackwater Changes Its Name to Xe," *Associated Press*, February 13, 2009.
180 James Glanz and Andrew W. Lehren, "Guns firing, contractors fed chaos," *New York Times*, October 25, 2010.

At the very time of these October 2010 Wikileaks revelations of misbehaving U.S. contractors in Iraq, Afghan President Hamid Karzai was demanding that Washington withdraw all its contractors. The U.S., even with another 30,000 "surge" troops in place, feared grave risks to rebuilding efforts, and argued for keeping many contractors. Note: This, despite strong evidence from Greg Mortenson (of *Three Cups of Tea* fame) and other locally-led project managers that armed and often undisciplined foreign "protectors" only attracted Taliban violence.

Basic problems? The private firms, not answering to any authority but their company bosses, became notorious for brutality and violence against local citizens. And for endless financial scandals – remember not just Blackwater, but Richard Cheney's old firm Halliburton. The latter won huge, non-tendered contracts. It became known for obscene budget overruns, as well as for its damaging insensitivity to Iraqis. [181]

A lot of the PMCs' costs went into boondoggles, embezzlement and worse. Several times, brave whistle-blowers brought evidence to superiors or the Pentagon. Here, according to an Associated Press survey, is the treatment they got:

One after another, the men and women who have stepped forward to report corruption in the massive effort to rebuild Iraq have been vilified, fired and demoted. Or worse. For daring to report illegal arms sales, Navy veteran Donald Vance says he was imprisoned by the American military in a security compound outside Baghdad and subjected to harsh interrogation methods. There were times, huddled on the floor in solitary confinement with that head-banging music blaring dawn to dusk and interrogators yelling the same questions over and over, that Vance began to wish he had just kept his mouth shut.

He had thought he was doing a good and noble thing when he started telling the FBI about the guns and the land mines and the rocket-launchers

---

[181] Victims of alleged Blackwater crimes will take little comfort in this apparent evidence of impunity reported by James Risen in the *New York Times* of October 20, 2010: "Nearly four years after the federal government began a string of investigations and criminal prosecutions against Blackwater Worldwide personnel accused of murder and other violent crimes in Iraq and Afghanistan, the cases are beginning to fall apart, burdened by a legal obstacle of the government's own making."

- all of them being sold for cash, no receipts necessary, he said. He told a federal agent the buyers were Iraqi insurgents, American soldiers, State Department workers, and Iraqi embassy and ministry employees... 'It was a Wal-Mart for guns,' he says. "It was all illegal and everyone knew it.'

So Vance says he blew the whistle... For his trouble, he says, he got 97 days in Camp Cropper, an American military prison outside Baghdad that once held Saddam Hussein, and he was classified a security detainee. Also held was colleague Nathan Ertel, who helped Vance gather evidence documenting the sales ... according to a federal lawsuit both have filed in Chicago, [they alleged] they were illegally imprisoned and subjected to physical and mental interrogation tactics "reserved for terrorists and so-called enemy combatants."

Corruption has long plagued Iraq reconstruction. Hundreds of projects may never be finished, including repairs to the country's oil pipelines and electricity system. Congress gave more than $30 billion to rebuild Iraq, and at least $8.8 billion of it has disappeared, according to a government reconstruction audit.

... 'If you do it [blow the whistle], you will be destroyed," said William Weaver, professor of political science at the University of Texas-El Paso and senior advisor to the National Security Whistleblowers Coalition.[182]

American PMCs are definitely mercenaries, in that they are paid outside of government forces to perform military or quasi-military duties. Indeed, they are above the law wherever they operate. "Security" became a catch-all mandate for PMCs in Iraq. Also in Afghanistan, where – since President Hamid Karzai could not trust Afghan soldiers – private American bodyguards watch over him. Terrible PR, of course; but Karzai, to stay alive, had little choice.

What does all the above mean? It shows that both through regular forces and private contractors, the Pentagon has sold Congress on a sky's-the-limit approach to defense. Professing that almost any step it takes is to save lives or money, in effect it fails on both counts. Its heavy, culturally insensitive way of fighting appears to serve as a recruiting tool for terrorists. And its relentless hyping of "heroes" and "high-tech wizardry" tries to make war sound glorious. Militarism – the *cult* of the military, not its sober respect – exalts violence as the only way to

---

182 Deborah Hastings, "Americans Tortured in Iraq – Those Who Blow Whistle on Contractor Fraud in Iraq Face Penalties," *Santa Barbara News-Press*, August 24, 2007.

fight a war of ideas. It keeps Congress and public focused not just on "our brave boys" (and they are). It sucks politicians into spending both on new toys, and on *old* ones meant for fighting the last war. Getting drones into action to replace far costlier fighter-planes took years.

Does massive spending on equipment and contractors leave America with a more effective army? Not at all. Washington's coddle-the-Pentagon culture neglects a crucial detail: the quality of its serving officers. Tim King is a former Air Force Intelligence officer and is now a senior fellow in research and policy at the Ewing Marion Kauffman Foundation. In a shocking 2011 article in *Atlantic,* he analyzed why the stifling, one-size-fits-all U.S. armed forces bureaucracy is driving top young officers out before their peak years. The "talent bleed" (from early-resigning officers) results, he argues, from a "deeply anti-entrepreneurial personnel structure. From officer evaluations to promotions to job assignments, all branches of the military operate more like a government bureaucracy with a unionized workforce than like a cutting-edge meritocracy."[183] Promotions imposed from on high, with little input from local superiors or aspiring candidates, produce cookie-cutter forces instead of cutting-edge ones. Promotions are scheduled at fixed times for all, with little room to fast-track obvious stars. Result: the stars leave and the duds get eased out. This leaves far too many mediocrities – often time-servers just waiting for their turn at the end-of-career arms-industry trough.

The exit rate for officers became a crisis during the Iraq and Afghan wars. But for decades, studies had warned about the talent hemorrhage. King cites a "widely circulated 2011 report" from the Strategic Studies Institute of the Army War College. It detailed the cost of the Pentagon's risk-averse bureaucracy: "Since the late 1980s... prospects for the Officer Corps' future have been darkened by ... plummeting company-grade officer

---

183 Tim King, "Why Our Best Officers are Leaving," *Atlantic,* January-February 2011.

retention rates. Significantly, this leakage includes a large share of high-performing officers." [184]

In sum: Wild, mantra-driven spending to support a "strong national defense" seems to give the U.S. the worse of all possible worlds. It fattens an out-of-control defense budget at a time when budget deficits are driving politics to cut almost anything except defense. And America is getting what for this largesse? An increasingly unimaginative military machine that, apart from a tiny handful of newborn "experts" on counter-insurgency, regularly stands accused of poor generalship. (That means generals whose only answer to almost any military morass is to "stay the course" or – all generals' historic refrain – "send more troops.") The U.S. is paying through the nose to be led by the nose...to *weaker* defense, not stronger.

The Other Iraq War: "Infoganda"

Calling a fibber a liar, author Susan A Brewer leads off her review of the March 2003 Iraq invasion with this: "...President George W. Bush declared that war would make Americans safer and the Iraqis free. Such assertions masked the real purpose: the expansion of U.S. influence in the Middle East." [185]

Out-Wilsoning President Wilson, Bush went on to promise a decisive clash between "civilization" (i.e., whatever the U.S. wanted) and "barbarism" (whatever its adversaries wanted). Extolling America's "mission" – cf. France's *mission civilisatrice* and Kipling's "White Man's burden" – he added in September 2002 that "the United States will use this moment of opportunity to extend the benefits of freedom across the globe... We will actively work to bring the hope of democracy, development, free markets, and free trade to every corner of the world." [186] Heck, if the terrorists could dream of a worldwide Caliphate

---

184 Casey Wardynski, David S. Lyle, Michael J. Colarusso, "Towards a U.S. Army Officer Corps strategy for success: retaining talent," *U.S Army Professional Writing Archive*, Volume 8.2, February 2011.
185 Susan A Brewer, *Why America Fights: Patriotism and War propaganda from the Philippines to Iraq*, Oxford University Press, p.230.
186 *Ibid.*, pp. 230–231.

from the Philippines to Old Arabia's Andalusia, why couldn't Americans dream big?

To seize and hold Middle America's imagination, Bush and Co. went far beyond old-fashioned "wartime information" as mastered by the Brits and Americans in the Second World War. This time, the White House invented a strategy closer to George Orwell's *1984* than Winston Churchill's 1944. Its own descriptions of its techniques are eloquent: "Infoganda," "iron message discipline," "24-hour-a-day news management," "winning every news cycle,", "perception management" and "expectation management." Said one presidential aide: "We're an empire now, and when we act, we create our own reality." [187]

Stage management became "infotainment" – especially aimed, it would seem, at female voters. Remember Bush's macho, May 1, 2003 landing on the deck of the aircraft carrier *USS Abraham Lincoln* in that crotch-enhancing flight suit? Alas, his huge "Mission Accomplished" banner became a graphics-based version of – might one say? – premature ejaculation. Seven years later, U.S. imagery was drooping. It no longer signalled "Mission Accomplished!" But "Man the Lifeboats!" And later, something like "let's cling to some Iraqi bases near the oil-fields until the end of time."

Chapter 3 showed that, just before the 2003 Iraq invasion and in its early months, the U.S. media notoriously took a vacation from journalism. They became cheerleaders – and not only via the Fox Network with its handsome chief reporter-cheerleader Geraldo Rivera. Offering journalists to be "embedded" with troops paid brilliant dividends. Embedded journalists saw only a grunt's-eye view of the war, often through a slit in a troop-carrier or tank. With few exceptions, they missed the big picture. They forgot analysis, in favor of bonding with the soldiers they were covering. Said Pamela Hess, a United Press correspondent, the U.S. forces favored embedding because that got them more positive and memorable coverage. Why? Because reporters "turn to mush" around "gung-ho, polite 18-year-

---

187 *Ibid.*, p. 233.

olds."[188] Result: a blizzard of (hi mom!) human-interest stories, and almost zero interpretations of the war through Iraqi history, culture, society or customs. Few revelations about the profound changes occurring around reporters outside the "embedment." And certainly almost nothing about the massive suffering of the Iraqi people in their now-lawless land.[189] A snow-job without snow.

Another snow-job was technological 'gee-whizzery.' The 1990-91 *Desert Storm* war started this new era of cyber-reality, of video-game distraction. Life and death in the field became shock-and-awe on the TV screen. Disappearing dots on-screen, alas, were blown-up human beings. Fireworks seemed to explode only skies. But below, in cities, real people died, ripped apart or incinerated. A key advantage of this development for the military: their PR officers became TV programmers, indeed monopolistic news managers. How? By controlling the cockpit footage of rockets blasting scenes below, then giving their own official commentary on what they say happened. Journalists at the Doha Press Center of George W. Bush's "Second Iraq War" first had to sit and watch gripping-if-fuzzy video exploits while a military PR officer proudly explained how U.S. missiles destroyed targets. When one journalist asked about Iraqi casualties, he earned a cough and a disapproving stare. The spectacle, as French analyst Debord warned, became the truth – by smothering debate.

In Roger Stahl's words: "...whereas propaganda engages with argument and narrative, the spectacle presumes an audience that does not. And whereas propaganda seeks to answer the question of why we fight, the spectacle loses itself in the fact that we fight... the spectacle operates mainly through the disappearance of debate... both *technofetishism* and support-the-troops rhetoric most literally satisfy...the dominant order's monologue of self-praise, where a seductive vision of the military apparatus itself begins to appear as the reason for its existence..." Debord's spectacle is a 'permanent opium war'..[and]

---
188 Cited in Brewer, p. 232.
189 Paul McLeary, "Embedded with a night patrol in Fallujioh," *Columbia Journalism Review*, February 2, 2006.

"the bloodless, antiseptic battlefield could be said to be a quest for the cleanest opium..." [190]

Bush and the Pentagon outdid themselves to glorify military culture. True, you do that in wartime – but not as wildly as the 2003-onward U.S. image-molders did (see above Jessica Lynch and Pat Tillman). With an all-professional volunteer army, most soldiers came from poor, undereducated families who were soft touches for unquestioning patriotism. When you witness battles more exciting, heroic and purposeful than anything you see in Tuscaloosa, joining up looks like a wonderful way to "Be All You Can Be" (an old U.S. Army recruiting slogan). Romanticized military PR drew in, as we've noted, a disproportionate number of unemployed and/or non-white recruits (42 percent from 'minority' communities). The "infoganda" therefore didn't upset too much the middle and upper classes. They had the leisure and education to think more carefully about the war – if they cared to bother. In the end, they had fewer sons or daughters on the combat line. In Rumsfeldian terms, they had "no dogs in that fight."

On arrival in Iraq, U.S. troops did not, as Deputy Secretary of Defense Paul Wolfowitz had promised, have to duck flowers tossed by deliriously happy Iraqis. Rather they dodged bullets and bombs from resisters that Rumsfeld, with his usual felicity, termed "dead-enders." Rioters sacked every ministry except the Oil Ministry – the only one guarded by U.S. troops. Rumsfeld dismissed the looting of Iraq's world-renowned National Museum with a shrug: "Stuff happens."

Then, with the cheerleading, Arab-mocking U.S. press banging its drums, TV viewers watched as a U.S. *Gauleiter* (Jay Garner first, then desert-booted, tie-wearing L. Paul Bremer) strutted about ordering Iraqis to work for obscenely overpaid U.S. contractors. The contractors were allegedly there to rebuild Iraq – and, suspected many, Cheney's old firm Halliburton.

---

190 *Ibid.*, pp. 31-32.

The first TV pictures made terrible PR: One of the U.S. soldiers pulling down Saddam's statue planted a U.S. flag on it. A few minutes later, a scream from Washington replaced this with an Iraqi flag. Then a military-run fiasco rolled out over weeks and months and years. A key reason: Rumsfeld's Defense Department won the turf war, as mentioned, with the more thoughtful State Department. He simply ignored State's detailed plans for rebuilding Iraq and restoring its civil society. Rumsfeld's bullying and blundering became high policy. Setbacks got dismissed with his trademark obfuscating and dismissive "wit."

Result: the U.S. remained mired in Iraq eight years later. Then, it could only hope that the rough-and-ready Shia-led democracy they imposed on Iraq could stabilize the country. Alas for logic and geostrategy, next-door Iran's Islamic Republic – the magnetic, historic centre of Shia Islam – seemed likely to play an even larger role in Iraq once the Americans left. This, at a time, when Israel and the U.S. insist that a soon-likely nuclear-armed Iran is their worst enemy. This is not quite the "remaking of the Middle East" in the safer, freer, more democratic mold that "W" promised. It's the logical end-result of blind, stubborn, arrogant U.S. militarism.

In the final two years of the Iraq war, more experienced generals, a much smarter Defense Secretary (Robert Gates) and especially a more farsighted U.S. president (Barack Obama) finally managed the U.S. official – though partial – escape from Iraq in August 2010. In June that year, U.S. military deaths stood at 4, 407. [191] Iraqi civilian deaths, the usually unspoken cost of the "liberation:" 105, 408. [192]

Discreetly but firmly, the expansionist U.S. military got its reward in Iraq: control of enough bases on stand-by outside Baghdad to secure U.S. oil supplies and support a government friendly to Washington. Time will tell how useful these bases

---

[191] U.S. military deaths: http://www.defense.gov/news/casualty.pdf
[192] Iraq Body Count: http://www.iraqbodycount.org/. A September 20, 2006 UN report claimed that Iraqi civilian casualties were widely considered under- reported: informal estimates ranged up to 600,000 .

are – or whether future Iraqi governments will tolerate them. The world energy supply, and even more unstable Iraq politics, may also undermine their value. [193]

How innocent of U.S. 'imperialism' are the bases (once naughtily termed "enduring camps")? The June 4, 2007 transcript of a National Public Radio interview with senior news analyst Daniel Schorr gave a hint:

The new word from the White House is that American troops would be stationed in Iraq permanently on the Korean model. The analogy is a little strained. South Korea has no internal insurgency to worry about. The plan for permanent bases in Iraq must have been long in the making. The president [George W. Bush] ignored a recommendation of the Baker-Hamilton Commission that he state that America seeks no permanent bases.

The building of four bases along with the gigantic new embassy in the green zone on the Tigris River has been moving along quickly. The bases will have mile-long runways to accommodate the largest American planes. The Balad Base north of Baghdad covers fourteen square miles. The new embassy, which will be the largest American mission in the world, will be complete with swimming pool and commissary.

Retired General Anthony Zinni says their permanent bases are quote, "a stupid idea," unquote, that will damage America's image in the whole region. These huge installations must have more than Iraqi stabilization in mind. Ex-president Jimmy Carter said in a speech in February of last year that the reason we went to Iraq was to establish a permanent military base in the Gulf region. And few are missing the point that bases in Iraq will keep American might on Iran's doorstep. [194]

The Nation magazine reported On August 27, 2007 a total of 75 U.S. bases in Iraq. After the Americans announced an August 31, 2010 departure of "combat forces," five massive bases (including the world's largest embassy, with 3,000 staff) will remain. Their activities: "crucial intelligence and logistics support. In many cases special-forces teams are embedded with

---

193 Andrew Lee Butters, "Iraq's political disarray likely to remain after U.S. departure," *TIME*, April 28, 2010.
194 "All Things Considered," *NPR*, June 4, 2007. By August 2010, as its last combat troops left Iraq, Washington called these bases "fortified compounds." But former ambassador Ryan C. Crocker hinted that, if overall security demanded, the U.S. and Iraq might have to "joint relook at the post-2011 period" (Michael R. Gordon, *New York Times*, August 18, 2010).

the Iraqi troops as advisers and mentors." [195] The mega-bases will house between 35,000 to 50,000 soldiers.[196] In mid-2010, all these figures were evolving downward.

Semantic fudging continued into 2010-11. Will the remaining rather large corporal's guard of Americans actually fight? Or will they just hide in their bases, and do training and intelligence? It's a safe bet that, whatever else they do, they will help defend Iraq's oil wells and pipelines. It's not cynical to say that, just realistic. Supporting the fudge in August 2010, two leading Iraqis spoke in favor of keeping the Americans around much longer. First, you could read on August 12 from this astonishing Iraqi source: "Iraqi Army chief Lt. Gen. Babakir Zebari told the *Telegraph* this week that his troops won't be ready to protect the nation until 2020 - nine years after the Obama administration intends to bring all U.S. troops home." [197]

Then, if you have a sense of historical irony, enjoy this comment from Saddam Hussein's loyal no. 2 man, Tariq Aziz: "For 30 years Saddam built Iraq and now it is destroyed. There are more sick than before, more hungry. The people don't have services. People are being killed every day in the tens, if not hundreds. "I was encouraged when [Obama] was elected president, because I thought he was going to correct some of the mistakes of Bush. But Obama is a hypocrite. He is leaving Iraq to the wolves." [198]

Boots versus Sandals: the Psychology of Asymmetrical War

On March 20, 2003, when George W. Bush launched his "Iraqi Freedom" invasion of Iraq, the Pentagon still believed in airplanes and tanks. That's largely what had won George Bush Sr.'s "Desert Storm" January-February 1991 Iraq war – called the "Mother of all Battles" by Saddam Hussein. Within

---

195 BBC website, November 28, 2008.
196 Obama spells out Iraq departure," *Associated Press*, February 27, 2009.
197 CBS/AP, *Daily Telegraph*, August 12, 2010.
198 Martin Chulov, "Saddam Hussein deputy Tariq Aziz calls for US forces to stay in Iraq," *The Guardian*, August 5, 2010.

months, Western inspectors found that all the U.S.-trumpeted motives for Bush Junior's invasion were based on lies or flimsy excuses – none affecting vital U.S. interests. Again: arms of mass destruction (none found, just vague, hypothetical plans); Saddam's alleged ties to Al-Qaeda (non-existent); Saddam's payments to families of Palestinian suicide bombers (an annoyance to Israelis, but hardly a significant U.S. interest); concern at Saddam's human rights abuses (this never bothered U.S. Defense Secretary Donald Rumsfeld when he held a cordial meeting with Saddam on December 20, 1983 as Ronald Reagan's special envoy); a wish to spread democracy to the Arab world (news Bush forgot to convey to the Saudis and other Arab dictator pals).

Quickly after the 2003 invasion, attention turned from motives to running a devastated Iraq – whose army, the nation's only possible stabilizing force, the Americans promptly and frivolously disbanded. What remained was a shattered post-war country suddenly dominated by revived sectarian hates. And by U.S. soldiers and administrators whose ignorance of Iraqi history and culture was breathtaking.

A perceptive article by Stephen John Morgan on the *InfoWarp* website of March 15, 2007 spells out the U.S.-Iraqi intercultural dialogue of the deaf:

...US troops booted down the door of Arab values and brought the worst of all possible insults upon them by dishonoring and humiliating them. In a region and culture, both Arabic and Muslim, where one's dignity and honor are to be defended at all cost, including one's life, the US shamed the Iraqi nation, the Arab nation and the Muslim world. This, in a culture where shame is the worst possible of destinies – unlike the guilt based societies of the West...

It is a reason why the humiliation and shaming of the Palestinians has made it the cause célèbre of the Arab and Muslim world and also explains the ferocity of the eventual resistance to the US occupation in Iraq and its condemnation of by Arabs and Muslims worldwide. The occupation is felt and empathized as a humiliating, shameful, dishonor perpetrated by the infidel, United States upon Arab and Muslim brothers and sisters...

For Arabs and Muslims their honor and the shaming of themselves and their brethren is something which cannot go unavenged. One must be prepared to die for it. It is linked to the culture of retribution, where a hurt or death brought upon another of one's family, tribe or clan must be avenged and this now extends to one's sect, nation, ethnicity and common religion...

It would take a leap of the imagination for the Administration to realize that the aim of the insurgency is not to win, but to take retribution and to heap shame upon them. Culturally, this would even be the case should they be able to win militarily! Humiliation not annihilation is their payback for the occupation. Thus, withdrawal is the only option for the US, since they cannot uproot an emotional motivation by military means. It is not just that the US cannot succeed in an asymmetrical war, but that they cannot win a psychologically asymmetrical conflict. Withdrawal will be a victory for the insurgents. But regardless of all this, sometimes eating humble pie is the most emotionally intelligent course. [199]

Eerily, all these points apply as much to Afghanistan in 2011 as to Iraq in 2009. But in the Afghan case, a uniquely pointed source of humiliation and anger emerges from the country's long history of foreign occupation. Archeological research shows evidence of invasion from East, West and North back to Paleolithic times. But just to take the best-known invaders of the modern era: Alexander the Great (330 B.C.); Arabs, bringing Islam (7th century); Britain (intermittently, 1839-1919); Soviets (1979-89). America tried its luck for the first time in the late 1980s by arming Afghan *mujaheddin* – and some Arab volunteers such as a wealthy Saudi dreamer called Osama bin Laden. Although the Afghans and Arabs dominated the hills and valleys, the Soviets dominated the air. That is, until the U.S. supplied its turbaned, circumstantial Cold War allies with shoulder-fired Stinger ground-to-air missiles. See the movie *Charlie Wilson's War*.

Drones, Phones and Internet: Asymmetrical Technology

Anybody who visited the Pakistani and Afghan sides of the Khyber Pass between 1850 and 1950 witnessed a marvel of technology: illiterate Pathan (or Pashtun) tribesmen, armed with a clamp and a few tools, producing perfect copies of Western, mainly British, rifles and pistols. Sometimes the

---

199 Stephen John Morgan, "Insurgent psychology – Honour, Dignity, Shame and Humiliation – the roots of an endless war," www.InfoWarp.com, March 15, 2007.

perfect copies would blow up when fired, but they were the heart of a highly-skilled gun culture. Today the huge, dusty gun markets of Peshawar, Darra and Sahakhot on Pakistan's North-West Frontier carry on the tradition. They also sell trafficked originals of *Kalashnikovs* and other guns. A copied *AK-47* costs fifty dollars – including the right to test it by firing it down the street outside the shop. In Pathan villages, you still see 10-year-old boys hauling around their rifle, with bandolier bullet-belt proudly criss-crossing their chests. Locals will tell you of ancient vendettas with the next village perpetuating murders this young boy may later have to avenge. He may also learn the ancient craft of copying enemy weapons.

The Pathans – whose totally ungovernable tribal areas even Pakistani officials can enter only with a Pathan guide – are not the only tech-savvy tribe or group. Pakistani Taliban have also become skilled at using the Internet, and use it effectively for spying and propaganda. They are also brilliant at adapting vehicle- and personnel-killing improvised explosive devices (IEDs) to new Western counter-measures. Never mind body-armor – insurgents can run faster without it. They can also use coded radio faster than Western field translators can translate and pass along messages to the right officers. And they can buy night-goggles and sniper rifles as war surplus with the fortunes they make selling opium (over 90 percent of world production).

But the Americans wield technology that trumps all of this. The heart of it is the massive eavesdropping capacity of Washington's National Security Agency (NSA). Its huge arrays of computers, multi-billion-dollar budgets and thousands of top crypto-analysts scour the world. Analyzing media (radio, TV, Internet) and private telephone and e-mail conversations anywhere in the world it wishes, the NSA taps the phones of foreign political, military, guerrilla and even spy chiefs. With such a resource, the U.S. puts cosmic secrets on the U.S. President's desk often before a foreign leader's own colleagues know them.

The question then is: If the Americans are so smart, how is it that Iraqi insurgents and the Taliban could for so long run rings around Western troops? One reason is that Taliban and *al-Qaeda* leaders long ago gave up using traceable electronic communications – except in brief tactical or propaganda situations:

"As many wanted *al-Qaeda* and Taliban figures have been killed or captured after being tracked down through their satellite phones, the militants have either stopped using these communication gadgets or become cautious and selective in their use. Osama bin Laden, his deputy Dr Ayman al-Zawahiri and other Al-Qaeda figures also ceased using their satellite phones and faxes. Afghan Taliban leader Mulla Muhammad Omar too appears to have given up the use of the satellite and mobile phone. This is the major reason of their staying alive and remaining free eight years after the US invasion of Afghanistan and the fall of the Taliban regime in late 2001. They are obviously using more traditional means of communication such as couriers, hand-written letters and audiotapes."[200] But even couriers are risky: tracking them finally led to bin Laden's death.

This communications impasse may help explain why, after almost ten years in Afghanistan and swearing to stay "as long as it takes," Americans and Westerners in general are quietly getting ready to bail out – even if it means supping with the Taliban and Pakistani ISI (military spy service) "devils." But the West's frustration runs deeper than blocked intercepts.

There is tech-smart and ground-smart. When the imperial British invaded Kabul in 1839 with 20,000 troops, they had top-of-the-line rifles, grenades and cannons, as well as well-trained horses. When the remaining British community of 16,500 (including 12,000 civilians) had to withdraw in January 1842, they took their army's know-how on a 90-mile trek to Jalalabad. But the Afghans knew the hills and valleys. They ambushed and murdered all 16,500 British, men, women and children – all except Dr. William Bryson whom, bloodied and exhausted,

---

200 Rahimullah Yusufzai, "Intercepting the Taliban," *The News*, Peshawar, July 21, 2009.

they allowed to escape to tell the tale and warn off other invaders.

Western weapons and tactics have changed since then. Traditional Afghan weapons and tactics have too. But the Talibans' decisive edge – the ability to hide in, and foray from, the ancient dusty hills remains. They will sit there, to use the American boast, "as long as it takes," their patience outlasting that of the attention-deficit Westerners.

They vividly remember that, after arming Afghans and jihadists to drive out the Soviets in February 1989, the Americans went home – as Defense Secretary Robert M. Gates later said, leaving Afghanistan and Pakistan "holding the bag." We have already seen that America also left Afghan rebel groups, including some *al-Qaeda*-style groups, holding several hundred shoulder-fired Stinger ground-to-air missiles. To defeat the Soviet invaders, the U.S. had handed out to these guerrillas between 2,000 and 2,500 *Stingers*. In December 2001, *Slate* magazine alleged that between 200 and 300 of these remained in *al-Qaeda* or Taliban hands.[201] In November 2002, a Stinger-like Soviet-made SA-7 missile narrowly missed bringing down an Israeli airliner in Africa. Meanwhile, the CIA was buying back Stingers from Afghan rebels at extortionate prices – totaling more than all U.S. humanitarian aid during the just-ended war.

Stingers or not, America's abandonment of Afghanistan after the Soviets decamped left the future *al-Qaeda* fanatics in control. They built the training bases that eventually sent airplanes into New York's Twin Towers. When the Americans leave again, as they must and will, whom and what will they leave behind? What is their best option? The least awful?

Why (Obviously) the Locals Always Win

The main reason local insurgents have an edge is that they're fighting for their own country – home, family, livelihood. Nationalism usually fuels fury against invaders even more than

---

[201] Robert Mackey, "Another Stinger Plot Misfires," *New York Times*, May 22, 2009.

does religion. Anger at foreign occupiers was eventually a critical factor in driving the Americans out of Iraq. It will prove still more central among ferociously nationalistic Afghan tribes. As with the 19th-century British, Afghans also enjoy an enormous advantage in knowing the local landscape, languages, culture and customs. They know how to negotiate with local enemies and allies – whether through bribes, sympathy or threats, or all three. These factors confer, as sportsmen say, a "home advantage," but one infinitely more tangible.

Xenophobia – hate of and resistance to foreigners – can fuel wars for decades, even centuries. "Foreigners," indeed, may be from other tribes or nations, or simply from different language or religious groups. Sometimes differences between hostile groups are spectacular – Russians vs. Chinese and Japanese in the late 19th century. Or extremely minor, when deliberately cherished and exaggerated by insecure nationalists. Michael Ignatieff's splendid book *Blood and Belonging* looks at how Serbs and Muslims, Irish Catholics and Protestants, and even Quebec separatists played their nationalist cards.

In a subsequent book, *The Warrior's Honor*, Ignatieff applies Freud's theory of the "narcissism of minor difference" to explain how two peoples, secretly feeling they are the same in spite of mutually hostile propagandas, take pains to inflate trivial distinctions. After the 1990s Balkan wars, Serbs, Croats and Muslims all tried to invent different spellings or pronunciations for essentially the same Serbo-Croation language. Ignatieff cites a conversation with a Serb irregular who explains why he hates Croats: "First, these are Serbian cigarettes; over there they smoke Croatian cigarettes. Second (after troubled reflection), Croats think they're better than us; they want to be gentlemen; they think they're fancy Europeans. Third (this time after no pause) we're all just Balkan shit." [202]

The flip-side of "local" xenophobia (patriotism?) is invaders' contempt for the locals. Whatever the pretexts or propaganda 'justifying' invasion, sooner or later the guys with big guns

---

[202] Michael Ignatieff, *The Warrior's Honor: Ethnic War and the Modern Conscience*, Metropolitan Books, New York, 1998.

abuse the guys with smaller guns. In Iraq, the American cult of guns and the military merely brought this universal law into play earlier, and more viciously.

Two memorable examples: the aforementioned financial and human-rights abuses of many expatriate contractors; and Iraq's Abu Ghraib prison scandal. Some U.S. contractors' violent abuses are well known. In financial terms: vast overcharging, crooked books, disappearing money – but also sweatshop exploitation of dismally paid Asian workers, failure to employ more than a minimum of unemployed, thus unhappy, Iraqi workers. Halliburton didn't do much for human reconstruction in mass-unemployment Iraq: in mid-2004, barely a quarter of its employees in this well-educated country were Iraqis.

All this left deep marks in Iraqis' minds. Iraqis came to see Americans not as decent, friendly helpers, but as gun-crazy, America-knows-best, to-hell-with-the-'*hajis*' occupiers. Such behavior contributed mightily to the image of America as a garrison state. Many Americans looked like henchmen from outposts of empire run by England's 17th-century royal-chartered East India Company. When Bush the "Wilsonian idealist" promised to bring the rich benefits of free enterprise to Iraq, he and Cheney seem to have had in mind benefits for U.S. contractors. They brought not enterprise capitalism but crony capitalism – with the U.S. taxpayer picking up the tab. All as part of a "war effort" that caught-unawares U.S. citizens had to salute: for it came under the umbrella of the newly-revered military. [203]

But the most notorious contractors' scandal – intersecting with guilty military abusers – was the Abu Ghraib Prison horror. Once again, esteem for the military covered up a multitude of crimes. This time: physical and psychological torture, sodomy, sadism, humiliation, and murder. Leaked photos of the Iraqi prisoners' ordeals swept the world – including the Muslim world. Naked prisoners piled on top of each other like cordwood, another blind-folded and in danger of electrocution, another covered in feces, and still another lying

---

[203] For a good summary of the "reconstruction" boondoggles and rip-offs, see Pratap Chatterjee, *Iraq, Inc. – a Profitable Occupation*, Seven Stories Press, New York, 2004, p.248.

naked on the ground – and daintily held on a leash by a female soldier, Lynndie England. The prison boss, General Janis Karpinski, was also a woman. Both women inevitably added symbolically to the humiliation of macho-but-prudish Muslim males. (Note: most of the criticized soldiers were either women or low-ranking men – a fact Karpinski blames on the army's sexist and protect-the-brass culture). Once again – and although U.S. civilians did some of the torturing – the U.S. military became an exemplary recruiting agency for al-Qaeda.[204]

Taking the U.S. "liberation" of Iraq overall, it turned out to be an all-points disaster for both Iraq and the U.S. From beginning to end, military hubris, gunslinger bravado and self-glorification blinded America to either the big picture or the Iraqi people's tragic, family-level "little picture." From 'forgetting' to keep statistics on Iraqi deaths to turning a blind eye to endless "collateral-damage" shoot-outs likely killing thousands of innocent civilians, the U.S. military disgraced itself. Few at home cared for the dead Iraqis or their looted, destroyed economy. Americans, weeping at yellow ribbons wrapped around trees, and at U.S.-flag-draped coffins (banned from view until reaching hometowns), still loved their military. It was now in their hearts, their minds, their fantasies and their blood. It was all part of a grand, brave, high-tech Hollywood movie praising the USA at its finest.

Seven years after the invasion, Iraq struggled to attain its pre-war economic health. In many places, the country still resembled Berlin in 1945. Its Bush-ordained "democracy" was years from being stable, its touted elections taking an eternity to produce a government even tolerated, much less respected. The northern Kurds looked organized enough to run a real country. The big winners were the "folks" next door – the nuclear-weapons-bound Iranian theocrats who were America's bête noire.

---

204 See Office of the Secretary of Defense and Joint Staff, *Taguba Report With Annexes (AR 15-16 Investigation of the 800th Military Police Brigade)*: http://www.dod.gov/pubs/foi/detainees/taguba/

They were also, as noted, Israel's *bête noire*. But logic went AWOL in Bush's planning of the Iraq invasion. Who remembers now that old-fox Ariel Sharon, after helicoptering a gullible George W. Bush over Palestinian lands to show why Israel "needed" them, also egged Bush on to depose Saddam Hussein? (The Iraqi dictator had sent Scud missiles against Israel during the first Gulf War in 1991). Sharon and Bush met less than two years after 9/11. America then had a decent chance – by keeping most of its troops in Afghanistan – of eliminating both the Taliban and Osama bin Laden. Instead, Bush took Sharon's counsel, as that of his own pro-Likud advisers, and siphoned off his soldiers from Afghanistan to attack Iraq. Iraq, a country that didn't threaten the U.S. directly at all.

But the 2003 Iraq invasion also nicely dovetailed with the Bush family's extraordinarily intimate sharing of interests with Saudi Arabia.[205] The Saudi royals feared Saddam's military ambitions. By curbing Iraq's oil production for several years (though hoping to control it later), Bush would also enrich the Saudis by marginalizing a major competitor.

The cost of Iraq? We just saw the U.S. Body Count figure of Iraqi deaths: 105,408. But other estimates go higher. *Lancet,* Johns Hopkins, Associated Press, and Opinion Research Business Survey numbers range from about 110,000 to just over one million civilian deaths. One suspects a lot of guesswork there. Confusingly, Wikileak's October 22, 2010 divulging of masses of new classified U.S. war documents cited 'only' 109,000 dead counting both sides, and 66,081 dead Iraqi civilians – many killed by other Iraqis in Sunni-Shiite murders." Whatever the figures, cases of permanent injury or disfigurement of Iraqi civilians are estimated in the hundreds of thousands, or low millions.

Lifelong Iraqi traumas are likely in the same range. Depleted uranium shells raised cancer rates, for example in Fallujah. "Several mental health care professionals suggest the number of untreated or under-treated people nationwide reaches into

---

[205] See next chapter, and Craig Unger, House of Bush, House of Saud - a 30-year History of Deceit, Oil and Greed, Gibson Square, London, 2007.

the millions," reported the *San Francisco Chronicle*, "and the consequences could permanently harm generations. 'Iraqis are being traumatized every day,' said Dr. Said al-Hashimi, 54, a psychiatrist who runs a private clinic and teaches at Mustansiriya Medical School in Baghdad. 'No one knows what will result from living through this continuous trauma on a daily basis.'" [206]

We cited American losses as 4,415 military deaths. But hundreds of thousands more U.S. veterans are physically maimed, or suffer Post-Traumatic Stress Disorder (PTSD). Troops in the field (including Iraq and Afghanistan in late 2010) are seeking mental-health care at a rate of over 100,000 a month. And suicides often run higher each month that combat deaths. The American Medical Association reported in 2009 that active-duty U.S. troop suicides were running at a 28-year high. [207]

A 2008 RAND Corporation study noted that almost one in five service members, of 300,000 veterans, returned from Iraq and Afghanistan with symptoms of PTSD or major depression.[208] Suicides are common and constant partly because Army treatment is either absent or lackadaisical. Among returned troops, an *Al Jazeera* documentary cites an epidemic of suicides from seeing brutality during multiple tours. [209] The financial cost of George W. Bush's "Mission Accomplished" had already passed *three trillion* dollars by 2008 – and was still exploding.[210] But that's only money. If Vietnam is any precedent, the damage to American society in broken lives, families, suicides and crime may last half a century.

In Afghanistan, constantly perfected rocket-firing drones allow the U.S. to advance its war tactically, while sabotaging it

---

206 James Palmer, "Protesters plead for peace - Civilian toll: Iraqis exhibit more mental health problems," *San Francisco Chronicle*, March 19, 2007.
207 Bridget M. Kuehn, "Soldier Suicide Rates Continue to Rise," *Journal of the American Medical Association*, March 18, 2009.
208 Emily Mullin, "Overstressed military mental health system examined," *Scripps Howard News Service*, November 12, 2009.
209 "The War Within," *Al Jazeera* English, April 8, 2010.
210 Joseph E. Stiglitz and Linda J. Bilmes, "The true cost of the Iraq war," *Huffington Post*, September 7, 2010.

strategically. Killing a few Taliban or *al-Qaeda* technically represents a military gain. But with all-too-frequent "collateral" civilian casualties in drone attacks, these raids incur a huge political – as well as human – loss. Indeed, since for every civilian killed inadvertently, observers claim you may create several new Taliban enemies, aren't such military 'successes' therefore eventually *military losses* as well? They also undercut, of course, the already feeble credibility of a notoriously corrupt and incompetent Afghan government. And this too can make it harder to recruit for the Afghan Army – again a *military* setback.

More terrifyingly, nuclear-armed Pakistan, theoretically America's ally in fighting the Taliban, is known to play a double game. Its Inter Services Intelligence (ISI) Directorate has stayed close to the Taliban – and indeed several terrorist groups – as part of a strategy to fight India. This complicity, combined with the anti-West teachings of thousands of *madrassa* schools, has enhanced American paranoia. And cost American lives. This in turn tempts the U.S. to use weapons as its main strategic tool, neglecting the terrorists' oft-proclaimed "mental battlefield." In August 2010, Pakistan President Asif Ali Zardari warned that America's anti-Taliban war was being lost "because we have lost the battle for hearts and minds." [211]

Debased COINage?

As top *al-Qaeda* spokesman, strategist and operations chief, Ayman al-Zawahiri frequently says (see top-of-this-chapter quote), winning hearts and minds is the very essence of the anti-West battle. U.S. counter-insurgency experts 'coined' the acronym COIN for their doctrine of splitting civilians from insurgents, and focusing more on protecting constituted local authority than on chasing terrorists. This entailed gluing the West to the government in place, warts and all – a policy with its own risk of discredit. COIN also required bribing some

---

211 Tom Peck, "War against the Taliban being lost, says Zardari," *The Independent*, August 4, 2010.

Iraqi terrorists (mainly Sunnis) to cooperate. Naturally, all this required more troops – the usual Pentagon refrain. And this, in turn, revived 'mission-creep' arguments about "another Vietnam quagmire."

On Afghanistan, top U.S. strategists split into military and political camps. The military – Joint Chiefs Chairman Michael Mullen, General David Petraeus and (until his dismissal in June 2010 for disloyal indiscretions) General Stanley McChrystal – argued for the counter-insurgency (COIN) strategy that the latter two reinvented. Broadly, this approach allowed Americans to proclaim the official "end of combat operations" in Iraq on September 1, 2010 – and ostentatiously, if far from completely, to get out. Leaving up to 50,000 troops behind was not quite an evacuation.

Obama's civilian or "political" camp, devoted to his re-election and led by Vice-President Joe Biden, argued for a more definitive anti-terrorist victory, using more Afghan Army troops in traditional anti-terrorist roles. This camp warned against a Vietnam-style quagmire, but still argued for this more classic "Vietnamization" approach – using many more Afghan troops. Perhaps their North Vietnam analogies were a bit risky. For it's hard to imagine the illiterate, tribally-divided, often corrupt Afghan Army ever being as disciplined as the ideologically united, brilliantly commanded Vietcong of General Vo Nguyen Giap.

Such policy contradictions are intrinsic to insurgencies. "There is a legitimate debate," argued James Dobbins in *Foreign Affairs*, "over how deeply the U.S. military should invest in counterinsurgency capability at the expense of conventional capacity. But no one seriously argues that counterinsurgency tactics are not necessary to resist insurgencies... As the anti-counterinsurgency faction admits, present U.S. efforts have reduced the risk of an attack on the United States originating from Afghanistan to near-zero. It is reasonable to argue that the cost of sustaining these efforts at current levels is too great to bear indefinitely and to urge instead the acceptance of higher risk. This trade-off between cost and risk is ultimately what the debate between the president's civilian and military advisers has been about." [212]

America can project its military force around the globe with aircraft carriers, long-range troop transport planes, stealth bombers, and pin-point guided missiles. It can invade, and send divisions, tanks and guns of every caliber. Such armament may indeed win tactical *battles*. But it can't win *wars* or create lasting peace. That's why COIN – sophisticated counterinsurgency – will remain part of the military mix as long as Afghanistan burns. And why, as we now see again, why "gentlemen warriors" should not belong only to the Victorian Age.

Annoying the Patriots

For war and peace exist essentially on the ground, in people's minds. The Pentagon has a duty to do its job, and to support its troops' morale with memories of home. But parading the "American Way of War" and the "American Way of Life" too ostentatiously among poor, terrified populations draws fear, envy and anger. Illustrating the invaders' "superiority" with guns galore is inevitable – although the British initially won friends in 2003 Basrah with bicycles, no sunglasses, and berets instead of helmets. Scaring locals with bearded, trigger-happy mercenaries in one-way-mirror sunglasses is thoughtless as policy and reality. Building gigantic PXs with "Mainstreet USA Food Courts" – however good for troops' morale – hurls in the face of hungry local peoples the shocking fact of invasion, intrusion and occupation by high-living foreigners. Foreigners who regularly displayed contempt for local customs and religion. Within days of the U.S. invasion of Iraq, in fact, "U.S. soldiers drew on racial and religious prejudice to refer to enemy fighters as 'sand niggers,' 'rag heads,' and '*hajis*.'" [213] The latter term was especially offensive because it mocked one of the five bed-

---

212 James Dobbins, "Your COIN Is No Good Here: How 'Counterinsurgency' Became a Dirty Word," Foreign Affairs, October 26, 2010.
213 Susan A Brewer, Why America Fights – Patriotism and War Propaganda From the Philippines to Iraq, Oxford University Press, 2009, p. 234.

rock duties of all Muslims – to go, at least once in a lifetime, as a pilgrim (*Hajji*) to Mecca.

Such coarseness to local people (all-too-familiar under wartime stress) may have softened a little, as a few generals realized the damage it could cause. Generals McChrystal and Petraeus understood this danger, and tried to discourage cultural offences to local people. But this lesson remains: Almost any "rescue" mission, if it drags on, becomes an occupation. And it guarantees the hostility of the 'rescued.' This turns most short-term victories into long-term defeats, with bad impressions outliving the good. This result is certain when the liberators betray their all-too-obvious intention of sticking around for "a few more years" and keeping – oh, just a few little bases. Inevitably, the occupier wants these in perpetuity. Opening bases is easy. Shutting them isn't. Abandoning them may just perpetuate imperialist nostalgias – see the Philippines, Haiti and that monster U.S. embassy in Baghdad: 3,000-plus employees (including trainers previously under military control) and 1,168 vehicles (159 missing through sloppy surveillance and accounting).

This overwhelming, continuing U.S. presence in Iraq implies two things: domination and permanence. In Muslim societies, where shame is a predominant value, both are anathema. However glad Iraq's Shia-run government may be to keep benefiting from American training of police, soldiers and other personnel, ordinary Iraqis see the gigantic U.S. embassy, and imagine control of oil, security – and, indirectly, the shape and values of their new society. The simple, involuntary message of the embassy: America, behind the scenes, is still paramount in this proud, ancient land of Mesopotamia with conservative Muslim values.

The only mitigating hope is that henceforth the more culturally sensitive State Department will control many of America's "critical missions" in Iraq, especially training. Remember that when Defense Secretary Donald Rumsfeld won his turf battle on Iraq with Secretary of State Colin Powell, he basically scrapped the State Department's thorough and thoughtful reconstruction plans. In their place: his bumble-and-bungle, Uncle-Sam-knows-best military horror-show designed to cow the populace and secure oil supplies and future bases. Both Defense and State approaches convey a certain 'idea of America.' Take your pick.

No idea of America has 'won' as a positive force in either Iraq or Afghanistan. Instead, both these countries got thousands of tons of more weapons, and hundreds of thousands of foreign soldiers. Much of this military effort was vital, at least in Afghanistan, to try to clean out *al-Qaeda* installations. But in the end, the big-picture contest remains *U.S. arms versus Muslim ideas*. Now a war for security has become a logistical problem: how to abandon Afghanistan *en masse*, but leave behind – maybe in tribal areas not ceded to the Pashtun Taliban? – "just a few" permanent U.S. bases. Given what Afghan history repeatedly teaches, any bases at all will be too many, and they may block a political solution.

In the face of America's militarist outlook stands Israeli philosopher Amos Oz. His old lesson [cited after this book's title-page] remains: "To defeat an idea, you have to offer a better idea, a more attractive and acceptable one." [214]

Oz is no pacifist. On defense, he's a realist: "I do not discount the importance of force. Woe to the country that discounts the efficacy of force. Without it, Israel would not be able to survive a single day. But we cannot allow ourselves to forget for even a moment that force is effective only as a preventative — to prevent the destruction and conquest of Israel, to protect our lives and freedom. Every attempt to use force not as a preventive measure, not in self-defense, but instead as a means of smashing problems and squashing ideas, will lead to more disasters, just like the one we brought on ourselves in international waters, opposite Gaza's shores." [215]

That's a philosophical and policy balance that neither the U.S. nor its along-for-the-ride allies in Afghanistan have yet achieved. Yet such a balance must underpin the West's strategy in the volatile lands of Islam. The "war" issue is not drones

---

214 Amos Oz, "Israeli force, adrift on the sea," *New York Times*, June 1, 2010.
215 *Ibid.*

vs. guerrillas, boots vs. sandals. That's plumbing, almost quartermaster stuff. The issue is the folly of improvising war strategy against opponents' improvised roadside bombs. Along with understanding other nations' sense of their own dignity, the West's failure to understand this disconnect between ideas and arms is the most fundamental reason of all why the "locals" will always win.

Besides, those troublesome "locals" have wonderful allies: the U.S. thought-leaders who keep the world out of America. We looked at them in Chapter Three: the media, schools, churches, Congress, even pop-culture intellectuals. Thanks to their dedicated work to ignore the world, and to promote America first, last, only, always, and forever, the U.S. public is ripe to buy Pentagon war propaganda as the finest Authorized Bible since King James.

This propaganda includes entrenching America's weird, war-fuelling alliance with Saudi Arabia. In spite of recent reforms by King Abdullah, the desert kingdom remains the homeland of Osama bin Laden and his maybe-not-quite-alienated family. It's the homeland too of the Salafi-Wahhabi imams – who, though ordered to tone down their West-hostile messages, are still 'educating,' through a multi-continent network of oil-funded *madrassas*, a new generation of bigots, bullies of women, and suicide bombers.

Let's ponder a staggering perversity. America's leaders, by refusing to limit their country's oil consumption, channel billions of dollars each year to a country where, claim serious observers, many Muslims still yearn to destroy America. [216]

---

[216] Operation Free, a clean-energy lobby run by retired senior military officers, estimates the cost of U.S. oil imports at $700-million a day. (See Joe Klein, A Reactor Revival," *TIME*, November 8, 2010). According to the U.S. Energy Information Administration (EIA), the Saudi Arabia figure for August 2010 was 1,080,000 barrels a day. With crude prices at around $80 a barrel, that would seem to be about $88-million a day). See the EIA website listing the top countries exporting oil to the U.S. in order of importance: Canada, Mexico, Saudi Arabia. Canada sells the U.S. roughly twice as much oil as Saudi Arabia. Strategic differences: Canada doesn't run Salafi *madrassas*, and it exports its oil over land. Both arguments obviously apply to Mexico too.

Europeans tax gasoline heavily. The U.S. – flattering its dream of "freedom" via cheap gas at the pump, Henry Ford's affordable, mass-produced jalopies, and go-wild road movies, rejects "taxes on liberty." *Easy Rider, Bonnie and Clyde*, and *Thelma and Louise* all pumped up the myth. Heck, why fight a great American illusion?

In the "war on terror," America funds both sides: its own armies, and (indirectly) its enemy's. For more detail on why and how, read on.

We're borrowing money from China to buy oil from the Persian Gulf to burn it in ways that destroy the future of human civilization. Every bit of that has to change – Al Gore

In one generation, we went from riding camels to riding Cadillacs. The way we are wasting money, I fear the next generation will be riding camels again – King Faisal

Chapter Five /

DRINKING THE SAUDI KOOL-AID

On January 10, 1901, wildcatters burst open the Spindletop Gusher at Beaumont, Texas. On March 3, 1938, after six years of exploration, U.S. geologists discovered Saudi Arabia's first commercial oil field in Dhahran, Eastern Province. Beaumont and Dhahran would define a bizarre and complex Arabian-American alliance making oil the lifeblood – and curse – of the world economy to this day. They also laid the groundwork, both financially and politically, for an intensification of U.S. militarism. By definition, the military-industrial complex needed oil. And it needed lots of oil-fueled money to fund always ballooning military "preparedness."

For if the U.S. didn't have an enemy, America's militarized culture always wanted to be ready for one. It needed a Pentagon tail to wag the American dog. If a big, tank-and-plane-consuming war was not available (or became outdated) after 9/11, an endless guerrilla war – say, a "war on terror" – would do just fine. The Saud family's absolute monarchy could supply the oil for U.S. armies; and the jihad-mongering Salafi clergy could supply the cause and the fighters to combat the Americans. Washington could fund both just by buying oil.

Let no one say the Saudis are backward. With their centuries-old desert cunning, and mastery of modern economics and technology, they're geniuses at tightrope-walking. But they couldn't finance today's quicksilver-like wars without big-time

American accomplices. Comrades-in-oil. Comrades-in-arms. Comrades in Ike Eisenhower's military-industrial complex.

Who's On First?

Abbott and Costello's classic skit, just cited, mocks ambiguity in identifying players. From the outset, the Ryadh-Washington axis has been rich in contradictions and misheard names. Also in conflicts of interest. Some of these have been internal to each country; others between the two countries. Within Saudi Arabia, three overlapping tensions have made the oil discovery a mixed blessing: the Sunni-Shia split, the Saud-Wahhabi pact, and ultra-rich versus poor.

The first tension pits the Sunni Muslim majority against the country's Shia Muslim minority. Originally a conflict over the Prophet's succession, this is now a set of complex disagreements over beliefs and rituals. Perhaps 15 percent of Saudi Arabia's 27 million population (almost a third being expatriates) are Shia Muslims – regarded by the Sunni majority as barely tolerable heretics.

Worse for the Sunnis, Shias are concentrated in the oil-rich Eastern Province, of which they constitute about a third of the population. Inevitably, Sunni control over partly 'Shia' resources there carries the germ of resentment. And the natural link between Saudi Shias and the powerful Shia elite of neighboring Iran across the 370-kilometer-wide (at widest) Persian Gulf worries Ryadh's Sunni theocracy. At relatively short rocket range, it's a major perceived security risk.

Another may be tiny next-door Bahrain, whose 1.2-million population is almost 70 percent Shia. Pan-Shia threats to Sunni overlords there came to a boil in February-March 2011. Then Bahrain's Sunni self-proclaimed King Hamad ibn Isa Al Khalifa let hirelings murder democracy demonstrators, mainly Shias, with live fire. Bahrain is linked to the large Shia population in the Saudi Eastern Province by the 25-kilometer King Fahd Causeway. Will Shias at both ends follow the 2011 Arab uprisings all the way, and try to topple their Sunni masters? Time will tell. Meanwhile, at Al Khalifa's request, 1,000 Saudi and Emirates' soldiers entered Bahrain in late March 2011 to help put down Shia (and other) democracy demonstrators. Repression was brutal.

Bitterness between Sunnis and Shias in this whole region makes continued antagonism a certainty. Divided by history-rooted theologies, economic class, lifestyle and psychology, Sunnis and Shias generally despise and distrust each other. Saudi Arabia's fanatical Wahhabis "are incensed by the Shia 'infidels' in their midst, whom they detest with a passion that words can barely describe. For the Wahhabis, the Shias are daring to profess what, to them, is anathema to every truth revealed by the Prophet to the Muslim faithful." [217]

Over recent decades, both U.S. "neocon" strategists and a few nostalgic British Arabists have toyed with the idea of seizing the Eastern Province oil-fields to create an independent "East Arabia." This new country would leave the religious cities of Mecca and Medina to the Wahhabi-Saudis, while (hoped the 'Anglo-Saxons') keeping the "Shia" oil-fields under indirect Western control. For now, this is pure fantasy. But over time, how much more indecently rich can the Saudi royals become while keeping their Shias – and indeed millions of poor Arabs elsewhere – in misery?

Golda Meir once joked that Moses was not all that beloved of the Jews because, after leading his people all over the Middle East, he dropped them off in the only spot (Israel) with no oil. But he dropped the Shias off in an ocean of Saudi (as well as Bahraini and Iranian) oil. In a cosmic economic crisis of rocketing oil prices and spreading Wahhabi-inspired terrorism, a Western move to split Saudi Arabia between oil and God might not, in the long run, prove entirely science fiction. In the spring of 2011, indeed, the unthinkable in Arab nations seems to be just whatever tomorrow morning's news comes up with. That year's domino-game of Arab re-awakening may need years to run its course. Much, indeed anything, can happen. Until

---

217 John R. Bradley, *Saudi Arabia Exposed – Inside a Kingdom in Crisis*, Palgrave Macmillan, New York, 2006, p. 78.

a miracle replaces it, oil is forever. Alliances, as we saw with Tunisia's Ben Ali and Egypt's Mubarak, are not.

Observes John R. Bradley in *Saudi Arabia Exposed*: "What would stop the Shiites of the (Saudi oil-rich) Eastern Province, who have little incentive to support the regime that oppresses them and damns them as infidels, from welcoming U.S. forces if they rolled into the Eastern Province to 'liberate' Saudi Arabia oil fields?" [218] Another, supporting question: Who on earth would weep for the medieval Saudi oppressors? Other Arab dictators? Where are they now? Maybe North Korea, Ryadh's only rival as a hermetic society? OPEC, which would welcome the Eastern Province overnight?

The second tension arises from the Saud-Wahhabi relationship. In 1747 the Al Saud family made the faith-for-protection deal with the family of Ibn Abd Al-Wahhab alluded to earlier. This agreement was to be perpetual. And 260 years later, both sides have stuck to it. The Saud family culture remains in many ways, and in spite of a veneer of modernity, rooted in the brutalities and simplicities of desert culture. Slicing off heads and hands, and cooping up women, are just the most visible examples. [219]

Al-Wahhab, for his part, managed through the original pact to impose on Saudi society an omnipresent clergy purveying a backward, dogmatic version of a pure, original Islam. Backwardness? Until 1985, the current blind Wahhabi imam believed that the earth was a flat disk – until a royal-family passenger on the U.S. space shuttle *Discovery* testified to him that the earth was in fact a globe. Dogmatism? In 2002, 14 teenage girls burned to death in their school because members of the Wahhabi Committee for the Promotion of Virtue and Prevention of Vice blocked their escape: the girls, rushing to survive the flames, were not wearing their Wahhabi-prescribed black cloak and head coverings. [220]

---

218 Ibid.,P. 83.
219 See the cheerful *BBC* interview with Ryadh's main executioner Muhammad Saad al-Beshi, who sometimes allowed his children to help him clean his sword – in Unger, p. 86.
220 The royal family is literally above the law. Although King Abdullah has personally set a higher standard, scores of other royals ignore the Wahhabis' moral strictures, especially when abroad. Women, alcohol and gambling

The alliance between the Saudi royal family and the homegrown strict-observance Wahhabi, or Salafi, version of Islam originally fought what it considered polytheistic Shia heresies. More subtly, it still does. But now the alliance focuses more on mutual advantage: the clerics support the royals, and the royals defend the clerics' strict version of Islam. The Saudi royals do this not just at home, but abroad. They pour billions into building Wahhabi-style mosques and *madrassas* (Islamic schools) in otherwise more moderate Muslim societies. These schools, focusing on rote-learning of the Koran, teach religious intolerance and contempt for Western values. Several royals are also suspected to have contributed financially to the jihadist wars of Osama bin Laden and others like him.

The third tension: rich versus poor. Cry for Argentina, but don't cry for Saudi Arabia if that East-West split happens in coming years. For the ruling Saudis, Gulf petro-emirates and Gaddafi-era Libyans have kept their obscene profits for themselves – while barely sharing a *ryal* (about 27 cents) with their impoverished Arab "brothers." This, as repeated scandals prove, while often horribly mistreating underpaid (or unpaid) Filipino, Sri Lankan and (fellow-Muslim) Pakistani and Indonesian servants. One day, will the rich Saudis be forced to share, or be overthrown? Or will renewable energies finally – in 50 years? – replace oil? [221]

---

are routine entertainments for the petro-rich Saudi playboys. The word 'hypocrisy' does not seem to be a very familiar term to them – no doubt because witnesses have serious motivations not to talk.

221 Maids in private homes often become slaves. Beatings, rape, unbearably long hours, primitive sleeping accommodations, starvation diets, unpaid wages, and withheld passports are rife among the 1.5 million impoverished overseas maids. One Saudi employer and his wife, denounced in August 2010, drove 24 nails into the body of a 49-year-old Sri Lankan maid. See "Nails removed from 'tortured' Sri Lankan maid," BBC World website, August 27, 2010. Disgustingly, in the light of the Koran's urging to treat others with kindness and compassion, many immensely rich Saudis violate elementary decency. The same, alas, applies to many wealthy Kuwaitis, Emirate Arabs and Lebanese. All, in their own minds, 'good Muslims.' See a confirming story about a Pakistani maid in Saudi Arabia, citing *Human Rights Watch*: "From 12:00 pm to 2:30 am my employer beat me with an electric cable...[he] said, 'you have only two choices: either you work without a salary or you

Before going further, it's worth remembering who the Saudi royal family really are. They are essentially a greedy, accidentally oil-rich, extended family descended from (as most royals everywhere are!) a tribe of bandit-warriors. Their roughly 7,000 "princes" (about 200 of whom count in politics and the economy) keep almost all the country's fabulous oil riches for themselves. With few exceptions, they spend it with staggering profligacy, with scant regard for their own people and even less for the impoverished millions of Arabs without oil. Many princes, ignoring the strict morality they impose at home, have squandered fortunes abroad. "In the eighties, [King] Fahd and his entourage spent up to $5 million a day ...in Marbella, Spain. ..his fleet consisted of eight aircraft, including five Boeing 747s...[He traveled with] 400 retainers...and 25 Rolls-Royces and limos." [222] Ostentation today is less blatant, but still general. Ask the managers of the swishest hotels in London and Paris – which, by the way, often belong to the petro-princes.

There was one outstanding exception to this indecency: King Faisal, who reigned from 1964 to 1975. A personally frugal man, he modernized wherever possible, and put the kingdom's finances in order. For this, he was assassinated by a half-brother's son. The dying Faisal asked, to no avail, that his killer's life be spared. Much of Faisal's legacy is his very example, as fondly recalled by another impressive man, Sheikh Ahmed Zaki Yamani, Saudi Arabia's oil and minerals minister for 25 years: "He [Faisal] was modest in a glorious way. He lived in homes that today a middle-class Saudi would not accept. He never took money from the Treasury for himself." (Interviewer: "Yamani says this as though this fact alone makes the king unique.") "He was a reformer. He was strongly for the education of women. At that time, it was forbidden. He used to send girls from his own pocket to study outside the country. One of his achievements was to abolish slavery, and I was an instrument

---

die here, if you die, I will tell the police that you committed suicide,'" Rafia Zakaria, "Maid to order," *Daily Times*, Lahore, July 12, 2008.
222 Unger, pp.83–89.

in that. He was a believer in the Arab cause and in Islam, without being a fanatic." [223]

To his credit, King Abdullah, whose reign began in August 2005, has shown remarkable new vision. Prudently – at a pace he judges his Wahhabi allies and Saudi society can bear – he has invested heavily in education, notably at university level. He has made cautious steps to respect women more. Amazingly, he has initiated inter-faith dialogue with Jews and Christians, working in tandem with Spain. Instead of ranting against Israel at every turn, as Crown Prince in 2002 he produced a peace plan – later approved by the Arab League as the "Arab Initiative." It still more or less fits the consensus of nearly all sincere peacemakers. It implies Israeli withdrawal from Palestinian lands in exchange for full normalization of relations with all 22 Arab states. Israel never responded officially to the proposal, though former Prime Minister Ehud Olmert said it was "a step that I can't help but appreciate." Abdullah has also put down local *al-Qaeda* and other terrorist groups, setting up a daring system of re-education for violent dissidents.

Also to Abdullah's credit: Though often uneasy with the probing investigations of *Al Jazeera* (he did ask the Emir of Qatar to tone down certain attacks on Saudi Arabia), he has supported Egypt's moves to tame Salafi broadcasters. In September 2010, Cairo, with his agreement, shut down 17 TV stations preaching anti-Shia and anti-Christian messages. A pacifying move by both Egyptians and Saudis. But it still matched Arab governments' increasing moves to limit freedom of speech.

Apart from controlled media, many Saudi practices profoundly trouble Western observers. Among them: obviously, the aforementioned harsh judicial punishments, and the segregation and total veiling of women. But also women's legal inequality and lack of basic rights; banning of churches; and the yawning gap between awesomely rich and desperately poor. Saudi apologists cite not only Islam and "ancient desert traditions." They say they fear "immoral' Western customs – the latter, we know, not being much of a problem for vacationing princes.

---

[223] "Farewell to riches of the earth," Gyles Brandreth, *The Telegraph*, June 25, 2000.

Oil, Israel and Illusion

How did the U.S.-Saudi contradictions begin? The U.S., led by Texas oil interests, simply became addicted to Saudi oil. This started at the height of the Second World War. In February 1943, President Franklin D. Roosevelt proclaimed that "the defense of Saudi Arabia is vital to the defense of the United States." This made the Saudi kingdom eligible for military assistance. The first U.S. military mission to Saudi Arabia, under General Ralph Royce, came in December that year. King Abdulaziz Al Saud, founder of today's Saudi Arabia, welcomed his American visitors in the Red Sea port of Jeddah. Agape and agog, the Americans attended a grand banquet featuring 10 slaughtered sheep – with their eyeballs served as a delicacy. No alcohol or smoking, but presents of royal robes and gold daggers for all 11 Americans. The American gave the king a radio transmitter and offered him (an opportunity graciously declined) a ride in an airplane. [224]

On February 14, 1945, to formalize the fast-developing relationship, President Roosevelt and King Ibn Saud met on the *USS Quincy* in Egypt's Great Bitter Lake – just weeks before Roosevelt died. They signed an understanding to swap affordable Saudi oil for U.S. security. The two chiefs of state agreed that the Saudis would keep fairly cheap oil flowing to the U.S. economy in exchange for the U.S. protecting the Saudi throne. This understanding in turn created two risks. The first was of squeezing the U.S. between its commitment to Saudi security and its commitment to eventual Israeli security – the latter naturally, and powerfully, backed by America's Jewish community. [Israel became independent on May 14, 1948].

The first notable conflict here – the "tank war" – happened under president Dwight D. Eisenhower. On February 16, 1956, an anonymous tipster called United Press International to "warn" that eighteen M-14 tanks on a Brooklyn pier were headed for Saudi Arabia. At the time, the State Department

---

224 David B. Ottaway, "The King's Messenger - Prince Bandar bin Sultan and America's Tangled Relationship with Saudi Arabia," *Washington Post*, May 3, 2008.

was holding up an Israeli arms request for $50 million. After Jewish protestors forced Eisenhower to suspend the tank shipment, a furious Saudi embassy cried betrayal. Eisenhower quickly released the tanks to the Saudis – but promised much-needed spare parts for Israel's forces, plus "most careful scrutiny" of Israel's $50-million major-weapons request. America's dilemma was clear in this State Department memo: "If the shipment were canceled, it would unquestionably provoke the Saudi Arabians to the point where our future relations would be seriously jeopardized; they would probably proceed to buy arms from the Soviets; the negotiations for renewal of the Dhahran airbase would be difficult, if not impossible; and vital U.S. resources [oil] could be lost." [225]

This oil-vs-Israel trap became almost a routine. And it strains the U.S.- Saudi relationship to this day. The most dramatic clash occurred when the Saudis organized an oil embargo with its OPEC cartel colleagues to punish the U.S. for re-supplying Israel's arms during the 1973 Yom Kippur War. This caused huge gas-pump line-ups and gasoline price increases in the U.S. The Saudis also saw the embargo as a way of raising prices to compensate for a U.S. dollar that had fallen in paper value by a third, largely because of U.S. Vietnam defense spending. The "Nixon shock" of 1971 (ending the U.S. dollar's convertibility to gold) confirmed this drop and helped stiffen Saudi determination to keep prices higher. The U.S. public could now see the Arab-Israeli conflict had an oil dimension too.

This would not be the last time. America was 'trapped' again between Ryadh and Jerusalem when *New York Times* columnist, Thomas L. Friedman, revealed then-Crown Prince (and now King) Abdullah's aforementioned peace plan (later termed the "Arab Initiative"). [226]

President George W. Bush, sworn to back the Israelis no matter what, ignored this promising plan. As he did – apparently guided by his Likud friends – all other compromise proposals: the Geneva Accord, the Quartet Roadmap, the Clinton

---

225 *Ibid.*
226 "Abdullah II: The 5-State Solution," Thomas L. Friedman, the *New York Times*, January 27, 2009.

Parameters. The Saudis still resent this American rejection. But even the more peace-oriented Obama Administration seemed less than eager to promote the Saudi ideas. Like Bush and Co., Obama seemed reluctant to take big risks for peace. America's perpetual electoral cycle clearly reminded him of how brief and fragile were his opportunities.

As a result, the whole Saudi-U.S. agenda – oil, Israel-Palestine, Iran, potential Saudi mediation with the Taliban, showed no startlingly constructive results. Even after two Obama-Abdullah summits, the Ryadh-Washington relationship remained cordial, but cool. It only chilled, but seriously, when Obama, against Abdullah's advice in January 2011, not-so-gently pushed Egypt's fellow-autocrat Hosni Mubarak from office.

Cutting to the core of the strange U.S.-Saudi relationship: the Saudi royals have a double marriage – and we're not talking of Islam-authorized wives. Put more pointedly, the royals are caught in their double "protection racket." On one hand, the Wahhabis keep a lid on popular discontent as long as the royals uphold their Falafi-Wahhabi doctrine. On the other, the royals have to keep their oil flowing at reasonable prices, failing which the U.S. *could*, though more or less in theory, withdraw its military support for the throne. The Saudi royals are masters of these twin balancing acts.

Americans are really the ones caught in an absurd situation. Since politically, U.S. politicians are terrified of raising gasoline taxes (there being a national election every two years), Americans end up consuming far more oil than they might if prices went notably higher. Result again, in technicolor: in the "war on terror," the U.S. is funding both sides: its own military, and the jihadists who still, on the sly, are likely drawing funding from more than a few Saudis.

Holding Hands in Crawford

Craig Unger's revealing book *House of Bush. House of Saud* shows vividly how the Bush and Saud families intertwined for almost 30 years. Vice-president H.W. Bush (later president no. 41) cultivated the royals assiduously under President Reagan. He continued this as president. But his son, George W. Bush, unblushingly outdid him. The charming April 6, 2005 picture of Crown Prince Abdullah (later king) and George Bush hand-in-hand at the president's Crawford, Texas ranch tells the story. Cozy? Late-night comedian Jay Leno offered this naughty caption for the photo of the grinning, eye-locking, hand-holding pair: "What happens in Crawford stays in Crawford." [227]

A similarly fond Crawford picture shows a shirt-sleeved Bush sprawling in his cowboy boots as long-term Saudi ambassador Prince Bandar camps tie-less on an easy chair. The Bushes and the Saudis are plainly old buddies. Much of the credit for that, and for keeping the whole relationship intimate, belonged to Prince Bandar, the monarchy's ambassador to the U.S. for a remarkable 22 years (1983 to 2005). Some observers regarded Bandar as virtually a member of both Bush cabinets.

Unger cites a heartfelt letter from Bandar to George H.W. Bush on the eve of the latter's defeat by Bill Clinton in November 1992: "You are my friend for life, one of my family." When the final votes confirmed Bush Sr.'s defeat, Bandar said he told King Fahd that he wanted to resign: "It was like I lost one of my family, dead." But, as Unger noted, Bandar stayed on as ambassador and consoled himself by adding still more rooms to his 38-room estate in McLean, Virginia. [228]

For bitter humor – and endless irony – on the Bush-Saudi inter-family compact, you could do worse than to see Michael Moore's superb polemical documentary *Fahrenheit 9/11*. But the basic facts were already known, and make one marvel, if not cringe. In a nutshell, the Saudi royal family are old friends and clients of the wealthy bin Laden family. The bin Ladens were the Sauds' favorite builders – they won the main contract for refurbishing both sacrosanct Mecca and Medina. Osama, before he segued into terrorism with his $30-million inheritance, was

---

227 This section owes a great deal to the excellent book by Craig Unger: *House of Bush, House of Saud – The Secret Relationship Between the World's Two Most Powerful Dynasties*, Gibson Square, London, 2007.
228 Ibid., p.152.

personally known to several royals. In fact, a few months before Bush Senior launched "Operation Desert Storm" against Saddam in 1991, Osama easily won an audience with Bandar's father, Prince Sultan bin Abdul Aziz. Prince Sultan was then Saudi defense minister. Having just defeated the Soviet Union in Afghanistan (with much U.S. help, especially those helicopter-destroying, Stinger shoulder-borne missiles), a cocky 33-year-old Osama told Sultan that there was no need to let half a million infidel foreign troops "occupy" Saudi Arabia's holy soil. He, Osama, could chase Saddam's army from Kuwait – with "faith" and 100,000 battle-toughened jihadists.

Ominously, Osama warned Sultan that allowing "Crusaders [Christians] and Jews" to invade the Muslim world's hallowed ground, the royal family risked more than Saddam. By calling in America and its allies to ensure Saudi security, the ruling clan was putting in jeopardy its religious legitimacy. The Salafi-Wahhabi clergy would feel betrayed. They would consider themselves released from the ancient pact to back the Sauds in exchange for imposing Salafism.

King Fahd took the risk, and announced he would allow hundreds of thousands of mainly U.S. troops onto Saudi soil. When they started arriving in August 1990, Saudis discovered that they included not just Christians, but Jews and – even worse – women, of course 'obscenely' uncovered. The trauma galvanized many now-unemployed Arab Afghan fighters, as well as devout Saudis.

Osama still tried to avoid crossing the royal family. As an alternative to welcoming foreign troops, he urged a boycott of U.S. products. Buying American, he pointed out, meant putting money into Israeli pockets to oppress the Palestinians. A logical stretch, and definitely a long-shot way of holding back the U.S. military.

Over following months and years, Osama and his allies began their well-known escalation of terrorist actions: the World Trade Center bombing (February 1993); the "Blackhawk Down" incident (October 1993); bombing of the U.S. embassies in Kenya and Tanzania (August 1998); bombing of the Khobar military complex (June 1996); and crashing a suicide-boat into the *USS Cole* (October 2000). The Khobar attack, in Saudi Arabia itself – and near the eastern oil-fields – cut to the heart of the U.S.-Saudi alliance: oil for security. Even more than the other events, Khobar triggered a strong Saudi response against terrorism – including against the Sauds' old friend Osama.

These spectacular events obliged not just the Saudi royals, but Osama's own family, to denounce him officially as the bin Ladens' black sheep. But the bin Ladens are a big family, and so are the Sauds. It's hard to believe there was not at least occasional "back-channel" communications still going on.

This weird situation gets scarier: By stunning coincidence – the same royals who knew Osama and his family are, as we just saw, close friends of the Bush family – including both father George H.W. Bush (president no. 41) and son George W. Bush (president no. 43). At only one remove, the president of the United States became the sworn enemy of a family (the bin Ladens) close to his intimate family friends (the Sauds). It's one thing for the linchpin royal, Prince Bandar, to make sure that Sauds and Bushes always got what they wanted: for the U.S., oil; and for the royals, a secure throne. But historically, the Bush-Saud friendship meant that George W. Bush (after 9/11) and the royals both shared another "link:" Osama bin Laden himself. A Hollywood movie with such a script would get laughed out of Tinseltown. (Well, Michael Moore did think of it... and laughed all the way to the bank).

The evening of 9/11 unmasked how close – and ironic – that link really was. Soon after the New York and Washington attacks, authorities found that 15 of the 19 hijackers were Saudi Arabian citizens. Yet two days later – when U.S. airspace was closed to outgoing and incoming flights – a luxury charter aircraft took off secretly from Tampa, Florida. On board: a son of Defense Minister Prince Sultan bin Abdul Aziz and the son of a senior Saudi military commander. From several points in the U.S., members of the bin Laden and Saud families converged on Boston's Logan Airport. With special clearance from the White House (allegedly at the request of George H.W. Bush via Bandar), they were allowed to fly home to Saudi Arabia – *without even being questioned*. Astonishing: surely at least the bin Ladens, as relatives of Osama, were natural candidates for police and CIA interrogation. Yet the Bushes allowed them to escape even the slightest official interest.

Long before, the bin Laden clan had publicly disowned Osama. But as one former U.S. anti-terrorist chief said, "blood is thicker than water." On February 26, 2001, several close relatives had joined Osama bin Laden in Kandahar to attend his son Muhammed's wedding. And according to Carmen bin Laden, estranged sister-in-law of Osama, several bin Laden family members may have kept on sending money to Osama. [229] Several rich Saudis kept giving money to Islamic charities suspected of funding terrorism. That same month, intelligence operatives spotted two of Osama's sisters taking cash to Abu Dhabi airport. There, said a *New Yorker* piece, they were "suspected of handing it to a member of Osama bin Laden's *al-Qaeda* organization." [230]

But hard proof of systematic Saudi funding for *al-Qaeda* – especially by royals – never surfaced. America has preferred, for diplomatic and commercial reasons, not to look too hard. Besides: logically, insist Saudi apologists, had royals sent Osama money, they would have been funding their own destruction. Because the king had allowed infidel foreign soldiers into Saudi Arabia for Desert Storm, Osama had sworn to bring down the Sauds' royal house. It's no secret that the Salafi-Wahhabis despise the West and its "decadent" infidel culture – and Saudi royals who sneak away to enjoy its immoral delights. In spite of recent royal educational reforms, the Saudi *Ulema* (constituted body of religious leaders) still basically turns young Saudis against Western liberties and values.

Possible Saudi terrorist backing remains a foggy issue. But bearing in mind the country's history, theocratic make-up, and the everyday anti-West discourse of so many Saudis, the fog may be smoke – as where there's smoke, there's fire. Or at least brush-fires: a Saudi called Shaykh Muhammad Abu Fa'id is

---

229 *Ibid.*, p. 178.
230 Interview with John L. Martin, cited in *Ibid.*, p. 230.

identified as a top financier and "manager" for the youthful Somali jihadists of *Al-Shabaab*. [231]

This only adds piquancy to the U.S.-Saudi hand-holding in Crawford. Americans' "special relationship" with the Saudis collides not only with antithetical values. It collides with America's very special relationship with Israel. And complicates working with either Ryadh or Jerusalem, Washington has to close its eyes to the old, intimate friendship between Sauds and bin Ladens. Bin Ladens who, though their "rejected" black sheep Osama knocked down the Twin Towers, had enough clout with the White House to defy a post-9/11 no-fly ban. And amazingly, to steal out of the U.S. – heavens, as though they had something to hide...

Before Obama, another thing always hidden in plain sight was George W. Bush's almost incestuous relationship with the Saud family. If his father, George H.W. Bush, had developed the relationship, his son almost made it into one big, happy, transcontinental family. When his father got restless young "W" into the Texas oil industry, Saudi investors kept a close eye on him. One Saudi bailed out floundering Harken Energy while Bush Jr. was on its board. Not only would such helping the son please the father. The son's having a presidential dad made him attractive as a next-generation ally – *Inch'Allah*, even a future president? By the time George W. ran for president in the 2000 election, he came surrounded by Saudi friends and money. "By a conservative estimate," calculates Unger from various sources, "$1,476-million [almost a *billion* and a half dollars] had made its way from the Saudis to the House of Bush and its allied companies and institutions. It could be safely said that never before in history had a presidential candidate...been so closely tied financially and personally to the ruling family of another foreign power..." [232] Only allegations? But serious ones that Unger plainly opens to challenge.

Include as inner-circle Bush-the-Younger backers his father and vice-president Richard Cheney (of oil-field services firm Halliburton). Together they made "W" the Big Oil candidate,

---

231 See *Wikipedia* under "al-Shabaab."
232 *Ibid.*, p. 200.

and put a Big Smile on Saudi faces – as well as on Texas oil-patch faces. As Unger points out: "Never before had the highest levels of an administration so nakedly represented the oil industry. Between them, the president, vice-president, national security advisor, and secretary of commerce had held key positions in small, independent oil companies...[and] major publicly traded companies (Halliburton and Chevron)." Others with personal stakes in, or links, to oil: the secretary of the army, U.S. trade representative, and both president's and vice-president's chiefs of staff. [233] The national security advisor (later secretary of state) had headed the Chevron board's committee on public policy. She ended up with a supertanker named after her: the 129,000-ton *SS Condoleeza Rice* (a name quickly changed to the *SS Altair Voyager* for obvious reasons). See Google "Images" online for a picture of this fine-looking ship.

None of this *of course* implies corruption or conflict of interest. It simply notes that the Bush administration and Big Oil were kissin' cousins who kissed quite a bit. They smooched a lot too – hey, hands across the ocean! – with their Saudi petro-cousins. When Bush Jr.'s regime took power, a Saudi embassy official allegedly crowed: "Happy days are here again!"

The Obama administration may have a leader whose middle name is Hussein, but that doesn't make Barack Obama an enthusiastic friend of the Saudis. His interest in the Saudis naturally includes a concern for energy. But it seems as much to be a hope for improving U.S.-Muslim relations. In itself, that's a tricky agenda. Remember when Obama in August 2010 courageously defended the principle of religious freedom in the case of the proposed mosque near Manhattan's Ground Zero?

A startling proof of Obama's *Realpolitik* with Ryadh was his administration's 2010 decision to shield Saudi nationals from possible evidence that many high-placed Saudis had long funded Al-Qaeda. The previous two Bush administrations had originally ignored such proof, for Osama bin Laden was, or had been, a U.S. ally fighting Russians in Afghanistan. Obama had no such excuse for shielding suspected high-ranking Saudi

---

[233] *Ibid.*, p. 222.

terrorism-funders from U.S. law. But a lawyer-ally offered another excuse – as blunt and refreshing as you could wish. Elena Kagan, Obama's solicitor-general (before joining the U.S. Supreme Court in August 2010), simply argued that going after the Saudi royal family would harm U.S. foreign policy. She said that *even if evidence proved* [author's italics] that top Saudis had helped back *al-Qaeda*, "the princes are immune from petitioners' claims." Why? Because of "the potentially significant foreign relations consequences of subjecting another sovereign state to suit." [234] With some 7,000 princes, quite a sovereign state.

This was certainly not a personal decision by Kagan. Obama had to agree. Her record of encouraging study of *Shariah* law as Harvard law dean, generously financed by the Saudi royals – may have been a coincidence. But both the "shielding" and *Shariah* decisions hint again at the extraordinary persistence of Saudi power in the United States.

If anything, after BP's spring-summer Gulf of Mexico oil fiasco in 2010, Obama had little inclination to build Bush-like complicities with the oil industry. Whip-sawed between needing to encourage offshore drilling to preserve domestic oil supplies, and worries about another catastrophic spill, Obama stayed correct but cool to the industry. And stayed coolly correct with the Saudis.

His alternatives: environmentally dangerous Canadian tar sands; decades-to-develop alternative energies (solar, wind, biomass, tidal, etc.); pushing Detroit on higher-mileage-per-gallon performance; or – the smartest, but most unpopular solution – raising gasoline taxes. As we'll argue later, the latter would cut consumption, lower imports, keep U.S. money at home, and *maybe* put *al-Qaeda* on a diet.

Almost certainly, the Bush-Saudi agenda will prevail until at least a possible second Obama term. Houston, Ryadh, and bought-and-paid-for members of Congress will work hand in glove with the Pentagon and Madison Avenue on one message to Americans: "Defending America's security and prosperity"

---

234 Eric Lichtblau, "Justice Dept. Backs Saudi Royal Family on 9/11 Lawsuit," *New York Times*, May 29, 2009.

with cheap gasoline must trump common sense. Doing so, they will drive America – in Hummers and overweight SUVs – to global warming, pollution and new pretexts for unnecessary wars. That's not paranoia. Given the record of the Bush-Saudi cabal, it's pretty certain.

There has been, and still will be, a cost to America for this Bush-Saudi coziness. Pre-9/11, there was clearly a lackadaisical attitude to security with Saudis visiting the U.S. Although repeatedly and strongly hearing from the president's chief counter-terrorism czar, Richard Clarke, that an attack on the U.S. possibly involving Saudis was imminent, the Bush White House did nothing. Instead, it set up a "Visa Express" program in Ryadh allowing Saudis to get a U.S. visa *without even appearing in person.* A breathtaking lack of routine caution.

In the end, the odd bed-follows of Ryadh and Washington will keep billions of dollars flowing each year to the wrong people: Pentagon budget-bloaters, mega-rich Arab sovereigns, plus the terrorists who – one way or another – seem always to siphon off their unfair share of the loot. The impoverished tens of millions of oil-poor Arabs will get nothing for sensible education or basic health. Instead, from America's Saudi "allies," billions will flow to Salafi-Wahhabi *madrassas* all over the Muslim world.

So what? Well, the most radical Islamic schools systematically attack western values and the West itself. The schools' quality varies, but too many *madrassas* are little short of jihadist factories. In these, with barely a bit of math and reading, almost the only subject studied is the Koran – interpreted by Wahhabi-trained teachers. The tens of thousands of "graduates" of these *madrassas*, essentially boys, emerge with a view of the world that augurs badly for peace and reconciliation with the West.

Wahhabi doctrine often attacks even good Muslims who dare to interpret the Koran differently. The Shias of course, but even more the peace-loving, love-preaching Sufis and "peaceful jihadist" Ahmadis. In the spring of 2010, Taliban fanatics attacked a Sufi shrine where poets and musicians had gathered for centuries. The shrine had brought a message of peace and tolerance to the Pashtuns who straddle the Afghan-Pakistan border – the very place where Osama bin Laden's version of 'love' thrives. About 10 years earlier, Saudi Arabia built a Wahhabi-style *madrassa* at the end of a path leading to the shrine. Almost immediately, the Wahhabi-brainwashed *madrassa* students tried to halt the shrine's Sufi "heresies." Said the shrine-keeper: "My family have been singing here for generations...But now these *madrassa* students come and tell us what we are doing is wrong. They tell women to stay at home. This used to be a place where people came to get peace of mind. Now when they come here, they just encounter more problems."

Finally, the Taliban blew up the shrine – "blaming the shrine's administrators for allowing women to pray and seek healing there." [235] Fanatical Muslims also blew up two other Pakistani Sufi temples on October 7 and 25, 2010, killing a total of 15 faithful, including several women and children. The previous July, two suicide bombers had killed about 40 worshippers at a famous Sufi shrine in Lahore. [236]

Is this what America's twin-brother Saudi ally is doing with the Niagara of dollars American consumers and politicians seem incapable of linking to their oil addiction? It's quaint to call America and Saudi Arabia mere odd bed-fellows. The truth is infinitely more sinister: As we have repeatedly noted, blissfully (or willfully) ignorant Americans are funding not only their own bloated military establishment. They are training new generations of America-hating jihadists to fight hapless U.S. troops – good soldiers brainwashed to believe they are fighting for "liberty," not a Murder Inc. cabal of oil barons. Put a tad more politely by the *New York Times's* Thomas L. Friedman: "... we send Saudi Arabia money for oil, even though we know that some of it ends up financing the very people we are fighting, because confronting the Saudis over their ideological exports

---

235 William Dalrymple, "The Muslims in the Middle," *New York Times*, August 16, 2010.
236 "Bomb at a Sufi shrine in Punjab: At least eight dead," *AsiaNews. it* website (Asia News). October 25, 2010. The Wahabbis are not the only concern about tolerance in Islam. Taking just 2010, Muslim fanatics have killed (in places of worship) scores of Egyptian Copts and Iraqi Christians.

seems too destabilizing. (Addicts never tell the truth to their pushers.)" [237]

Alas, both these wordings sidestep another problem. Among the many charms the Saudis offer the world, systematic opposition to fighting global warning is part of their oil-everywhere package. American politicians are too lazy, and too in hock to the oil industry, to register, much less analyze, such facts. They completely miss the big picture: a coherent Saudi strategy of keeping America's gasoline dope-fiends hooked. The Saudi dope-*dealers* get along very well...with a little help from their OPEC friends. The more you get into the corrupting, oozy, spider-web-world of oil, the more you realize, with cynics, that "there is no such thing as energy policy – only energy politics." To paraphrase MacBeth's witches, the oil-pushers' motto is "Double, double, oil and trouble." Huge, lethal, worldwide trouble.

OPEC: Fill 'er Up, at Whatever Price We Want

Americans have taken cheap gasoline as a natural right ever since Will Rogers said during the 1930s Great Depression: "We are the first nation in the history of the world to go to the poorhouse in an auto-mo-bile." Today we don't have poor-houses. But we have a very poor understanding of how oil feeds wars. Especially when God-fearing American presidents link up with God-fearing Arab theocrats floating on an ocean of oil.

The Saudis, with about 20 percent of the world's proven oil reserves, can move the world market enough to significantly influence gas-pump prices in the U.S. and Europe. But not enough, and not for long enough, to totally control the world market. In 1960, they found a way to leverage their influence as a kind of "swing producer" – in effect the key one.

With Iran, Iraq and Kuwait, Saudi Arabia responded to a 1960 Venezuelan initiative to create a Geneva-based (later Vienna-based) cartel to control the market decisively. The Saudis could

---

[237] Thomas L. Friedman, "The Great (Double) Game," *New York Times*, July 31, 2010.

then more readily control world prices by raising or lowering their oil production. Supposedly, they would do so in concert with the other cartel producers – though a little cheating on production quotas quickly became everybody's game. Now this cartel – called the Organization of the Petroleum Exporting Countries (OPEC) has 12 members. The new ones: Qatar, the United Arab Emirates, Libya, Algeria, Nigeria, Angola, and Ecuador. You will note that the list is not exactly a hit-parade of liberal democracies. So their stability may be somewhat at risk. As may be the stability of Saudi Arabia itself?

Uneasy Lies the Head that Wears a Crown

Historically, we've seen that the Saudis, with the Salafi-Wahhabis, have created a worldwide network of new potential jihadists. In coming years and decades, who knows how many more of these may filter back to challenge a theocracy already feeling shaky? The royal family, at odds with democratic ideas but compelled to try a few, must also look over its shoulder at the real anti-democrats, *al-Qaeda*. Another Saudi risk – thinking in decades – is that the world may finally wean itself away from oil. Let's ponder these short-term and long-term fears.

The royals' recent fear – *al-Qaeda* – has long been rooted in the royal family's own promotion of Wahhabi-Salafi education. Even today, public schools teach a xenophobic, anti-Semitic view of the world. Such teachings definitely formed the current generation of jihadists, including Osama bin Laden himself. But as *al-Qaeda* began (between 2003 and 2005) killing Saudis on Saudi soil – even targeting counter-terrorist chief Prince Muhammed bin Nayef in August 2009 – Ryadh dramatically changed its attitude. Instead of shaping terrorists, it would chase them. Now Saudi Arabia follows a three-pronged approach to domestic (and even international) terrorism, a strategy that even foreign intelligence colleagues admire.

First, it sends highly-trained commandos to kill jihadist leaders and stop bombings. Second, it runs a broadly successful rehabilitation program for lower-ranking jihadis – re-educating them, and even finding them jobs and wives. (This is not Guantánamo...). Of 349 graduates of the rehabilitation program, only 20 have returned to terrorism – a low rate of recidivism that most Western correctional systems would envy.

The third prong is counter-intelligence. In late October 2010, the Saudi intelligence service passed along the decisive tip that prevented the bombing of *UPS* and *Fedex-Qatar Airways* planes – the notorious "printer-cartridge" plot. Using the Saudis' intimate knowledge of Arab, Gulf and Islamic cultures, plus unlimited oil-generated funding, Prince Muhammad has planted spies throughout his region. They play lethal cat-and-mouse with *al-Qaeda*.

"The Saudis have really stepped up their efforts in Yemen," said Theodore Karasik in the fall of 2010, an analyst with the Institute for Near East and Gulf Military Analysis in Dubai. "and I'm under the impression that they've infiltrated *al-Qaeda*, so that they can warn the Americans, the French, the British and others about plots before they happen." Saudi intelligence has also stopped terrorist outrages in at least Pakistan, Iraq, Somalia and Kuwait. [238]

Apart from fear of *al-Qaeda* – its jihadists are still almost certainly financed by certain Saudi and Gulf princes and sheikhs – the Al Saud dynasty now suddenly has to fear democracy. In recent decades, the family toyed and tinkered with local democracy. But it showed no intention of loosening its reins. Now the 2011 Arab uprisings have leapt out of Saudi TV screens into the minds and conversations of millions of idle Saudi youth. The sudden toppling of several Arab dictators, and threats to others, forces the royal family to look at survival strategies.

It has several in its repertoire. John R. Bradley's *Saudi Arabia Exposed – Inside a Kingdom in Crisis* analyzes each. [239] First strategy: "reaffirming and reasserting the adherence of the family to Islam." Although this is mainly a counter-*al-Qaeda* strategy and one to "buy off the Wahhabi establishment," it also anchors the family in a country where, as home to Islam's holy cities,

---

238 Robert F. Worth, "Tip on plot shows shifting Saudi role," *International Herald Tribune,* November 1, 2010.
239 Published by Palgrave Macmillan, 2005, pp. 209–213.

religion is omnipresent. Second strategy: "engage in denial and blame others:" Zionist conspiracies make a trusty scarecrow, as do nebulous crimes by "followers of Satan." Third strategy: "throw money at problems." And especially at the people. When King Abdullah returned in February 2011 from a medical trip, he announced a $37-billion stimulus package including help to families and students. Cynics call this "bribery" to buy off unrest. (All frightened Arab rulers did the exactly that). Be that as is seems, this was easily affordable balm – though not exactly chump-change. Fourth strategy: "outright repression." Saudi military support for the Bahraini royal family in April 2011 fit that bill perfectly.

This is the classic dictator's dilemma: Will repression stop unrest, or stir it up? Chances are the Al Saud family is going to be facing this for a long time, probably alternating reform and repression. Ryadh's March 2011 sending of 1,000 troops to help crush demonstrating Bahraini Shias gives some idea that this will not be a dainty business.

We've already touched on the potentially deadly threat to the Al Sauds from the Shia community around the Eastern Province oil-fields. With them, even more than with all Saudis, royal policy has zigzagged between mild reform and harsh repression. In an Al Saud nightmare world, as we hinted, the Shia danger might in some distant future even split the country: simplistically, holy cities for Western Sunnis, oil for Eastern Shias. That's not on any credible horizon. But it may explain the Al Sauds' extreme nervousness with the Shia revolt against their Sunni little brothers in Bahrain. If the Bahraini Shias (a 70 percent majority) overturn or "constitutionalize" Bahrain's royals, could their success inspire Eastern Province Saudi Shias? With the U.S. Fifth Fleet at anchor in Bahrain, a messy prospect.

Apart from brooding on such political hypotheses, the Saudi royals do have a legitimate long-term, fear: slowly depleting oil reserves. For now, 90 percent of total Saudi export and state revenues come from oil. Oil makes up 40 percent of the kingdom's gross domestic product. In spite of OPEC and its (fragile) solidarity, a slow slide to lower oil prices could cripple the

Saudi economy. Then, generations of young Saudis who never got a modern education, or learned to work, just might revolt against the Saud family and its selfish extravagances. For now, they appear too happy to be bought off.

All of that is mere speculation. But it's not outside the realm of plausibility. For the foreseeable future, the Saudis will maintain their ability to use oil to squeeze America and the West. With their petro-state allies, they did so in 1973-74. Saudis and their friends then stopped shipping oil to the West, quadrupling the world price. After the 1973 Yom Kippur war, prices stabilized at 10 percent higher than pre-war prices. Such a boycott is still theoretically possible, though unlikely because it harms both producers and consumers.

In the very long run – with radical energy conservation, more energy-efficient vehicles, airplanes and ships, and faster development of new energy alternatives, the West *may* be able to call the shots – or at least better resist Saudi and other producers' pressures. Don't worry about oil running out. Scaremongers, including the Saudis, have cried wolf countless times. But the black stuff just keeps bubbling up. Here, there, though not yet quite everywhere.

Since 2003, major new oil finds have popped up, among other places, off Brazil and the North Polar Circle, reaching to coastal Greenland and Alaska. The Gulf of Mexico has seen expanded offshore drilling – with the occasional catastrophe such as BP's dramatic summer-of-2010 *Deepwater Horizon* explosion. Even this gigantic spill, though triggering endless lawsuits, soon became a hiccup for new drilling. We are in a race, as always, between rising consumption and new discoveries. And both sides run on high-octane greed.

Energy economist Richard Heinberg confirmed much of this in his sobering 2003 study of alternative energies vs. oil: *The Party's Over: Oil, War and the Fate of Industrial Societies*.[240] He saw no miracle, or combination of miracles, in alternative energies to prevent a severe energy crisis in coming decades – maybe

---

240 Richard Heinberg, *The Party's Over: Oil, War and the Fate of Industrial Societies*, Clearview Books, Forest Row, East Sussex, pp. 137–184.

as early as 2020. But deep conservation, he said – along with a drop in lifestyles – must be part of a replacement to oil. "If there is any solution to industrial societies' approaching energy crises," he argued, "renewables plus conservation will provide it." But he sees oil producers thriving for a long time. The Saudis know this, the Americans know it. And both will continue to bet on oil for a very long time. Probably until an insoluble crisis is upon us. If you're older than 60, you can safely leave the big worries to your children.

But America, following Europe, can somewhat delay the day of reckoning, and gain many other benefits. The key again to reasserting U.S. (and western) geopolitical power: a hefty U.S. carbon tax. This would lower oil consumption, encourage energy-saving, strengthen the U.S. balance of payments – and above all, reduce the flow of dollars to preachers of anti-West hate. For how long can the Texas and offshore oil-patches, their congressional puppets and the Sarah Palins of this world prevent this? And continue to hand American security to the oil-fueled jihadists? Five, 10, 20 years? Or more? Blinded by anti-tax ideology (no matter what the tax's purpose or size), the fiscal jihadists are, in the end, only feeding the bomb jihadists.

Their short-sightedness leaves one agape. But that's democracy. That's a certain America – or rather an America certain that it escapes the laws of logic, math, and (as for unsustainable, unjustifiable, sky-high military budgets) the law of gravity.

But let's take comfort where we can. The 2011 Arab uprisings put Washington-Ryadh relations on a more realistic, if already less harmonious, basis. The reality: Ryadh will buy off reformers, even while intimidating them. Oil will continue, as *Bloomberg Businessweek* predicted in March 2011, to be Saudi Arabia's "cash register that pays for social stability." [241] America won't dare push reform within Saudi Arabia; it will only tut-tut when the Saudis send troops abroad, as they already have, to bolster neighboring autocracies.

A distant cloud in the desert sky: Saudi Aramco, the well-run state-owned national oil company, will over time find it costlier

---

241 Peter Coy, "Why Saudi Hope Still Floats," *Bloomberg Businessweek*, March 7-13, 2011.

to find and produce oil. This, while a rising population makes heavier demands. Moreover, "Aramco oil may be as much a curse as a blessing," went on the *Bloomberg* article: "it breeds complacency, feeds corruption, and finances the puritanical strain of Islam, Wahhabism, which speaks against that corruption." A vicious circle.

As the Saudis face these challenges, their monarchy shows few signs of bowing to its people's even modest democratic demands. Might this embolden Washington to franker talk with the Wahhabi kingdom? How about something like: "Stop funding those awful Wahhabi *madrassas* in Asia and Africa that 'educate' the next generation of jihadists."

Whatever happens next, let's raise a toast to the fast-fading Saudi-Bush love-fest – that bizarre, hand-in-hand-in-Crawford cabal that made crony capitalism look, well golly, almost familial. The U.S., a virtual colony of Ryadh? No more. So that toast? Maybe one in Jim Jones's suicidal *Kool-Aid* laced with top-grade West Texas Intermediate crude.

The lesson of this century is that Europe will only be peaceful if the Americans are on this continent – Margaret Thatcher.

Who do I call if I want to call Europe? – understandably overused quote from Henry Kissinger.

Chapter Six /

EUROPE-AMERICA DISCONNECT

"Eurabia." The term strikes a dagger into the heart of Christian (or Judeo-Christian) Europe. Coined by Egyptian-born British writer Bat Ye'or, a pen-name for Gisèle Littman, the neologism evokes a nightmare: that Muslim immigration into Europe, and high Muslim birthrates, may in few decades make Islam not only a cultural and theological tidal-wave, but a political force dominating Europe. And probably a cause of civil war. For Islamic zealots, the "reconquest" of Europe would be the mirror image of Catholic Spain's "Reconquista" of the Muslims' mythic medieval Andalusia – *Al-Andalus*. In Europe's cities, already empty churches suggest a losing battle between steeples and minarets.

"Tolerant" Old Andalusia may or may not be fact. Some scholars support the idea that Muslim overlords treated Christians and Jews better than when the shoe was on the other foot – Crusaders did drench Muslim Jerusalem in blood. Other scholars dispute the *Al-Andalus* "myth" as modern Muslim propaganda. Still others claim that tolerance was intrinsic to Andalusian cuture, Christian or Muslim. Still others allege that subjection of non-Muslim subjects to unfair taxes and denial of certain careers constituted tolerance only if compared with violent persecution.

On balance, Muslim Andalusia did see a flowering of Jewish culture. Twelfth-century Jewish philosopher Maimonides engaged in spirited debate with Muslim polymath Averroes, paving the way to secular European thought. [242]

---

[242] For a gripping tale of Jewish Andalusia, see Erna Paris, *The End of Days: A Story of Tolerance, Tyranny, and the Expulsion of the Jews From Spain*,

Whatever the Andalusian truth, there is no doubt about two things today. First, that a clash of Muslim vs. Christian cultures is making all Europe tremble. Second, that Europe has a millennium of experience with Islam, while America has essentially – since 9/11 – a decade. In intellectual and scholarly terms, and in spite of some impressive U.S. studies, Europe's universities and writers are an unparalleled source for understanding Islam.

Paradoxically, this unequal cultural experience may have magnified with the election of President Barack Obama. Although personally acquainted with Asian Muslim education as a child, Obama clearly shows less knowledge of, and interest in, Europe. He skipped key European summits (the 20th anniversary of the fall of the Berlin Wall, a NATO summit in Lisbon). And by all accounts, he has built no close relations with European leaders. America's transatlantic links – its multifaceted cultural, wartime collaborations, and Cold War solidarity with Europe – seem to be atrophying. This is an almost universal complaint of European statesmen.

The danger here? Precisely at a time when the closest possible Europe-America exchange of ideas is crucial, the deep political, economic and cultural affinities between "allied," European-shaped continents are weakening. America's growing economic and demographic ties to Asia and Latin America also 'dilute' Europe's perceived importance to America.

This may deprive the West of opportunities for confronting radical Islam intelligently. Europe's generous welcome to Muslim immigrants and refugees since 1945 only deepens the Europe-America disconnect. So does America's obsession with Israel as the lodestar for its Middle East policies. That relationship is so intense and omnipresent that Muslim countries seem an afterthought – a source of oil and gas, or of intelligence and security benefits. And a cartoon image of corrupt petro-sheiks and terrorists.

Europe-American cooperation at the technical level of anti-jihadist security is strong, and getting stronger. But broader possibilities of pursuing realistic immigration and multicultural integration rarely get discussed. Long-term, they are the

---

Prometheus Books, Amherst, New York, 1995.

heart of the matter: finding ways for Judeo-Christian societies and Muslim cultures to coexist. Americans are understandably concerned with a closer-to-home issue: illegal Latin immigration pouring over their southern border.

Result: Europe's rich and varied experiences of filtering, welcoming and integrating Muslims barely reach U.S. radar screens. When they do, it's usually 'bad' news: banning of minarets, face-covering, praying in the streets, and polygamists' abuse of social benefits. The slow, quiet integration of the majority of ordinary Muslims doesn't make headlines.

America shapes its actions mainly on its 9/11 trauma. And on a vision of the Muslim world rooted not in Muslim history or culture, but in the jihadism that its recent, big-footprint military invasions aggravate. Europeans and Americans have lessons for each other. They can learn from each other's historical and strategic perceptions. Day-to-day counter-terrorist security is vital, though one-dimensional. Yet even in this, deepening the Europe-U.S. dialogue on Muslim culture, history – and even theology – could be quite profitable.

To measure the Europe-America disconnect on Islam, let's glance first at Islam's long history in Europe. Then at Europe's colonial and post-colonial dealings with Islam; its diverse policies on Islam today; current Islamic challenges to Europe; and the resources, governmental and intellectual, that Europe could offer an America taking a broader approach to dealing with Islam – worldwide and at home.

Islam's Early European Rise and Fall

Scimitars slashing and fired by faith, Muhammad's early followers screamed out of Arabia in the late 660s, across North Africa and, from Gibraltar in 711, up into Spain. The internal borders, caliphates and emirates of their empire varied over the centuries. But the Muslims stayed nearly 800 years until Spain's "Catholic Monarchs," Ferdinand and Isabella, defeated them at Granada in 1492 – the year Columbus discovered America.

Muslims' cultural influence on Spain remains deep, manifest and irreversible even today.

The second Muslim invasion of Europe came in the East from Turkey's Ottoman Empire, even as Islam fell in the West. For about 600 years, from 1299 until a few years preceding its official dissolution in 1923, this empire bridged Eastern and Western worlds. At its peak in the 15th and 16th centuries, it ruled much of western Asia (i.e. the eastern Mediterranean or today's "Middle East") and North Africa, as well as swaths of the Balkans. The 1389 Ottoman victory over Serb forces in Kosovo's Field of Blackbirds became a myth of Serb humiliation and patriotism that burned for centuries.

Serbian strongman Slobodan Milosevic exploited that legend to provoke vicious wars that dissolved 1990s Yugoslavia in a series of "ethnic-cleansing" bloodbaths. Backed by Serb clergy, intellectuals and captive media, Milosevic agitated the scarecrow of "Turks" (Muslim Kosovars and Bosnians) allegedly raping and murdering Christian Serbs. The result: half a million displaced persons, almost a quarter of a million dead. These included – included the Serb-directed massacre of 8,000 men and boys at Srebrenica, a crime for which the supervising Serb general, Ratko Mladic, 'miraculously' escaped over a decade of supposed search by tens of thousands of NATO troops and the Serbian security services. For many Serbs, Mladic remains a hero. Fear of imagined "Islamic hordes" apparently still trumps justice and shame.

To understand the haunting image of Islam in 20th and 21st-century Europe, one should remember that these lingering perceptions matter, no matter how outdated, twisted and convoluted they may seem. At some level, Ottoman warriors "at the gates" of Poitiers (732 A.D.) and Vienna (1529 and 1683) still climb over "Christian" city walls into the imaginations of Europe's school-children. These even learn that their morning croissants recall the Islamic crescent. For many history-drenched Europeans, Islam has been – counting from 711 to 2011 – a 1,300-year-old threat. Fear of Muslim attack and enslavement lurks in their DNA, not in Manhattan's Ground

Zero. And it's not just in Southern and Eastern Europe. The Ottoman Empire shaped much of today's "Middle Eastern" cultures: from architecture to food to music to even oppressive political habits. Indirectly, it stretched a finger into Chechnya, where many of today's toughest itinerant jihadists come from.

Colonialism's Bitter Fruits

A third wave of Muslim influence on Europe marked the 19th and 20th centuries. During that time, British and French colonialism soaked up a wide and intimate experience of Islam. Already, since about 1600, Britain's East India Company ran much of India's princely states. Direct governance from Westminster spanned roughly the period from 1889 to 1947. Along with exposure to Hinduism, the British dealt with Muslim princes and peoples, accumulating an impressive fund of lore and scholarship.

For their part, the French gained their modern Muslim experience mainly from colonizing North Africa. They also developed a rich scholarly experience of Egypt (since Napoleon), and later Iran, Iraq, Syria and Lebanon – the latter two via League of Nations and United Nations mandates. Even today, France is a leader in Islamic studies through its universities and its remarkable *Institut du Monde Arabe* in Paris. A complementary academic body: the *Institut National des Langues et Cultures Orientales* (*INALCO* – or, traditionally *Langues O*).

In London, the British Museum opens a dazzling window on Islamic cultures. Its Room 34 on the Islamic World opens into several other galleries. Among them: the Islamic Middle East, Pre-Islamic South Arabia, a Gallery of Ottoman Science in the 19th Century. The physical and online resources of the Oxford Centre for Islamic Studies attract researchers from everywhere.

A fourth phase of Muslim-West intermingling started in World War I. Muslim troops from North and West Africa fought in great numbers for the French army in both world wars – especially in the 1939-45 war when much of the old French army was in German prisoner-of-war camps. The decisive role of mainly Muslim colonial soldiers finally became widely known to the French public in the 2006 French movie *Les Indigènes*. Thousands of Indian Muslim soldiers also fought with British forces in both wars.

The 1947 independence of India and Pakistan opened Britain's door to a huge and lasting influx of Muslims. France's post-1960 waves of African decolonization also facilitated Muslim immigration. As did the end of France's Algerian war in 1962. France needed immigrant workers to fill menial jobs and help fund French pensions.

By 2010, Islam had displaced Protestants as France's second largest religious group – about six million in a national population of sixty-five million (Jews are a distant third). As in Belgium, Switzerland, Holland, and even Denmark and Sweden, French public discourse reflects three concerns. Anti-immigrant fears are far more pronounced than even in the U.S.. Europeans fear terrorism among immigrants and their descendents. But mostly, they resent "reverse colonization" – the creeping introduction of Islamic mores in public places: minarets, swimming pools, schools, food- stores; and symbolic extremism such as head-to-toe face-covering clothing for women.

Facing re-election in 2012, President Nicolas Sarkozy systematically played off anti-Muslim fear. Panicked by polls showing astonishing gains by attractive new far-right *Front National* leader Marine Le Pen, he stirred the xenophobic pot to a boil. His new 2011 Interior Minister Claude Guéant sang insidious songs from Sarkozy's play-book. "Some French," he intoned, "don't feel at home [in France] anymore." The March-April French-inspired, UN-authorized military engagement against Muammar Gaddafi's Libya heightened fears of new waves of "illegal immigrants" – that is, 'hard-to-assimilate' Muslim refugees.

Occasional Islamist attempts at terrorism – even by French- or British-born Muslims – raise understandable fury about Muslim "ingratitude," "disloyalty" and "cowardice." Several dramatic terrorist events have occurred in both Britain and France. British and French internal security police have stopped many other tragedies through smart sleuthing and infiltration of violent groups. Paris anti-terrorist "investigating judges" (who interrogated and jailed Carlos the Jackal) are tough and deeply immersed in terrorist culture. So are UK authorities, interfacing with millions of Muslim immigrants, and with decades of fighting Irish terrorism behind them.

Before 9/11, Europeans, like Americans, missed huge dangers in spite of highly suspicious activities. A Hamburg mosque was a hotbed of jihadists, including 9/11 pilot Muhammad Atta. But Germans have a long experience with non-jihadist terror, including the Red Army Faction (1970-1998). So does Italy with its Red Brigades (1967-late 1980s).

Spain, with its centuries-old familiarity with Islam, only tightened its anti-jihadist work after the 2004 Madrid train station massacre (191 dead, 1,800 wounded). But its anti-terrorist focus before that was directed at Basque ETA killers. In January 2011, after murdering 829 individuals and wounding or kidnapping thousands, ETA (again) announced a "permanent, general and verifiable" ceasefire. The Spanish government declined, having seen this movie before. [243]

Today, often via Interpol or specialized anti-terrorist networks, Europe as a whole fights terror with well-honed instincts strengthened by a cultural and historical grasp of the origins of Islamic aggression. Europeans and Americans now fight a common anti-terrorist war. Each partner brings unique skills to the table: American technology and financial savvy meshed with a longer, more intuitive, European cultural perspective.

Important caveat: When dealing with France on Muslim issues, America should be aware of a persistent trap: colonial overhang: France's attitude to Arab and Muslim societies still betrays a remarkable mix of condescension, myopia and state connivance in corruption.. We have already seen how Paris intellectuals were befuddled and frightened by the January 2011 collapse of Ben Ali's Tunisian autocracy. But government officials, convinced that they "know all about" Tunisia and North Africa, were equally caught with their papers down. Only minutes

---

243 Fiona Ortiz, "Spanish government rejects ETA ceasefire move," *Reuters*, January 10, 2011.

before Ben Ali decamped in shame, French ambassador Pierre Ménat informed Paris that Ben Ali would soon restore order. In the weeks following Ben Ali's escape, French newspapers presented an orgy of more embarrassing evidence. It detailed top-level complicities of both French politicians and media stars in Tunisian freebie tourism and sweetheart real-estate deals. All Ben Ali and his still-greedier wife Leila wanted was a little reciprocity: unquestioned political and military support, open doors everywhere in Paris, and fawning coverage in the French media.

Twin Failures of 'Integration'

Beyond terrorist concerns, how has Europe coped with its fast-growing Muslim communities? It has tried two approaches – assimilation and "multiculturalism" – with many variations and extremely uncertain results.

The French are really the only people to try outright, color-blind, religion-blind assimilation. This finds its roots first in the French Revolution's ideal of "equality," the national motto along with liberty and hoped-for fraternity. The ideal ignores hyphenated citizenship. It teaches loyalty to a powerful state as incarnation and tool of the national interest. A second, reinforcing, event was France's now-cherished 1905 law separating church and state. This law aimed at removing the all-powerful Roman Catholic Church from affairs of state. But now it has become a kind of "lay religion" of all who want to keep Muslim women visibly out of schools and government offices. Today's "state-and-mosque" separation concept has its own untranslatable tern: *la laïcité*. It makes the state owner of places of worship, leaving clergy salaries to the faithful.

In recent years – and largely in reaction against Islamic (especially face-covering) costumes – France has banned Islamic scarves and flamboyant religious symbols in schools and government offices. And, since 2010, it has banned so-called *burqas* (actually *hijabs* or Saudi-style *niqabs* in streets. Fear and anger at terrorist events fuels these reactions. But so does a simple, old-European "enough is enough" feeling that the very physiognomy of "our Christian" nation is being overwhelmed by aliens perceived as aggressively foreign, and possibly dangerous. Many of these stalwart "Christians," by the way, haven't seen the inside of a church – except for funerals and tourism – in decades. But they identify with a "homeland" skyline of steeples, not minarets.

Under President Nicolas Sarkozy, France has emphasized the ideas of "nation" and "identity" almost as much as its revered "Republic." Immigration, plus sky-high unemployment among young Muslim North and West Africans, threaten local violence – remember the car-burning 2005 *banlieues*? They also allegedly favor terrorist-recruitment. Many young Muslims say they despise France, even booing La Marseillaise at soccer games. Sarkozy fired several of his few high-profile Muslim ministers in 2010. And the 36,000 municipal communities ("*communes*") had not even a handful of Muslim councilors. The neo-Fascist *Front National*, we've noted, snapped at Sarkozy's heels, driving him even farther right to an anti-foreigner stance as his 2012 presidential election approached. [244]

The assimilation model – which existed mainly in rhetoric and in official papers – failed totally at the level of jobs, promotions and elected representatives. It is as ritualistic and unevenly applied as is France's corollary myth of itself as "the country of the rights of man." Such rights do not notoriously reflect today's citizens' rights – say, against police. But they echo the 1793 Declaration of the Rights of Man and of the Citizen, thus set a heart-stirring tone.

Europe's "multicultural" model – proclaimed by most countries outside France (with Switzerland ambiguous, as often) purports to recognize various degrees of protection for

---

[244] Note the February 2011 appointment as Interior minister of Sarkozy's trusted, tough chief of staff, Claude Guéant. In his first major interview, Guéant attacked illegal immigration, ghettoization ("le communautarisme") of ethnic-religious groups, customs violating French law, and untraceable Muslim *hallal* meats. He promised a more serious effort to "assimilate" new arrivals, invited to adopt a French lifestyle and to respect French traditions. See: "Les Français veulent que la France reste la France," interview with Yves Bordenave, Arnaud Leparmentier and Élise Vincent, *Le Monde*, March 16, 2011.

immigrants' home-country cultures. Most Muslims in small groups have joined the mainstream reasonably well. But there is a hard-core of radical Islamic believers who insist on customs and dress that not only stand out egregiously, but often deliberately mock host-country mores. This usually includes abuse of social benefits (polygamy exploiting family allowances), subjection and covering of women, often genital mutilation, forced marriages, and horrific "honor killings." [245]

Death threats against welcoming-country "insults" to Islam are routine methods of dialogue. The famous Danish cartoons on the Prophet Muhammad drove cartoonist Kurt Westergaard into permanent police protection. So too did exposés of "anti-women Islam" drive Holland's Ayaan Hirsi Ali abroad. In December 2010, Danish and Swedish police stopped a jihadist Mumbai-style massacre by mere hours – it aimed at machine-gunning innocents for the years-old publication of the allegedly blasphemous cartoons of the Prophet Muhammad.

Dutch film-maker Theo Van Gogh got a knife in his chest for a film condemning alleged Muslim anti-women practices. A fanatic (seemingly a Dutch-origin Muslim sympathizer) killed Dutch anti-immigrant politician Pim Fortuyn in 2002. Assassin Volkert van der Graaf explained that he wanted to stop Fortuyn from "scapegoating" Muslims in his election campaign.

Britain – home of the notorious "Londonistan" of jihadist preachers – has seen grave acts of terrorism. It is now tightening tolerance for violent Islamists. The 2005 London Tube and

---

[245] The notorious 2010 case of a native French woman in Nantes arrested for driving in a head-to-toe *burqa* made French headlines for much of that year. Sandrine Moulères was married to Algerian-born "cleric" and businessman Lies Hebbadj. He was "accused of four counts of benefits fraud and breaking employment law." Police found he was living with several other women and collecting their family-allowance benefits. Knowing his public, Hebbadi said the others were really just "mistresses" – and in France, of all places, having a mistress should surprise nobody. A new law forbidding people from "hiding their faces in public spaces" came into effect on April 11, 2011. Given that barely a few hundred women in France covered their face, one Belgian Muslim woman critic called the law "killing a fly with a bazooka" (see "Une loi sur la burqa, c'est 'tuer une mouche avec un bazooka,'" Catherine Gouëset, *L'Express*, May 19, 2010. .

bus bombings killed 52 and injured 700. Other outrages were barely headed off.

An anti-Muslim backlash is now well underway in these and most other "multicultural" European nations. Scandinavian parliaments now harbor strong anti-Muslim "patriotic" parties. In 2010, even a normally tolerant Dutch public elected a decisive number of anti-Muslim Freedom Party candidates led by demagogue Geert Wilders.

Germany is reacting strongly against its huge Turkish minority for alleged abuse of social benefits and refusal to integrate. On October 19, 2010, Chancellor Angela Merkel declared that "*multiKulti*" had "failed entirely," and that immigrants should not only learn German, but adopt "Christian values." This, after the runaway success of a book (*Germany Abolishes Itself*) by senior banker official Thilo Sarrazin saying roughly the same. Sarrazin warned that with too-tolerant immigrant and integration policies Germany was committing suicide. Now, he said, Germany had two societies: the historic, native Garman one, and an indigestible foreign one, with different languages, religions, cultures and customs.

A few weeks after Frau Merkel's condemnation of multiculturalism, British prime minister David Cameron denounced "state multiculturalism" in almost identical terms. He attacked publicly-funded Muslim groups that "live separate lives, apart from each other and the mainstream," and hesitate to criticize terrorism. "Frankly," he argued, "we need a lot less of the passive tolerance of recent years and much more active, muscular liberalism." He demanded that immigrant (i.e. Islamic) groups subscribe to values intrinsic to Britain's identity: "Let's properly judge these organizations: Do they believe in universal human rights - including for women and people of other faiths? Do they believe in equality of all before the law? Do they believe in democracy and the right of people to elect their own government? Do they encourage integration or separatism?" [246]

Not to be outdone, President Nicolas Sarkozy chimed in five days later to say of multiculturalism: "My answer is yes, it

[246] Oliver Wright and Jerome Taylor, "Cameron: My war on multiculturalism," *The Independent*, February 5, 2011.

clearly is a failure... We've worried too much about the identity of the person arriving in France, and not enough about the country welcoming him...We don't want a society where communities coexist beside each other. If you come to France, you agree to melt into a single community, the national community. If you don't accept that, you don't come to France." [247]

As of March 2011, French media – always delighting in a soul-wrenching ideological debate – were wringing their hands over how politicians, press and intellectuals were betraying shibboleths of tolerance and national "fraternity." Surprisingly, given Jewish suffering under Hitler and the Vichy regime, several stars of this rush to the far right were Jews: Élisabeth Lévy, Philippe Cohen, Éric Zemmour (a media comic-iconoclast) and even (depending on the day, the topic, the opportunity and the 'misquotation') that venerable all-purpose gadfly Alain Finkelkraut.[248]

Obviously, at least the first three of these, who call themselves "sovereignist intellectuals," were ricocheting off the political unpopularity of President Nicolas Sarkozy. As "Sarko" entered the homestretch for the May-June 2012 presidential and legislative elections, he pillaged ideas and slogans from the far-right *Front National*: fear of foreigners (ah, Sarkozy, that charming old Hungarian-French name), of Roma, of immigration, of Islam, of crime. Proudly, the son of Pál István Ernő Sárközy de Nagy-Bócsa could boast, as he sometimes did before Jewish audiences, of having a Greek-Jewish grandfather. In today's terms, Sarkozy was a typical Frenchman – though not a *stereotypical* one.

In electoral mode, Sarkozy peddled fear of France's losing its Astérix- Joan-of-Arc identity. Ostentatiously visiting historic Catholic churches and convents to highlight France's "Christian heritage," he said he was only underlining how church and state could coexist. And, by implication, how mosque and state *had* to exist.

---

247 « Sarkozy - le multiculturalisme: un échec », *AFP-Le Figaro*, February 10, 2011.
248 "Ils décontaminant la pensée FN," Ariane Chemin, *Le Nouvel Observateur*, March 10-16, 2011.

But his constant glorification of *la laïcité* (very roughly 'secularism') managed to convey the idea that the hapless "old-stock" French were drowning in a sea of 'ungrateful' and 'presumptuous' – indeed abusive – newcomers.

Translation of "newcomers:" Muslims, even more than blacks, as such. The 2011 Arab uprisings didn't help matters. They unleashed a flood of new Muslim refugees to Italy and France. The "foreign peril" is a classic scarecrow for bankrupt politicians – especially when it presents, as it does in today's Europe, a major challenge to mainstream citizens' culture and self-image.

That crafty old *Front National* founder, Jean-Marie Le Pen, loved to mock rightist politicians like Sarkozy who tried to fish in his xenophobic waters: "Voters always prefer the original to the copy." Now the FN 'original' is blonde, female, a handsome early fortyish, and tactfully reassuring. This new FN chief, Marine Le Pen, still takes her father's France-first line – but softly, "sensibly," logically. (In this case, few French prefer the scary, Holocaust-minimizing 'original' father to the likeable second-generation 'copy.'). By March 2011, Martine's soaring polling numbers were traumatizing Sarkozy's national UMP majority.

Issues of identity and immigration will not go away. They will poison French and European politics for years. Sarkozy's spring 2011 national debate on Islam – like the one raging in the U.S. Congress and in other European nations – inevitably scapegoated moderate Muslims. This finger-pointing tactic, in turn, may turn angry "rejected" Muslim youth to less moderate paths. [249]

A telling sidebar to multiculturalism: Canada. As in many public policies, Canada floats somewhere in the middle of the Atlantic Ocean – half-American, half- European. A country of immigrants like the U.S., it offers both enormous physical and social space to newcomers. Building on its English-French linguistic duality, it elaborately welcomes ethnic pluralism. Instead of the U.S. melting-pot model, it has built a "mosaic"

---

[249] Éric Fassin, " Le multiculturalisme, entre modèle et crise," *Le Monde*, February 26, 2011.

society. Canada's 1969 Official Languages Act made French and English the official languages of all federal administrations. "Equality for two opened the door to equality for many."

At least, that's the official myth. In reality, the long-overdue "equal" recognition of English and French stirred up new, previously unimagined "rights" for immigrant communities of other backgrounds. Suddenly, in 1970-71, they complained of being "second-class citizens." This stampeded Prime Minister Pierre Trudeau's Liberal government – eager to gain votes in the immigrant-rich western Prairie provinces – into improvising a "multicultural policy." Later Ottawa expanded this into Canada's 1988 Multiculturalism Act. Bizarrely for national unity, this not only ordered all federal departments to "respect" ethno-cultural diversity; it ordered them to "enhance" it. Unite by dividing, so to speak. Canadians, used to sticking together via constitutional ambiguities, have generally bought the story.

Disproportionate crime among some immigrant youth groups have in recent years shaken the consensus. A few notorious homegrown Islamic terrorist plots have also caused serious new doubts. Critics allege that "too-tolerant" Canadian-style multiculturalism has allowed even a few born-in-Canada Muslim youth to turn to violence. [250]

On the positive side, and unlike either U.S. or European cases, you find even fairly recent immigrants occupying significant jobs: Canada's last two Governors-General (a symbolic quasi-head of state post) were female refugees: one Chinese, the other Haitian. Ministerial benches seat immigrants or their children in any portfolio. Countless such arrivals or their descendents populate business, academia and the media. Against this, a noisy American minority still contests even the American birth of Hawaii-born President Obama. Both U.S. and Canada seek to integrate immigrants – but they do so very differently, and with different results.

For powerful and unique historical reasons, the Canadian model will never work either in the U.S. or Europe. In the U.S., because its national "melting-pot" narrative is bluntly assimilationist; in Europe, because both spontaneous assimilation

---

[250] Isobel Teotonio, "Toronto 18 attack was to mimic 9/11," *Toronto Star*, June 23, 2009.

and generous multiculturalism have manifestly failed. Now Europe's pendulum has plainly swung back to specific, law-enforced assimilation.

Europe is now toughening its welcome to immigrants in general, and Muslims in particular. This more "realistic" policy has led to a serious, continent-wide debate on Islam. This is probably both dangerous and healthy. Will it, for example, open the door to Germany's terrifying racialist atavisms? Will it feed the fortunes of France's neo-fascist *Front National*? Of the British National Party? Of bigoted Dutch and Scandinavian anti-immigrant parties? Or will it clear the air and lead to a more lucid accommodation between "native" citizens and newcomers? A French debate on Islam looks to be highly controversial – as it was even within the governing UMP party. [251]

The risk of more divisiveness is unavoidable, though it can be lessened by courageous, enlightened leadership. The upside of debate: Maybe European nations will grow more comfortable with diversity by probing their evolving identities. Maybe, through frank discourse, thoughtfulness and hope can replace demagogy and fear. A tall order.

U.S. and Islam – Say Little, Think Less

For long, the U.S. public also avoided open, frank analyses of Muslim life in America. It tended to focus on fuzzy hopefulness, local anecdotes of understanding or conflict, incantations about "unique" American liberties, and a few dramatic media events such as the sad, September 2010 comedy of a Florida pastor holding his nation to ransom by a threat to burn copies of the Koran. Given President Obama's powerful public analysis of the black-white race question, and his personal childhood experience of Islam, he could and should lead a probing national reflection on Islam in the world and in America. This is a potentially explosive issue, of course. But are silence or vagueness more pacifying than genuine, open debate?

---

251 Ruadhán MacCormaic, "Sarkozy's party divided over debate on Islam," *Irish Times*, March 9, 2011.

Unfortunately, the most prominent debate on Islam in America was organized in March 2011 by Republican Congressman Peter King. But it was focused on unmasking Islamist extremism. It was not a fair-minded review of Muslims' place, problems and contributions in America.

U.S. and European politicians and researchers should compare notes far more often. Their diverse experiences, theories and methods might mesh together more to both sides' benefit. Nearly every approach presents country-specific aspects. But overall, more comparisons could probably prove fruitful. The U.S. may have some lessons for Europe (such as electoral promotion of Muslims?). And Europe for America (possibly unsuccessful social experiments?).

Bottom-line: Europe can offer America incomparable historical, intellectual and policy resources on Islam. The U.S. should look more at these, and broaden its one-dimensional, all-security dealings with Europe America should draw on European, especially French and British, scholarship and expertise on the Muslim world. Why, indeed, 10 years after 9/11, isn't there a U.S. university or think-tank program of the scope of Paris's *Institut du Monde Arabe*?

For both foreign policy and personal-leadership reasons, Europe and America have never recovered their intimate, broad-based relationship forged by the Second World War and the Cold War. Restoring and updating this should be a priority for both sides – for the old partners' relative estrangement is harming collective action on the "war on terrorism." In practical terms, President Obama needs to listen much more to Europe. He should develop real relationships with its leaders. For its part, Europe needs, with U.S. help, to figure out how to resolve its wobbly speculations on its foreign-policy identity. Can it finally define a united front in a world it alternately sees as "multi-polar" (U.S., Europe, Russia, China) or bipolar (U.S. and China) – or merely a *Pax Americana* world? Can it finally find a single European phone number for Henry Kissinger? So far, Europe Union efforts to speak up, organize itself, and dynamically contribute to world affairs are rather dismal.

To elicit new European collaborations, Obama could start by taking two decisions, both demanding courage and adroitness. First, citing a budget crisis, he could face down the big-spending Pentagon/Congress/arms industry partisans of endless war. This would have to be a sustained, multi-year effort – perhaps initially with backing from deficit-cutting hawks of whatever persuasion, even Tea Party. Having demonstrated America's need for military frugality, he would at the same time press Europeans – as he did in Libya in March-April 2011 – to share U.S. defense burdens more fairly. Second, Obama could swallow hard and announce a clear, specific plan for a fair settlement of the Israel-Palestine impasse. Ideally, he would do this in consultation with fellow members of the "Quartet:" the European Union, Russia, and the United Nations.

Europe could help with both decisions. It is eager to stand in for some of America's military roles, especially in UN peacekeeping. And besides continuing to contribute money to Palestine, it could advise realistically on the Israel-Palestine logjam. Europe's media and publics are far better informed on the Middle East than are America's.

Again, Europe can count more only if it can finally decide on its collective identity, and on what it wants to achieve in the world. To share America's worldwide challenges, Europe must learn how to wield both hard and soft power on a global scale. What is sure: America is weaker because it has almost "lost" Europe as a strong, ally. An ally able to make sense to Washington, and to help Washington make sense to the world.

Is the Muslim culture gap between America and Europe a myth? For the answer, look back again at America's parochial, U.S.-centric public education system. Even if America decided today that its young should seriously study Islam and world history, it would take at least a generation to forge a more informed, people-supported foreign policy. Europe is not the whole answer. But ignoring its example and its inspiration is folly – a self-blinding risk to more enlightened U.S. national security.

PART III – WHAT COULD GO MUCH BETTER

Everything I know about Islam I learned on 9/11 – Placard protesting new mosque near Ground Zero in August 2010.

There are millions of good Americans who practice the Muslim faith who love their country as much as I love the country, who salute the flag as strongly as I salute the flag – George W. Bush, shortly after September 11, 2001.

Chapter Seven /

INDISPENSABLE 'IMPOSSIBILITIES'

In all too many ways, we've seen, America already resembles a garrison state. Harold D. Lasswell defined this in 1941 as a state run by "specialists in violence." It aims at the "supremacy of the soldier," backed by a cabal of propagandists and bureaucrats. It's enamored with itself and drunk on the idea of its own superiority – its unchallengeable, world-dominating military power. Does that sound familiar?

In the 2002 *National Security Strategy of the United States*, President George W. Bush, egged on by his even more hawkish National Security Advisor Condoleezza Rice, promised that: "Our forces will be strong enough to dissuade potential adversaries from pursuing a military buildup in hopes of surpassing, or equaling, the power of the United States." Read in Beijing or even Moscow, these words must have looked like an invitation to a new arms race – not at all an unpleasant prospect for the U.S. arms industry and the Pentagon.

Pass the Ammunition... Forever

Glorifying military power is not just a Republican Party vice. Democrats, especially in office, are just as eager to support the "national defense consensus." For consensus it is. Through lobbies, election funding, and threats to term a member of Congress "weak on defense," the consensus stifles debate on whether a war, a weapons system, a base or Pentagon budget deserves support. Arms lobbies, the military, politicians, evangelical pastors, and even cheerleading media – all parts of the consensus – make sure that the consensus stays solid. And that there is always a more or less plausible threat somewhere in the world to justify a U.S. military action or presence.

That's the perspective of "permanent war" outlined in that oft- cited 2010 book by Andrew J. Bacevich called *Washington Rules: America's Path to Permanent War*. Bacevich makes his point early in the book with Hillary Clinton's first national defense speech as secretary of state. She cited Thomas Paine's famous words: "We have it within our power to begin the world again." Then she added: "Today... we are called upon to use that power." [252]

Bacevich, himself a military man, warns in his book that the unspoken assumption of all U.S. presidents, including Obama, is that they can and should exercise what Teddy Roosevelt in 1904 called "international police power." George W. Bush, in Iraq, argued that the U.S. had a right and duty to launch "preventive wars." Much of this chest-beating is nonsense, mere self-delusion. Ask Binyamin Netanyahu or Hamid Karzai: America blinks as often as it thinks.

Now what should America be thinking to escape permanent war and the demons of militarism? Given the ingenuity and entrenched interests of the "national defense consensus," clear aims are probably futile. But let's pretend. Let's see if there are ways to arm less, and imagine more. To counter jihadist hate with constructive ideas instead of destructive armies. To devise smarter people-helping" options instead of smarter drones. To fashion policies for taming hostile Islamic energies and building peace-favoring strategies.

Consider two stages for developing strategies of hope for both Islam and the West: a) eliminating war-provoking obstacles to peace; and b) promoting proven, practical pathways to a happier world for ordinary human beings. The first consists

---

[252] Cited in Andrew J. Bacevich, *Washington Rules – America's Path to Permanent War (American Empire Project)*, Metropolitan Books, New York, 2010, pp.19-20.

of clearing the political and psychological "decks" in order to aggressively pursue the second. The challenge: how to balance the two as circumstances stand, and change? That will be the purpose of following chapters.

So far, the U.S. establishment has not coherently tried to use diplomacy, backed by arms and money, to "clear the decks" that we examine next. It proceeds only tentatively, piecemeal and erratically: a ritual, hesitant try at Israel-Palestine; a quick shot (immediately abandoned) at Jammu and Kashmir; a lip-service appeal to curing America's oil addiction.

Then, customarily, the U.S. returns to focusing almost exclusively on military power and elusive victories. Instead of this all-military approach, let's see how the U.S. could find *more security* with a mix of 'defensive' military actions and 'strategic' non-military approaches. Less "hard power," more "soft (or 'smart') power." Less tactics on a treadmill, more long-term prevention and reconciliation. Less arms, more ideas – many of which can and should build on successful *Muslim* peace-building initiatives.

But first, some inspiring words, then the "decks" – the solution-blocking impasses.

Clearing the Decks With Obama?

Deep improvement in U.S.-Muslim relations will take miracles. The key one will be translating fine U.S. words into actions. President Barack Obama set the tone for a more positive U.S. relationship with Islam in his landmark June 4, 2009 Cairo speech. Called "A New Beginning," it remains a well-intentioned but hesitant start. According to Muslim spokesmen everywhere, and even independent studies, if Obama's soaring words of respecting Muslims don't soon lead to concrete action demonstrating respect and fair play, the Salafi-jihadist war on the West will continue unabated. Ordinary Muslims are watching. And until the U.S. makes some real changes in policy, they will sit on the fence – many with secret admiration for Osama bin Laden, even dead.

What changes? What "miracles?" Consider seven obstacles to peace that the U.S. needs to try even harder to remove – just to make it conceivable to *begin* remaking the world. These are obstacles to a world where – as Spain and Turkey urge – we could engage a genuine "dialogue of civilizations." The challenges look insurmountable. But perhaps that's why we have history – to remind us that the insurmountable may only take a little longer. Like the fall of communism. Like a racially-reconciled South Africa. Like a China and India that can now finally feed their peoples. Like an Arab world aflame for democracy after a poor Tunisian fruit-seller set fire to himself.

Observation: Almost none of the obstacle-removing below requires much, if any, use of U.S. military might. There are other places (Korea, for example) where danger invites the American military to stay. But in building a happier world, especially healthier U.S.-Muslim relationships, U.S. power needs to discover restraint. Sometimes policy, based on too-eager use of arms, looks like a solution in search of a problem. Then it becomes a problem itself.

Reality check after November 2, 2010: Riding-high Republican legislators signaled that they would sabotage any worldview less 'exceptionalist' (read militaristic) than their own. They hated Obama's irreverent 2008 comment: "I believe in American exceptionalism, just as I suspect that the Brits believe in British exceptionalism and the Greeks believe in Greek exceptionalism." [253] Crudely, the Republicans translated exceptionalism as keeping the dollars flowing to their Pentagon and arms-industry puppet-masters. For some, a weakened Obama administration also meant that the Israeli *Likud* lobby could more easily foot-drag Palestinian peace talks into a ditch. Both of these developments bode ill for peace and reconciliation with the Muslim world.

Were the outcomes of U.S. inaction not so tragic, it would be laughable even to raise the seven "impossible-to-solve" problems that follow. The only certainty: If they are not raised at all, they will continue to be unsolvable. The list below is not

---

253 Jonah Goldberg, "Mocking American Exceptionalism," *Real Clear Politics*, November 10, 2010.

a reasonable program; it's a dream agenda. It's a wish-list for a world that may not yet exist. But even wishing has to precede new beginnings. What, then, are these peace-blocking problems?

1. Settle Israel-Palestine -

The first issue blocking peace between Americans and the world's Muslims is the eternally festering, and intolerable, Israeli occupation of Palestinian lands. The Israeli-Palestinian impasse threatens both U.S. and world security. President Obama has grappled with this. But he hasn't dared to press hard enough to settle it. Instead, failing to scare Netanyahu into extending a freeze on new West Bank settlements, he ended up trying to *bribe* him with a cornucopia of money and weapons. Netanyahu sneered at this, knowing he could likely get it all anyway with *no* concessions.

The outcome remains uncertain. But clearly, it will only find a solution when Obama finds the courage to go to Jerusalem (with Quartet support) to spell out to the Knesset a fair, two-state solution that America will accept, fund and guarantee. Failing agreement, America will focus on defending its own national interest – which may require significant financial and diplomatic reappraisals.

Given close Israeli-AIPAC coordination, the time to announce this new U.S. position would have to be just after the start of Obama's second term. But the announcement would, after much gnashing of teeth, turn out to be profoundly in the interest of Israelis, Palestinians and Americans. For it is the only chance to give both Israeli and Palestinian children a peaceful future. Make no mistake: the only long-term alternative to something like this will be war without end – dangerously radicalized on both sides.

The State of Israel deserves respect, security and legitimacy. The world community must stand by Israel and guarantee its existence with all reasonable means – political, economic and even, if necessary, military. For many reasons, and not just the Holocaust, Israel's security is sacred.

But so is the Palestinians' security. Dispossessed, and betrayed by their own leaders, Arab regimes and the West, they have had none for over 60 years. The only lasting solution to the two-peoples-one-land conundrum will be internationally assured security for two equal states, Israel and Palestine. Israel, as the "regional superpower," must now accept what top American generals have publicly said: that failure to come to terms with the Palestinians has become a major security problem for the U.S. – and for all Western countries.

Year after year, TV has shown home-made or imported Islamist rockets trying to hit Israeli towns, sometimes succeeding and killing children. Until the Israeli Wall, TV showed suicide bombers blowing up innocent people in Israeli restaurants and buses.

But honest TV has also shown young Israeli soldiers humiliating Palestinian men and women in front of their children; checkpoints lethally blocking sick babies and pregnant women; Israeli bulldozers demolishing Arab villages and homes; Palestinian olive-groves destroyed by fanatical, Army-protected settlers; American-supplied F16s blasting Palestinian refugee camps; Israeli snipers killing Palestinians (often stone-throwing teenagers) apparently at random; and invisible Israeli missiles killing from the sky "suspected" but untried terrorists – often along with "accidental" victims. Very occasionally, miscreant soldiers may face a secret army inquiry; but the Israeli Defense Force's 'understanding' of its own seems limitless.

Hundreds of millions of TV-watching Muslims seethe at these sights. They see America as an accomplice of brutal colonialism, because it finances and arms the Israelis unconditionally. Jihadists everywhere – including in the cities of Europe and North America – vow vengeance not just on Israel, not just on America, but on the entire West because of these sights.

The IDF, the national army, has often saved Israel, and bravely so. But its massively-documented mistreatment of Palestinian civilians, collateral damage from "pinpoint" drones, and sly support for gun-slinging illegal settlers, have also put Israel seriously at risk. IDF's behavior at checkpoints, for example, has outraged many Jewish observers having witnessed army-Palestinian contact up close: "Everyone in Israel knows," wrote Ami Isseroff as far back as 2004, "what happens at the checkpoints established in the Palestinian areas, except possibly the government. Everyone understands the day to day inhumanity and brutalization of Palestinians that goes on there. Even the most gung-ho Greater Israel zealot, if they are not insane, must understand that humiliation and intimidation of ordinary people is bad for Israel as well as being an immoral act. It breeds resentment and hatred... As they are run presently, checkpoints are probably breeding more terrorists than they are preventing terrorism. Even those who don't care at all about Palestinians should recognize that this is *bad for Israel* [his italics].[254]

Now that was in 2004. But surely treatment of Palestinians has improved during the long recent years of a sporadic "peace process" and enhanced Israeli-Palestinian collaboration? Here's how a key checkpoint looked to a couple of shocked Americans, Alain and Katia Salomon, in March 2011. Because their report is very recent and this well-educated Jewish couple are highly credible, it's worth citing at length:

We reached the Kalandia checkpoint between Ramallah and Jerusalem on Friday, March 11, at 9:30 in the morning. We chose to get off the bus with everyone else, even though as foreigners we could have stayed on.

We were stunned by what we saw: dwarfing cement structures, barbed wire, cameras. As we lined up we could see an Israeli woman soldier inside a multifaceted concrete blockhouse, peering out at us. Ahead of us there was a tunnel of bars just wide enough for one person. At its end a turnstile was blocked electronically from somewhere.

As we entered this narrow space I looked at the barbed wire further on. We are Jewish, and began to weep. How was it possible that our own people, who have gone through such suffering, can inflict this ordeal, intended to humiliate and intimidate another people?

And then we were seized by fear. If there had been a surge of panic or a fire, we would all have been trampled, for there was no escape. The stories of women giving birth here, some losing their babies, came painfully to mind.

---

[254] "Checkpoints – conscience and good sense," Ami Isseroff, *MidEastWeb, Middle East Web Log,* July 28, 2004.

After that narrow corridor we stepped into a small area, again in front of a metal turnstile. Many of us were wet, as it had rained in the morning, and it was cold. There were not that many people waiting but only one or two people were let through every 10 minutes or so. There was no bench in this space, nowhere for old people or children to rest. One child started to cry, another complained of her feet being frozen because her boots were wet...

A couple with a child showed us their appointment slip for a hospital consultation at noon, an unlikely target now, even though they had arrived at 9:30, as we had. As noon approached a few men turned back; it was too late for prayers.

At 12:10 it was finally our turn. We could see the people controlling the turnstile. There were several young Israeli soldiers inside. They seemed to be having a very good time, laughing, horsing around, like all youths. We want to believe that they had no clue as to the moral and physical suffering they were inflicting with their very slow control process. Do they have orders to slow everything down on Friday mornings in order to discourage the men who come to pray? Or perhaps to reduce the numbers of people who want to spend the weekend with their families?

One can easily imagine the feelings of resentment that are born from this experience. This treatment is unwarranted from the perspective of legitimate security imperatives; it is degrading and inhumane and not understandable coming from a nation that wants to be perceived as democratic, a nation among nations. [255]

Year after year, tales of IDF abuse of civilians, even children, seep out from troubled soldiers. Former IDF commander Eran Efrati, sickened by routine ill-treatment of Palestinian children, explained in 2009 why he still dreamt about screaming Palestinian kids: "You take the kid, you blindfold him, you handcuff him, he's really shaking... Sometimes you cuff his legs too. Sometimes it cuts off the circulation.... He doesn't understand a word of what's going on around him. He doesn't know what you're going to do with him. He just knows we are soldiers with guns. That we kill people. Maybe they think we're going to kill him... A lot of the time they're peeing their pants, just sit there peeing their pants, crying. But usually they're very quiet." [256]

---

255 Alain and Katia Salomon, "A morning at an Israeli checkpoint," *International Herald Tribune*, March 31, 2011.
256 "Israeli troops ill-treat kids," Katya Adler, *BBC World News* website, August 6, 2009. Ms. Adler reported that in 2008 the IDF arrested 7,000 Palestinians, including 700 children.

Hundreds of thousands of young Israelis have served at checkpoints over the years, and not all have acted like brutes. But their families, and the Israeli public, can scarcely claim they "have no idea" what their "boys and girls" saw on IDF duty. Moreover, hundreds of thousands, in fact millions, of Palestinians have watched how many Israeli soldiers behaved.

One wonders what the price will be for both sides. On the Palestinian side, surely resentment. On the Israeli side, probably desensitization. To the extent that the media cover abuses (only non-American ones much bother), the Muslim world draws its conclusions. And these do not lead to sympathy for those who arm Israel. "Arab anger over the Palestinian question," General David Petraeus told the U.S. Senate Armed Services Committee in March 2010, "limits the strength and depth of U.S. partnerships with governments and peoples [in the region]." [257]

There can be no truce between the West and Islam until a just solution unites Israelis and Palestinians. No single problem in the world, by ricochet, threatens Western troops, cities and civilians so powerfully. After 9/11, as we saw, Saudi Prince Alwaleed bin Talal offered New York Mayor Rudy Giuliani a $10-million check, adding that U.S. Mideast policies may have contributed to the Twin Towers horror. Giuliani famously returned the check, and the prince's comment was grossly insensitive. But it contained a grain of truth: there *is* a link between the Mideast impasse and peace elsewhere. And today, when senior U.S. officials link the U.S. Mideast stand-off to violence against U.S. soldiers in Iraq and Afghanistan, they are just stating the obvious.

U.S. weapons have become a big part of the Israel-Palestinian dispute – on one side. Ironically, they might also prove helpful to both sides: in guarding and guaranteeing borders. Peacekeeping, border-policing and nation-building are not popular with the American military. Condoleezza Rice famously

---

[257] "U.S. general: Israel-Palestinian conflict foments anti-U.S. sentiment," *Haaretz Service*, March 17, 2010.

sniffed that "We don't need to have the 82nd Airborne Division to escort kids to kindergarten." [258]

But U.S. military support for Israel-Palestine peace might prove a robust peacekeeping alternative to normally supine UN forces. Americans would actually fight to defend an Israel-agreed border, and Israelis would insist on having their U.S. friends as part of any border-watching team. The Palestinians might prefer Europeans more sympathetic to their aspirations; but they would accept Americans. Americas or Europeans? Ideally both: Friendly guarantors of any background should be welcome, if ever there is a peace to keep.

The early 2011 Arab uprisings, we noted, have created a new Middle East checker-board. Soon, Prime Minister Binyamin Netanyahu began again talking about an "independent" Palestine with "provisional borders" and the IDF on the Jordan River. At first glance, this is something of an oxymoron: sovereignty with foreign occupation. But Israel's isolation has seriously weakened its strategic position. Maybe, just maybe, the post-Tahrir Square momentum will make serious negotiation with the Palestinians a little more attractive to Israelis.

2. Sort Out "AfPak" – Cockpit of Armageddon?

A second "insoluble" crisis poisoning Muslim-West relations also dates from 1947: the India-Pakistan disagreement over Jammu and Kashmir. In reality, the dilemma is now much broader than that. It closely embraces three countries: India, Pakistan and Afghanistan. A lasting solution must bring in all three – as well as several outside powers. ("AfPak" is a charming neologism of U.S. security circles: they correctly see Afghanistan and Pakistan as a single theater of operations.)

Pakistan – a poor, terrorist-infected, deeply corrupt nation with a history of nuclear proliferation – is arguably the world's most dangerous state. Likely at least 50 percent of its 170 million people are illiterate, and live on less than two dollars a day.

---

[258] "Surge Incapacity," James Traub, *Foreign Policy* magazine,

Its education system is a disaster, having been starved to feed and arm a huge army with only one presumed "enemy" – India.

Millions of young men (15 percent of the adult population in 2011) have no work; countless others occupy dead-end jobs. Ill-adapted religious education will likely drive both groups higher in future. Women's rights, as in many Muslim countries, are grossly neglected, and in rural areas are subject to cruel "traditional" laws. Both internal and next-door (Afghanistan) jihadists threaten Pakistan's stability. Religious fanatics – though unlikely soon to be able to seize power – intimidate even top leaders, tragically weak and too terrified to defend religious tolerance. A leading governor and a Christian cabinet minister fell to assassins' bullets in February-March 2011.[259] Proudly possessing between 100 and 110 nuclear weapons (as of March 2011), Pakistani holds the only "Muslim atomic bomb." With Chinese help, they are even equipping strategic rockets with MIRV technology, allowing multiple warheads on a single rocket.[260]

The U.S. and Pakistan share a bizarrely ambiguous relationship. Officially strong allies, they also deeply distrust each other. Americans believe (correctly) that the Pakistan Army's Inter-Services Intelligence (ISI) Directorate is working hand in glove with Afghan Taliban – as well as funding terrorism against India. Noting the barely challenged rise of Pakistan's Islamic extremism, Americans and Westerners also deeply worry about the security of Pakistan's nuclear weapons. When Wikileaks revealed this in 2010, "publication of the [diplomatic] document so angered Pakistan's army chief, Gen. Ashfaq Kayani, that he told journalists there that the Pakistani people believe that the "real aim of U.S. [war] strategy is to denuclearize Pakistan...."[261]

Details of the Jammu-Kashmir puzzle are complex. The contest is basically Pakistanis' ethno-cultural-religious solidarity

---

259 "Pakistan – la faible voix des modérés," Frédéric Bobin, *Le Monde*, March 8, 2011.
260 MIRV means Multiple Independently Targetable Re-entry Vehicle.
261 "New estimates put Pakistan's nuclear arsenal at more than 100," Karen DeYoung, *Washington Post*, January 31, 2011.

versus India's legal and political argument. Pakistan emphasizes that the local populations are largely Muslim. India insists that the territory – absorbed into India because of its Sikh maharaja's 1947 decision to join India with his 77 percent Muslim subjects – is vital to its multicultural identity, and even security. The two countries have fought three wars over Jammu and Kashmir. Estimates place cost of the impasse at over 77,000 dead since 1990, including 47,000 deaths in "militancy-related" incidents in Indian-administered Kashmir. Thousands more died between 1947 and 1990. [262] Tensions continue to flourish. With suspected support from Pakistan's military intelligence, Islamic terrorists (essentially nationalists?) still threaten India – whose armed forces, by all accounts, brutally suppress dissent. A fall-2010 Indian offer to ease restrictions did not win decisive local support. [263]

A few brave Indian intellectuals have taken a stand in favor of Kashmiris' United Nations-sanctioned freedom to choose India, Pakistan or independence. India has always vociferously rejected this free choice. Arundhati Roy, acclaimed Indian novelist and activist, accuses the Indian government of a vicious occupation. This includes, she and many others allege, crushing of civil and democratic rights, widespread torture and murder, and ruthless censorship. Herself repeatedly threatened with death by Hindu nationalists, and denounced by Indian authorities for "treason," she describes Gaza-style explosiveness: "...India's military domination ought not to be confused with a political victory. Ordinary people armed with nothing but their fury have risen up against the Indian security forces. A whole generation of young people who have grown up in a grid of checkpoints, bunkers, army camps and interrogation

---

262 "Armed Conflict Report: India-Kashmir," *Ploughshares* website, February 2010. This site, embracing reports from the *Washington Post, Associated Press* and the *Asian Centre for Human Rights,* cites widely varying numbers, but a May 2009 report from the *Asian Centre for Human Rights* counts 20,000 civilians among the estimated 47,000 post-1990 dead within Kashmir.
263 For a political analysis of the sources of "seemingly endless" Kashmir conflict, see Sumit Ganguly, *Conflict Unending,* Oxford University Press, New York, 2001.

centers, whose childhood was spent witnessing "catch and kill" operations, whose imaginations are imbued with spies, informers, "unidentified gunmen," intelligence operatives and rigged elections, has lost its patience as well as its fear." [264]

Both sides refuse to compromise. And both sides reject Kashmiri independence. This is a shocking and tragic disgrace for both India and Pakistan. For six decades, they have chosen to invest hundreds of billions of dollars in arms and armies instead of in their impoverished peoples' development. That's the simple fact. It enrages both sides, but neither can deny it.

Some glimmerings of hope appeared in early 2011. But for every positive sign there appeared to be a negative one. Visceral suspicion between India and Pakistan has so far torpedoed substantive progress. [265]

Until this issue is resolved – by statesmen yet unknown – it will feed jihadist fervor, especially throughout Asia. As with the Israeli-Palestinian dispute, it would be silly and presumptuous to float hypothetical solutions here. It's enough to note this: Kashmir's Islamic warriors already identify with their brothers in Afghanistan, and draw further fury from the Palestinian drama. Muslims and Hindus have centuries of disputes to eclipse. Even the decades-old UN Military Observer Group can barely help stabilize a Line of Control. Now, with both sides being armed with nuclear-tipped missiles, the urgency of a final settlement is blatantly obvious. Noting the dangers from this fight to the rest of the world is just holding up a mirror to reality.

As "AfPak" perils and costs balloon, some Americans are finally asking the fundamental "why?" question. "When one looks across the Arab world today at the stunning spontaneous democracy uprisings," argued Thomas L. Friedman in March 2011, "it is impossible to not ask: What are we doing spending $110 billion this year supporting corrupt and unpopular

---

[264] "Kashmir's fruits of discord," Arundhati Roy, *International Herald Tribune*, November 10, 2010.
[265] "In hope, not expectation – neither government looks strong enough to get far with peace talks," *The Economist*, February 17, 2011.

regimes in Afghanistan and Pakistan that are almost identical to the governments we're applauding the Arab people for overthrowing?" [266]

Friedman correctly noted that Pakistan's ISI spy service is in many ways a "twin" of Mubarak's *Amn Al-Dawla*, the State Security Police. The columnist explained their common tactic: "Pakistan's military leaders play the same game Mubarak played with us for years. First, they whisper in our ears: 'Psst, without us, the radical Islamists will rule. So we may not be perfect, but we're the only thing standing in the way of the devil.' In reality, though, they are nurturing the devil. The ISI is long alleged to have been fostering anti-Indian radical Muslim groups and masterminding the Afghan Taliban."

So, Pakistan: Ally or adversary? Both, it seems, and that is what makes it fiendishly hard for the West to be either present, or absent, in "AfPak."

The only realistic approach to peace there is to seek a broader peace in the whole region. Pakistan's respected journalist Ahmed Rashid has outlined an approach taking into account the interests and roles of all potential players: Pakistan, India and Afghanistan, of course; but also Iran, Russia, China, the U.S. and the European Union. The Central Asian republics of Turkmenistan, Uzbekistan, and Tajikistan may also play a role.

"There is no more a political solution in Afghanistan by itself," wrote Rashid in 2008, "than there is a single military solution. Nor can a solution be reached through a piecemeal approach to Afghanistan and Pakistan such as the one the United States has pursued since 2001. The leading players – the United States, the European Union, NATO and the UN – need to agree on a new global compact and launch a united international political and diplomatic initiative to help this region resolve its problems." [267]

---

[266] "The $110 billion question," Thomas L. Friedman, *New York Times*, March 6, 2011.
[267] Ahmed Rashid, Descent Into Chaos – Pakistan, Afghanistan and the Threat to Global Security, Penguin Books, London, 2008, pp. 415–418.

Rashid sets out changes both Pakistan and India must make to reduce mutual paranoia. The Pakistani army – still the nation's strongest organized entity – has to begin seriously backing the civil government, respecting politicians, and reforming ISI. It must also stop fishing in troubled Islamic waters abroad.

The May 2, 2011 killing of Osama bin Laden raised an even more shocking suspicion: the world's top terrorist was found in a spectacularly fortified mansion a short walk from a prestigious Pakistani officer-training school – iself a short drive from the country's capital. Is it conceivable that the powerful ISI didn't know bin Laden was there? Imaginable that no one in Pakistan was part of bin Laden's support system? These questions tested, and still test, already deeply distrustful U.S.-Pakistani relations.

India, for its part, needs to play a more transparent role in Afghanistan: its Kabul embassy and *four* regional consulates stir Pakistani suspicions of anti-Pakistan scheming. Why else would India need so many consulates in Afghanistan?

Iran? Obama will have to swallow hard, and at least engage Teheran within a multinational "AfPak" initiative. Iran has long demonstrated that it can act for better or worse in Afghanistan. It cannot be ignored. Russia, China and the others all have interests. At a minimum, they could support reconstruction and help stabilize an eventual peace.

Rashid's perceptive book on all this was short-listed for the 2009 Orwell prize. A perfect evocation for the "AfPak" puzzle...

3. Cure U.S. Oil Addiction

Can you stand hearing this again? Still another "impossible" task: escaping the grip of oil, especially for automobiles and trucks. The U.S. barely pretends to wean itself from oil's pollution and its unimaginable political-economic costs. It dabbles in experiments with alternative energies, toothless conservation measures, higher proposed mileage-per-gallon minima – and Gulf hurricanes of green-talk. So far, this is useful tinkering.

It allows the international oil industry to smirk with fear. For it knows the big fight for an oil-cure must be won in American public opinion (thus the media) and in Congress. The belief that God wanted Americans to have cheap gasoline dies hard. So far, the debate animates mainly a few serious commentators able to link expensive fuel to folly. *New York Times* columnist Thomas L. Friedman is, as noted, one of the best. But getting through to Middle America and Congress is another matter. Both seem to live in worlds where knowledge arrives slowly, and convictions rarely change.

A good example of Congress's autism is politicians' ability to ignore easily available, credible information contradicting its received beliefs. Tone-deaf and blind, it pays scant attention to anyone on oil except the oil industry and the base-seeking Pentagon. Medically, "autism" concerns "restrictive and repetitive behavior," with seeming unawareness of one's surroundings. Voting the same way year after year, whatever the changing facts, fits that definition.

It's no longer just lefty 'green' people who argue for developing alternate energies. An elite group of retired admirals and three- and four-star military and air force generals argued with devastating clarity in 2009 that *oil addiction* is a *clear threat to America's national security*:

"Many of our overseas deployments were defined, in part, by the strategic decision to ensure the free flow of oil, to the U.S. and to our allies. Many of the troops we commanded were aided by air cover from high-thrust delivery systems that only an energy-intense society can provide. Many of these same troops were often burdened and imperiled by battle-field systems that were energy-inefficient. Some of the attacks on our troops and on American civilians have been supported by funds from the sale of oil. Our nation's energy choices have saved lives; they have also cost lives...

...As we consider America's current energy posture, we do so from a singular perspective: We gauge our energy choices solely by their impact on America's national security. Our dependence on foreign oil reduces our international leverage, places our troops in dangerous global regions, funds nations and individuals who wish us harm, and weakens our economy; our dependency and inefficient use of oil also puts our troops at risk." [268]

The retired officers added that "climate change, national security, and energy dependence are a related set of global challenges." To his great credit, Republican Senator Richard Lugar immediately endorsed this report. But he's known more as a statesman than a Republican. The report is plainly a hard sell to a now Republican-dominated House of Representatives. Many such Representatives still deny climate change, and think of oil as "Drill, baby, drill!" House Speaker John Boehner, never accused of being a statesman, is known as every lobbyist's best friend. Will he listen to his oil and defense-industry cronies? Or to the deeply informed retired brass? It's still safe to invest in oil...

Friedman has argued passionately for both a carbon tax and a gasoline tax. Both would be dissuasive of oil use. They are, for those who like big words, "Piglovian" (after economist Arthur Pigou). Or in plain English, "sin" taxes. Both taxes are, if you wish, pro-environment taxes on all use of carbon, the key human cause of global warning.

An across-the-board carbon tax punishes all use of oil, gas, coal and petroleum products, including diesel and aviation fuel. A gasoline tax targets hydrocarbon use in trucks, buses – and in the biggest polluters of all, personal automobiles. Responsible for about one-quarter of all U.S. fossil-burning pollution, these vehicles' use of gasoline or diesel fuel can vary significantly with the price of fuel. But taxing such fuel is an explosive political issue. The automobile being a mythic symbol of individual freedom, populist politicians usually portray a "gas tax" at the pump as a "tax on liberty" itself. Thus an "anti-American" tax._

Like free trade and rent control, a carbon tax pits many pro-tax economists against public opinion. But the case for

---

268 "Powering America's Defense: Energy and the Risks to National Security," *Military Advisory Board, Center of Naval Analyses*, May 2009.

punishing carbon and gasoline use is overwhelming. All that requires to work is for America to elect only intelligent, courageous, honest, public-spirited members of Congress. Alas, as Henry Kissinger and others have noted, the skills required to get elected are not the kind you need to govern in the public interest.

Friedman sees a gasoline tax almost as a magic bullet. It cuts pollution, by discouraging excessive driving. It keeps money in the U.S. to fix decrepit roadways. It encourages Detroit to make more fuel-efficient vehicles. It strengthens the U.S. dollar. It helps U.S. taxes support a strong American foreign policy. It reduces money sent to petro-kingdoms still suspected of funding terrorism.

Friedman cites John Hopkins University foreign-policy specialist Michael Mandelbaum, author of a new book called *Frugal Superpower*: "A gasoline tax 'is not just win-win; it's win, win, win, win, win... A gasoline tax would do more for American prosperity and strength than any other measure Obama could propose.'" [269] Friedman's last word: If Washington doesn't pass a gasoline tax, it will be "morning again – in Saudi Arabia." And in Beijing, Moscow, Teheran and several other capitals. For Mandelbaum's overriding thesis is that the U.S., by its wild-spending military adventures, may have speeded its decline to the status of threadbare imperial power. [270]

There's no obvious active military role in reducing U.S. oil consumption. On the contrary, the Pentagon's ethos of more and more interminable wars does exactly the opposite. The military establishment's only contribution is to promote huge, permanent military bases abroad to "protect American oil interests" – such as in Saudi Arabia (from Qatar and Bahrein) and Iraq. The need 'justifies' the bases – then the bases 'prove' the need. The same circular argument applies to U.S. wars in Muslim countries:

---

269 "Win, Win, Win, Win, Win...," Thomas F. Friedman, *New York Times*, December 27, 2008.
270 Michael Mandelbaum, The Frugal Superpower: America's Global Leadership in a Cash-Strapped Era, Public Affairs, Perseus Books Group, 2010.

The U.S. "must fight" there to "defend itself;" but its presence in Muslim lands invariably *forces* the U.S. to defend itself.

America's adversaries may use Islam as part of their rationale. But the other part of their reasoning (as in Iraq and Afghanistan) is clearly patriotism: defending their homeland against foreigners. What's so hard to understand about that?

4. Tame the Pentagon

It's probably far too late to tame the U.S. military. America's passionate, unquestioning belief in "strong national defense" is now the foundation-stone of American *identity*. This proceeds from the core idea of American "exceptionalism' – the conviction that God ("In Whom We Trust") assigned the U.S. a unique role in re-ordering the world in its own perfect image. President Woodrow Wilson articulated – and carelessly pursued – this idea at the start of the 20th-century: to "make the world safe for democracy." At the start of the 21st century, President Barack Obama kept the idealism: "To overcome extremism, we must also be vigilant in upholding the values our troops defend – because there is no force in the world more powerful than the example of America." Fine. But instead of preaching hubris-driven unilateralism, Obama pressed for international cooperation. And with the 2010 mid-term elections, he found that Congress preferred the Old might-is-right America. Among several setbacks, the "reset" with Russia had to struggle harder to stick.

We have seen how most of the vehicles that form American public opinion essentially sustain this view that America is "God's Country." This may or may not be a harmless conceit. Plenty of other countries claim as much – and not just the Israelis – a Chosen People with a Promised Holy Land. At one time or another, the Chinese, Japanese, Indians, Germans, English and Serbs have presumed that God spoke their language. (The English, plainly, were right). France didn't need God, for it had Louis XIV, Napoleon and de Gaulle. Besides, if you're lucky enough to live in France, it may seem self-evident that

God, were there one, made the place. The German phrase for living well is *Leben wie Gott in Frankreich* – to live like God in France. But for self-blinding illusion amid the fog and rain, the English win again, thanks to Shakespeare's *Richard II*: "This other Eden... Demi-paradise... This blessed plot, this earth, this realm, this England."

Impressively, Americans trump all this today. They glory in a deep conviction of moral superiority, and stiffen backs and chins at their Manifest Destiny, Monroe Doctrine, and American Way of Life. They especially ache to believe that everybody else wants to be just like them. They are a stubborn lot – intractable nationalists who don't usually even *want to know* what Kipling's "lesser breeds" (i.e. everybody else) might think. It's not just their chest-beating political establishment that expounds America's supremacy. As we saw, it's every opinion-shaping institution in the country: schools, churches, media, movies, TV, academics.

Linked to the military – as this effusion of self-congratulation inevitably is – the bragging is not so harmless. No doubt the French export language and culture by setting up a worldwide network of the *Alliance Française* to showcase France's wonders. Other nations follow: Germany's *Goethe Institutes*, Italy's *Dante Alighieri Societies*, Spain's *Cervantes Centers*, and now China's *Confucius Institutes*. But it looks a bit less innocent when a self-described military superpower keeps building bases abroad... while shutting down (in 1999) 150 overseas office-libraries of the U.S. Information Agency.

It's also worrisome to be fighting Muslims abroad with "exit deadlines" on which generals make fools of their political masters. First, in the spring of 2010, General Stanley McChyrstal publicly ridiculed President Obama's national security team (getting fired for his trouble). But not before publicly lobbying for a massive increase in troops. Instead of the 40,000 he asked for, he got 30,000 more – a saw-off with the 20,000 that a deeply skeptical Vice-president Joe Biden recommended. Then, over the summer of 2010, Obama repeated that his "drawdown" of U.S. troops from Afghanistan would start in mid-2011. Within weeks, Marine Corps Commandant James Conway publicly suggested that this might be "giving our enemy sustenance" and that U.S. Marines would be in Afghanistan for many years. Even semi-loyal General David Petraeus mentioned a longer stay – this, after he assured Obama that, after agreeing to a 2011 drawdown date, the military would not welsh on its agreement.

Petraeus and the Pentagon continued chipping away at Obama's insistence on an Afghan exit strategy. Bob Woodward's September 2010 book *Obama's Wars* spells this out. [271] The generals despised the White House's political calculations: Obama said the public would allow him only two years on Afghanistan. They simply refused Obama's request to define an Afghan exit strategy – so Obama had to write his own plan. Recounting a shadowy but sharp war between the White House and top generals, Petraeus actually threatened Obama with a public fight (subtext: those brave generals against the Chicago wimp). Petraeus told his staffers that the president of the United States was "[expletive] with the wrong guy." [272] Probably he meant "singing" with the wrong guy – no doubt from the same hymn-book, but with Petraeus's choice being *O Worship the King* (Petraeus) and Obama's being *Blest Be The Tie That Binds* (White House and Pentagon). Masters of mission creep, the top U.S. military played Obama for a weak-kneed community organizer. First, they demanded more troops for Kabul, then barely saluted when – against his understandable fear of a new Vietnam – he gave them 'only' 30,000, with two provisos: Give me a credible exit plan, and promise not to start changing your tune and lobbying for more troops and a longer war.

Obama clearly wanted to avoid Afghanistan being labeled "Obama's War." His elaborately staged troop farewell with Biden in Baghdad in 2010 already aimed at leaving "Bush's War" as Iraq's only label. But the generals, in a shocking campaign of insubordination, seemed determined to stick him with both labels: Afghanistan and Iraq. The 50,000 U.S. troops they left ambiguously behind in Iraq will help make their point. These

---

271 Bob Woodward, *Obama's Wars*, Simon & Schuster, New York, 2010.
272 Cited in *The Economist*, September 25-October 1, 2010.

soldiers camped in out-of-town bases under a cheerful-sounding Operation New Dawn. But they may still face more fighting – which broke out within days as *al-Qaeda* in Mesopotamia sprang back to life.

The generals also disloyally began an almost immediate PR blitz suggesting that the Bush-started Afghan war wouldn't really "draw down" many troops in mid-2011 as Obama announced – but likely several years later. Obama's Big-Picture political vision was of scant interest to the generals. They may have imagined they were giving realistic, honest, professional advice. But, unlike Obama, they didn't have to get re-elected. Ever. Meanwhile, will President Karzai and the Taliban (helped by Pakistan's ISI) come to a deal and make America irrelevant?

On November 11, 2010 (appropriately on U.S. "Veterans Day"), Obama spectacularly caved in to the generals. Defense Secretary Robert Gates, Secretary of State Hillary Clinton, and chairman of the Joint Chiefs of Staff Mike Mullen all came out in the *New York Times* to say that the Afghanistan draw-down date was really more like 2014. That pesky three-year extension was absolutely, adamantly, sort of, er, not really the slightest change from 2011."The president has been crystal clear," insisted White House spokesman Tommy Vietor, "that we will begin drawing down troops in July of 2011. There is absolutely no change to that policy." Except that two senior Cabinet members and the top military man had just said it had changed – in reality, if not in weasely rhetoric.

Exquisite rationales made 2011 sound like 2014 all along. Gates assured that the non-delay was to convince the Taliban that the U.S. would continue "coming after them" after the earlier, transitional non-deadline. Michael O'Hanlon of the Democrat-friendly Brookings Institution, rushed out to provide another justification. The 2014 date made sense, he said, because the Afghan Army and police were scheduled to increase their numbers to their planned goal of 350,000 by 2013. "[2014] is far enough away to allow lots to happen, yet it is still close enough to debunk the myth of an indefinite foreign occupation of the country." The "myth"...

A third rationale might be that Obama, after "singing" with General Petraeus, had decided to ignore again his anti-war Democratic base and go with the Pentagon flow. Indefinite foreign occupation? Never! Until you remember what Petraeus told Bob Woodward about Afghanistan in his book *Obama's Wars*: "You have to recognize also that I don't think you win this war. I think you keep fighting. It's a little bit like Iraq, actually... Yes, there has finally been progress in Iraq. But there are still horrific attacks in Iraq, and you have to stay vigilant. You have to stay after it. This is the kind of fight we're in for the rest of our lives and probably our kids' lives." [273]

Our kids' lives. At last, loud and clear, the "consensual" military-industrial complex fantasy: a *multi-generational* war that you never have to explain or leave. Why? Because people will forget why they got into it in the first place...

The bars in U.S. officers' messes echo with clinking tumblers of *Jack Daniels*. "Defense" industry lobbyists splurge on Maseratis. Snouts-in-the-trough Members of Congress join fancier golf clubs. America finally achieves a "strong national defense." Until next time.

So don't count on 2014 being the end either. As of November 2010, the score was: Generals 3, Obama 0. If, before his first term ends, Obama doesn't play the public's war fatigue against the generals' predilection for endless war – and win that fight – the score of his presidency's final year will be: Generals 4, Obama 0. And the battle to regain political control of the military will essentially be lost.

Woodward clearly delineated the civil wars pitting the "politicals" (mainly Obama's personal campaign staff), desperate for an exit strategy, against the "militarists" yearning for a success strategy. The generals defined the latter as they did in Vietnam and Iraq: If you can't defeat the enemy unequivocally, at least declare victory, scrounge a fig-leaf, and get the hell out. Or try to keep a nice little war going indefinitely: budgets, glory, promotions, maybe later jobs with a still-vibrant 'defense' industry.

---

273 Quoted from Woodward's book by Steve Luxenberg in the *Washington Post*, September 22, 2010.

Cynical? Not at all. Just remember how Pentagon generals and admirals reacted in August 2010 when Defense Secretary Robert Gates tried to cut only 50 of their superfluous comrades. Their screaming perfectly illustrates how – in league with the defense industries and their Congressional messenger-boys (and -girls) – the military-industrial complex still resembles a Florentine cabal-cum-Teamsters Union. How does mess-gossip work? Leak Cabinet dissensions. Undercut a presidential policy in the media. Accuse the president of being "weak on defense." And you're home-free. (Do anything but resign on principle).

Some generals and top industry-crony bureaucrats fear that Gates has got their number – and finds it too big. "Pentagon officials said the [Gates compressions]... were aimed at more than a number. Mr.Gates said he wanted to flatten a bureaucracy that had experienced significant 'brass creep,' swelling to 'cumbersome and top-heavy proportions.' He complained, for example, that a request to send a dog-handling team to Afghanistan goes through no fewer than five four-star headquarters." [274]

That's not walking softly and carrying a big stick. It's five generals walking the same dog. It's hundreds of generals and admirals applauding Petraeus's half-prediction, half-plea, for unending war. In proposing his cuts, Gates gamely insisted: "No sacred cows." But back to the kennel: All these events and opinions highlight a military "tail" that's perilously close to wagging the political "dog." When generals publicly scheme against their President, where is the piously-vaunted submission of soldiers to elected officials?

And what about officers' pricey, all-too-comfy lifestyles? One would like to call this high-on-the-hog living – but retired General Arnold L. Punaro cheerfully describes it in canine terms again: "When you have a head dog, you also have a deputy dog, then a deputy deputy dog, and a deputy deputy deputy dog," deplored General Punaro. "The layers are suffo-

---

[274] Ginger Thompson and Thom Shanker, "Generals Wary of Move to Cut Their Ranks," *New York Times*, August 26, 2010.

cating the bureaucracy." [275] Doggone it, if this is not evidence of out-of-control "militarism," what is?

We are far from the anti-Vietnam War protests of the 1960s and '70s. Then, a people's army of conscripts created a vast pool of the disenchanted. Today's all-volunteer professional army – supplemented by hapless reservists and tens of thousands of mercenary contractors – isolate war from most taxpayers. Only immediate families of U.S. dead and wounded really feel the pain. And unless completely caught up in the militarist mystique, only these are likely to oppose ill-advised or wrongly fought wars.

Generals win, civilians lose. And the civilians' sons and daughters struggle with maiming and PTSD – Post-Traumatic Stress Disorder – until the end of time. But, cluck the generals, *we* are the battlefield, not those messed-up kids. Why fiddle with long-term nation-building for a peaceful Afghan society when you can game the system and keep an endless war going? Militarism? Civilian control of the military? Hey, whose in charge here anyway?

5. Avoid a New "Operation Enduring Occupation"

To raise that question is to hit a wall of denial something like this: "We (America) cannot leave Muslim lands because we're still fighting there, and hope to win." Or, perhaps in President Obama's case, he hopes to simply "manage" conflict in Muslim countries. The point here is that *because* U.S. troops fight in proud Muslim lands, their presence as "invaders" drags on, stirring up inevitable patriotic resistance. Then a war rages on indefinitely. America, at some level, knows this. It realizes that it is riding tigers. Besides, its military-industrial establishment gains money and prestige from these wars. And the politicians' ever-short attention spans – abetted by a never-stopping, military-lobbyist-dominated electoral cycle – ensures that it takes forever to withdraw troops without a credible "victory."

---

275 Jason Linkins, "Generals Push Back on Robert Gates' Budget Cutting, *The Huffington Post*, August 26, 2010.

Meanwhile, campaigns roll on, urging citizens to "support our troops." No problem there. But for some reason, you never see posters urging people to "support our politicians." That is, their policies – that mysterious shell-game of shifting goals and deadlines that somehow keeps the war-show on the road.

After a decade of frustrating, seemingly futile, wars in Iraq and Afghanistan, America may finally be grasping this simple fact: Most peoples don't like foreign occupiers. Remembering 4th-century B.C. Afghanistan – call this the Alexander-the-Great syndrome. Famously, Pashtun tribesmen made life a nightmare for Alexander, as they did for the 19th-century British (twice) and 1980s Russians.

At each occupation, invaders seem to have learned nothing from their predecessors. "At the time" [when we invaded Afghanistan in 1979], deplores ex-Soviet General Ruslan Aouchev, "we hadn't taken account of the British experience. And in turn, the [U.S.-led] international coalition ignored ours." [276] On February 15, 1989, Mikhail Gorbachev saw the last bedraggled Soviet troops crawl home via the Amou Daria River's Friendship Bridge. He recalls that Moscow's aging Politburo had seen Afghanistan as a cakewalk to stabilization. "Instead," he sighed, "we got exactly the opposite: greater instability, a war with all its destructions, and appalling side-effects for our own country." [277]

It is now almost universally recognized that George W. Bush's Iraq war was a monumentally stupid error. Before and after being elected president, Barack Obama called it a "dumb war." Informed observers, including British and French generals, call the current Afghan war unwinnable. With different weapons, tactics and timetables, it resembles another Soviet-style disaster.

Given that the U.S. thought it had learned some lessons in 1960s-'70s Vietnam, wading into two more quagmires (Iraq and Afghanistan) does not seem like the quintessence of

---

276 Marie Jégo, *Le Monde*, Paris, August 26, 2010.
277 Ibid.

history-rooted wisdom. By now, even trigger-happy Pentagon geniuses must realize that they have met that old truism: "It's easy to get into a war, but not so easy to get out." And this truism too: While an invading power may allege an ideological, geopolitical or economic motivation, to the involuntary 'host' people, the 'guests' always look like – well, foreign invaders. Then, intolerable occupiers. This is an age-old reflex that Americans ought to understand, but rarely do when it's found in other peoples: patriotism.

Adding to the anti-occupier stew, especially in Iraq, is now a catastrophic religious-political dimension: jihadism. This brings the "war on terror" to homeland America, as well as to Canada, Australia, Europe, Africa, even India. The Afghan Taliban, though fanatically religious, are essentially patriots whipped into die-hard nationalists. Alas, the U.S. presence in Afghanistan has also stirred the pot among the Taliban's anti-West friends elsewhere. These thrive (as "fellow Muslims") in Iraq and (with a little help from Islamabad's ISI secret services) especially Pakistan. Also – with various local labels and goals – in Yemen, the Horn of Africa, the Philippines, Indonesia, and North Africa. In short, across a huge swath of the Middle East, Africa, Central Asia and East Asia, U.S. willingness to throw hundreds of thousands of troops into Muslim countries has not achieved its aim of security. It has actively generated *in*security for both the U.S. and its allies.

Even the European Union's cautious ambassador in Afghanistan, former Lithuanian foreign minister Vygaudas Usackas, publicly recognized this in August 2010. "Some observers think" that foreign troops "keep the war going," he agreed – even though NATO believed that if they left too soon, "Afghanistan would fall into chaos and civil war." [278]

Foremost among the beneficiaries of America's long excursions to Muslim lands are the Shiite Iranians. With the firestorm of anger (and distraction) that U.S. military enthusiasm has lit, Teheran today emerges stronger everywhere. East and west

---

278 Rémy Ourdan, *Le Monde*, Paris, August 30, 2010.

(Afghanistan and Iraq), its traditional adversaries lie weakened. Afghan Taliban fight a nine-year guerrilla war. Iran's Shiite allies dominate neighboring Iraq's struggling government against ragtag Sunni *al-Qaeda*. Dangers north and south are quiescent. Hated Israel (and despised Sunni Saudi Arabia) tremble at the fast-approaching day of Iran's possible nuclear armament. And Israel fears a looming rain of Iranian rockets that may fall again from Hezbollah in Lebanon and from Hamas in Gaza.

This all-round American shooting-itself-in-the-foot is largely imputable to ill-thought-out U.S. military adventures. That's why – in spite of momentum, myth and the military-industrial establishment – America must face this fact: However grave the provocation, U.S. invasion and occupation of Muslim lands will almost invariably *cause* more harm than good. It will make more enemies than friends. American military "cures" will be worse than virtually any local "disease."

This is certainly not to plead for unilateral U.S. disarmament. At a minimum, China – already aggressively extending its naval power – and perhaps even always-touchy Russia, may constitute serious future risks. Weird North Korea remains a wild-card. And pacifism is not a reliable antidote to any dangers of war.

It would be folly to plead for a permanent moratorium on all possible American military action abroad. There will always be occasions when the U.S. must enter the fray – start with the two world wars and 1950s Korea. But such interventions should be for critical situations where human lives or international security are clearly threatened. They should, moreover, be rare, timely and limited to achievable goals. America's spearheading of the March 2011 Libyan no-fly zone was a good example. Peacekeeping – saving lives – should be a primary activity. The Congo and Rwanda would have been defensible interventions. But American leaders were distracted by elections and silly sex scandals. At the time, they didn't pay attention, or didn't care when they did. They failed to defend civilization, so millions died horribly.

Bottom-line: There are other, *non-military* means for America to exert decisive influence for peace and security. These are much cheaper in blood and money. They can be incomparably more effective than boots and bullets. And that's the theme of our final chapters.

President Obama has already set a precedent for enhancing non-combat U.S. activities among Muslims. In the fall of 2010,. he reversed the Bush-Rumsfeld folly of putting the Defense Department in charge of Iraqi reconstruction. Henceforth, the State Department is supervising reconstruction – and, in liaison with Defense, keeping a close eye on training of Iraqi security forces. With luck, State's less gung-ho, more culturally sensitive, staff will choose to favor many of the educational and social reforms cited here later.

6. Entice the Saudis to Join the World

As we've often noted, Saudi Arabia exports two products: oil and Salafi-Wahhabism. The latter is the world's most backward-looking version of Islam, and a core jihadist faith. Again, fifteen of the nineteen September 11 murderers were Saudis. Ryadh finds little useful work for its money-spoiled youth. If in future it can't find them satisfying real jobs, it may be sitting on a volcano. In time, this will spew out still more terrorists.

We needn't recap the many sins of the Al-Sauds' absolute, theocratic monarchy. But it's fair to say it's a truly weird anachronism, with customs and values no modern, civilized nation would tolerate. Apart from chopping off heads and hands, it treats women like infants and as the devil's own handiwork. In terms of human equality, freedom, democracy and decency, Saudi Arabia is not part of the "Free World: (The *Economist Intelligence Unit*'s democracy index places Saudi Arabia as no. 160 in the world; Gaddafi's Libya scored 158). It's merely a handy service-station for Western cars, trucks and airplanes. And a bottom-fishing buyer (with profits from U.S.-European oil purchases) of crown-jewel Western properties.

As the 2011 Arab Spring shook other autocracies to their foundations, the Al-Saud family knew that its Western client-protectors wouldn't flinch at continuing to back them – and their oil. "Did you hear it?" asked one sarcastic British journalist. "The clamour from Western governments for democracy in Saudi Arabia? The howls of outrage from the White House and Downing Street about the shootings last Thursday, the suppression of protest last Friday, the arrival of Saudi troops in Bahrain on Monday? No? Nor did I.... Why [does the West apply a double standard to Ryadh]? Future weapons sales doubtless play a role. But there's an even stronger imperative. A short time ago, French bank Société Générale warned that unrest in Saudi Arabia could push the oil price to $200 a barrel." [279]

Yet might this bizarre country have a role to play in making a better world? To play a credible, trusted role, it would have to make far greater reforms in its own educational, social, religious and anti-terrorist norms. Specifically, it would have to remove even lingering suspicions about unofficial Saudi sympathy for *al-Qaeda*-type subversion outside the kingdom.

But let's dream. What might these contributions be?

First, economically. There already exists a Kuwaiti-based Arab Fund for Economic and Social Development. In 2010 it held assets of $9.3-billion. In petro-prince terms, small change – but a start and an example. The Arab League, though mainly consultative, also deals with trade and monetary coordination. But the Arab world remains a region of large, impoverished nations and smaller, extremely rich oil-and-gas kingdoms. If pan-Arab solidarity meant anything, the richer nations would help the poorer infinitely more.

However implausible this seems now, why not press the Saudis much harder – along with the smaller oil-and-gas kingdoms, plus Algeria, and later Iraq (perhaps even Gaddafi-looted Libya) – to set up, for the entire Arab world, a massive Arab Investment and Development Fund? Half of it in grants for non-religious education (math, science, literature, world history)

---

[279] George Monbiot, "Our dependence on petrol leaves despotic Saudi monarchy high and dry," *Mail & Guardial Online*, March 18, 2011.

and health; half for micro-credit investment in small business? For the development fund, the acclaimed United Nations Arab Human Development Reports could provide a diagnosis of needs and blueprint for reform. Such a fund need not duplicate existing international efforts. For example, it might simply amount to a vast, refocused expansion of the Kuwait-based Arab Fund for Economic and Social Development.

If Ryadh preferred, it could choose to spread its wealth unilaterally, as it already largely does. But ideas are vital too. Ryadh should be made to understand that its intolerant Wahhabi exports are utterly unwelcome, and a severe blow to Western trust. The Saudis should not defend an activity that even *risks* favoring recruitment for Osama bin Laden's movement.

If the Saudis were serious about creating a modern, tolerant international Arab society, they *could* fund Arab-language translations of, say, 20,000 classic books from all world civilizations. Then load them on e-readers (like Kindles) to be handed out free of charge to Arabs everywhere. This would instantly put an open-minded cat among the Wahhabi pigeons. It would also create an intellectual and cultural basis for rapprochement with the entire non-Arab, non-Muslim world. For now, this is fantasy – a far likelier project for the West.

If the Saudi royals – again, more plausibly the West –wanted to be *really* daring, they could put most of the translated books (and thousands more) online via *Wikibooks* or *WikiSource* – not to make a bad pun – 'royalty-free.' Why translations? The first UN *Arab Human Development Report* (2002) noted what later editions confirmed: "...the total number of books translated into Arabic during the 1,000 years since the age of Caliph Al-Ma'moun [a ninth-century Arab ruler who was 'a patron of cultural interaction between Arab, Persian, and Greek scholars'] to this day is less than those translated in Spain *in one year*." [author's italics].[280] Obviously, online publication of current Arab literature is also a priority – demanding brave decisions against censorship.

To return to the real world: One struggles to imagine the Saudis *ever* funding anything like either of these revolutions.

---

280 Fahed al-Fanek, *Al-Ra'I*, Amman, Jordan, July 4, 2002.

Their whole history and mindset, plus their power-sharing pact with the Wahhabi clergy, militates against it. Opening minds is more the specialty of modern-thinking Hamad bin Khalifa Al Thani, the Emir of Qatar. It should also be a cosmic priority of the West. The above proposals could make one of the most constructively subversive actions Western strategists could possibly support in "fighting terror." Nevertheless, should a future Saudi king wish to surprise the world...

Secondly, the Saudis could consider a more dynamic role as peacemaker. Already we have seen that King Abdullah floated a bold and realistic plan for Israeli-Palestinian peace. For memory: In February 2002, as Crown Prince Abdullah, he showed *New York Times* columnist Thomas L. Friedman a proposal for full, normal relations with all Arab states in exchange for Israeli withdrawal from all occupied lands. As President Obama's new Palestinian-Israeli talks began in September 2010, the plan still looked reasonable – to everybody except Israeli settlers and their right-wing friends. [281]

Riyadh's enormous wealth – and perhaps embarrassment for its past fostering of terrorism? – could lead it to reposition itself as an honest broker between Muslims and West. It could offer more insistently to become the generous banker of any Israel-Palestine agreement. To encourage this, the U.S. shouldn't reinvent the secretive crony relationship of the Bush-Saud years. It should just nudge the Saudis toward internal reforms allowing it to follow economic, social and cultural reforms in Arab and Muslim worlds. Washington should encourage Ryadh to even more Abdullah-style diplomatic daring to try to break peace-paralyzing log-jams.

How? And this could become a third Saudi signature, by taking a longer look at energy. The U.S. should engage the Saudis more imaginatively in this area they are both extraordinarily sensitive to. Counter-intuitively, the Saudis should look not only at oil and gas, but at *alternative* energies – especially solar. A useful point of departure is a 2005 book by the late Matthew Simmons: *Twilight in the Desert: The Coming Saudi*

---

281 "Saudi Time," Thomas L. Friedman, *New York Times*, September 7, 2010.

Oil Shock and the World Economy. Simmons, respected in Ryadh as in Texas, noted that new oil exploration was "coming up empty." He urged a gradual move to natural gas, as a first step to diversification.

The U.S. could help deepen Saudi-U.S. cooperation on sustainable energy sources. Given the vast deserts in both countries, solar energy is an obvious priority. Indeed, it already has been in Ryadh for a generation. An old idea – but who in the West knew about it? Or saw the dazzling potential for marrying Saudi deserts, ideas and riches?

In itself, the Saudis are wise to plan for a still-distant post-oil era. But developing its specialty of solar energy even faster could bring Saudis immediate benefits. First: diversified income from Saudi-developed solar equipment. Second: sophisticated experimental and industrial jobs for the millions of dangerously underemployed Saudi youth – now heavily educated in the Holy Koran. Third: a focus of national pride that could lead to still more progress in education. Fourth: desalinization – the production of drinking water. Clean, safe water is a priority for every country in the world – and is critically needed in poorer countries.

Becoming known as a "green" superpower that supports education, health, small business, solar energy, and abundant clean water could prove an immensely attractive goal for the Saudis. If they look at the world's view of them today – as selfish enemies of global ecology measures – such changes represent an Allah-sent opportunity. And, in passing, green is not a bad trademark color for the homeland of Islam.

Is all this a deep-desert mirage? Just to take alternative energies: "Who needs" more energy, argued a leading oil magazine even 30 years ago. "To some observers, Saudi Arabia's effort to develop solar energy is decidedly a coals-to-Newcastle situation. With close to 113.5 billion barrels of proved oil reserves, Saudi Arabia hardly requires more energy." [282]

But even then, visionaries such as internationally respected Shaikh Ahmed Zaki Yamani, longtime Minister of Petroleum

---

[282] *Aramco World*, September-October, 1981.

and Mineral Resources, could warn: "The oil won't last forever." In the event of a miraculous Israeli-Palestinian settlement, Saudi solar expertise could also become a celebrated new Arab bridge to Israeli researchers who also dabble in solar. Saudi-Israeli energy for tragically neglected Palestine? Unthinkable? Why? And why not bring in Palestinian solar engineers too?

7. Integrate U.S. Muslims

Muhammad in Manhattan. The summer 2010 outcry against the Ground Zero Muslim community center revealed a still-powerful undercurrent of fear among and against American Muslims. It's not easy to be a Muslim in America. And it's not easy being a 'traditional' American trying to understand Islam. [283]

American Muslims are at the crossroads of any worldwide Muslim-West accommodation. As in Europe, anti-Muslim prejudice in America is growing, despite serious efforts to combat it. [284] A bigoted Florida pastor stupidly threatened in September 2010 to burn a stack of Korans – a provocation that caused General David Petraeus, American commander in Afghanistan, to warn that it would put U.S. troops in even more danger.

Why the anti-Muslim backlash? September 11, of course – a trauma Americans will never forget or forgive. Then almost a decade of "war against terror" in Iraq, Afghanistan, and Africa has deepened mainstream anger, as the U.S. relives nightmares of Vietnam-style quagmires. A final reason: many Muslims, in appearance, clothing and ideas, clash with America's historic self-image – dating to Pilgrim times – of being a "Christian nation." (Jews, after earlier facing deep prejudice, now pass religious-patriotic muster. Indeed, in the minds of many born-again fundamentalists, they pass as sort of 'honorary Christians'

---

283 Laurie Goldstein, "American Muslims Ask, Will We Ever Belong?" *New York Times*, September 5, 2010. Also Bobby Ghosh, "Islamophobia: Does America Have a Muslim Problem?" *TIME*, August 19, 2010.

284 "Islam in America – It's part of the fabric of life, but protests reveal a growing hostility to the religion of Muslims," cover-story, *TIME*, August 30, 2010.

for giving America both the Bible and Jesus...). The dismissal of Muslims as "un-American" is strongest, moreover, wherever the born-again, pro-Israel version of Christianity thrives.

Another source of anti-Muslim anger: the casually exercised power of some U.S. media in picking up and dramatizing prejudice. Even in the face of demonstrable error. Is Barack Obama a Muslim? A quarter of Americans still think so – citing his middle name Hussein. Is he foreign-born, thus ineligible to be president? Twenty percent of Americans think that too, even though his Hawaii birth certificate has graced the Internet for over two years. Foreign, black and maybe Muslim? Well, he is black, but the rest is nonsense.

The United States has far fewer Muslims per capita than France, Germany, Great Britain, Spain or Canada. See Muslims as a percentage of total population: Canada (2%) France (6%); Germany (4%); Spain (1%). In other European countries developing anti-immigrant parties: Holland (5.7%), Denmark (2%); Sweden 2%). Anti-Muslim feeling exists in all these countries.

The percentage of Muslims in the total U.S. population? An "unscary" 0.8%. But for all the reasons given above, Muslims and other Americans plainly aren't yet comfortable with each other. And they probably won't be for some time. Besides the trauma of 9/11 which affected all Americans, hundreds of thousands of returning U.S. troops are bringing memories of being blown up or shot at by Muslims. Many U.S. Muslims find it understandable that foreign Muslims attack 'occupiers,' even though these soldiers are their American compatriots. The point is, as from Vietnam, the battlefield's psychological poison will continue for decades to seep into the American mentality. Much of this, again from Vietnam, will haunt U.S. veterans as the aftershocks of PTSD – Post-Traumatic Stress Disorder. This terrifying pathology will continue for decades, quite unfairly linking Muslims to shattered dreams, broken families, and suicides.

Meanwhile, even long-established American Muslims feel humiliated by social exclusion, airport profiling, and anti-mosque protests – New York's Ground Zero being the sum of both sides' self-images and anguishes. "Sacred ground" there confronted "freedom of religion." Examples of mutual misunderstanding abound already, and there will be many more. Even when peace seems to reign, prejudice lurks just below the surface. The well-publicized case of Dr. Mansoor Mirza of Sheboygan Country, Wisconsin, gives the flavor. Many of the same patients who revered Dr. Mirza as a doctor screamed vicious insults at him about Islam at a public meeting about a new local mosque. [285]

Can all this change? Of course – as it has changed with every other once-'exotic' ethnic, cultural or religious group entering America. But rarely has a single decade of terror and war so shocked mainstream Americans – associating fairly or unfairly a whole category of relatively recent arrivals with "anti-Americanism." The assimilation of Muslims into mainstream America will take longer than for the Jews, Germans, Irish and Hispanics. But much less time than the centuries of slavery that oppressed blacks. Not to mention native peoples still on the fringes, who continue to await admittance through America's front-door.

The key in all cases of prejudice? Remember this almost automatic equation: ignorance leads to fear, and fear leads to hostility. With Muslims, America – and virtually all Western countries – still linger between ignorance and fear, but with anti-immigrant hostility fast growing in Europe.

This is not all the fault of long-established Christians and Jews. When you see paragons of tolerance such as Holland, Denmark and Sweden dipping into anti-immigration anger, you have to ask: Is this because the Dutch, Danes and Swedes have suddenly become vile racists? Or have a few too many Muslim immigrants abused their hosts' hospitality by rejecting local values, culture and traditions, maybe cheating at social welfare through polygamy, and imposing the subjection of women?

Why do some Muslims insist on *hijabs* or slit-eyed *niqabs*, the torture of genital mutilation, and even murder of women (grotesquely called "honor killings")? Muslim apologists often

---

[285] Bobby Ghosh, *Ibid.*

shift the blame for such crimes or affronts to "ancient cultures, not Islam." But when only Muslim, or mainly Muslim, countries practice such horrors, are these denials credible?

The Dutch saw a daring anti-Muslim film-maker Theo Van Gogh stabbed to death in the streets of Amsterdam. They saw a brave Somali immigrant, Ayaan Hirsi Ali, hounded out of the country by death threats. Happily, a few young Dutch Muslims condemned these crimes. But a new atmosphere of terror colors Dutch-Muslim relations. In Denmark, Islamic thugs still plot to murder a cartoonist who in 2005 drew some cartoons they judged sacrilegious. Brave Danes have stood up for him – saying, in effect, that "multicultural tolerance" does not give anybody a license to kill.

In the U.S., with its tiny percentage of Muslims, such horrifying individual murders are rare. But many remember that in February 1993, even before 9/11, Muslim extremists tried to blow up the World Trade Center. And today, hardly a month goes by without hints or evidence of Islamic terror on U.S. soil.

Before tarring all Americans with the racist brush, Muslims should recall that after both 1993 and 2001 World Trade Center outrages, America *reached out* to Muslims – imperfectly, no doubt, but clearly. They didn't mobilize hysterical crowds screaming "death to Muslims!" They tried to understand, yet pursue justice through the courts. Immediately after 9/11, George W. Bush tried to dampen anti-Muslim hysteria by saying "Islam is a religion of peace," and visiting a mosque. His Cabinet colleagues routinely made similar statements to reassure Muslims.

One struggles to imagine a Muslim country where, if Christians were the terrorists, such generosity would be thought normal. Egyptian Muslims have defended Coptic victims of other Muslims; commendable, but that's not quite like forgiving Copts for being perpetrators.

The last half-century has seen unprecedented Muslim immigration into Western countries. We are living through a fast telescoping of experience in which, for the first time ever, Muslims, Christians and Jews are living in stable, quite tolerant societies. (Old Muslim Andalusia made a good try for the time). But all will need time to adapt. There will be slip-ups and setbacks, mistakes and misunderstandings. But the die is cast: In the West, we must all live together, one way or another. With luck, perhaps something like the 1992 cry of Rodney King for black-white reconciliation will echo in our minds. After a brutal beating by white Los Angeles police, Mr. King tried to stop a black backlash with the simple, plaintive words: "Can we all get along?"

In "non-traditional" immigration, there are three sources of prejudice. The first flows from plain, ancestral host-country prejudice. This can fade with good laws, good teaching, good friends and good intermarriages. The second source is host-countries' too-accommodating welcomes (think Holland) that lead to local citizens' resentment, in turn earning them immigrants' too-prompt accusations of "racism." The third, happily rarer, source, comes from immigrant-origin citizens aggressively affronting local culture and abusing social protections. In France, the Western nation with the most Muslims per capita, North Africans' booing of the *Marseillaise* at soccer games and polygamous social-benefit scams have badly scarred intercultural relations.

Welcoming cultures owe basic courtesy to their new compatriots. The latter, remembering how eager and grateful they once were to come, owe respect and loyalty to their chosen land. Both groups need to work to make the transition easier. Common sense? Of course. But how common is common sense? This, even more than tolerance, inter-faith and intercultural dialogue, is what could best speed two-way integration of Muslims into America's mainstream.

America has always swallowed up, then embraced, its newcomers. It can do so again with Muslims. But success will demand national and local leadership – by responsible Muslims and others. It will require media, schools, and churches, synagogues and mosques to stretch imaginations. This will take a generation or even two. But it must be seen to be happening, even as much deeper and wider changes take place.

Can the U.S. military assist Muslim integration by welcoming more Muslim recruits? A military melting-pot is an attractive idea. But in the current state of inter-faith unease in the U.S., and with isolated violent incidents, it's a tricky option. Muslim-Americans will want the military to adapt to Muslims in ways that will test goodwill, and even trust. But one shudders to recall the Fort Hood murders leading to the arrest of Major Nidal Malik Hasan. A few scattered cases of Afghan soldiers turning their weapons on U.S. and British comrades raised fears too. Islam in the Army will not be a quick or easy accommodation. But it must happen, to clear the air for broader, non-military, collaboration.

All of the above "impossible-but-indispensable" changes could help lay groundwork for a more stable world. A world where Islam and the U.S. (with its allies) might focus on improving life for hundreds of millions of people now held back by unholy war between Islam and the West. A war arguably aggravated by the U.S. passion to seek massive military solutions – so often a source of tragic backlash.

What deeper, non-military changes America might invest in? Why and how might these work? And who might inspire and direct them? Most of all, can new "smart options" or "soft options" constitute – more than massed armies – a more effective contribution to America's "national defense?" The few examples to follow may give some idea.

Common sense is the most widely shared thing in the world... because everybody thinks he possesses it so richly - Molière

You can't cross the sea merely by standing and staring at the water - Rabindranath Tagore

Chapter Eight/

MAYBE COMMON SENSE AS POLICY?

Lesson from the mess the U.S. left behind in Iraq: America's armies can't make Muslim countries stable, "free" and prosperous. As Gorbachev reflected on the Soviets in Afghanistan, foreign armies do exactly the opposite. So what's the secret of a more stable world? Just faster development of free markets?

Free markets are vital, but not enough. They're rough-and-ready remedies that allow a lot of short-term pain for long-term gain. China's dazzling economic success rests on dictatorship, trampled human rights, muzzled media, hit-and-miss health care, a brutal prison system, corruption (bribes, building-code and baby-food scandals) and a mountain of capital-punishment corpses. The spectacular stories of the other fast-development, Big Four "BRIC" nations – Brazil, Russia and India, as well as China – all provide overreaching ironies.

Even with recent neighborhood police reforms, Brazil may need decades to fix its miserable, crime-infested *favelas*. Its airport infrastructure is a mess before the upcoming World Cup. And its native peoples simply remain excluded from society. Russia still faces rampant alcoholism, plummeting longevity, horrific violence, omnipresent corruption, phony justice, and grossly-neglected basic services (e.g. 2010's untamed summer fires). Software giant India bumps along on appalling roads and railways, and allows hundreds of millions to starve while corrupt warehouse-owners hoard food surpluses. It blew $39 billion in a cell-phone license scandal while vital food subsidies faltered. Since all's well that ends well, let's not dwell on India's

October 2010 near-miss fiasco in organizing the Commonwealth Games.

Yet all four BRIC countries, against reason and morality, are running obscene military budgets. They all squander money that should go to their nation's health, education and infrastructure. Part of the reason for such wasteful military spending is that the United States sets an irrational, inflated standard for it. The U.S. also pump-primes its defense industries with high-tech weapons exports that most smaller nations don't need. The Russians, French, British, Chinese and even Israelis also export arms. But arms don't build anything. Sometimes they offer a vague "security" – but in reality, they heighten neighbors' paranoia and cause arms races.

Smarter-than-"Strong" Defense: Resist and Reconcile

Are there better ways to ensure "security?." Half a dozen well-chosen non-military contributions could ensure U.S. security far better than what is now basically an all-military approach. USAID's programs can be very good, though they tend to favor pilot projects, not transformative, long-term reforms. Or they promote U.S. "commerce" – such as exporting subsidized wheat or cotton surpluses that then undercut competitors in poorer countries. [286] Truly transformative reforms look to the long haul. Instead of sending soldiers or bureaucrats, they send citizens with a built-in "multiplier effect" – that is, they train trainers, or at least their own replacements.

The following non-military proposals aim to show that ideas, in the end, are infinitely more powerful than arms. Why? Arms can only force people temporarily to do things they don't want to do; but ideas can "get people to do things" voluntarily, cheerfully and permanently. Good things instead of bad things. Good things that families, children, women and men actually *need*. Such "soft options" aim to treat human beings as more

---

[286] This "farm income stabilization" costs the U.S. roughly $20 billion a year – $3 billion for cotton alone. See: L.D. Jackson, "The Shame of U.S. cotton subsidies," *Political Realities* website, November 9, 2010.

than "collateral damage" of war. People's happiness – not the comfort of legal constructions called "states" – should be the central purpose of peace, and of life itself. Didn't somebody's Declaration of Independence talk of "life, liberty and the pursuit of happiness?" Politicians and their allies who ignore these goals are guilty of dereliction of duty.

"Soft" options, by the way, do not reflect soft-in-the-head thinking. On the contrary. They are the hardest of the most-hard-headed options. For when combined with a robust, "low-boot-print" counter-terrorist defense with small, elite overseas forces, they can complete a perfect defense-serving "resist-and-reconcile" strategy. That is, a policy of combating terrorists while helping ordinary people build fulfilling lives. This two-track approach can both deal expediently with the "alligators" (terrorists) and drain the "swamp" of bad education, unemployment and lethargy that supports them. It aims to defeat fanatics' tactical assaults; but strategically, it aims to build deep solidarities with the alienated millions of mainstream Muslims.

This is not a new strategy. It's what the U.S. used during the Cold War: George Kennan's (and Harry Truman's) military, economic and counter-espionage "containment" of Soviet power. This entailed a huge range of hearts-and-minds peace-building activities. Examples? The Marshall Plan for European recovery, the foreign-student Fulbright scholarships, the multilingual *Voice of America*. Joseph S. Nye, Jr., a former assistant secretary of defense, deplored in a 2004 *Foreign Affairs* article that George W. Bush's America had only kept the military side, while ignoring, even ridiculing, the peace-building side. "The Bush administration may dismiss the relevance of soft power," said Nye in his summary, "but it does so at great peril. Success in the war on terrorism depends on Washington's capacity to persuade others without force, and that capacity is in dangerous decline." [287] This ability to attract individuals – and nations – depended, and still depends, solely on the spectrum of people-helping activities coming under "soft power."

---

287 Joseph S. Nye, Jr., "The Decline of America's Soft Power," *Foreign Affairs*, May/June 2004.

"Strong national defense" is surely "smart defense." And "smart" implies a duty to seek solutions that work – not comforting incantations that suffocate innovative thinking. Smart defense solutions end or prevent conflict; they don't provoke, celebrate or perpetuate it. On Afghanistan's 2011 "draw-down" horizon may loom a battle royal between the White House and the U.S. Afghan field commander, General David Petraeus. It pits Obama's political wish for a "steep and deep" draw-down, aiming for the exit before his 2012 re-election bid, against Petraeus's "small and shallow" troop reduction, allowing an open-ended war.

But before caricaturing Petraeus as merely a big-army, corporatist warmonger, take a glance at his November 2010 reading-list, obtained by *Boston Globe* columnist H.D.S. Greenway. In addition to books on Afghanistan's cultural and political history, *Mujahideen* tactics against the Soviets, and Winston Churchill's classic *The Malakand Field Force*, it includes – the softest of soft options! – Greg Mortenson's *Three Cups of Tea*: on building girls' schools in Taliban territory.[288] Just the right mix for "resist-and-reconcile?"

Education: It's All in the Mind, Heart... and Jobs

Cutting to the quick: The single most effective weapon against terrorism is education. Useful, mind-opening education that encourages curiosity and sound values, including tolerance. Already hundreds of thousands of Pakistani boys attend those Saudi-inspired and – funded Wahhabi *madrassa* schools we have often mentioned. They emerge with a world vision that is not only shockingly limited, but extremely bigoted. Many will emerge as fodder for the next generation of bin Ladens.

If you look at where Muslim terrorists come from, it's often from Islamic schooling totally ill-adapted to securing jobs for its graduates. Instead, such schools program graduates for unemployment, dependency, resentment, social frustration, and

---

288 H.D.S. Greenaway, "The Reader of Kabul," *Boston Globe*, November 8, 2010.

bitterness. This pattern exists in many Muslim countries where extreme Islamic education prevails.

Indeed – and one should not underestimate the power of this – such economically useless schooling condemns many young men to years of sexual frustration. To marry, young Muslim men must usually be able to support a bride, starting with a house. The social cost of being denied family fulfillment is deep humiliation, an affront to manhood. But the physiological cost for vigorous young men is downright explosive. If ever Western decision-makers could overcome their misplaced embarrassment about the subject, they might discover this: sexual frustration (physical and psychological) may be a key reason why jihadist Islam finds no trouble recruiting suicide bombers.

Two thousand years ago, St. Paul said that "it is better to marry than to burn." In the context of today's Muslim terrorism, his often-mocked wisdom rings true. Not as the *only* reason for terrorism, of course. But as an important factor.

Terrorism, poverty, economic stagnation, blighted social, family and sexual lives – these are some of the "secret" costs of poor or irrelevant education. The West needs to wake up to them. Working with Muslim governments, it needs to make enormous, very long-term investments in modern schools that lead to good jobs. Such a change in priorities wouldn't weaken U.S. "defense." On the contrary, it would strengthen it. By transferring funding from military overkill to useful education, it could enhance *real* U.S. defense – through a long-term reduction in terrorist temptations.

In the very long run, yes, but the long run starts now. And to secure long-run solutions, of course, you sometimes need to secure the short run militarily – to counter terrorists today. But unless America and its allies make a huge effort now to drain the pool of new terrorists, these will keep coming, and keep multiplying.

Once again: Opponents of such long-term investments in non-military security will quote the old saw: "How can you empty the swamp when you're up to your elbows (or thereabouts) in alligators?" That's why a two-faceted approach makes sense: a) continue a robust, short-term military effort to keep terrorists at bay; but b) start, as of now, making the violent jihadist option less attractive to young boys not yet of insurgent age. We should divert youth from 'education' that teaches them only how to become a martyr in the next world. We need to give them tools to find employment, family and identity in *this* world.

Such a diversion need not take religion out of their lives. It should merely ensure that obsession with backward-looking, nihilistic religion doesn't cripple their lives. As in advanced countries, a reasonable religious education could exist in parallel with modern, jobs-preparing education.

A realistic model may be Turkish. The government of Prime Minister Recep Tayyip Erdoğan's moderate-Islamic Justice and Development Party (AKP) has developed a compromise: a religious-secular curriculum called *imam-hatip* (religious vocational schools). Ankara teaches this curriculum to over 100,000 pupils in over 500 schools. It allows girls as well as boys to attend. These hybrid schools offer a decent modern education. But they also allow a significant amount of religious and ethical instruction. Roughly 40 percent of classroom time goes to religion, Islamic law and Arabic; and 60 percent goes to mathematics, science and literature. Compare this with the Wahhabi-type *madrassas* where the Koran, Islamic law and Arabic take up 90-100 percent of class time.

Both passionate Islamists and dogmatic secularists criticize the *imam-hatip* system. Many Islamists want more Islam; secularists deplore any preaching. But *imam-hatip's* hybrid nature seems to ensure that it contains, even soothes, these ideological tensions. Paradoxically, the system works well for many faith-leaning students *because* of Turkey's powerful secular tradition.[289] It smoothly combines private religion with public secularism.

Observers suggest that this relatively open-minded secular tradition – established by the republic's founder, Kemal

---

[289] For a fuller analysis of this phenomenon, see a fine article from which much of this is drawn: Nichole Sobecki, "Muslim world turns to Turkish model of education," *Global Post*, August 12, 2010.

Atatürk, and long guaranteed by the army – is precisely why *imam-hatip* schools can operate in Turkey. Turkish Islam is not Iranian or Saudi Islam, where the state is a theocracy. It's not Afghan or Pakistani Islam, where obscurantism and sectarianism plague believers. But it is Islam. It represents a pragmatic balance which evolves, one way or the other, with political and social currents. By definition, it *seeks balance* – which the Wahhabi *madrassas* do not.

Several Muslim nations have looked into the Turkish model. Many find it a tempting experiment in educating young Muslims, while curbing extremism. Among foreign admirers: both Afghan and Pakistani education ministers. On February 1, 2010, they signed a cooperation agreement with Turkey on "modernization of Islamic education." Several other nations have come to study the Turkish model, and suggest they may try it – precisely to curb more extreme religious models. Among major new fans: Russia and Bulgaria. One Turkish school – Kayseri's Mustafa Gerimli *imam-hatip* School – has offered multinational classes to 325 youths from Afghanistan, Albania, Azerbaijan, Bosnia, Georgia, Kazakhstan, Kosovo, Kyrgyzstan, Macedonia, Romania, Serbia, Thailand and Ukraine.

All these nations face a similar challenge, though to often very different degrees: how to accommodate a 'moderate-Islamic' education with 'pragmatic-secular' teaching. No doubt, each test country will wish to adapt the Turkish hybrid system to its own specific history, culture and needs. But the seed-idea is compromise: neither all-religious nor all-secular. Westerners, with very different histories and realities, might not love this hybrid idea – because it includes 'unfamiliar-thus-scary' Islam. But the model attracts many governments and pedagogues in Muslim countries. It attracts them exactly because it seems a sensible, forward-looking approach. A way to be both Muslim and modern.

The key, as with all education systems, is teachers and textbooks. The books are the easy part. Many exist already, at least for 'pragmatic' subjects such as math and science. Possibly some countries may be able to adapt and translate the Turkish textbooks. But training teachers, principals and education directors will take much longer. For that requires changing minds, not texts.

Suggestion: If the West wants to encourage such (it seems) extremism-curbing hybrid models, why not ask Turkey to coordinate the effort worldwide? Why not fund a network of joint Turkish-local-country teacher-training schools with one or two billion dollars diverted from arms purchases? The payoff in terms of real education, democracy, development, and even security could be astounding. Might some of 2011's newly-sobered petro-kingdoms also be persuaded to chip in?

The West should obviously avoid direct involvement in curriculum, even while assessing whether such a system is really beneficial to Western ideals. Meddling in content – especially religious – would plainly be the kiss of death. It would outrage both Muslims and secular patriots. The simple goal here would be to "replace Saudi Arabia with Turkey." Or at least to *compete* with Saudi Arabia's dangerous, deadening Wahhabi doctrines. If the Saudis don't like it put that bluntly, then remind them of what their *madrassa* graduates have done, are doing, and might still do. For example, with Pakistan's "Islamic" A-bomb.

According to Istanbul's *Hürriyet Daily News* of February 1, 2010, picked up by Karachi's *Dawn*, Afghan Education Minister Frarooq Wardak said "I visited a few *imam-hatip* schools in Ankara and saw that they give a balanced education there... I have asked Turkish officials to establish some *imam-hatip* schools in Afghanistan. Learning from their experiences, we will be able to achieve a balance in our own Islamic education system... We would very much like to use Turkey's experience in overcoming gender disparity in education. We have requested that they establish some girls' schools in Afghanistan." [290]

Citing again Nichole Sobecki's article in *GlobalPost*: "Through education you are, in one form or another, controlling the political socialization of the upcoming generation," said Iren Ozgur, a Turkish-American academic at New York University who has studied Turkey's *imam-hatip* system... If they can find a way to

---
290 *Dawn*, Karachi, February 1, 2010.

transfer the fundamentals of these schools, then in effect Turkey would be helping to spread a form of Islam that is more liberal and moderate across the Middle East." [291]

Pakistan may have too many other problems to make decisive, long-term Turkish-style education reforms. It groans under burdens of heart-wrenching poverty, illiteracy, corruption, a shaky democracy, the threat of A-bomb insecurity, flood-damaged infrastructure, tension with India over Jammu-Kashmir, a restless military, American pressures, and out-of-control terrorism. But even to survive, it has to undertake education reforms. That over 60 years after independence Pakistan still can't manage to produce a modern Muslim society is a scandal.

Critics of long-term approaches love to dismiss starting action now with the old alligator-and-swamp tale. But if you don't start draining the terrorist-fomenting swamp at least part of the time, you're condemning yourself to several lifetimes of draining swamps. To eternal war. Meanwhile, the alligators will get you for sure.

Opening and enriching minds is the very hallmark of civilization. Education must be the paramount contribution that societies, including the West's, can make to a more peaceful world. We don't have to design or run the education model. But we can fund it.

In 2009, the world, "led" by America's largely unchallenged Pentagon spending, spent over $1.5-*trillion* on "defense." [292] Worldwide spending on education that same year came to roughly $1.7-trillion. [293] Very roughly the same amount. U.S., Chinese, Pakistani and Indian defense budgets, among others, continue to project growth. All should be ashamed.

Spending so much on guns, instead of more on teachers, pupils and schoolbooks, is not just immoral. It's crazy and self-defeating. It's lousy "national defense." For it guarantees perpetual conflict. The Romans were wrong to say: "If you want peace, prepare for war." Mankind's experience says: "If you want war, prepare for war." And yet, in Washington, partisans

---

291 Sobecki, *GlobalPost*.
292 Source: Stockholm International Peace Research Institute (SIPRI).
293 Source: UNESCO Institute for Statistics.

of big-bucks, *military* "strong defense" – always stronger than anybody else's, always growing – inevitably get their wish. And they will. Especially if, by ignoring education, and sending big armies and careless drones to provoke Muslims, they invite Wahhabi *madrassas* to 'educate' the other side, their graduates blowing up civilians, soldiers – and cities? – for decades to come.

Public education in both Pakistan and Afghanistan is in an indescribable mess. Less than two-thirds of Pakistani children finish *elementary* school. Less than three percent get to university. Only 12.6 percent of Afghan girls over 15 can read or write.

The Turkish model may not be a cure-all. But it's about the most promising approach on offer. The U.S. and the West should support it massively. Then get out of the way and let the Turks and other Muslims make it work.

Find Peace Through Culture, Not Technology

A last suggestion for education: Don't neglect either liberal arts, such as literature and philosophy, or the cultural arts, especially music. The West's broader education, favoring curiosity and exploration, pits critical thinking against infallible authority. The arts, by favoring personal expression either alone or in groups, are known to promote a gentler, more supple outlook on the world.

A number of new studies, moreover, have shown a disturbing link between a purely scientific or technical background and an attraction to terrorism. [294] Of course, you can argue that often complex terrorist operations require some technical knowledge, and that this may draw recruiters to such candidates.

But there's also a cause-and-effect way of viewing the tech-terrorist phenomenon: Do prior, purely technical studies in fact shape rigid, "black-or-white" mentalities prone to terrorism? Check the biographies of all the 9/11 attackers, and you'll be shocked: nearly every one had culturally limited, mainly

---

294 John Allemang, "Can the liberal arts cure jihadists?" *Globe and Mail*, Toronto, September 3, 2010. Allemang credits Martha Nussbaum in her book *Not for Profit* for exploring this hypothesis.

technological backgrounds. Start with the leaders of *al-Qaeda*: Osama bin Laden was a civil engineer; his no. 2, Dr. Ayman Muhammad Rabaie al-Zawahiri, was a surgeon; 9/11 mastermind Khalid Sheikh Muhammad was a mechanical engineer; Mohamed Atta, who crashed the Boeing 767 of American Airlines Flight 11 into the North Tower, was an architect specializing in high-rise buildings; Hani Hanjour, who crashed American Airlines Flight 77 into the Pentagon, was a wanna-be pilot. The most dangerous recruiter of English-language jihadists in 2010 was Yemen-based, American-born Anwar al-Alawki – a civil engineer.

None of these terrorists studied in any formal way the great works of world literature and philosophy – the works that teach right from wrong, diverse cultural contexts, psychological complexity, human solidarity, and universal values. Or the freedom of the individual to question authority. None is known to have had an artistic dimension. All they had was technology and a narrow, dogmatic reading of the Holy Koran.

In any reformed system – like the Turkish – teachers must teach curiosity and questioning. They must teach some version of what the West calls "liberal arts" or (the distinction is often moot) "humanities." These are disciplines that study and teach critical thinking, our common humanity, and a tolerance for dissent, difference, diversity and debate. Literature, philosophy, and world cultures and history are foundations of this approach. Many argue that such "humanistic" studies incidentally teach sympathy, mercy, loyalty and trust. The Koran teaches some of that. But in more fundamentalist countries, it does so within a system that all too often (as with some Western religious groups) prefers legalism to love. One likes to think that teaching the humanities, and drawing heavily on many world sources, might even bring believers closer to the core of Islam.

The "cultural" arts? Drawing, painting and sculpture help children and youth express emotions they might not otherwise discover. These arts can also, above all, inspire them with a sense of beauty in a violent, ugly and cynical world. Film and film studies can deepen understanding of the human heart, and open minds powerfully to other cultures, religions, emotions, and ways of seeing the world. A Sorbonne medical professor once made Plato obligatory reading in first year – he wanted students to understand human beings, not just human bodies. In the same vein, a University of Toronto political science professor made Erich Maria Remarque's novel *The Black Obelisk* essential reading. Why? To teach how the anguish of civilized societies under severe economic stress can dissolve into brutal dictatorships. Weimar Germany's hyper-inflation, among other factors, led straight to Hitler.

Music may be the most healing of all the arts. It is the most deeply embedded in the human brain: in patients losing their minds to Alzheimer's Disease, memories of music are the last thing to flee.[295] Many countries' schools recognize the fundamental, irreplaceable value of music: Russia and North America are among the leaders. But South America may offer the best model. Venezuela's musical-education *El Sistema* trains hundreds of thousands of children a year in classical music. The entire country plays or sings. *El Sistma* emerged from the brain of José Antonio Abreu's work with his Social Action for Music program. Abreu believed that collaboration to create beauty made the symphony orchestra the ideal model for human harmony. One graduate of *El Sistema*, Gustavo Dudamel, became conductor of the Los Angeles Philharmonic at age 28.

This Western model need not deter other cultures: many of today's finest 'Western" classical musicians are Chinese, Japanese, Korean or Indian. They could equally well be Iraqi, Egyptian or Jordanian – as Daniel Barenboim and Edward Said demonstrated brilliantly with their West-Eastern Divan Orchestra. If one were to take a single model for arts-and-beauty education – and as an education in brotherhood and peace – this Middle-East but world-embracing Barenboim-Said orchestra might be the very best. It teaches mutual respect,

---

295 See Vanessa Dylyn's 2009 prize-winning documentary *The Musical Brain*. This stars the singer Sting, and is based on a book by McGill University Professor Daniel J.Levitin, *This is Your Brain on Music: The Science of a Human Obsession*, Plume (Penguin Group), 2007.

collaboration, and joyful harmony. Is there a better definition of a peaceful world?

Education must touch the heart as well as the mind. Children, especially in conflict-ridden countries, struggle to understand the world. And to communicate with it. Giving them intellectual tools is excellent. Giving them artistic means to express their emotions, sense of beauty, and yearning for human solidarity can teach them to feel – not just alive, but part of mankind.

Taking Care of Business:
Open Markets, Micro-credit, Training

Which tools of economic development directly help impoverished populations? Which ones leave most freedom for local and individual initiative? These are undoubtedly freer markets, micro-credit, and small-business training. These three are "soft," "smart," alternative-to-military options into which America should put lots of imagination, will-power, money – and in some cases, know-how. They should be trademarks, even foundations, of American foreign policy. Of American *defense* policy.

Take note: Although the West peddles propaganda about free trade and open markets, it rarely practices what it preaches. Both the U.S. and Europe (thanks mainly to France and Germany) block agricultural imports from developing nations. And almost all nations – never having read David Ricardo on "comparative advantage" – still discourage foreign imports or investments that 'threaten' their pet industries. France did so with trains (Canada's Bombardier and Germany's Siemens vs. France's Alstom). Even with its "crown-jewel" *Danone* yogurt! It may soon try to keep cosmetics (*L'Oréal*) from those plain-faced Swiss.

The U.S. played block-the-foreigners in February 2011 with a $35-billion U.S. Air Force tanker aircraft, 'adjusting' (claimed the losers) tenders for Boeing against Europe's EADS. Some economic chauvinists try to hide their vote-grubbing game by baptizing industries they want to save as "national champions."

From the preceding paragraph, you may have guessed at one specialist of this rooster-crowing: French President Nicolas Sarkozy. He mouths free-market slogans in Brussels for the European Commission, then shouts them down in Paris. But everybody plays the "champion" or "home-jobs" game. "Sarko just does it with more shameless panache.

The heart of this debate – and its link to Islam and world peace – is markets for Asian and African textiles, clothes, commodities and agricultural products. Even though giving lip-service to welcoming these, the U.S. sabotages liberalization. First, on textiles and clothing, it drags in U.S. labor standards that have next-to-zero pertinence in most Muslim countries. Most of these nations are at radically lower stages of development than the U.S. And as much as one should stop the worst of the sweat-shops, many of these (including for children, alas) are all that stand between workers' survival and death. As we saw on commodities and other agricultural products, raw, brutal protection for U.S. (and some other Western) markets are the norm. In both cases, the basic U.S. crime is hypocrisy. Forcing Bangladeshi and Pakistani cotton and clothing exporters to raise their prices is just an automatic, if indirect, subsidy to Texas, Mississippi and Arkansas.

To make matters worse, the U.S. government subsidizes exports of peanuts and many other farm products. The Third World needs desperately to sell these, as well as coffee and sugar, to create jobs for its peoples. Remember that key reason why Islamists can seduce young Muslims? Lack of jobs. But U.S. politicians tremble to take an electorally perilous stance in favor of the desperate, legitimate needs of poorer nations. These are needs readily open to satisfaction. But only if the U.S. actually *practices* the free-market dogmas it rents its unionized garments over.

Note that the very countries where wide-open textile, clothing and agricultural markets could create stabilizing jobs are the very Muslim countries where the U.S. faces mortal danger. Unstable, nuclear-armed, *al-Qaeda*-infested Pakistan is the main one.

The U.S. has a free trade agreement with Israel. It also has one with the West Bank Palestinians. But Gaza remains blockaded. Unemployed young men there now have little or no hope of a career, or even marriage. Can we not imagine what barring imports (thus jobs) does to the dignity and hopes of these young men, and their women? Can't we remember what their despairing alternatives already are? If Israel and America dislike Hamas (which Israel originally helped create, to counter the Palestine Liberation Organization), it's time to think again. The most certain, indeed insidious, way to undermine Hamas extremists would be to help improve the entire Palestinian, including Gazan, economy.

Micro-credit – when prudently regulated – is probably the single, most liberating economic tool ever invented for stagnant, impoverished and unstable countries. It can be a decisive tool for spurring entrepreneurship among the poor and powerless. Jonathan Swift spoke of very small loans to help launch the 18th-century Irish Loans Funds. The Marshall Plan dabbled with them. But in our time, the hero of the worldwide micro-credit play is a farsighted Bangladeshi called Muhamad Yunus. His Grameen Bank has become the model for a worldwide system of small loans to motivated-but-penniless small business persons. He and his bank received the Nobel Peace Prize with this citation: "for their efforts to create economic and social development from below."

Below, in most poor countries, especially means women – of which more shortly. Unfortunately, micro-credit seems to work almost everywhere in the world except the U.S. Cultural, political and financial particularities seem to get in the way. The same applies to cooperatives, of which the Yunus model is a variation. Yet micro-credit, in spite of Koranic strictures against loan interest (called usury) works on a huge scale in Bangladesh, a Muslim country.

To spread micro-credit's benefits much further in Muslim and Third World economies, the U.S. should not try to impose an American model of lending to entrepreneurs. It should simply consider supporting in any way it can experienced, ethical micro-credit experts such as Dr. Yunus. More reasons why come in our next chapter – on the vital peace-promoting role of women. [296]

Small business training – on how to start and run a successful business – is the third lever to get poor people on their feet. This is definitely a U.S. specialty. It should, with adaptations to local cultures, become a central American contribution. It can offer vehicles for personal independence to millions of dangerously unemployed youth. "National defense" again?

Imagine the positive impact on Muslim unemployment of these three changes – freer trade, micro-credit, and small-business education. Just to create a "nation of shop-keepers?" That's how Napoleon dismissed England before it invented the Industrial Revolution. With practical, "little-people" policies, you could put millions of angry young men (and women) on their feet and into business. And thousands of *al-Qaeda* recruiters out of business.

The West is supposed to be good at free enterprise. Why then doesn't it help implant it on a huge scale where it could do world-changing good? Where it could help solve the cruelest problems for overseas Muslims, while creating prosperous, likely more accepting, new partners? 'Taking care of business' with Muslim peoples is just pursuing U.S. "national security" by other means. Softer, smarter – far, far cheaper – means.

Getting the Message: Media To Excite and Reconcile

Another thing the West thinks it's good at: developing and using media. Developing, for sure: radio, TV, the Internet, e-mail,

---

[296] Like traditional bank lending, however, sound micro-credit requires reasonable regulation to avoid abusive interest rates and excessive defaults. See Lydia Polgreen and Vikas Bajaj, "India Micro-credit Faces Collapse From Defaults," *New York Times*, November 17, 2010. See also widespread abuse in the Indian state of Andhra Pradesh, but also the wealth-creating benefits of "microfinance institutions" (MFIs): See "Overcharging, micro-lending is under attack, unfairly," *The Economist*, November 17, 2010. In 2010–11, Dr. Yunus also ran into serious trouble over an accounting issue discovered, then forgiven, by his Norwegian donor. According to several international allies, jealous enemies at home, especially the prime minister, used this and other pretexts for attacking his Grameen Bank to settle political accounts (see "Haro sur le 'banquier des pauvres,'" *Le Monde*, Febuary 3, 2011.)

Facebook, Twitter instant messages (SMSs), Skype video – and who knows what next week will bring? But using media intelligently to present Western ideas and values to the world? Using them to initiate dialogue with Muslims worldwide?

Apart from a small percentage of good, excellent, even sublime cultural "products" (usually on a pay-extra basis), the U.S. and the West have offered the world a stew of shock and shlock: violence, pornography, and an ocean of trivia such as game shows, phony "reality shows," emotionally exploitative talk shows, money-grubbing "evangelical" shows, gambling shows, bikini or wrestling gawk-shows, crime-and-scandal "news" shows. It's probably safer not to ridicule afternoon soap-operas. The mothers and housewives lobby is just too intimidating. But overall, the ratio between awful and tolerable media offerings runs at about 90 percent ghastly to 10 percent decent. And that's if you're not too big a snob. You can cite a handful of fine exceptions, but basically, TV is still Newton N. Minow's 1961 "vast wasteland."

Using media to speak to overseas Muslims in local languages is a good idea. But it's hugely tricky. The original BBC mandate is not a bad guide: inform, educate, entertain. Each of those three goals has its limitations. In the end, education and entertainment are probably more reliable than politically-slanted news.

Inform? An array of Arabic and Muslim networks and stations now brings world news to the Muslim world. Most of these subscribe to Western news services such as Associated Press, ITN (television packages), Reuters, BBC, *Agence France-Presse* and *Deutsche Welle*. *Al Jazeera* English has successfully launched a worldwide TV network competing with *BBC World*, *CNN* and later-arrival *France 24*. But American international broadcasting efforts, apart from heavily financial *MSBC*, are not as influential as before. At least at the start, they served too much propaganda of the America-the-Beautiful kind. *Voice of America*'s previous fine Arabic service ended up, by a frivolous decision, being drowned in the pop-music and snappy news briefs of Arab-language *Radio Sawa*.

For the past 15 years or so, a rich new academic field of "media, conflict, peace and security" has developed in several countries: Costa Rica, Scandinavia, Britain, Canada, the U.S., South Korea and a few others. Specialists there produce books, articles, curricula and colloquia. Core idea, in *The Economist*'s succinct question: "Is a broadcast worth a brigade?" [297] Can responsible journalism favor peace better than armed force? This field can offer many insights, but few dogmas. Its practitioners believe the self-evident fact that news media exert a powerful influence on issues of war and peace. But they can't agree on *exactly how* truth-seeking journalists should draw lines between honest coverage and propaganda. Selecting stories, framing them, illustrating them, editing them, and interpreting them all present choices. Thus opportunities for shaping perceptions. The best, if unscientific, approach to fair coverage seems to be to hire skilled, conscientious professional editors and reporters.

To help Muslim media thrive, Western institutions already offer scholarships and exchange programs to overseas journalists. The highly reputable Medill Journalism School of Northwestern University now runs a strong academic and "learn-by-doing" program in Qatar. Foundations can and do financially support start-up media likely to lean toward tolerance and compromise. Ideally, scholarships should come from independent foundations, not directly from governments. But Washington could offer generous tax breaks to steer such funds to journalists. A current problem: Most of America's great media-backing foundations (remember Freedom Forum's Newseum mistake) have gone parochial: help for internationally-minded journalists is slim.

One excellent example of a multicultural experiment, too-soon abandoned, was Sarajevo's Open Broadcast Network – originally funded by George Soros. A U.S. military representative voted to stop funding to this valuable vehicle for a tolerant peace. Not needed to end the war in people's minds? The October 2010 elections in Bosnia-Herzegovina ended in a more

---

297 "Is a Broadcast Worth a Brigade?" *The Economist*, December 1994.

radical ethno-cultural polarization than before. In the 1990s OBN had brought together Muslim, Serb and Croat journalists in the same newsroom. For several years, it was the most respected TV network in the Balkans. Then America pushed for its privatization – and Bosnia-Herzegovina reverted to separate ethnic stations. [298]

Offering several thousand scholarships for Muslim journalists, especially from conflict zones, could prove extremely valuable. Such scholarships, to expose journalists to the widest spectrum of approaches, could take students to any Western country contributing to the project. But donors should encourage each scholar to take at least one course in conflict resolution, or media studies in relation to inter-cultural conflict.

Educate? Already the Internet bursts with fine offerings, including plenty of free distance-learning courses from respected institutions. MIT pioneered giving away nearly all its courses online; now other universities imitate this. If the West wants to develop its educational contribution at pre-university levels, it needs to: a) consult education authorities in key countries where youth unemployment is heaviest; b) identify with them high-value, practical courses (mainly vocational?) likely to help young people find work; c) adapt and translate the best courses into local languages where each course can serve a real need; and d) cooperate with local educational authorities to try to secure recognition of new diplomas for distance education; e) advertise availability of new courses; f) get out of the way, and let the best available locals run the show.

The key standard: Will each course help students actually find useful, paid employment? It's time to be crassly practical, and not create still more uneducated, unemployable "graduates:" "The Devil finds work for idle hands."

Entertain? As with education, business and any other Western attempt to help: leave content to the locals. Offer scholarships to individual artists, but let them find their own way.

One valuable exception: tours and appearances by inspiring artists – both in Muslim countries and in the U.S. and the West

---

298 Disclosure: For two years, the author served on OBN's volunteer international board of directors.

generally. Again, music may be the most universal and easy-to-share of the arts. The unforgettable *Concert at Ramallah* of Daniel Barenboim's and Edward Said's West-Eastern Divan Orchestra spectacularly linked minds and hearts through Western classical music. Young Arab and Israeli musicians, with help from Spain and Germany, eclipsed even the intractable Israel-Palestine conflict. Only for a few hours – but the chords and memories continue to echo.

The West – if only better to educate itself – might also fund tours to the West by renowned Muslim musicians. Islam has a rich musical history. Though not well known in the West, its haunting scales and chords and moods still color Spanish music today. Istanbul hosts several respected jazz groups. Its "Jazz in Ramadan" festival took place in August 2010 in the Topkapi Palace. Among popular Muslim singers, Sami Yusuf and Yusuf Islam – both peace-praising artists – are loved by millions. You may remember Yusuf Islam: he used to be Cat Stevens.

An entertaining – and remarkable – new cultural link emerged in 2011 between disabled young Americans and disabled young Syrians. Inspired by a 2010 Damascus conference of disabled youth, it's an adventure comic-book starring fictitious Muslim superhero *Silver Scorpion*. It draws U.S. philanthropic money from the Open Hands Initiative – its name recalling President Obama's "open hand" to the Muslim world in his famous June 2009 Cairo speech. *Silver Scorpion* aims at nothing less than rescuing humanity from hate and prejudice. A disabled superhero attacking racism and bigotry? Why not? "It's 2011. Little baby steps won't do," a young man called Hashash told *TIME*: "We want our superheroes to save the world." [299]

Can you talk of entertainment without humor? Apart from high-brow classical or jazz, you have to make room for laughter. There are precedents for making Muslims laugh – preferably at their own jokes. The Canadian Muslim-Christian sitcom *The Little Mosque on the Prairie* (later picked up in the U.S.) is a good example of sugaring the pill of tolerance in an often

---

[299] Claire McCormack, "Can a Disabled Muslim Comic-Book Superhero Save the World?" *TIME*, March 11, 2011.

dogmatic or disoriented Muslim world. An Australian tension-breaker, especially for its youthful Muslim-mixed audience is the TV show *Salam Café*. In the UK, Shazia Mirza, a 28-year-old British stand-up comedian of Pakistani extraction, gets away with some very edgy stuff in English: e.g. "Why am I like a suicide bomber? It's me, me, me!" Could she dare say that in Urdu? In the U.S., Ahmed Ahmed presented a film called *STAND UP: Muslim-American Comics Come of Age* in these terms: "We can't define who we are on a serious note because nobody will listen. The only way to do it is to be funny about it." One UK Muslim music group sang Louis Armstrong's famous *Blues in the Night* lament "My Momma done tole me" as... "My *papadum* told me." Well, music is the food of love...

An obvious problem: All these comics are aiming at audiences in Western countries – to achieve a kind of immigrant catharsis. To reach overseas Muslim audiences, they would have to rewrite their material not only to meet local languages, but local mentalities and customs. Humor can be universal. It can also fall flat disastrously in the wrong context. A model well adapted to both North African and French audiences is the slapstick Moroccan-TV series *Islam School Welkoum*. It's about the misadventures of French-educated young Muslims running into a by-the-Book (i.e. the Koran) Moroccan imam. It conveys the right mood, perhaps. But it could never have come straight from America or Europe.

Humor as an anti-terrorist weapon is well worth pursuing. It could include clever ridicule, subtle irony, or even slapstick – but *only* if totally scripted by target-country Muslims. For – you may have noticed – terrorists don't have much of a funny-bone. A weapon we neglect, but that the French have always cherished: *Le ridicule qui tue*. It especially kills hypocrisy. Prime targets: *al-Qaeda* leaders who send youth, even handicapped youth, to suicide – but who don't seem to send many of their own children to blow themselves up. Michael Moore showed the same, if less directly suicidal, phenomenon in *Fahrenheit 9/11*: None of his war-happy Congressmen seemed to have sent their own offspring to Iraq. How touching to see how 'leaders' on both sides look after their kids...

Thank Heaven for little girls – sung by Maurice Chevalier in the film *Gigi*.

... *a great many more than 100 million women are 'missing.' These numbers tell us, quietly, a terrible story of inequality and neglect leading to the excess mortality of women* – Amartya Sen, *New York Review of Books*, December 20, 1990. [India's 2011 census showed that the 2001 sex ratio of 927 girls per 1,000 boys aged 0-6 had fallen in 2011 to 914 girls. Costs of dowries and weddings led many parents illegally to use pregnant women's ultrasound tests to abort "burdensome" girls].

Chapter Nine /

FREE THE WOMEN, SAVE THE WORLD

Ultrasound – used to abort girls. Baby girls buried alive. Others condemned to die of starvation or from lack of medical care. Acid in faces for daring to attend school. Noses cut off for fleeing a violent husband. Genital mutilation. Pregnant or eloping girls strangled to defend family 'honor.' Underage girls forced to "marry" disgusting old men who already have several wives. Burnt alive for 'insufficient' dowries. Agonizing death in childbirth. Vicious beatings by husbands and in-laws. Kidnapping and enslavement for prostitution. Divorce on a husband's whim. Unspeakable rape and murder in civil wars, even for girls under 10. Destitution and abandonment in old age...which may come at age 30 or 40. In the Third World, including much of the Muslim world, girls and women are expendable, exploitable, and executable as the devil's own witches. These are fates known to hundreds of millions of Third World girls and women, many of them Muslim. The world doesn't want to know about them. And when it does, it does little to help. Usually nothing.

Open Season on Girls and Women

These crimes against girls and women dwarf in numbers every wartime massacre, every genocide. They are the reasons why the levers of freedom – education, health, entrepreneurial assistance, media empowerment – can help women incomparably more even than men. Hundreds of millions of women in Asia and Africa face lives of living hell and premature death. Men, and too-often men's religions and male "spiritual guides," don't give them a chance. Thousands of young women in Afghanistan die horrible, unattended deaths in childbirth. Hundreds of others, battered by husband and husband's families, take the only route to freedom: cooking oil, a match, and long days or weeks of screaming for oblivion as their deep-burnt flesh falls off.

For context: Not all the crimes in this chapter's opening paragraphs result from Islam. China and mainly Hindu India too account for much of the suffering. India's caste system and China's now slightly softened "one-child" policy are major culprits in killing or aborting girls. But India also has over 161 million Muslims, Pakistan over 174 million, and Afghanistan 28 million. At village level, these three countries are among the world's cruelest for women. Indonesia is the world's largest Muslim country at over 203 million believers. There, women have a much better chance – though they can still face public whipping and private brutality.

Another dimension: Female infanticide often comes from cultural considerations. More often from Sophie's-Choice economic calculations. Islam itself, through the Prophet, forbids it. But in practice, many Muslim countries – exceptions being Egypt to a large extent, and Tunisia – tolerate barbaric anti-female practices: 'honor" killings and facial mutilations are the worst crimes, and a disgrace to manhood itself. Some Arabian Peninsula countries impose on women unbearably hot, black full-body clothing and face-masks – while their men stroll comfortably in heat-reflecting white robes. Some Muslim countries, with no contradiction from imams, treat women as chattel or witless children. They tolerate genital mutilation, allegedly for 'cultural' reasons. And some, applying *Sharia* law, deny women equal rights in court.

A few countries – the most self-proclaimed Islamic one is Iran – tolerate whipping, even (when the world is not watching) stoning, of women for alleged sexual misdemeanors. A 2010-11 case was the unspeakable horror facing Iranian mother-of-two Sakineh Muhammadi Ashtiani. First threatened with stoning, then whipping, then hanging for alleged adultery, she became another symbol of men's barbarism in the name of Allah. Thanks only to the embarrassment of a huge international outcry, her death sentence was finally stayed indefinitely. But in spite of denials, as of October 2010 stoning for adultery was allegedly still on Iran's *Sharia* books. Afghanistan's devout Taliban took in hand pregnant widow Bibi Sanubar in August 2010. They gave her 200 lashes publicly, then shot her in the head for alleged adultery.[300] In "moderate-Islam" Bangladesh, village elders and Muslim clerics citing Sharia law in January 2011 had 14-year-old Hena Begum whipped to death. Family members of her married alleged lover had already beaten her up the day before. Her grief-stricken father was further fined a crippling $700. [301]

Even in 'moderate' Indonesia, women are publicly whipped for selling rice in daytime during Ramadan. In Somalia, for wearing bras. In Sudan, for wearing trousers. In Saudi Arabia, for walking outdoors without a close male relative. In Malaysia, for drinking a beer in a night club. In the latter case, the prime minister's (Muslim) religious adviser explained comfortingly that "after all...the whipping is fair – the *rotan* [rattan] used is thin, not thick, and the officer is well trained in appropriate caning." [302] In modern-minded Cairo, 83 percent of Egyptian women and 98 percent of foreign women in a 2008 survey of 1,010 women reported being insulted or groped on the street. [303]

These are crimes and abuses that Islam cannot explain away, or entirely excuse, merely by blaming another Muslim sect or local "culture." Some version of Islam *is* the culture guiding each such offending country. Moreover, it isn't Christians who

---

300 *Agence France Presse*, August 10, 2010.
301 *BBC News South Asia* website, February 2, 2011.
302 Virginia Haussegger, "Imagine if Australian women were flogged for drinking a beer ," *National Times*, Sydney, March 1, 2010.
303 Daniel Williams, "Covered Up, and Harassed, in Cairo, *New York Times*, June 23, 2009.

blow up mosques and temples in Pakistan, Afghanistan and Iraq; it's fellow Muslims – who also kill Christians. It isn't in the Christian states of Nigeria that courts have issued *Sharia* sentences of death by stoning for adultery. As in Iran, the stoning sentences of Nigerian Muslim women Safiya Husaini Tundun and Amina Lawal were suspended only because of international outrage.

Some Muslim idealists, though pleased to believe how kind and tolerant and respectful of women the Koran is as a Holy Book, are brave enough to deal with how it is actually *applied* across so many cultures. Out of respect for the Word, they do not dismiss widespread misdeeds committed in the name of Islam. They condemn them, but with very limited effect. Question: Can Islam face its scandals as openly and vigorously as – after outrageous footdragging – Christian churches have finally faced up to pedophilia, crushing of aboriginal cultures, corrupt clergy, embezzlement, and the admittedly un-Christian disgrace of their own denominational divisions?

Educate a Girl: Educate a Family, a Village, a Country

Many Muslim countries – Syria, Iraq, Egypt, Tunisia, Indonesia, even fairly recently Saudi Arabia – have invested heavily in education, including for women. Many have not. They have denied literacy to girls and women as "inferior" under certain interpretations of Islam. Pakistan – set up expressly to be a model Muslim society – has betrayed its own people by failing to educate the masses. But especially, by failing to educate girls and women. Pakistani adult literacy in 2009 was 69 percent for men, and 45 percent for women. In hard-to-control but devout "Tribal Areas," both figures were much lower. In predominantly Hindu India – part of the same former British *Raj*, thus starting with a similar political and socio-economic modern history – literacy rates in 2009 were almost 77 percent for men and 55 percent for women. India's population is still around 14 percent Muslim and rural, facts likely giving its Muslim areas literacy rates closer to Pakistani rates. According to the Muslim-run website *Indian Muslims:* "The Muslim literacy rate [in India] ranks well below the national average, and Muslim poverty rates are only slightly higher than low-caste Hindus, according to a November 2006 government report." [304]

Keeping people ignorant is the world's oldest instrument of oppression. Keeping girls and women "pregnant, barefoot and in the kitchen" echoes this – as does the now-satirical German *Kinder, Küche, Kirche*. (Since the rise of Angela Merkel, Germans have added *Kanzleramt*...). Male political and religious leaders almost everywhere have made sabotaging women their stock-in-trade.

A few brave victims of Third World female oppression dare to confront their oppressors. Millions more have died for their pains or been brutally shut up. Neda Agha-Soltan died in June 2009 on a street in Teheran, murdered by a state thug for standing up to Iranian despot Mahmoud Ahmadinejad after his crooked 2009 presidential election. You will have seen this beautiful, talented girl on TV, lying on the street among horrified friends, her blank eyes looking skyward as her life slowly bled away from mouth and chest.

Nicholas D. Kristof, justice-pursuing op-ed columnist of the *New York Times*, has highlighted many cases of often illiterate women braving death to face down tormentors. In the extraordinary case of Pakistan village-girl Mukhtar Mai, he chronicled a story of repeated rape, kidnapping and attempted murder. Defying her attackers, corrupt local police, and later even Pakistan President Pervez Musharraf (who found her international notoriety "embarrassing"), she used foreign donations to found schools and cultural facilities. She inspired many other women to stand up to brutality and lawlessness. Result: rapes throughout her region have fallen dramatically. Mukhtar couldn't read before. Now, attending her own school, she can. Her example has shown millions of women and men that knowledge can illuminate and strengthen the spirit.

Every day, however, countless other women die in obscurity in usually covered-up, so-called Islamic 'honor" killings.

---

304 Carin Zissis, *Indian Muslims* (collective blog), June 22, 2007.

Or they die beaten to death by an abusive husband. Or simply through starving as the last family-member to be fed. In July 2009, 27-year-old, mother-of-five Fadia al-Najar was tortured in Gaza by her father, then beaten to death with an iron chain, in an "honor" killing. He overheard his long-divorced daughter talking on the phone with a man. The Gaza-based Al Mezan Center for Human Rights denounced such killings as "murder" that "cannot be lawfully justified." It added: "the leniency with which the authority treats the perpetrators of such crimes, who usually allege that they were acting to preserve the honor of the family, has contributed to the noticeable increase in honor killings." The authority, of course, was the devoutly Islamic Hamas government. [305]

A last, hopeful, word about girls' education. American mountain-climber Greg Mortenson nearly died after getting lost in the Karakoram Mountains on the border of Pakistan, India and China. Impoverished Pakistani villagers rescued him. In gratitude, he promised to return to build a school. Raising money and consulting village elders each time, he returned to build over 130 schools in Pakistan and Afghanistan. In his book *Three Cups of Tea* (which sold in the millions), he explained how he first listened to local elders, won their confidence, then worked with Muslim clerics to deliver the goods. Local warlords and even Taliban almost always left his schools alone. Some enrolled their own children, including daughters. Some Taliban actually became teachers.

Won't many girls' schools continue to be burnt down? Yes, if they appear, through construction and staffing, to be creations of despised foreigners. No, if they emerge from listening to local village leaders. "Aid can be done anywhere, including where Taliban are," argues Mortenson in a typical column by the *New York Times*'s Kristoff. "But it's imperative the elders are consulted, and that the development staff is all local, with no foreigners." [306] The old Alexander the Great-British Empire

---
305 Kevin Flower, "Rights groups decry Gaza 'honor killings,'" *CNN World*, July 30, 2009.
306 Nicholas D. Kristof, "Dr. Greg and Afghanistan," *New York Times*, October 22, 2010.

lesson: Afghans hate invaders. Corollary: most Taliban, ardent patriots like all Afghans, will sometimes negotiate with *respectful* foreigners.

Confirming that Afghan-rooted and -run schools, even for girls, can thrive: CARE has 300 *unburned* schools in Afghanistan, reports Kristoff; the Afghan Institute of Learning, run by a local woman, Sakena Yacoobi, has the same number, also unburned. Both examples rest on the closest possible relationships with local elders.

As early as 2008, Kristoff had pointed out the relative costs and benefits of schools versus soldiers. "Suppose that the United States focused less on blowing things up in Pakistan's tribal areas and more on working through local aid groups to build schools, simultaneously cutting tariffs on Pakistani and Afghan manufactured exports. There would be no immediate payback, but a better-educated and more economically vibrant Pakistan would probably be more resistant to extremism." [307] A U.S. soldier in Afghanistan costs $1-million a year – enough claims Kristoff, to fund 243 schools.

Not a few U.S. soldiers agree with Mortenson's approach. The Pentagon placed a large order for his book, and invited him to speak. Before getting fired for mocking his political bosses, then-U.S. Afghanistan commander General Stanley A. McChrystal raved about the book too. Plainly many soldiers, up to their whatever in alligators, already see how to drain the swamp.

Educating girls and women as *the* key to development is now mainstream thinking. Its spin-off benefits to families and communities seem endless. Former UN Secretary-General Kofi Annan has termed girls' education "the single highest-returning social investment in the world today." Lawrence Summers, then-director of the White House National Economic Council, and former World Bank chief economist, adds: "hard statistical evaluations fairly consistently find that female education is the variable most highly correlated with improvements in social indicators." Even Goldman Sachs tells Japan to exploit

---

307   Ibid., "Make schools, not war," July 15, 2008.

the "untapped resource" of its women to get out of its economic stagnation. [308]

If the U.S. were to make a truly intelligent shift in its defense priorities – and get the biggest possible "bang for a buck" in these tight-budget times – it would follow the advice of Mortenson, Annan, Summers, and almost every leader in Third World development today. It would adopt a strategy making girls and women its *number one* priority. And it would use primarily NGOs and local villagers to guide its work. Not combat soldiers.

This initiative has to include new methods of child-centered (not rote) learning – and teachers trained in this approach. In the Muslim world, as already argued, the U.S. should look for local models to support – notably the promising Turkish hybrid model. At very least, the "Turkish compromise" can offer broad inspiration: a curriculum mainly practical and pragmatic, but with some well-supervised teaching of religion. Forget "U.S. know-how." The U.S. *doesn't* really 'know how' faraway Muslims think and learn. Washington should look for local wisdom and models, then support them. Inevitably, the locals will ask for U.S. ideas too.

The same local focus applies to books. With these, look first for mother-tongue, culturally relevant materials. If these meet reasonable standards, get behind them, and train teachers to train other teachers to use such materials. Scholarships and literary awards for promising textbook (and even fiction) authors might also help. As could backing literacy NGOs with valuable experience. Two such North American organizations are: Canada's CODE (Canadian Organization for Development Through Education) and its U.S. partner, The International Book Bank.

Will time and technology change these NGOs' model for shipping books? In time, the new technologies of e-readers and Print-on-Demand (POD) will likely be part of their efforts. Both could reduce distribution costs dramatically, and give every child access to thousands of the world's best books – in English

---

[308] All cited in Julia Mouldon, "When you educate a girl, everything changes," *Huffington Post*, September 5, 2009.

and other languages. Hopeful projects for a strategic "soft-option" approach.

Two last thoughts – two sides of one coin – on why early education is critical for girls. On one hand, in most of the developing world, families tend to see girls as a burden, a drain on family finances, and a loss of lineage. Girls eat, they are weaker for heavy work, they need dowries, and they marry into other families, abandoning elderly parents. If a girl does not get schooling before age 12, her life is over: by 14, if not earlier, she will be married and illiterate, soon pregnant, unaware of health precautions (much increasing her risk of dying in childbirth), and condemned to poverty – for herself and her parents. If she can't find work or a husband, she may have to sell her body to survive. You can read and hear all about this tragic sequence in a shockingly instructive video on *YouTube* called "The Girl Effect."

One the other hand, an educated 12-year-old girl becomes a resource. Education offers her hope and tools to thrive as an adult, make smarter decisions, find decent work, and maybe even make some money to send back to the old folks. She will be able to read health advice, find a better-paid job. When she marries, she will (as women tend to do) watch out for the whole family's welfare. She will create a virtuous circle of better health, higher income, and an escape from helplessness. For herself, her family and, with like-minded women, her village. A lot of such villages make a happier nation.

Get a Life, for a Woman

Female health in many countries is a daily, life-or-death affair. Education in itself greatly helps improve girls' and women's health. Teaching hygiene, birth control and balanced diets (where there is a choice of diet) all flow from schooling. So too can psychological health. Learning how families can get along better is a big part of a woman's happiness. In fact, it's a truism to say that "if the woman is happy, everybody is happy." That's a lesson not only for economically poor countries – but it's essential there, maybe even life-saving. Schools can also teach how villagers and larger communities can cooperate better. Students of conflict prevention and resolution concluded long ago that – *as a rule* – women tend to seek consensus and accommodation. Not always. But usually. Women's physical, mental and psychological health clearly ties into peace in a community – whether village or nation.

A new pro-women Western strategy has to deal with the many physical hazards women in poor countries face. Rape, forced exposure to HIV/AIDS, lack of birth control, unsafe child-birthing, and lack of pre- and post-natal care are among the gravest problems. Without birth control, women become enslaved to large families, and families to poverty. Perhaps the most unforgivable and unnecessary health hazard for poor women today is death while giving birth. The causes and statistics, resembling 18-century Europe's, are sickening:

The major causes of maternal (in childbirth) death are well known. With primitive or no care, they became a murderous plague: obstetrical hemorrhage, infection, ectopic pregnancy, childbed fever, eclampsia and obstructed labor are routine killers. Unsanitary conditions multiply dangers. Heart and kidney failure and HIV/AIDS put nails in young women's coffins on a heartbreaking scale. A Reuters story on the website *IslamOnline. net* puts this massive tragedy in context: "A woman hemorrhages to death as she lies screaming in agony in a Spartan hut in a remote region of Afghanistan. There is no doctor or midwife to help and the hospital is several days journey away. Women die this way every day in Afghanistan, a country with one of the world's highest maternal mortality rates. About 1,600 Afghan women die in childbirth out of every 100,000 live births. In some of the most remote areas, the death rate is as high as 6,500. In comparison, the average rate in developing countries is 450 and in developed countries it is 9." [309]

The World Health Organization (WHO) and UNICEF figures put Afghanistan's maternal death figures two-thirds lower – but

---

309 Tan Ee Lyn, "Death in childbirth: a health scourge for Afghanistan," *IslamOnline.net*, May 1, 2008.

Afghanistan still comes second only to Sierra Leone in this awful record.

HIV/AIDS is a special scourge for African and Indian women. It is often spread through men's refusing to wear condoms with prostitutes. It demands urgent attention. Millions of women face death as a result of careless or uncaring men – and so do their babies. This is a health problem that is, in reality, a social, moral and educational one. To deal with it: publicize the danger, educate both men and women, supply condoms. The plague is "fixable" with informed action, determination, training of paramedics, contradiction of dogmatic, criminally negligent clergy and politicians (e.g. the Vatican and former South African President Thabo Mbeki). Plus, of course, huge, sustained budgets.

But HIV/AIDS also results from rape – endemic in many countries. The Congo sees a minimum of 15,000 rapes a year – rapes of unspeakable violence and gruesomeness. Most victims' ages: *seven* to 21 – with many far beyond that. In many Muslim countries, rape thrives because of war or civil war, a culture of family shame (twistedly called "honor" as an excuse to kill girls). The crime also benefits from impunity for authority figures, police complicity in committing and covering up rape, and Islamic courts. "Following the Holy Qur'an," such courts apply the rule that it takes two women witnesses to balance one man's testimony: thus rape requires two witnesses to incriminate a man, a practical near-impossibility. In some Muslim countries – of Central Asia (Kyrgyzstan), the Caucasus (Chechnya) and parts of rural Africa – a respected "tradition" allows men to kidnap a girl, then force her to "marry" him. Culture? A tolerating religion? Or both?

The U.S. has made token protests against worldwide rape. It has published reports and made fine speeches. But it has not yet thrown into the fight the kind of political and financial resources required to make a real difference. In Muslim Sudan's Darfur province, a few thousand disciplined, foreign Muslim troops, with ample U.S. air support, could have stopped mass rapes – carried out by *janjaweed* Arab Muslim marauders with

Khartoum's complicity. Is it impossible to violate Sudan's sovereignty and to suffer international anger for "invading still another Muslim country?" Valid arguments, up to a point. And that point might be met by imposing tougher – and certain – anti-rape penalties.

The U.S. could also have invoked Bernard Kouchner's postulation of a "duty to intervene" in his 1987 book of that name – inspired by his combat against futile hand-wringing over Biafra atrocities, including mass rapes. Out of this developed at the 2005 UN World Summit a "Responsibility to Protect" – a duty for the world community to act under the Security Council to save local populations threatened with violence.

An earlier version of this idea had led President George Bush Sr. to demand that Saddam Hussein stop killing Kurdish refugees. His son, George W. Bush, backed by hapless UK prime minister Tony Blair, stretched to breaking point a similar doctrine to invade Iraq in 2003.

More recently, in March 2011, armed with Security Council Resolution 1973, a coalition of Western and Arab countries set up a Libyan no-fly zone to save the Gaddafi-threatened people of Benghazi. The colonel had sworn to "hunt down" his opponents there "in every house, every room, every cupboard, and without mercy." The resolution spoke of many crimes and "abuses" – but omitted "rape" as such.

Adding this word might not have helped Iman al-Obeidi, a woman who burst into a Tripoli hotel on March 26, 2011 to tell foreign journalists that she had been handcuffed, then gang-raped, by 15 of Colonel Gaddafi's goons. Before being hooded and hauled off screaming by Gaddafi agents, she won worldwide publicity. A regime-launched lawsuit termed her accusations "a grave offense." This, after trying to threaten, then bribe, her and her family to recant. [310] The Gaddafi Gang, true to form, ended by smearing the victim as a "drunk prostitute."

Nobody, it seems, is willing to talk of a "duty to intervene" or "responsibility to protect" if the goal is 'only' to stop rapes. "Oh well," one imagines male politicians shrugging, "that kind of

---

310 "Alleged Libya rape victim charged over claim," *CBS/AP*, March 29, 2011.

thing has been going on forever, and it's not as bad as killing." Such attitudes seem especially true at the UN, where Asian, African and Middle Eastern nations – including many Muslim ones – find no throbbing sense of urgency in protecting women from "local traditions." Meanwhile, as in the Congo, rape is often so vicious that many women consider it *worse* than death.

In general, the UN has grossly failed in its duty to protect women, even in notorious conflict zones such as the Congo and Darfur.[311] With a Secretary of State called Hillary Clinton, who has made defending women a lifetime mission, the U.S. could and should make women's health, including the very unhealthy matter of rape, another key part of a new foreign policy. A policy that gives more space to women, and less to weapons.

Back to our central argument. Quite apart from a humanitarian concern for women's mistreatment, protecting these pre-eminent, natural peace-builders is brilliant, hard-nosed *national defense*. For these women are raising the next generation of young men. Will these men enter adulthood as educated citizens with good values, and dreams of making a decent life? Or will they – being intellectually and morally stunted by poverty and a dysfunctional family – become angry, unemployable misfits? "Losers" who turn to furious fantasies of death? Jihadism thrives on nihilism, beautifully wrapped in despair and out-of-context verses from the Koran. Given half a chance, women can civilize and uplift men. They can dissuade them from violence and fighting. Keeping Muslim mothers and daughters healthy, happy and fulfilled is a *strategic national defense bargain* for the U.S. and the entire West.

As with education, Western investment in Third-World health-care works best when woven into as much local expertise and methodology as makes sense. Western medical priorities are not always as useful and affordable as those determined by local personnel. Former South African President Thabo Mbeki, it's true, made a mockery of that principle by long denying the basics of HIV/AIDS. His stubborn arrogance killed his citizens on a horrific scale. But he was surely a bizarre exception.

---

311 Josh Kron, "U.N. Knew of Rebels in Area of Congo Rapes," *New York Times*, August 25, 2010.

An excellent example of careful listening, then strong, targeted action is the Bill & Melinda Gates Foundation. Focusing on health in poor countries, the Foundation has a clear grasp of the central role played by women in all societies. In June 2010, the Foundation pledged $1.5-billion to a joint effort with the United Nations to improve the health of developing-world women and children. This would represent a "comprehensive approach through 2014 to help women deliver babies safely and plan healthy families with access to contraception, while incorporating current vaccination and nutrition programs," summarized Reuters. "That is in addition," said Melinda Gates, "to grants that we already make in vaccines, diarrhea, malaria." UN Secretary-General Ban Ki-moon emphasized at the time: "The women and children are always last in line for health issues... It's just morally unacceptable ... This is a real human rights issue." [312]

Again, our point here is that *helping women is smart national defense.* Compare the Foundation's far-sighted $1.5-billion for women to the *monthly* $5.7-billion the Pentagon is spending for its no-win, Afghanistan military *cul-de-sac.* [313] If Congress were thinking straight, it would stop presuming that "national defense" only meant short-term feeding of the military-industrial beast. An astute Congress, White House – and even Pentagon – would look at the deep, solid payoff from their "strongest" security allies: women. Doing well by doing good? Yes. Today's ultimate soft option builds tomorrow's hard security.

Diamonds Are Not a Girl's Best Friend

A third part of a free-the-women program should support female entrepreneurship. Freedom takes many forms, but its ultimate underpinning is economic independence. "Jobs" for

---

312 Maggie Fox, "Gates Foundation gives $1.5-bln for women's health," *Reuters*, June 8, 2010.
313 Columnist Amy Goodman claimed that the cost was more like $8 billion a month ($2 billion per week). See "Afghanistan and the arithmetic of austerity," *King Features Syndicate,* March 2, 2011.

women is a worthy aim. But helping women to run their own lives as business owners is even better.

Promoting small business – and the freedom to grow them bigger – ought to be as natural to Americans as breathing. Individual initiative *defines* Americans. In some countries, everybody secretly yearns to start a revolution. In others, they dream of becoming civil servants. In America, foreigners can't step off the plane without tasting the air and scheming to start a business.

The basic ingredients for starting a business, even in a tiny Pakistani or Afghan village, are the same as everywhere: a little capital or credit, a bit of imagination and common sense, a product or service – and a ferocious desire to make a decent life for oneself and one's family. Oh yes, and for a woman, you might need a husband's permission. But mainly, you need the confidence to dare.

America can help with asked-for advice. Its most important contribution might be just to encourage women's ambition, and their will to become self-reliant. In fighting the war for women's – and men's – dignity, Americans would not be dodging bullets and bombs. They would not be navigating strange battlefields and unmarked roads infested with Improvised Explosive Devices. As business mentors, they would be swimming like fish in water. Supplying information, ideas and experience, they could understand this "war" and feel good about it.

Perhaps the best-known, most transformative of aids to women in business is micro-credit. Also known as micro-finance or micro-lending, it offers very small loans to help would-be entrepreneurs in impoverished countries get going. We already traced micro-credit's modern form to Bangladesh. There, thanks to the Grameen Bank launched by Dr. Muhammad Yunus, hundreds of thousands of women have started small businesses and strengthened their independence. They have also greatly contributed to their communities. Yunus believes deeply in "social businesses" that help others, as well as the borrower.

His Grameen Bank offers a life-changing model now being widely copied. Its training courses are well-organized, practical and easy to apply. They teach most aspects of small business, technical and personal. They are particularly strong on management and motivation. Grameen's training goals: arouse curiosity; stimulate interest in micro-credit; encourage self-learning; learn and share with others; and discover the individual's role in organization and community.

Grameen is infinitely more than a lending bank. It's a people's university for self-reliance and social service. Its "four principles" are discipline, unity, courage and hard work – "in all walks of our lives." On these principles, Yunus built "16 decisions" – making a detailed, down-to-earth blueprint for women to change their own, and their family's, lives. The list is simple, direct and entirely focused on living responsibly. Here's the guide to women's commitments – worth reading carefully to grasp how revolutionary the Grameen approach can be for whole families and communities:

1. We shall follow and advance the four principles of Grameen Bank — Discipline, Unity, Courage and Hard work – in all walks of our lives.
2. Prosperity we shall bring to our families.
3. We shall not live in dilapidated houses. We shall repair our houses and work towards constructing new houses at the earliest.
4. We shall grow vegetables all the year round. We shall eat plenty of them and sell the surplus.
5. During the plantation seasons, we shall plant as many seedlings as possible.
6. We shall plan to keep our families small. We shall minimize our expenditures. We shall look after our health.
7. We shall educate our children and ensure that they can earn to pay for their education.
8. We shall always keep our children and the environment clean.
9. We shall build and use pit-latrines.
10. We shall drink water from tube-wells. If it is not available, we shall boil water or use alum.

11. We shall not take any dowry at our sons' weddings, neither shall we give any dowry at our daughters' wedding. We shall keep our centre free from the curse of dowry. We shall not practice child marriage.
12. We shall not inflict any injustice on anyone, neither shall we allow anyone to do so.
13. We shall collectively undertake bigger investments for higher incomes.
14. We shall always be ready to help each other. If anyone is in difficulty, we shall all help him or her.
15. If we come to know of any breach of discipline in any centre, we shall all go there and help restore discipline.
16. We shall take part in all social activities collectively.

Keeping these commitments is sometimes hard. But the clarity and common sense they breathe are electrifying. In the first nine years of Grameen's micro-lending, it put on a path of hope almost seven million borrowers, of which 97 percent were women. Yunus being Muslim, did he get flak for charging modest interest, while the Koran forbids interest? He replies that the most common Muslim religious query was about why so many women got help...

Yunus and his Grameen Bank are now legends in the development world. They jointly won the Nobel Peace Prize in 2006. Their citation: ... "for their efforts to create economic and social development from below." In August 2009, President Obama awarded Yunus the U.S. Presidential Medal of Freedom. The Yunus-Grameen approach has now spread almost everywhere in the Third World as a crucial tool for women's entrepreneurship and dignity.

As with education and health, in business too women are seen as the 'solution' with the greatest potential for peace and cooperation. Why don't more men want to follow a path such as Dr. Yunus's 16 decisions? No doubt, many are working hard in the fields, growing food while protecting their family. But this is an agenda that any enlightened man could support. Many men who've seen their wife raise up the whole family already do.

Is small business a cure for terrorist-feeding unemployment as well? If you read behind the headlines telling flashier big business stories, small business is doing that already. Even in advanced countries, it's small business, not huge firms, that create most jobs – on average, about two-thirds of all jobs. As early as 2002, Grameen created a "phone-ladies" program. This Village Phone Program won the 2004 Petersburg Prize for its innovative approach to technology in development. Some 55,000 Bangladeshi women in 28,000 villages had by then set up neighborhood cell-phone systems. They charged a tiny amount per call, and served over 80 million customers. "Small" business indeed!

So, "national defense" here? Doesn't a society's economic stability underpin political and social stability? Isn't such stability a condition for preventing conflict? And isn't *preventing* conflict smarter than flying in thousands of troops to fight wars you *didn't* prevent? Wars that large numbers of troops only end up sustaining? If America really "means business," it should subsidize fees for Dr. Yumus's courses, and for business-training courses like them. Such courses plainly help build stable, prosperous societies across the Muslim world. And they strengthen those proven peace-builders and "war-preventers" called women.

Expensive? A highly credible report estimated in 2008 that it cost $2,123 to sustain *one* American soldier in Afghanistan or Iraq for *one day*. [314] The author was Steven Kosiak, soon after hired by President Obama as hatchet-man for defense at the powerful Office of Management and Budget (OMB). Kosiak's 2008 estimate of $775,000 per year per soldier may already be creeping past *one million dollars a year per soldier*. Take any competing figure you want – then compare it to these fees for Grameen business-training seminars: $30 a day (plus $25 training manual for the whole course).

---

314 Steven Kosiak, study on costs of war, *Center for Strategic and Budgetary Analysis*, 2008, p. 38.

Let's be a bit polemical. In lasting, bang-for-a-buck terms against soldiers, armor and drones, which makes the better deal for long-term, strategic national defense?

Burqa-free Radio

A final field for leveraging women's talents is media. For women to gain acceptance and credibility in society, they need to find voices. These can speak most dramatically through radio, TV, film and the Internet. In the West, women journalists thrive. As reporters, TV anchors, editors, managers, they are everywhere. Their participation in collecting and presenting the news came about slowly, and mainly in the past 30 or 40 years. But it's now universally welcome – and impressive.

In a few parts of the Muslim world – Indonesia, Egypt, Qatar spring to mind – women can also do well in the media. Maybe, if on TV, they will run into a debate on head-covering – even on mainstream *Al Jazeera* Arabic. [315] But generally, in such partly westernized Muslim countries, they are free to do good work. Unusually, *Al Jazeera* began in a BBC-style model, especially in English. (Many of its original Arab-language staff came from BBC Arabic Television).

However, in much of the Muslim world, female journalists work in conditions of condescension, discrimination, hostility, even physical danger. Death threats to women journalists are routine in many Muslim societies. Their 'crimes?' Alleged "indecency" of hair, makeup or dress; covering news embarrassing to Islam; or just being women. Worse, from the Islamists' viewpoint, women journalists tend to focus less on warlords, and more on the human cost of conflicts. Since that cost often includes oppression of women, they attract extremist anger for threatening male supremacy.

In Afghanistan, media executives first used women on radio – no burqas needed. TV came later, but it exposed female reporters and presenters to grave risks from Taliban. Since TV sets

---

315 Rob Quinn, "Female Anchors Quit Over Makeup and Hair," *Daily Telegraph*, June 2, 2010.

are far rarer than radios in Afghanistan, they allow abundant coverage of social issues beyond normal conflict reporting. But women's news progress in conflict zones is still dangerous, whether in print, or on the radio, TV or Internet. Names get known, as do addresses.

On September 17, 2009, the highly-regarded Institute for War and Peace Reporting (IWPR) commented on one week's tally: three murdered female journalists in Iraq and Afghanistan. All were probing social or human-rights issues threatening the male-Muslim establishment: "Women journalists have demonstrated particular tenacity and bravery in Afghanistan, Iraq, Uzbekistan and other Islamic countries, reporting on the human costs of conflict and the efforts of mostly male-dominated power structures to undermine democracy," said Anthony Borden, executive director of IWPR, which supports local journalists in conflict areas and maintains extensive programming in Iraq. "Women are vital agents of democratic change in these societies, and the recent tragic killings demonstrate the depth and violence of opposition to their efforts." [316]

Said one of the soon-to-be-murdered women, Iraqi Sahar Hussein al-Haideri, about the lives of women journalists: "Our psychological state is unbalanced because we live and think in fear and worry, and always think about our destiny and that of our family members, relatives and friends," she told the *UK Press Gazette* in early 2010. "But I have never thought about quitting, as journalism is my life and I really love it." [317]

Al-Haideri was shot to death for covering the public murder of Du'a Khalil Aswad, a 17-year-old Yazidi girl in the Kurdish-Iraqi town of Bashiqa. Du'a had fallen in love with a Sunni Muslim Arab. After she was dragged from her home, she was surrounded by a mob of 2,000 hysterical men who stoned and kicked her to death. If you can bear it, you can watch this horrific scene online, hearing the call of the local muezzin and seeing local police standing around to watch the spectacle. Her brother and uncle cast the first stones. You can also see many

---

316 *IWPR* website, September 7, 2009.
317 Ibid.

excited men filming the scene on cell-phone cameras, no doubt for their later enjoyment.[318]

This ghastly and heart-breaking "honor killing" is precisely a priority topic for female Muslim journalists. Although this murder occurred in a public square, countless others, say local women in Muslim countries, happen in the shadows. In 2002, a United Nations report estimated that about 5,000 "honor killings" occur worldwide each year. Notable crime scenes: Egypt, Jordan, Lebanon, Morocco, Pakistan, Afghanistan, India, Saudi Arabia, Persian Gulf countries, Iran. The sickness has even spread to North American and European immigrant communities – often hushed up because it is "culturally sensitive." [319]

The other problem facing Muslim journalists is censorship. In 2008, *Reporters Without Borders* listed that year's Afghan media environment as 156th out of 173 in the world, with 1st being most free. Consistent anti-government reporting in many oppressive Muslim countries – take at random Egypt and Tunisia before 2011's Arab Spring– can get you jail, a beating, torture, or worse. A still riskier accusation is that of "insulting Islam" – since Islam, though "one religion," has many sects and variations of belief and ritual. As a result, killings between sects blot and blur Islam's unity. Sunnis, Shias, Ahmadis, Ibadis, Kharijites, Alawites and Sufis may be the best known, but there are other groups, as reviewed here in Chapter 1. Unfortunately, some of their members take difference of any kind as a reason to kill. Again: It's not Christians or Jews who blow up mosques; it's other Muslims. But to report too probingly on this is perilous at best, especially in local languages.

Islam, like many religions, does not cherish freedom of expression. Orthodoxy, dogma and tradition come first. On real or imagined affronts to religion, Muslim reactions have often proven vociferous, even violent. In 1998, Iranian Ayatollah Khomeini famously issued a death-order *fatwa* against Salman

---

318 The Yazidi sect contains elements of Islam, but also of Christianity and Judaism. It is passionate about purity in all forms, notably in marrying within one's own caste – apparently Du'a's great sin. Sunni extremists say Yazidis are devil-worshippers and must convert to Islam or die.
319 *Wikipedia*, 2010.

Rushdie for alleged sacrilege against the Prophet Muhammad in Rushdie's novel *The Satanic Verses*. The 2005 worldwide Muslim outcry against Danish newspaper *Jyllands-Posten*'s cartoons for the same offence showed this volatility again. By the time a weird and bigoted Florida "pastor" called Terry Jones threatened to organize an International "Burn-a-Koran Day" in front of his church on September 11, 2010, not just journalists, but world leaders, jumped to attention. Among the horrified interveners: President Barack Obama, UN Secretary-General Ban Ki-moon and the Pope – not to mention Afghanistan commander General David Petraeus and the U.S. secretaries of State and Defense. Ah yes, and Angelina Jolie.

The London-based *International News Safety Institute* regularly reports on censorship and its more insidious form, self-censorship. So does Paris-based *Reporters Without Borders (RSF)*. Their reports make the mainstream news and often cause serious reflection. Sometimes they elicit positive action, such as freeing jailed journalists. *RSF*, the *International Press Institute*, the *International News Safety Institute*, the *Institute for War and Peace Reporting*, the *Committee to Protect Journalists* and other sites run regular updates tallying journalists' on-the-job deaths, death threats – and often imprisonment, torture and harm to journalists' families. A typical example from July 2010: "At least six women and children were seriously injured late today after a group of unidentified attackers threw grenades and opened fire on a home connected to television correspondent Zafarullah Bonari, according to Pakistani journalists... In a 2009 *CPJ* series, 'The Frontier War,' Sher Khan Afridi, president of the Khyber Union of Journalists, said six journalists houses had been specifically targeted because they were the houses of journalists." [320]

Not all attacks on journalists happen in Muslim societies, and not all concern women. As the *CPJ* example reminds, male journalists in many countries also face death or persecution. On September 9, 2010, *RSF* reported the murder of Alberto Chakusanga, host of an Angolan radio program critical of the government.

---

320 Committee to Protect Journalists website, July 26, 2010.

Latin American drug wars are also a major cause of killings – Colombia and Mexico being the most lethal countries. But journalist killings, beatings and jail-terms occur regularly under African dictatorships – and, more often than not, they go unpunished. On April 27, 2910, the Nigeria Union of Journalists (NUJ) condemned the murders of three colleagues: Edo Ugbagwu, 42, a court reporter who worked for daily newspaper *The Nation;* Nathan S. Dabak, 36, and Sunday Gyang Bwede, 39, working for a Christian publication, *The Light Bearer,* were all stabbed to death on their way to an assignment in the central Nigerian city of Jos. The NUJ denounced the "impunity" surrounding anti-journalist crimes. Jos is a focal point of Muslim-Christian antagonism and two-way massacres.

Returning to the American-Muslim conflict: the dangers faced by Muslim journalists in conflict zones are extraordinary – dangers religious as well as political. Both authoritarian governments and religious fanatics kill reporters and editors. Women journalists again face unique dangers, just because they are women.

In principle, for example, the Afghan media are free... unless you "defame" somebody (especially in authority). Or unless you produce articles or programs "contrary to the principles of Islam." Never mind that the law, or Islamic law, may be vague or open to wide interpretation. You can always try to explain yourself. "Dialogue" with those offended may consist of your getting kidnapped or killed.

In spite of all, many Afghan journalists try valiantly to do honest journalism, with women often among the bravest. Alas, the terrorists – themselves terrified by critics of their male-dominated system – are winning. They are discouraging women from training as journalists. Example: women entering Herat journalism schools during the first seven years of Hamid Karzai's regime fell from 70 to 30 percent. "[Women] have the same problems as male journalists, but stronger," said Vincent Brossel, *Reporters Without Borders* Asia director. "Some of them have been threatened by the Taliban and extremists because they are women." [321]

Such persecution also occurs in non-Muslim Asia. On January 12, 2009, Maoist guerrillas hacked to death Uma Singh, who worked for a private radio station in the Janakpur area of southern Nepal. "Known for her strong point of views on women's rights, caste and dowry systems and also for various political issues, the brave journalist was attacked by around 15 men armed with traditional Nepali curved knives (known as *Khukhri*). Uma, who was under 30 and the first female journalist to be killed in Nepal, was taken to the hospital, but soon she succumbed to injuries." [322]

These awful threats to women media professionals measure agonizingly the vast potential of female journalists to change society. Giving such women security, training, encouragement and opportunities should figure among the West's top priorities. *Al-Qaeda* and the Taliban know well that intelligent, eloquent women are profoundly subversive of their patriarchies. They sense correctly that most women despise war, and will try to change national and local narratives toward a more humane and humanistic society.

Reserving many more places in journalism schools for women is excellent; but providing personal security on the job and at home is vital. If the West's Kabul government really hopes to undermine its enemies, it should keep women in print, and especially on the air. They scare the medieval thugs more than a fleet of drones.

Is there any good news at all for Third World women journalists? It's scattered, and still modest. But it's going in the right direction. In Latin America, women are advancing quickly in radio and TV. Elsewhere, their progress is mainly anecdotal. In the 1990s, the UN-launched University for Peace in Costa Rica learned of West African female radio directors downplaying conflict-related news in favor of education, health and tribal

---

[321] 'Genevieve,' "Female Journalists Under Fire in Afghanistan and Pakistan," *The Epoch Times*, May 18, 2009.
[322] Nava Thakuria, "Woman Journalist Killed in Nepal," *American Chronicle*, January 21, 2009.

reconciliation.[323] In January 2007, *FEMNET News* announced a "Media for Women's Rights Project" in East and West Africa. The goal of its radio programs: to publicize women's rights. In August 2010, the President of Liberia opened "Liberia Women Democracy Radio" in Monrovia. Sponsored by the UN, it's the country's "first radio station dedicated to raising the voices of women and increasing women's access to information. The radio station also seeks to highlight gender issues and to provide practical training and exposure to female journalists."

In majority-Hindu India, relatively moderate-Muslim Indonesia and the mainly Christian Philippines, women journalists are generally succeeding, or at least advancing notably. But even there, they face hazards men don't – not often lethal, but harassment just for being women.

Of all the areas where women's influence can make a decisive difference for peace and security – education, health, business, and journalism – media work is the most life-threatening. Americans glory in the marvels of their free press. But instead of cutting back their coverage of the world, as they have, the U.S. media should stop treating freedom of speech as just a ritual topic for self-congratulatory colloquia. They should go, and help, where journalists have to risk their lives for it every day.

The U.S. government, without interfering in content, should generously support Third World journalists, including Muslim women journalists. U.S. "national defense?" These women's worldviews, values, competence and courage terrify the jihadists far more than do foreign soldiers. Female journalists' on-air appearances also inspire other women, who see them as role models. Brave combatants for truth, such women live, and too-often die, for their version of America's First Amendment.

---

323 Disclosure: The author was then director of the university's Institute for Media, Peace and Security.

No nation could preserve its freedom in the midst of continual warfare – James Madison, 1795.

The release of atom power has changed everything except our way of thinking... the solution to this problem lies in the heart of mankind. If only I had known, I should have become a watchmaker – Albert Einstein.

Chapter Ten /

FIGHT CHEAPER AND SMARTER, OR FIGHT FOREVER

New York, September 11, 2010. A brisk, sunny morning at Ground Zero. Just before 8:46 a.m., when the first plane had hit the North Tower. Tens of thousands of grieving family members and strangers bow heads, pray, and sing a beautiful, elegiac *Star-Spangled Banner* before victims' relatives read out the names of the 2,752 World Trade Center people murdered by Islamic fanatics. Three other pauses marked the South Tower attack and the collapse of both towers.

Two Frightfully Sincere Men of Religion

Two blocks away, at 51 Park Place, a few more thousand stood in front of a proposed new Islamic community center. A few hundred held signs exalting "American values" of tolerance and freedom of religion. A far noisier crowd shouted fury at this Muslim "provocation" and "insult to the 9/11 victims."

To poison the atmosphere further, an obscure evangelical "pastor," Terry Jones, had journeyed from Gainesville, Florida, to (in his mind) negotiate a deal with *Park51*'s Imam Abdul Rauf: Don't build your mosque near Ground Zero and I won't organize a public burning of a stack of Korans. Imam Rauf's project was to be called Córdoba House. It would, he said, recall 8th-to-15th-century Muslim tolerance for Jews and Christians. Alas, amateur historian and Republican politician Newt Gingrich insisted that the name "Córdoba" did not evoke tolerance. In every Muslim ear worldwide, he suggested, it echoed the clashing swords of Islamic triumph – the conquest of Christian Spain. The cat was among the peace doves: Córdoba House would become a focus of discord. And it would be renamed to its street address: as inoffensive *Park51*.

Only in America: Two earnest but stumbling clergymen of different faiths tangling over free speech, gross insensitivity, and mutual provocation. This, on a street and a day of reverence that they managed to turn into a circus and a screaming-match. Their interaction, however sincere, set Americans against Muslims, and Americans against Americans. A field day for the gleeful Taliban and *al-Qaeda*. In September 2010, *Al Jazeera* showed truckloads of Arab, Chechnyan and other *Mujahideen* pouring into northern Afghanistan and Pakistan to swell the terrorist and guerrilla ranks – while grinning Taliban leaders welcomed them with effusive speeches.

A typical early-morning visitor to Ground Zero, Tavis Moonan, told the press on the 2010 anniversary: "I don't know that there is going to be forgiveness for the individuals involved [the 9/11 murderers]… and for the motive for the event. There will be forgiveness for the faith, but the mosque debate certainly hasn't helped." He went on to say, with more hope than evidence: "But we are definitely united." [324]

Americans were manifestly *not* united, except in fear and uncertainty. Both reactions drew poison from the then-upcoming mid-term American elections. Fear and uncertainty will continue to grip Americans – until their leaders devise new approaches to jihadist dangers. And new strategies to neutralize them.

But no one can doubt this: Huntington seemed prescient. In America – and throughout the West – there was now a cosmic misunderstanding between Atlantic civilization and the children of Muhammad.

---

[324] Jeremy Kutner, "9/11 ceremony simple, poignant," *Christian Science Monitor*, Septmeber 11, 2010.

Einstein's Nightmare ... and Ours

The dangers are well known. Never mind the whole world's long-term threat of climate change. Much sooner, the U.S. and the West face risks of three world-changing explosions: uncontrolled weapons of mass destruction; out-of-control guerrilla-and-terrorist brushfires linked to *al-Qaeda*; and, within a generation, societal tensions in Asia caused by a shortage of girl babies – thus of future brides. Translate that as hundreds of millions of frustrated, angry young men.

Einstein warned about the horrors of atomic war, quickly demonstrated August 6 and 9, 1945 at Hiroshima and Nagasaki. To that menace, the Cold War added gigantic stocks of easy-to-replicate bacteriological, chemical, and radiological weapons, on top of enough nuclear weapons to blow up the civilized world several times over. One way or another – through too-loose controls, theft, bribery or even reinvention – evil regimes or stateless terrorists could use such weapons against vulnerable Western sites: cities, water supplies, electricity, Internet and/or communications infrastructures. North Korea, Pakistan and Iran are key danger-points to monitor, along with several loosely-policed ex-Soviet territories.

What is the likelihood of an *al-Qaeda*-style mass-destruction attack in coming years? Some serious observers predict a mass attack, or wave of major attacks, anytime between 2015 and 2020, possibly sooner. Gunmen might machine-gun city crowds: the 2008 Mumbai rampage killed 166 people, and police fear copy-cat plots elsewhere. In October 2010, alerts were warning of "white" European Islamic converts being trained in Pakistan and Yemen for similar outrages in Berlin, Paris and London. A few Christian European young women were marrying extremist Muslims – and, in full-covering *niqabs*, risked being used in terror plots. At least that was the nightmare police could see, shuddering at how religion, culture, love, sex, political correctness and law could serve them an inedible stew.

But if luck is the meeting of preparation with opportunity, so is terrorist catastrophe. *Al-Qaeda*, its acolytes and its cousins brag on websites such as *Inspire* and *Global Jihad* about preparing and training for other 9/11s. But what luck will they find – perhaps from failed or unstable Muslim states? Nuclear-armed Pakistan (*Al-Qaeda*'s supposed haven) has been tottering. Terrorists' fantasy attack is a nuclear blast or radiological dispersion device (RDD, "dirty" or "salted" bomb") killing or incapacitating millions in a major city. An online debate of the Council on Foreign Relations cites this objective from *al-Qaeda* spokesman Suleiman Abu Gheith: [We hope] "to kill 4 million Americans – 2 million of them children – and to exile twice as many and wound and cripple hundreds of thousands."*Al-Qaeda* claims that these numbers only reflect "justice:" vengeance for Muslim deaths it blames on the U.S. and Israel.[325] Murder on that scale would be the ultimate jihadist blow. And as with many other hypotheses floating about, nobody knows if or how – while half-expecting when.

Congressional witnesses confirm the uncertainty as to times and types of terrorism. In February 2010, Director of National Intelligence Dennis C. Blair warned of *al-Qaeda*'s obvious intent to "cause mass casualties, harm the U.S. economy, or both." In September 2010, Homeland Security Secretary Janet Napolitano warned that the United States might also face scatter-gun attacks of roadside bombs and Mumbai-style small-arms attacks. Other likely targets: chemical plants, ports, sports stadiums, hotels and famous landmarks. Most worrisome agents of such attacks: American-accented jihadists converted by Yemen-based, American-born Anwar al-Alawki. These junior jihadists are now often trained in chaotic, extremist-infested Somalia.

America's allies also face great danger. Canada, which has a growing Muslim population of 650,000 in a total Canadian population of 35 million, has broken up at least two significant gangs. The "Toronto 18" (11 of whom were convicted) had advanced plans to bomb key sites in Toronto. In August 2010, the "Mounties" arrested three more Muslims accused of trying to bomb Ottawa, and of sending money for weapons to

---

325 Graham T. Alison, "How Likely is a Nuclear Attack on the United States?" *Council on Foreign Relations* online debate, April 20, 2007.

fellow-conspirators to attack Canadian troops in Afghanistan. Muslim spiritual leaders denounced these attacks, as they have elsewhere in the West. But volunteer jihadists still seem vulnerable to terrorist propaganda.

The UK has a long history of resisting terrorism, Irish as well as Islamic. On July 7, 2005, terrorists killed 52 and wounded 700 in an attack on a London bus and the "Tube" (subway). Two weeks later, another such attack fizzled through incompetent bomb-handling. On June 30, 2007, British-born doctor Bilal Abdullah and his driver Khalid Ahmed crashed a Jeep Cherokee loaded with propane canisters into the gate of Glasgow International Airport. Jonathan Evans, head of Britain's MI5 counter-espionage and security service, warned on September 16, 2010 that it is "only a matter of time" before a new generation of *al-Qaeda* terrorists based in Somalia launch a major attack in the United Kingdom. Noting a similar risk from revived radical Irish Republican Army terrorism, Evans foresaw in Somalian *Al-Shabaab* or Yemeni threats "a serious risk of a lethal attack." The UK announced a "high probability" of new attacks just before or during the July-August 2012 London Olympics.

Risk Management Solutions Inc., a U.S. insurance-industry think-tank, predicted in 2008 many more years of terrorist dangers. It explained this partly in these terms: "The Palestinian-Israeli conflict dominates relationships between [Western] Coalition nations and Muslim states." Influential Muslims, whether political, economic or intellectual leaders, agree. So do published estimates of Western intelligence services. French counter-terrorism experts note that French troops in Afghanistan run extra risks because of perceived Paris discrimination against France's six million domestic Muslims. A new French "anti-burqa" law gives *al-Qaeda* new, mobilizing pretexts. French attacks on North African kidnapper/killers of French citizens drew even greater threats. As of late September 2010, France's entire transport system went on high-alert under the nation's *Vigipirate* plan. Among other moves, this puts soldiers with machine-guns into train stations and seals all public garbage-cans.

In August 2010, Germany shut down a hate-preaching mosque that some 9/11 killers, including leader Mohamed Atta, had attended. Europeans agree that the Schengen open-borders agreement inevitably makes it easier for terrorists to move undetected throughout the continent.

Cataclysmic terrorist violence in the West remains an explosion only waiting to happen. As defense, we have only vigilance, luck and prayers – until the West and Islam come to some kind of truce. Meanwhile, the risk of disaster is already woven into our subconscious – as deeply as was the Cold War's threat of thermonuclear incineration.

The second explosion has already begun – the spread of relatively small but deadly local terrorist insurgencies. Yemen, the Horn of Africa and the Maghreb host Al-Qaeda proxies, copycats or semi-autonomous field groups. In fall-of-2010 Yemen, the White House was grappling with a dilemma eerily recalling the "mission-creep" that dragged John F. Kennedy and Lyndon Johnson into a Vietnam quagmire. It's always a choice between cutting losses or sending "just a few more" soldiers and weapons to stifle the insurgency. We saw the same in George W. Bush's Iraq and now in Barack Obama's Afghanistan: a temptation to gamble on more war to get less war. Bush's famous "surge" in Iraq was perhaps partly effective militarily in some areas. But General David Petraeus's use of a few hundred million dollars in bribes to Sunni insurgents made the real difference. And it gave the U.S. just enough extra time to sneak out of a still-violent, still ungoverned Iraq with a fig-leaf over its defeat.

The third explosion is slow, invisible, but perhaps most dangerous of all. As briefly cited above, at the end of our generation's short road lies a problem that screams out for action: an end to the time-bomb lurking in female-fetus abortion, female infanticide and often-lethal mistreatment of girls. China, India and some other Asian countries are headed imminently for a yawning shortage of brides: in parts of India, only 80 baby girls are allowed to live for every 100 baby boys. [326] Multiply that

---

326 Kate Darnton, "Where Are The "Baby Girls? *Boston Globe*, September 1, 2010.

by even a few tens of millions, and you will see disaster looming: more rapes, more kidnapping, more trafficking of foreign women, more general crime – and likely legions of ready-to-explode, bride-less young war-age bachelors.

Today's female infanticide has set the stage for easily a hundred million young Asian men to live lonely, bitter lives. War, poverty, occupation, and rigid social customs guarantee the same fate to millions of young Muslim men. One way or another, they will satisfy their frustrations – social, professional, emotional and sexual. But peacefully? How many of these testosterone-loaded young men already seek to fight in armies, insurgencies or fanatical religious-ideological-nationalist groups? They will not all become monks. That's not alarmism. It's not some eccentric theory of sexual obsession. It's a cool assessment of reality.

The Israel-Palestine tinderbox is a powerful case in point. Tens of thousands of young Muslim men in Gaza, and in Israeli prisons, face a lack of education, careers, money – and brides – thus families denied. Their repression – however you judge Israelis' justifications – will lead to a new generation of humiliated, vengeful males. And of nothing-to-lose Islamic "martyrs." As some Israeli observers noted here earlier, such a result does not even make clever repression.

What can Washington do about these tensions? Not much with big armies. What's needed – in addition to astute, indefatigable anti-terrorism – is far-seeing diplomacy that favors all the "soft" or "smart" options examined here.

Again: A supporting reason for shifting from impractical armies to practical ideas is America's patent inability to fund endless wars. Even if Washington wanted to send more troops and weapons to fight guerrillas, it no longer has deep enough pockets. It's fast becoming a superpower long on rhetoric and short on cash (as well as results). Even as fast-rising rivals – commandingly China – defy it, America must finally start measuring the *costs* of its militarism. Now the question is not just: "What national defense do we need?" But: "What national defense can we afford?"

A Cheaper Date With Destiny

Let's consider first America's plausible defense needs. In coming years, the U.S. will likely fight on three battlefields: economic, physical, and cyberwar. None requires huge armies fighting, or based in, Muslim lands.

The economic battlefield? The hills are already alive with the sounds of monetary music. And of endlessly tangled trade disputes. Both come from the direction of Beijing. (And even Seoul).
[327] Pitching the *renminbi* artificially low to the dollar, China will never give up its role as "the world's factory." True, Chinese workers' wage demands – now often backed by strikes – may nudge up Chinese export prices somewhat. But adroit shifts of priority sectors will steer China to its most advantageous specialties. And theft of Western intellectual property will continue as long as the Chinese are... Chinese. That is, sharp, resourceful businessmen.

Beijing's commercial heft in the World Trade Organization will continue growing, as will its weight in U.S.-China trade negotiations. China's immense holdings of U.S. Treasury bonds also give it huge potential power over the U.S. dollar and economy – though some think the Federal Reserve could buy up enough of these bonds to defang the Chinese dragon. Already cynics, referring to Beijing, are saying: "You can't argue with your banker:" In mid-2010, China held over $900-billion in U.S. Treasury Bills ("T-Bills"). Already you can glimpse America's fear of China in its kowtowing (literally, in Barack Obama's case) to Beijing's growing economic power. And potential military power?

A telling analysis of how China is starting to replace America as the world's economic master appeared in *Bloomberg Businessweek* in November 2010. The magazine's Economics editor Peter Coy recalled that at the 1944 Bretton Woods conference (establishing the postwar monetary system), war-drained

---

327 Sheryrl Gay Stolberg, "Obama slips up in S. Korean trade negotiations," *New York Times*, November 11, 2010. The November 2010 G20 meeting in Seoul illustrated both trade and monetary phenomena – to America's embarrassment and frustration.

Britain wanted strong exporting nations (i.e. the U.S.) to dampen exports in favor of stimulating domestic demand. The U.S. was then, remembered Coy, the globe's "biggest creditor, bestriding the world like a colossus. That's China's part now..." Today, the U.S. was "reduced to the part that Britain played in the 1940s – a weakened power, running chronic trade deficits, and uncertain of how to restart growth." [328]

Adding insult to insult (though politely), German chancellor Angela Merkel turned down an identical request by Obama at the Seoul G20 meeting later that month. Even the pro-American *Economist* decreed in a November 11, 2010 leader that "America's unipolar moment has passed." Passed. As in past. This, barely a decade after the Bush Jr. administration gloated that it was "the world's only remaining superpower." Beijing's dazzling 2008 Olympics was just the coming-out party. On August 16, 2010, came the shocker: China had just surpassed Japan to become the world's second-largest economy. [329] Standard Chartered Bank predicted in a November 2010 report that China would overtake the U.S. as the world's largest economy around 2020. [330]

The significance of this? How the mighty have fallen, of course. We are witnessing a tectonic change. More to our point: How influential is military power if your economy is wobbly? Can you dominate geopolitics if you can't dominate the world economy? The signs of forced military retrenchment are on *this side* of the horizon. Even the signs of lost diplomatic clout. In NATO, the Europeans no longer ask "how high?" when America says "Jump!"

On the second – physical – field (land, sea, air), wars will continue to pit David (e.g. the Taliban, *al-Qaeda* and Somalia's *al-Shabaab*) vs. Goliath (the U.S.). And you know who won that one. Dumping and "surging" big armies into strange Muslim

---

328 Peter Coy, "The Keynes Solution," *Bloomberg Businessweek*, November 1–7, 2010.
329 Kevin Hamlin, Li Yanping, "China Overtakes Japan as World's Second-Biggest Economy," *Bloomberg News*, August 16, 2010.
330 Shamim Adam, "China to Exceed U.S. by 2020, Standard Chartered Says," *Bloomberg News*, November 14, 2010. This prediction echoed a similar prediction on January 21, 2010 by consultancy *PriceWaterhouseCoopers*.

societies and exotic terrain against smart, agile, elusive local fighters is self-defeating, even suicidal. To counter dangers in critical areas, what can the U.S. do? Intelligence link-ups with trustable locals, carefully chosen missions for special forces, and maybe a few discreet supply bases, might prove adequate to stop plots without infuriating resident populations. This is not trillion-dollar stuff. It's targeted, flexible, *affordable* defense.

The gigantic U.S. Navy, moreover, won't be fighting a Battle-of-Midway-style contest of a dozen dueling aircraft carriers. Flexing muscles against a surging Chinese navy in the Asian seas seems mainly political – to reassure smaller Asian nations fearing Chinese claims over resources under the East and South China Seas. A big U.S. Navy may caution China against possible later aggressions. But it essentially maintains America's "right" to an Asian presence.

In actual fighting terms? The U.S. Navy might end up ineffectively dodging Iranian speedboats with missiles able to sink oil tankers in the Strait of Hormuz – thus crippling U.S. oil supplies. Could missile boats even – thinking of the *USS Cole* – seriously damage a carrier? Maybe not. Or maybe yes. And remember: the latest, Nimitz-class carrier, the *USS George H.W. Bush*, cost $6.2-billion. Piloted air power from carriers? Modern aircraft are billion-dollar hammers hitting fleas. They dodge laser-guided or heat-guided missiles fired from the shoulders of bearded, sandal-clad guys hiding in hills.

The third unavoidable field of contest is cyberwar. This – plus outer space – is becoming the riskiest battlefield of all. For sabotage here could one day paralyze the entire military and economic infrastructure of the United States. That could mean physical isolation of vital defense computers, communications systems, and counter-technologies supposed to protect them. But protect them against *any* new threat? Science-fiction authors and even defense planners have long imagined, for example, a space-fired electromagnetic pulse that might fry all U.S. electronics systems.

As inventor of the Internet and modern computers, America might seem assured of keeping ahead of all comers for decades.

But that's dreaming. China, India and Russia produce much stronger crops of mathematicians and scientists. Their local elementary, secondary, undergraduate and graduate schools are cyber brain-factories. One day, they are likely to leapfrog over the U.S. in cyberwar skills and strategies. Russia's brutal mini-cyberwars against tiny Estonia in 2007 and Georgia in 2008 amply demonstrated Russian cyberspace savvy, and its determination to dominate this battlefield.

So do persistent efforts by "independent, unknown" Russian and Chinese hackers to penetrate Western computer networks. The U.S. still enjoys a lead in cryptology – but probably not for long. The fall 2010 "Stuxnet" worm that infected some Iranian atomic-industry computers might be one almost-last hurrah for American (and Israeli?) government hackers. Probably not yet. But in a few years?

Cyberwar also offers opportunities that the U.S. and the West no doubt already exploit: especially sabotaging jihadist websites, after acquiring useful insights and leads. The West can plant disinformation on Twitter and the various *Wiki* sites. And it can electronically block communications: See Israel's May 31, 2010 silencing of radios and phones to prevent live reporting from the Gaza-bound *Mavi Marmara* humanitarian-aid ship.

Cyberwar conducted at the highest levels will be costly. But on a cost-benefit comparison with big ground armies, cyberwar is a financial and political bargain.

Citing these three kinds of inevitable conflicts leads to considering a) the affordability of current defense budgets; and b) the shape of a more cost-effective, "smart-option" defense policy.

Mission Unaffordable

On September 15, 2010, Washington witnessed a sight to leave old Cold-War hands agape: a day-long Pentagon meeting of U.S. and Russian defense ministers... to swap tips on *cutting* their defense budgets. Defense Secretary Robert M. Gates and Defense Minister Anatoly E. Serdyukov instantly made enemies of their own constituencies: bureaucrats, defense industries and, loudest of all, generals. Every NATO country was also scrounging for savings. The significance: War is costing too much. In fact, too-heavy war machines are shrinking choices in foreign policy.

For the U.S. and its allies, this amazing U.S.-Russian meeting flowed straight from another event exactly two years earlier to the day: the September 15, 2008 collapse of New York investment giant Lehman Brothers. This, history will remember as the day the great world financial melt-down of 2008-2010 began. It forced everybody – governments, industries, property-owners, investors – to retrench and regroup. Cutting budgets became a religion, spending a sin.

In a 2010 book called *Frugal Superpower, America's Global Leadership in a Cash-strapped Era,* Michael Mandelbaum laid bare the limits of an activist U.S. foreign policy. Limits at a time of economic stagnation, ballooning entitlement programs, and a no-cost-spared war on terror: "[The Lehman collapse] accelerated a series of developments that will change the resources at the disposal of policy-makers in Washington, limiting the financial means available to conduct American foreign policy. The events of that day, in combination with trends in the American economy that were already under way and will expand in the years ahead, will reduce what the United States does in the world." [331]

The Lehman-triggered recession is only part of the federal government's straitjacket. Aggravating the recession's immediate effects will be *annual over-trillion-dollar deficits* at least as far as the next decade: $1.6-trillion for fiscal 2010 alone. Scarier still, much of this indebtedness is in politically unstoppable enrichment of "entitlement" benefits promised to America's fast-increasing elderly. This bounty includes the free-drugs bonus helpfully added by Republican George W. Bush. Now Tea-Party and Republican insistence on still more tax cuts have spooked even Democrats into favoring lower

---

331 Michael Mandelbaum, extract from *The Frugal Superpower,* cited in *Guernica – a Magazine of Art & Politics,* August 2010.

taxes. A pay-as-you-go America long ago went out the window. The question now is: Can the U.S. *ever* pay down even *part* of its out-of-control, almost $14-trillion national debt? The same angry, elderly Tea Partiers who want their entitlements hate taxes – so they demand that Washington go even deeper into debt to fund their entitlements.

As the unpopular Iraq and Afghan wars wind down (a mere hypothesis), and soldiers come home, Americans will turn inward again to domestic issues. An activist foreign policy, noisily "strong on defense," may start to look both pricey and questionable. Can a day of reckoning finally be on the horizon for the military-industrial complex? For a hard-up superpower? Will Americans, as after the Vietnam war, cool on U.S. "military adventures?" On their love-affair with militarism itself?

When the dust settles, a semi-broke America will be forced to accept a new, more affordable status in the world. This, because forced by its own war-weary people – and, above all, by its fast-emptying coffers. Will a diminished, retrenched America make Muslims love Americans? Probably not. But at least, if such an America pulls back some U.S. soldiers from Muslim lands, it will remove a major pretext to hate and demonize Americans. It will weaken the key *al-Qaeda* recruiting pitch.

A deeply retrenched America is neither possible nor desirable. America is too large and – with its language, culture, values and economy – too omnipresent to disappear. Paul Kennedy, in *The Rise and Fall of the Great Powers*, warned of "imperial overreach." But America's overreach is mainly military, thus capable of contraction as budgets falter. And contraction would be a very good thing – politically and even militarily – as well as unavoidable. Weaker defense budgets need not mean weaker influence in the world. That is, unless you define influence as essentially military. And unless you think "military" demands being the biggest in every single military domain.

There's another consideration – that old lesson linked to short-term vs. long-term "defense." In a November 2010 article on terrorism in Yemen, *The Economist* noted how U.S. air strikes there (often killing nearby innocents) had angered local people and encouraged *al-Qaeda* recruitment. (Afghan President Hamid Karzai says that every week.) Quiet training of Yemeni counter-terrorism specialists was useful, said U.S. friends; but any high-profile U.S. military action was self-defeating. "Tactical decisions must not undermine strategic objectives," the magazine quoted Rick Nelson of the Center for Strategic and International Studies as saying. "Simply capturing and killing bad guys is not a long-term solution." [332]

Unfortunately, capturing and killing bad guys is what traditional soldiers do. And inevitably, as we've seen, if you send thousands of troops to Muslim lands, they will do that on a scale large enough to recruit a new army of terrorists.

Looking again at the long-term – at strategy, not tactics – America doesn't need a new cause. It needs to reinterpret, trumpet *and apply* its old one: freedom, democracy, opportunity. It needs to pursue it with sustained, globe-surveying vision, out-of-the-box imagination, engagement of allies, and what you might call 'daring realism' – the wisdom and humility to try almost anything that helps *people*. Add to that, new listening skills. America must emerge from its self-regarding intellectual and emotional shell – or suffocate there. It must face the world as student, as much as teacher. For many of the "answers" to peace and security already lie in poor, dusty villages far off American radar-screens.

Supporting such a new U.S. worldview and strategy will require three things: getting America's accounts in order; focusing on culture and communication; and waking up the whole world to the single most powerful force for peace: women.

It's Still About the Economy, Stupid!

Getting America's budget under control is easy. All you need is a few ingredients: historical amnesia, a new Constitution, an efficient, intelligent, public-spirited Congress, a permanent truce in U.S. culture wars, and probably a national personality transplant. While waiting for these to come into play, maybe

---

[332] *The Economist*, November 6, 2010.

a look-ahead professor-president like Barack Obama could develop further his big-picture debate on budget priorities. He has already offered "education, innovation (lots of 'greenery' or clean energy), and infrastructure." Inspiringly – and correctly – he thinks America should be "out-innovating, out-educating, and out-building our global competitors and creating the jobs and industries of tomorrow." [333] But as time goes by, his plan should include these Congress-hated ideas: killing "earmarks" (pork); taxing gasoline; and cutting defense spending. Even Ike Eisenhower would approve of the latter.

The next five fiscal years, from 2012, will likely see a continuing (but slower) rise in defense expenditures – but perhaps a smaller proportion of defense in the overall budget: Now defense is "58 percent of discretionary spending and 20 percent of total federal spending (both based on FY 2011 estimates)." [334] The Pentagon's announced cut of $78 billion *over five years* is a flea-bite. To the innocent, this all sounds like the Pentagon is not yet planning to join Weight Watchers. And it sounds like ongoing wars and hoped-for promotions are still a good bet.

Anybody who thinks serious defense cutting has the slightest chance of out-shouting the serving generals, the defense industries, their Congressional puppets, and the Pentagon's religious-media cheerleaders, is living in a pacifist Disneyland. The pro-war people will never try to be fair, or even remotely factual. Take away their mantra of "strong national defense," and they would have to bring *reason* to defense appropriations.

Over time, creeping realities may start to sway opinion. Coming quickly into focus is bankruptcy of cherished entitlement programs. Just one example: Soon these programs will face crushing assault from tens of millions of new physically 'healthy,' but costly-to-maintain, Alzheimer patients – all under the elders' program called Medicare. The only question is: How long will it take for the "frugal facts" to turn minds toward more rational priorities than sky's-the-limit defense spending? A May 2010 report from the Alzheimer Association says that

---

333 "Winning the Future for Our Children," *White House* website.
334 *Institute of Public Accuracy* website, February 14, 2011.

America's current 5.1 million Alzheimer patients will rise to 13.5 million by 2050. The yearly cost of care will rise from 2010's $172-billion to over a *trillion* dollars in 2050.

Among the arguments Obama has to use are the following. First, allowing unsustainable, mammoth defense budgets to continue ballooning helps export this generation's already crushing debts to America's children and grandchildren. Second – and this is hoisting the in-love-with-the-military zealots on their own petard – out-of-control national budgets directly *weaken national defense*. That is the unanswerable point of Mandelbaum's brilliantly-documented-and-argued book *The Frugal Superpower*. Big-Defense backers, he proves, are actually *undermining* a strong defense.

Obama's third argument could undermine an all-military foreign policy even more decisively. But it would take even more time, patience and eloquence than the other two. This argument cuts to the very core of modern power: Power is becoming less and less military. It is becoming more and more economic. See, for example, China and Germany.

The Pentagon, and especially the U.S. Navy, has long worried about rising Chinese military expenditures. For much of the last decade, these have risen by 10 to 24 percent a year (not counting secret budgets) – though from a relatively low base. In 2010, citing the world economic slowdown, China said its defense budget rose "only" by 7.5 percent. Most observers believe that the real figures are much higher. Beijing claims it seeks only a "soft rise" to regional predominance. The U.S. and China's neighbors wonder how soft, how fast, and how high.

But how much of China's soaring status in the world depends on *military* strength? Quite a bit, no doubt – a population of over 1.3-billion in itself looks like a formidable potential adversary. The truth is even simpler: China's "defense" power is probably 90 percent economic. Watching Chinese economic growth surge routinely by 10 percent a year for nearly two decades, the world has a very good idea of China's deep and durable strength. China doesn't need to flex military muscle at every turn to get heard. Its domestic prosperity, trade and investments tell the tale. Without firing a shot, China has peacefully "invaded" Africa, Europe, and, to a lesser extent, Latin America. In satirical vein: Even "Monroe-Doctrine" territory, a few generals might warn...

America's *Wal-Mart*, among many other U.S. retailers, also knows a little about Chinese products. Western exporters (notably French and Germans) rush to Beijing to beg for multi-billion contracts. China is now a go-to economic superpower. It sits serenely facing the world, grinning like a porcelain Qing Dynasty *Fu-dog*, guarding its vast market, and maybe deigning to grant an occasional favor.

Ponder these unusual examples of how China's economic power is giving it diplomatic, even cultural, clout. In Beijing's September 2010 fishing-boat dispute with Japan, it only had to huff and puff and squeeze a few trade, immigration and tourist levers to force proud Tokyo to kowtow. At the same time, Paris and New York art dealers complained that collectors were turning away from Japanese art, and tripping over each other to buy Chinese art. Led the *New York Times*: "Two historic sales took place last week in Paris and New York. The dramatic contrast between the lackluster outcome of the French auction that dealt with Japanese color prints and the hugely successful American auction devoted to Chinese art in part mirrors the changing power balance between the two great cultures of the Far East." [335]

Mere anecdotal coincidence? Not at all. It's exactly how the art world has flourished in tandem with economic empire over the centuries: from Spain's Golden-Age Velázquez, to tulipmania Holland's Rembrandt, to the Victorians' gauzy light-show Turner, to Napoleon III's Manet, Degas, Renoir, Cézanne, and a kaleidoscope of other serviceable French geniuses – to America's late 20th-century parade of *Brillo* pads, *Campbell's Soup* cans, fetuses-in-formaldehyde, and Christ-bearing crosses in glasses of urine. Maybe this stuff is not quite obvious esthetic progress. But *Ars Gratia Artis* is routinely *Ars Gratia Imperii*. Advice to artists:

---

[335] "A Sifting Balance of Power," Souren Malikian, *New York Times*, September 24, 2010.

Wait for an empire, or at least a tulip-or-mortgage bubble, and your art will sell.

France too still sees 'empire' in every export. But for historical, industrial and psychological reasons, it has always invested heavily in military equipment, armies and *cachet*. This is vital now to keeping up *la gloire* – and to selling France's highly profitable arms exports. President Nicolas Sarkozy's 2011 leap to attack Libya's Muammar Gaddafi was especially dramatic, and politically effective. But economically, France drags behind Germany by almost every economic standard – except foreign direct investment. This severely limits its clout, especially within the European Union.

Germany, on the other hand, while doing a reasonable job of backing NATO militarily, dominates Europe politically. Why? Because of its dynamic industrial *economy* – the real "locomotive" of European prosperity, and bedrock of the euro. Germany's mind-space is far less in defense than in developing job-creating exports. Its famous *Mittelstand* – small- and medium-sized industries – employ over 70 percent of Germany's private-sector workers. Their high-quality products underpin Germany's reputation for excellence, hence its image of reliable, trustable power. [336]

In dealing with other countries, such excellence is almost a tangible "national defense" asset. It's a gauge and guarantee of power. America used to 'conquer' the world through admired exports. As the Ford Motor Company recently showed – generations after Henry Ford – they could still set international industrial standards.[337] From the viewpoint of national imagery,

---

336 Trust can be lost. Germany's reluctance to expose its soldiers to danger in Afghanistan has, for some, shown an "unreliable" nation that barely counts militarily. Chancellor Angela Merkel's astonishing neo-pacifist meandering over Libya in March 2011 confirmed this. Some close allies even said this proved that Germany could "no longer be trusted" and had ceased to deserve a permanent seat on the UN Security Council. A pity – but, in the interest of UN peacekeeping and its "responsibility to protect," the pendulum may swing back to a more realistic balance. Germany's economic might, and its willingness to fund peacekeeping, will likely guarantee this.
337 Steven Manning, "American Car Quality Tops Foreign Car Quality, Finds J.D. Power And Associates," *Huffpost Business*, June 17, 2010. Ford,

a highly-skilled nation exudes power. Prestige *is* power. And non-military exports strengthen the economy without addicting America to Pentagon contracts.

For military budget-cutters, here's a metaphor, though scarcely a likely paradigm: In 1948, Costa Rica *abolished* its armed forces. Savings went, and still go, to education, culture, health and local security. Plainly, this is unthinkable for the United States. It's a superpower with global responsibilities. But as a *symbol* of swords-to-plowshares thinking, and perhaps a motivation for greater common sense (sanity?), it should linger in the back of Congressional and media minds. The momentum to spend blindly on military *desiderata* is not unstoppable. It can be slowed with clear thinking, and with ferocious determination to reject featherbedding, routine cost overruns and gold-plating of everything in sight – including generals' perks.

A place where "Costa Rican" reasoning might make sense – even to Tea-Party super-patriots? – could be investing in better care for veterans and ordinary frontline soldiers. Cutting 12 aircraft carriers to, say, nine, could allow diversion of solid savings to a couple of surely uncontroversial needs: safer equipment (including armor) for soldiers; and kinder, longer-term care for the damaged bodies and minds of hundreds of thousands – soon millions – of war veterans sent to butchery by often misguided politicians. Weapons are essential to armies. But they're not as vital as human beings. War is iron and blood. And blood is sons and daughters.

Let's imagine now a "reasonable miracle." This would consist of Washington's accepting two ideas. First, that huge-army ground wars now (for both strategic and budgetary reasons) make no sense in the Muslim world, or indeed anywhere else. Second, that investing part of the savings from active-army cutbacks should go to a mix of smarter weapons, cyberwar skills, war veterans, and the "soft options" of helping build more peaceful, long-term Muslim societies.

---

said the authoritative Power consultancy, "showed some of the biggest gains in quality among individual brands, moving into the fifth spot. Porsche was the top scorer."

Affordable smarter weapons should continue pouring off the design boards. If carefully used, they can save lives, not kill "collateral" innocents. Developing cyberwar skills probably requires a new Defense Education Act favoring a mix of mathematics, the sciences (including social), and languages. Veterans? Seeing them treated generously would be one of the best ways to motivate the smaller forces required. .

Building a Muslim world more "reconciled" with the West requires a whole new style of dialogue. This includes support for healthy home-grown Muslim economic and social solutions. Let's look at both points.

Talking With the Muslim World, Not At It

A very affordable "Costa-Rican" priority for American foreign policy would be a much-expanded role for U.S.-Muslim communication – at a popular level. It's a natural and ideal way to strengthen U.S. defense. Remember what Ayman al-Zawahiri, *al-Qaeda*'s no.2 said: "We are in a battle, and... more than half of this battle is taking place in the battlefield of the media... we are in a media battle in a race for the hearts and minds of our *Umma* [worldwide Muslim community]."

Quickly: What have you heard recently about U.S. efforts to reach Muslim hearts and minds worldwide? About efforts to build cultural bridges *between* cultures – not just to hype the glories of America? What credible, well-adapted messages of respect and solidarity is America passing to overseas Muslims?

Muslims see fair play in the Middle East as a strict minimum. They can accept that America backs Israel strongly. But they would like at least acknowledgment that there is a Palestinian interest too. Typically, on Sept. 23, 2010, the U.S. said Israel's legitimacy is "sacred." Of course it is. But, say Arabs, isn't a future Palestine's legitimacy sacred too? In praising "security" for Israel, shouldn't the U.S. also promise security to Palestinians and an eventual Palestine? Both Israel and the Palestinian lands emerged from the same 1947 UN General Assembly Resolution 181 (II). Does that not, insist Palestinians, create some degree of "moral equivalence?" Or are Muslims (as well as Palestinian Christians) simply irrelevant?

George W. Bush did promise two neighboring states, Israel and Palestine. But his approach to Muslim Arabs was shockingly shallow. Instead of reaching out to listen, in essence he said to Muslims: "Now listen to us!" Bush wondered why Arabs and Muslims hated him – and thus America – so much. But he wouldn't waste time studying Middle East history and culture, or reviewing U.S. policies that enraged Muslims. He decided that America's unpopularity was just a quirky PR problem.

To fix that, he named three utterly ineffective cheerleaders in a row. All females (perhaps not a master-stroke to sway macho Islam), and none intimately in tune with Muslim mores. Job title: Under Secretary of State for Public Diplomacy and Public Affairs. First up: advertising executive Charlotte Beers (*Uncle Ben's Rice*). Her feel-good, America-the-Beautiful-loves-Muslims videos flopped. Next, State Department lifer Margaret D. Tutwiler took the mike. She handed it back after five months – just as America's Abu Ghraib Iraq prison scandals broke – and found another scandal-prone refuge in Wall Street. Finally, the third cheerleader – Texas TV reporter, "W" flack, and Republican apparatchik Karen Hughes – rushed to tell Saudi women that they were unhappy because they couldn't get a driver's license. Her audience replied that they were happy enough. Hughes never recovered. Aptly, she joined a big New York PR firm – perhaps to lobby for immigrants' driver's licenses.

Historical irony: In 2011, Obama's message on the Libyan phase of the Arab Spring came most strongly from three other female "cheerleaders." These ones, more policy-makers than cheerleaders, were anything but ineffective: Samantha Power, Susan Rice and Hillary Clinton. Their role in confronting the Mad Colonel elicited these delightfully "Dowdy" (i.e. 'undowdy') words from sharp-tongued *New York Times* columnist Maureen Dowd:

> They are called the Amazon Warriors, the Lady Hawks, the Valkyries, the Durgas.

There is something positively mythological about a group of strong women swooping down to shake the president out of his delicate sensibilities and show him the way to war. And there is something positively predictable about guys in the White House pushing back against that story line for fear it makes the president look henpecked.

It is not yet clear if the Valkyries will get the credit or the blame on Libya. But everyone is fascinated with the gender flip: the reluctant men — the generals, the secretary of defense, top male White House national security advisers — outmuscled by the fierce women around President Obama urging him to man up against the crazy Qaddafi. [338]

What's that brouhaha from afar? It's Boadicea, Joan of Arc and a jungle-full of Amazons screaming: "You go girls!" And surprise! These "girls" get along: Hillary has forgiven Samantha for describing her – in the heat of the Democratic Presidential Primary – as a "monster." Now that's peacekeeping.

Today's official U.S. approach to Muslims is more subtle than that of the three Bush cheerleaders. But the real problem is still not PR. It's policies. American spokespersons still have to defend U.S. policies (such as unconditional, one-sided support for Israel) that strike Arabs as deeply biased and unjust. Some people may not like that characterization; but few can deny that almost all Muslims see things that way.

Another lingering problem is the old George W. Bush self-cheerleading syndrome (W, you may recall, actually *was* a college cheerleader). This consists of extravagant self-glorification to shove "exceptionalist" America down everybody's throat – all for their own good, naturally. Perhaps a better way to make America look good to Muslims abroad might be to cheerlead a little for Islam – for example, to reach out to modern Muslims' greatest talents in every area (especially non-religious); then to visibly engage with them.

For a start, there is plenty of history to chew on. Much Muslim anger flows from grieving (if only subliminally) for mythic Andalusia – the ancient *Al-Andalus* where and when they were riding high as a leading civilization. Another good start for U.S. and Western "propagandists" would be to devour, and annotate, the UN Arab Human Development Reports.

---

338 Maureen Dowd, "Fight of the Valkyries," *New York Times*, March 22, 2011.

These, written by leading Arab scholars, are both a diagnosis of Arab ills and a blueprint for fixing them. This can include marginalizing abusive, crippling interpretations of Islam.

Washington has made some well-meaning media efforts. Funded by the U.S. Congress, the 24-hour-a-day *Alhurra* ("The Free One") Arabic TV network gives a U.S. view of world events, especially Middle Eastern affairs. Inevitably, this is not popular – because the *policies* are not popular. *Alhurra*'s U.S. sponsorship and tone also taint its news credibility. But it does run women's programs – including *Musawat* ("Equality") – that deal with women's rights issues that Arab-owned networks often don't cover. An example of *Musawat*'s courage: traditional Arab males hate its host, Nadine Al Bedair. She published a "blasphemous," mildly satirical, article proposing that Muslim women should have the right to four husbands (a parallel right to a Muslim man's possible four wives). Fanatics threatened one of her guests with stoning for saying that unmarried women – even if raped or abandoned – should be allowed to keep their babies.

Respected *Voice of America* radio used to broadcast in Arabic – until it was replaced in 2002 by trivial, teenage pop-music *Radio Sawa*. Even *VOA* sometimes struggled to compete in credibility with the long-established *BBC World Service*. But *Radio Sawa*, broadcasting from a Washington studio (though with Mideast bureaus) and largely funded by Congress, is a sad joke. Few Arabs trust its short, parochial, U.S.-centric news bulletins. And many commercial Arab stations play the same Enimen, Britney Spears and Lady Gaga music 24 hours a day. Again the irony: America, so proud of its technological skills, free press, lofty democratic message and vibrant culture, uses high tech to peddle its arguably 'lowest' products. Throwing money at nothing gets you... nothing. Bruce Springsteen's song had it right: "57 Channels and Nothin' On."

Influential websites encouraged by the U.S. include the *Arab Network for Human Rights Information*. Its mandate is to use the Internet: "to free the activities of human rights organizations from the restrictions they now face. We hope to give these organizations a megaphone to magnify their voices in-country and in the [Middle East] region."

Sending any message to the Muslim world often collides with U.S. domestic politics. Obama made the imaginative suggestion to former NASA head Charles Bolden that he try "to reach out to the Muslim world and engage much more with dominantly Muslim nations to help them feel good about their historic contribution to science ... and math and engineering." *Fox News*, true to its myopic, partisan view of the world, condemned the idea as a deviation from NASA's mission of space exploration. Walking and chewing gum at the same time seemed just too complicated for *Fox*. NASA could easily have stuck to its technological mission – but made a few inexpensive, but diplomatically useful, gestures by tipping its hat to the Muslim world's enormous Medieval role in math and science. Presumably *Fox*, as well as NASA, are using Roman, not Arabic, numerals.

Basically – and Lady-Gaga snobbery aside – any Western scientific, technological, and especially cultural, activity that can divert young Muslims from theological mountebanks is good. Even better, if it can engage them in collaborations with Western youth. Obvious arenas: student exchanges, and sharing culture (especially collaborative music) and sports. But the West can only break through to Muslim minds by listening far more than it talks. Another bromide, yes. But bromides are designed to bring calm.

Leading from Behind: (Muslim) Allies With Answers

Long-term initiatives to counter jihadist war are not yet coming from America. Understandably, Washington grapples almost exclusively with today's terrorist 'alligators' – active killers. It's not doing much to drain the swamp of tomorrow's alligators.

Many of the best investments in swamp-draining "soft" or "smart" options come field-tested from the Muslim world itself. Probably five large Muslim democracies, plus one enlightened

Muslim family-state, might guide the West in preventing long-term terrorism: Bangladesh, Malaysia, Indonesia, Turkey, India, and Qatar.

Bangladesh? Yes. Its economy – long thought a basket-case – now grows at six percent a year. Is it a coincidence that Prime Minister Sheikh Hasina is a woman, as is its Opposition Leader Khaleda Zia? And as are the holders of the key Foreign, Finance, Agriculture and Home (Interior) ministries? Only 15 of 345 Members of Parliament are women. That's virtually the same percentage of female Lower-House legislators as in the U.S. – except that in Bangladesh it's a constitutionally guaranteed percentage. The country's fast-rising, if still inadequate, cell-phone penetration rate is just over 35 percent. But it's turbocharged by the Grameen Bank's micro-loans to (in late 2010) 180,000 "telephone-ladies," a group growing by 10,000 a month.[339]

Fanatical male Islamists, it's true, have chased Bengali-language writer Taslima Nasreen to Sweden for "blasphemy" – and incidentally for her work promoting women. But the country as a whole is moving forward to improved women's rights. To acknowledge this, the West should open its markets far more to Bangladeshi textiles, a key export. In exchange, Bangladesh could provide unique advice on economic, social and political development spearheaded by women – advice, if applied, that could decisively discourage Islamist extremism. Can the West overcome its stereotype of the "Bangladesh basket-case" and listen to Dhaka's development case? The Nobel Peace Prize committee did so already – in honoring Grameen Bank and its Dr. Muhammad Yunus.

Malaysia is a guiding star for several reasons. It's democratic (after a recent authoritarian streak), economically advanced, smoothly multicultural, and it has a long history of promoting

---

[339] A sad shadow on Bangladesh: As mentioned, Prime Minister Hasina seemed in 2011 to be waging a political vendetta against revered Dr. Yunus of Grameen Bank. The full story is not yet told as of this writing, but several serious foreign observers note that Yunus's alleged misdemeanor is a minor technical point about serving as a bank officer beyond the authorized age. They also observe that there seemed to be no problem until the government came to believe that Yunus might enter politics against it.

women's equality. Westerners are familiar with Malaysia's high-tech manufacturing industries, and with Kuala Lumpur's soaring Petronas Twin Towers. But how many of us know that Malaysian women have zoomed to the top in Islamic banking? Fozia Amanulla, female chief executive of Eoncap Islamic Bank, credits women's success in Malaysian banking to a society that doesn't segregate men and women. Zeti Akhtar Aziz is the first female governor of Malaysia's central bank. Jamelah Jamaluddin in 2007 became the world's first woman to head an Islamic Bank. She is now an international superstar of the over-*trillon*-dollar Islamic banking sector.

Context of Malaysia's progress: If any of these accomplished women visit Saudi Arabia, they must be accompanied everywhere by a male relative. They may also find that local male counterparts will not shake hands, look them in the eye, or answer their questions directly. For understanding how women could advance in banking and business in other Muslim countries, "KL" (Kuala Lumpur) is the place to go. [340]

Indonesia is another key guide for Asia. As the world's largest Muslim country by population (230 million), Indonesia is not quite a paragon of honest government – corruption remains rife. But it has now run some pretty fair elections, is very prosperous, and relatively quite tolerant. Again best of all, it practices a 'moderate' version of Islam. The 2002 Bali night-club bombers who murdered 202 people remind us that *al-Qaeda*-inspired groups exist. But they are small, and are kept down by ruthless army-and-police security forces. They get often severe judicial punishment.

The main value of Indonesia, apart from its economic and democratic successes, is the relative live-and-let-live atmosphere of its Islamic model. It can give hope to young Muslims elsewhere for a saner, happier life than dreaming how to kill "infidels" and to win Heavenly virgins as a "martyr." The U.S. can and should point to the Indonesian example far more than it does. A former 'Indonesian' school-boy, Barack Obama, did just that on his wildly-welcomed visit to Indonesia in November

---

340 "High achievers in high finance," Liz Gooch, *International Herald Tribune*, September 27, 2010.

2010. Like Obama the black President in the White House for America, Indonesia makes wonderful propaganda for Islam just by existing. It can, and must, become a strong link between Islam and America.

Turkey may be the West's single best bridge to the Muslim world. Like Indonesia, it has developed over decades a solid, seductive modern society – but one whose ancient Muslim character echoes from thousands of minarets. Ankara is an old familiar U.S. ally within NATO, and a valiant war-partner in the 1950-53 Korean War. It has a modern, dynamic economy. Most vitally, it has devised a peaceful, though still evolving, *modus vivendi* between Islamists and secularists. Its much-admired hybrid Muslim-secular *imam-hatip* school curriculum has already led to aforementioned experiments in rigidly traditionalist Pakistan and Afghanistan – to the fury of Saudi-trained *Wahhabi* preachers.

Turkey still lags in many women's rights. One-third of village women are illiterate. In rural areas, "honor killings" of women remain shockingly common. But over 40,000 policemen have received training to deal with these scourges, and the government has run impressive TV campaigns against them.

Even in the large cities – Istanbul and Ankara, for example – women still face discrimination in the workforce, where they are only 25 percent of employees. Public administration and politics lack senior women. But the cities vividly display the contradictions of a society in fast evolution. In the streets, Muslim dress meets miniskirt. And women are increasingly taking leading roles in education, where many hold top university jobs.

Since the May 31, 2010 Israeli naval attack on its "Gaza Freedom Flotilla," Turkey has become extraordinarily popular in the Arab world. It has also inspired wide respect in the world for its 'loyal independence' from the United States. In 2003, it refused American requests to allow its troops to invade Iraq through Turkish territory. And in the 2010 Iran-West stand-off on nuclear weapons, it thumbed its nose at the U.S. by pursuing its own non-sanctions diplomacy on Iran, along with Brazil.

In future – whether or not it makes it (in a decade or more?) into the European Union – Turkey will continue to prosper economically. And thus diplomatically. The icing on the cake: Prime Minister Recep Tayyip Erdoğan, linking up with Spain's José Luis Rodríguez Zapatero, founded the 2005 "Alliance of Civilizations." This initiative seeks to resist religious and ethnic extremism through "international, intercultural and inter-religious dialogue." Originally proposed by Spain, then backed by Turkey, this could make Spain the West's most useful non-Muslim "guide" to the Muslim world. Reaching back to the seven centuries of its legendary *Al-Andalus* period, Spain has the historical, intellectual and moral authority to welcome Turkey's Muslim bridge to the West. To make the fabled 2005 "Ramallah Concert" possible, Madrid issued Spanish diplomatic passports to young musicians of Daniel Barenboim's West-Eastern Divan Orchestra (established with Palestinian Edward Said). An exquisite touch, turning protocol to serve culture and understanding.

If Turkey is arguably America's and the West's most instructive guide to the Middle East, it can help too with Turkic-language peoples of Central Asia: Turkmen, Afghans, Northern Iraqis, northern Iranians, Azerbaijanis. Notwithstanding its post Gaza-Flotilla discord with Israel, indeed perhaps because of it, Turkey will be able to help sway Arab people behind any eventual Israel-Palestine agreement. Erdoğan is now a hero in the Arab world. The West may need to ask him to spend there some of his well-earned capital of credibility.

Turkey's value as a guide for Westerners doesn't rest on perfection. In some ways, Turkey is still struggling to pull itself out of its old Ottoman Empire stagnation. But it compels attention for several reasons. It has a population of 80 million, three-quarters urban. Virtually 100 percent Muslim, it understands and reflects many dimensions of Islam: It is 80 percent Sunni and roughly 20 percent Shia, with a scattering of Sufis and smaller sects. Turkey accommodates beliefs and lifestyles from traditionalist Islam to resolute secularism – the latter a legacy of Mustafa Kemal's 1923 Revolution for across-the-board national modernization. Both Jews and Christians can testify that Turkey, with few exceptions, has historically respected and protected them.

Finally, Turkey matters because, one day, it may become a member of the European Union. For now, as elsewhere in the West, there is much anti-Muslim sentiment in Europe – and resistance to Muslim immigration. But one way or another, Turkey and Europe will probably grow closer, even as Turkey stays close to the Muslim world. There again is the key strategic question: Will Turkey become a bridge for Europe to the Muslim world? Or will it become a bridge-*head* for Islam in Europe? The economic, geopolitical, diplomatic and cultural factors in play, taken together, argue for the "bridge" view. Turkey will always be worth listening to. And it will be a source of invaluable ideas for the West's policies in the Muslim world.

India, a Muslim country? Not officially. It's a multicultural, predominantly Hindu, country. But it's home to the world's third largest Muslim population – at 161 million, less only than Indonesia's 203 million and Pakistan's 174 million. However, India's democracy is old and flourishing – reaching back to ancestral five-member *panchayati raj* village councils and British parliamentarianism. And therein lies its deep attraction as a model, partly 'Muslim" community. With most of the world's 50 Muslim-majority states being dictatorships of one kind or another, India's tens of millions of freedom-accustomed Muslim citizens could, if brought more into play, act as a democratic ferment. They could, just by telling their story to other Muslims, demonstrate that democracy and Islam can peacefully coexist in a single society.

That's a powerful and hopeful message to Muslims wherever rulers flout democracy, free expression and other civil liberties. With Indian government cooperation, the U.S. should look for ways to highlight this message. Prominent in business, the arts, entertainment and literature, India's Muslims are natural allies for democracy in the Muslim world. Political, geopolitical, cultural and theological complexities make international Muslim-to-Muslim links tricky – especially vis-à-vis touchy Pakistan. But if subtly encouraged, these might prove exceedingly fruitful.

A final, unusually open-minded state outside these mature or fast-maturing Muslim democracies is the Persian-Gulf Emirate of Qatar. Run with a firm but benevolent hand by Sheikh Hamad bin Khalifa Al Thani since 1995, Qatar is best known for its serious, hugely-watched international *Al Jazeera* TV networks. Through editorially separate Arabic and English networks, and with other language services in the works, *Al Jazeera* is now a respected, hard-hitting news organization. Its English network (AJE) alone may reach over a billion people worldwide, in competition with the *BBC*, *CNN* and other major mainstream networks. The originality and depth of *AJE*'s long-form documentaries attract much admiration.

Qatar's value as Western guide and inspiration to other Muslim peoples derives largely from *Al Jazeera*. But the Emir's imaginative range of diplomatic interlocutors – running from Israel, Europe and the U.S. to *Hamas, Hezbollah* and even *al-Qaeda* – also gives him extraordinary opportunities as a trusted go-between. Sheikh Khalifa Al Thani has several times tried to favor reconciliation of adversaries. His huge investments in education, culture and health (many of them piloted by his wife, Sheikha Moza bint Nasser Al Missned), demonstrate his intention to make Qatar an exemplary, progressive society with international reach. The "lessons" of Qatar: openness to the world, to different perspectives, to diverse cultures; tolerance; and pragmatism instead of ideology. The gas-financed Qatar "model" may only work in Muslim nations blessed by huge natural resources. But wealth is not the only secret. As oil- and resource-rich Nigeria (mixed Muslim-Christian), Gabon (mainly Christian), Congo and other unstable, unhappy oil-rich nations sadly show – if rulers lack the vision, public spirit and will to develop their countries for their people, rather than cronies, nothing good can happen.

If ever the West and Iran get beyond their passionate ideological and geopolitical differences (i.e. whenever, at a minimum, the ayatollah-based regime falls), the West might add Iran to any small group of Muslim nations with lessons to teach. Iran has a strong education system – especially in science and mathematics – in which women are extremely well represented. About 60 percent of Iranian university students are women; in science and engineering, their proportion rises above 70 percent. Even more promising: Against all other Muslim experience, Iran has far more girls than boys in primary schools: 1.22 girls for every boy. That's the world's highest ratio of girls to boys in elementary education. Surprisingly, much of this came *after* the 1979 Islamic Revolution.

Iran's current anti-women practices (has stoning really stopped?) make close West-Iran collaboration unthinkable. But one should keep an optimistic eye on Iran. And remember that its former president, moderate cleric Muhammad Khatami, first proposed, in a 1998 UN speech, a "dialogue among civilizations and cultures" to replace Samuel P. Huntington's Clash of Civilizations. Iran's ancient civilization is a vast cultural store-house. Alas, it may not be possible for the West, and even many other Muslim nations, to access this treasure until a more enlightened Iranian regime comes to power.

Persecuting human-rights lawyer Shirin Ebadi, their country's own female Nobel Prize-winner, was not good advertising for President Mahmoud Ahmadinejad and the Ayatollahs. Neither was arresting leading political opponents. But backing the thug who murdered in the street 26-year-old female student Neda Salehi Agha Soltan told us who the rulers really are.

There may be other potential guides for the West in Central Asia. But these nations are still too unstable and/or authoritarian to mix-and-match with the West, at least in ways that hope-seeking Muslims elsewhere could find exemplary. The West – instead of ignorantly lumping together all the world's Muslims as "terrorists" or crypto-terrorists – can find strategic peace with Islam.

This starts with crossing a few bridges of mutual Muslim-West advantage. Then with following Muslim guides who want peace as much as the West does. That is the essence of "soft power." It is the foundation of a jihad-defeating policy of "resistance and reconciliation."

Give Peace a Chance: Dilute the Testosterone

Consider this: Could radically expanded opportunities for Third World girls and women prove decisive in building a more peaceful world? Could making such opportunities a *central priority* of U.S. foreign policy "fight terrorism" more effectively – and lastingly – than ever-creeping military actions? Could a strategy of "soft" (or "smart") options – education, health, business, and media training – really prove a more cost-effective way to make our world secure? Could America – even while fighting jihadists militarily, and conducting robust counter-intelligence and cyberwarfare – profitably complement its "resistance" to jihadists with greatly enhanced strategic *reconciliation* with Islam? Specifically: Could Muslim women, far from being victims, become the vanguard of reconciliation?

Given the variety of Muslim cultures, such reconciliation can't impose liberty U.S.-style in a one-size-fits-all manner. It must embrace diversity of models and styles. But this is clear: a "reconciliation agenda" should focus less on governments and battlefields, and aim to reconcile *peoples*, highlighting girls and women. Such an approach will threaten certain Muslim cultures, but mainly in communities already held back by reactionary customs and religious leaders. Coincidentally, all of the most dogmatic variations of religion – say, within Judaism, Christianity and Islam – seem to keep their women covered, segregated and submissive.

All evidence since Lysistrata shows that freeing women, especially though education, creates virtuous circles of benefit for families, villages, nations, and the world. [341] It's no secret, and certainly no joke, that "males love fighting." And that most women, if given a chance, will seek conciliation. Massive evidence from past and current studies in conflict and its resolution illustrate this. Women may not all be pacifist angels – remember

---

[341] Veterans of the gender wars know well that Lysistrata, in the famous comic 411 BC play of that name by Aristophanes, organized the women of Athens to withhold sexual privileges from men who refused to negotiate an end to the Peloponnesian War. They stopped that war eventually – but re-ignited another one with their lovers.

Margaret Thatcher, Golda Meir and Indira Gandhi – but at least they don't drink testosterone every morning. Most of them normally do try to avoid the fighting that men thrive on. Giving little boys dolls and little girls toy guns doesn't change *la différence*.

Summing up again: Instead of focusing all its resources on a war of arms to kill or capture terrorists, America should now – *seriously* – be fighting a parallel war of ideas to liberate women. Specifically, loudly and persistently. That's not naïve. It's the hardest realism. It's the smartest, most tough-minded, most *strategic* way to defeat long-term terrorism. America should be fighting this other war – the war for the people (women) who have proven they can deliver peace. A war *for* women, defying the old one *against* them.

This war for women is at bottom a war for the economy. For putting people to work, helping them feed and educate their families, and giving whole families a boost up the economic ladder. And in the process, giving them a chance to build a happy, self-reconciled society. Nobel laureate Amartya Sen prophesied in 1998 that social opportunities, education and health care for women would help to solve the population problem which worsens all economic problems. But such solutions had to be "embedded in the economic fabric." [342] UN Secretary-General Kofi Annan argued for women as motors of development, and his UN Millennium Project called women's empowerment "vital for successful economic development." Speaking in May 2010, he said that "women's empowerment remains crucial for Africa's development and must be prioritized as the continent moves forward." [343] In September that year, he added that the world needed to "put investment in jobs and people, particularly girls and women, *at the heart of growth and development strategies* [author's italics]." [344] Annan's successor Ban Ki-moon carries the same torch. He presses hard for achievement of Jeffrey Sachs' Millennium goals for women.

---

342 Amartya Sen, "Empower women for development," *Times of India*, December 27, 1998.
343 Laura Lopez Gonzalez, "Kofi Annan, women's empowerment key to continent's progress," *Gender Links*, May 20, 2010.
344 *AllAfrica.com* website, September 20, 2010.

Writing in *Foreign Affairs*, Isobel Coleman, Senior Fellow at the Council on Foreign Relations, summarized the case in 2004: "Backing women's rights in developing countries isn't just good ethics; it's also sound economics. Growth and living standards get a dramatic boost when women are given just a bit more education, political clout, and economic opportunity. So the United States should aggressively promote women's rights abroad. And by couching its case in economic terms, it might even overcome the resistance of conservative Muslim countries that have long balked at gender equality." [345]

One Afghanistan observer, journalist Sally Armstrong, pointed out in October 2010: "... There is a direct correlation between the status of women and the economy — where one is flourishing, so is the other, where one is in the ditch so is the other. Every indicator says it's the women who can lead Afghanistan away from the abyss." [346]

The *New York Times*'s Nicholas D. Kristof, a tireless advocate for Afghan women, constantly stresses how education and small business point the way to peace and prosperity: "The best way to end oppression isn't firepower but rather education and economic empowerment, for men and women alike, in ways that don't create a backlash... schooling is possible even in Taliban-controlled areas, as long as implementation is undertaken in close consultation with elders and doesn't involve Westerners on the ground." He cites an amazingly successful women entrepreneur group called BPeace. Talking mullahs and elders into accepting and protecting them, members have created profitable factories of many kinds. One makes potato chips, another shoes. A third has 3,000 mainly female employees making jams, furniture, tailored and knitted clothing, and jewelry. [347]

Economic stability and opportunity obviously underpin any serious effort at peace. They do so far more than bigwigs with

---

345 Isobel Coleman, "The Payoff From Women's Rights," *Foreign Affairs*, May-June 2004.
346 Sally Amstrong, "To the Women of Afghanistan," op-ed in *International Herald Tribune*, October 27, 2010.
347 "What About Afghan Women?" Nicholas D. Kristof, *New York Times*, October 23, 2010.

their bags of "donated" money and homegrown guile. More than the ethnic and tribal chiefs jockeying for power. More than the tens of thousands of soldiers from some 38-odd Western coalition members. More too than Asian neighbors fishing in Afghanistan's troubled waters. All these will play shorter, sometimes even decisive, roles. But the deepest, longest-term, ground-up underpinning of security and reconciliation will come from the half of Afghanistan's population rocking the cradles of peace.

These "burqa brigades" offer unique advantages for peace. Women as peace-builders now attract impressive fans. UN Security Council Resolution 1325 of October 31, 2000 urged major roles for women in all areas of peacekeeping and peace-building. "I firmly believe," said NATO secretary-general Anders Fogh Rasmussen in October 2010, "that women can play a very important role in the prevention of conflicts and in peace-building." [348] Madeleine Albright spelled out her rationale: "Because women are often a principal victim of conflict, the women's perspective can be vital in seeking to prevent or to mitigate the damage caused by conflict. That assertion should not be controversial; it is simply common sense." [349]

Some critical roles only women can play in actual combat: frisking female suspects, "softening" the impact of violent house searches, comforting rape victims and children, interrogating women and even men. Some experts argue that women interrogators can more easily wheedle men into talking. Other observers, alas, can point out more sinister roles of women at Abu Ghraib and Guantánamo. But the splendid performance of an all-women Indian UN peacekeeping unit in Liberia demonstrated the real potential of women soldiers. Their presence radiated calm in local communities, encouraged local women to join police units, and gave many female victims of violence the courage to seek justice. In all, these 100-odd, highly disciplined women made an irreplaceable contribution to peace and security.

---

348 Katrin Bennhold, "Waging War and Peace With Women," *New York Times*, November 2, 2010.
349 *Ibid.*

"Having served in turbulent areas, including parts of northern India," said their female commander Seema Dhundiya, "they are well prepared.. These girls are experienced and have been trained. They have worked in areas of India where there was insurgency. They will do a good job, and the Liberian ladies will get motivated and inspired to come forward and join the regular police." [350]

Joanna Foster, a UN gender adviser, noted than women peacekeepers do not cause incidents of sexual exploitation as men often do. She went on: "Being pretty is a disadvantage here. Indian women are pretty so they are going to be whistled at and all sorts of things, but they will have to take it in their stride."

"But don't be deceived by the looks," commented an admiring male BBC journalist. "I saw an enthusiastic salute by one of the Indian peacekeepers almost knock a journalist's microphone half-way to Mumbai. Stand back - these women are serious." [351]

To a limited and scattered extent (as in Afghan schools), America is already trying to promote the lot of girls and women. But the effort is infinitely too modest. And it often draws Taliban attacks by brazenly posting signs outside projects to proclaim U.S. sponsorship. America can do the most good by being a little 'unAmerican:' listening to the locals, supporting their ideas, then standing aside to let them take the credit. Less is more. Modesty is success.

American Jihad: Resistance and Reconciliation

"It's going to take a generation," estimated Pakistani journalist Ahmed Rashid about the damage wrought by the George W. Bush administration, "before the world begins to see America in a different light. The Bush doctrine has been overburdened with lies, omissions, spin, altering the U.S. Constitution, two land wars, a burgeoning financial crisis that has affected the

---

350 Will Ross, "Liberia gets all-female peacekeeping force," *BBC World News*, January 31, 2007.
351 *Ibid.*

globe, and the spread rather than the containment of Islamic extremism." [352]

Rashid went on to do some math. "The enormous cost of the Iraq war has crippled the United States and almost certainly helped create the financial meltdown of Wall Street. According to one estimate, the cost of the wars in Iraq and Afghanistan which have now gone on longer than World War II, will eventually reach $3.0-trillion. In 2008 Iraq was costing American taxpayers $12.5-billion a month and Afghanistan $3.5-billion a month. That is already double the cost of the Korean War and costlier than the 12-year-long Vietnam War." All financed by borrowing, he noted, not new taxes. [353]

Did the U.S. political establishment learn any lessons from this – or even flinch at these numbers? Not at all. George W. Bush and *both* 2008 presidential candidates (John McCain and one Barack Obama) "proposed sending more troops to Afghanistan, to enlarge the Afghan army, and *carry out military incursions into Pakistan*, but troops alone will not provide security or put Afghanistan on the path of reconstruction." [354]

Indeed. But that's all a pretty good program to keep the endless-war folks smiling. Of course, it's only about money and self-defeating all-military strategy. In power, the Obama team spoke of loftier things. Well, vaguer, chest-beating things – that did include welcome hints of smarter options.

You can't blame Secretary of State Hillary Clinton for cheering up the Council on Foreign Relations. Or for hoping, on September 8, 2010, that the current century is a "New American Moment" when the U.S. "can, must and will lead." But did she make a classic, self-blinding, neo-imperial mistake: bragging about U.S. power and trying to pass that off as policy? She assumed that on any file, anywhere on the world, at any time, the U.S. should *seize* "leadership" – then order the locals to salute, click heels, and get in line behind the Yanks. Could leadership hubris be precisely America's problem?

---

352 Rashid, *ibid.*, p. 414.
353 *Idem*. Rashid drew these figures from "The Three Trillion Dollar War," Jospeh Stieglitz and Linda Bilmes, *The Times* (London), February 23, 2008.
354 Rashid, *Ibid*, p. 415. Author's italics.

There is now more evidence, it's true, of the U.S.'s consulting allies before 'leading' them. In fact, American hesitations in March 2011 during consultations with allies on a no-fly zone in Colonel Gaddafi's Libya ended up exasperating some allies – notably the U.K. and France. Damned if you do, damned if you don't, Washington might plead.

But the old U.S. presumption of leadership lived on in the latest (July 2009) State Department *Quadrennial Diplomatic and Development Review* (QDDR). Even as Secretary Clinton's own team of "smart-power," nation-stabilizing officials remained in limbo, this supposedly seminal text continued the old tradition. It assumed that the U.S. will always lead, and others follow. Its core idea: "Our success in exercising effective global leadership depends upon a robust and effective State Department and USAID working side-by-side with a strong military. By using all the tools of American power, we can pave the way for shared peace, progress and prosperity. This comprehensive approach is the essence of smart power." [355]

Boiler-plate, intra-departmental diplomacy. But nothing new. There's a grain of "resist and reconcile" in this document, but it doesn't accept the key premise: the failure and unaffordability of traditional U.S. militarism. Mrs. Clinton, though a pretty good team-player and national defense backer, may have to start publicly comparing military-budget overkill and the national-security potential of the "soft" or "smart" options she now guides. Columnist James Carroll makes the point for her: "The Pentagon counts its missiles by thousands, not by tens like other forces. The Navy has 11 carrier strike groups, while no other nation has more than one... But those carrier groups make another point, one about the disproportion of Washington's military in relation to its own investment in other kinds of American power, especially diplomacy. More personnel serve on just one carrier task force than the total of U.S. foreign service officers." [356]

Since the Balkan wars, added Carroll, the U.S. military has thrived on its big-time, big-army wars in Afghanistan and Iraq.

---

355 Document PRN: 2009/711, State Department, July 10, 2009.
356 James Carroll, "A misguided faith in might," *Boston Globe*, March 29, 2011.

But since then, "little or nothing has been done to strengthen other structures of U.S. influence in the world. Our illusions of martial supremacy have ruled us... the largest single factor in the shaping of current U.S. war policy, as previously, is the *institutionalized myopia of American militarism.*" [357]

The State Department's *Quadrennial Review* also fudges the strategic promise of soft-option reconciliation with Islam. "Smart power" presumably includes backing the "soft options" of deep, sustained, overseas economic and social development. Besides needing a new vocabulary, smart power demands smart thinking. "Strategic policy" supposes a strategy. And so far, the world has only heard that America intends to keep running the world – stunning arrogance as the globe splits into regional hegemonies, and witnesses how a fast-"rising" China runs economic rings around America.

With more daring and determination, Secretary Clinton should fill the ideas vacuum on Islam with a strategy that just happens to be her core passion: advancing women. She and the President wouldn't have to impose that cause on anybody at home, or even in many places abroad. But they would need to offer massive *practical* support to overseas Muslim women, especially their leaders (right down to village level). The same for women's supporters, wherever they need help. America should do so primarily in Asia and Africa –favoring Muslim societies where next-generation jihadism needs countering.

Muslim women, like other women of the developing world, have two open secrets. First, they know that education is their key to freedom. Even 10-year-old girls in Afghanistan defy the monsters who throw acid in their pretty faces on the way to school. Later, they will earn more diplomas, money and power than their men. Second, Muslim women know, as all development experts know, that to educate a woman is to educate a family, then a village, then a nation and the world. A new kind of *Al-Andalus* – without harems and subjection and dishonorable "honor killings" – lies on every Muslim girl's horizon.

---

357 *Ibid.*, book author's italics.

Barack Obama and Hillary Clinton make a formidable team to engage with Islam, especially its women. As of June 2011, they have less than 18 months to initiate a new outreach to the Muslim world – a world where America and Islam must start learning better to appreciate each other's qualities and values. Perhaps, broadly, these learnings for worldwide Muslims include America's optimism, enterprise, respect for the individual, and commitment to freedom and democracy. And for Americans, learnings about Islam's respect for family and community, spirituality, love of beauty, and devotion to a meaningful life. Both sides have complementary visions, and valuable lessons for the other.

Pursuing a policy of resistance to terror but reconciliation with Islam, America must continue stoutly confronting Islam's assassins. Cyberwarfare (including Internet and communications mastery and far more sophisticated propaganda war) should be a Western specialty. So should air power, especially better-controlled drones. Much larger special forces should displace huge, costly, jihadist-feeding ground forces. These forces should crush the nihilist Islamic murderers without pity – aided by cyberwar approaches that try to make jihadist communications deaf and dumb.

But at the same time, America needs to reconcile with Muslims equally eager to end "wars on terror." With security and peace-building in balance, America could then propose to both Muslim women and men a grand new East-West understanding. Neither a Clash of Civilizations, nor a New American Moment. But a genuine, mutually frank, Dialogue of Reconciliation including practical support for freeing Muslim men and women to live happy, fulfilling lives – the key, the *only* key, to a more modern, peaceful Islam.

Even with disagreements on short-term military defense, Republicans ought to be able to back such a resist-and-reconcile program as a strategic imperative. There is nothing in it that is alien to their principles. And much that Republicans claim as dogmas: deficit-reduction, democracy, free speech, free trade, and bootstrap progress via small business. If ever there were a chance for intelligent, visionary bipartisanship, this would be it. Indeed, for those reluctant to forget the mantra of a "strong national defense," resist-and-reconcile is an awesome bulwark for exactly that: stronger, *smarter*, longer-term national defense.

Both Americans and overseas Muslims passionately profess a belief in God's supremacy. Americans "trust" Him; Muslims "submit" to Him. Could this affinity prove an inspiring bridge to understanding? Maybe among partisans of inter-faith dialogue, and at the level of broad values. But theology and diplomacy make uneasy partners. Much of the time, when common sense, imagination and generosity can do the job of reconciliation all alone, maybe these wary interlocutors should give God a well-earned rest.

This is not an affair of courtesies and niceties. The West and Islam are alienated for deep historical, cultural, theological, geopolitical and economic reasons. With the Muslim world, the West faces a test of hard new thinking about often conflicting values – attitudes to women being a central disagreement. With mainstream Islam, obviously we need to seek out and build on shared values, not differences. We need to reject Al-Qaeda's grotesque polarization of the world into jihadists and Crusaders. We need to eclipse Huntington's Clash of Civilizations by "finding cures for cancer" (like fixing Palestine and Kashmir), and finding points of common interest.

Both America and Islam confront a new century of wrenching reflection. This, even as their opposing certainties harden – individual versus *umma*, freedom versus faith. Neither can reconcile with the other until both reconcile with a world changing at warp speed. Islam must finally join the modern world, or drag its many peoples down still farther. At a time when other previously ossified societies such as China and India soar, the stagnation of many Muslim countries will stand out even more.

Mainstream Islam should try harder to contain its wilder brothers. As in Pakistan, Afghanistan Yemen, Somalia and some other jihadist-challenged societies, *a-Qaeda*'s brutal fanaticism undermines Islam. Some Saudi and Gulf financiers have been *al-Qaeda* accomplices, whether direct or (think of the overseas

Salafi-Wahhabi madrassas) indirect. Many emerging Muslim reformers are already standing up to the hate-mongers. They sense that extremists are riding a whirlwind into quicksand. Into a future without a future for Muslim youth.

Three Voices of Reason: restraint, engagement, liberation

America? Its capacity for change still stirs in its bones. But its chauvinist mythology and paralytic, money-corrupted political system (spectacularly evident under the last Bush administration) have sometimes made it seem to careen around like a blind, rogue elephant – Iraq and Afghanistan being catastrophic examples. The closer you look at Washington, the more dismayingly true these harsh judgments seem to apply in certain quarters even today. The worst, but not only, offenders are – not to be partisan – Republicans or freelance rightists. If you shine a searchlight into extremist debate in the U.S. media, you see and hear a country losing its moorings. Indeed the sense of its very unity and nationhood.

Face inward, and these ideological dialogues of the deaf suggest a nation at war with itself. Face outward to America's world-girdling string of military bases, and you see the projection of a "garrison state." A militarist state where many good people – bent by mythology, custom and apparently incorrigible belief – have forgotten common sense and highest values, and have made guns and soldiers and war almost sacred. Apart from a vague sense of its own decline (a cyclical U.S. pathology), America is still a state camping ostentatiously on the certainty of its armed supremacy – and exceptional virtue. A state that, at ruinous cost, builds super-weapons that rarely seem to give it a sense of security. A state far too comfortable sitting on bayonets.

But there's another America. An America that could bolster its national defense" with fewer guns and better ideas. It was ideas, not guns, that toppled or terrified Arab autocrats in 2011. And these were the very ideas America and the West bragged of advancing, even while propping up dictators to stifle them.

These ideas are the West's trademark "weapons of mass construction:" freedom, democracy, individual dignity. They were exactly the ideas that allowed ordinary Arabs, with enormous courage, to cow the brutes who had stolen or stunted their lives. In hard-nosed national defense terms, supporting these ideas can help reform societies, instead of just (temporarily?) defeating insurgents. Supporting America's own defining ideals – instead of our Somoza-style "SOBs" – means redefining the "war on terror." It means no longer seeing this "war" as essentially (or exclusively) a military confrontation. It means seeing it as a contest of ideas. Of hope over fear.

As the youthful Arab idealists showed in 2011, *al-Qaeda*'s nihilist message of hate and martyrdom holds no or little appeal to most of the millions living diminished lives. At Tahrir Square, protesters repudiated *all* their masters – whether politicians, secret police...or terrorist "theologians." Mainly, they clamored for a happier version of *this* world, not "glory" in the next. They demanded freedom to live as they wished, to say what they wanted, to find a real job, to found a family, to get a life in a tolerant society. That's a message the West must respond to – with admiration and respect. Reshaped always to local conditions, it's a message of universal values, of individual fulfillment.

It shouldn't be hard for military-minded America to return to its own narration of these values and aspirations. For one thing, at a time of yawning deficits, a foreign policy actively pursuing values and practical, life-improving ideas would be far cheaper than endless "wars on terror." And it might lift the battle-battered spirits of both Americans and their allies. People can understand focusing on long-term peace-building with other human beings. They can't forever accept short-term, usually fleeting, guerrilla victories in "allied" states that stink of corruption..

How timely might the shift from big, complex land invasions to simpler, "people-smart" ideas prove? The time has plainly come. Just listen to three astute American voices. One is a clear-headed Republican defense secretary, Robert M. Gates (retiring in July 2011), who warns of big wars leading to big fiascos, both military and budgetary. The second is a man with an almost providential personal feel for Islam, President Barack Obama. The third – the passionate torch-bearer for women as agents of prosperity and peace – is of course Secretary of State Hillary Rodham Clinton.

Together, these three incarnate a 'radically sensible' new start in America's national defense. Together, they articulate a U.S. policy capable, some years hence, of ending all talk of Huntington's "clash of civilizations." A policy capable – with help from a liberated Muslim world – of discrediting the murderous fantasies of Osama bin Laden's acolytes.

Addressing West Point cadets on February 25, 2011, Gates spoke with a bluntness shocking partisans of "go-big-or-go-home" land invasions: "Looking ahead ... in the competition for tight defense dollars within and between the services, the Army also must confront the reality that the most plausible, high-end scenarios for the U.S. military are primarily naval and air engagements – whether in Asia, the Persian Gulf, or elsewhere. The strategic rationale for swift-moving expeditionary forces, be they Army or Marines, airborne infantry or special operations, is self-evident given the likelihood of counterterrorism, rapid reaction, disaster response, or stability or security force assistance missions. *But in my opinion* [author's italics], *any future defense secretary who advises the president to again send a big American land army into Asia or into the Middle East or Africa should 'have his head examined,' as General MacArthur so delicately put it.*" [358]

President Obama had already learned this lesson. He showed surprising skittishness in March 2011 about even imposing a no-fly zone on Libya as Colonel Gaddafi's forces pushed back Benghazi rebels. No-fly was a British-French-Arab League idea that, to prudent statesmen, looked like the possible beginning of a third U.S. war after Iraq and Afghanistan.

Obama's reluctance to "attack" Libya (as Gates dissuasively termed a possible no-fly zone) was one proof of the president's sensitivity to Islam. For years, jihadists and even moderate

---

[358] "Gates challenges cadets to change army culture," Jim Garamone, *Pointer View,* February 25, 2011.

Muslims had seen American anti-terrorist wars as "invasions of Muslim lands."

In his acclaimed Cairo speech of June 4, 2009 the president had already eloquently outlined a much broader, more activist policy of reconciliation with Islam. He touched on many specific issues: terrorism, Palestine, nuclear arms, entrepreneurship, religious tolerance. But his bedrock arguments concerned democracy and women. Both he praised as vital to peace and prosperity.

On democracy, he said: "... I have an unyielding belief that all people yearn for certain things: the ability to speak your mind and have a say in how you are governed; confidence in the rule of law and the equal administration of justice; government that is transparent and doesn't steal from the people; the freedom to live as you choose. These are not just American ideas; they are human rights. And that is why we will support them everywhere..."

On women's rights, he insisted: "... a woman who is denied an education is denied equality. And it is no coincidence that countries where women are well educated are far more likely to be prosperous... Issues of women's equality are by no means simply an issue for Islam. In Turkey, Pakistan, Bangladesh, Indonesia, we've seen Muslim-majority countries elect a woman to lead... Our daughters can contribute just as much to society as our sons. Our common prosperity will be advanced by allowing all humanity – men and women – to reach their full potential ... the United States will partner with any Muslim-majority country to support expanded literacy for girls, and to help young women pursue employment through micro-financing that helps people live their dreams." [359]

Let's leave the last word to Hillary Clinton. Since becoming Secretary of State in 2009, she has traveled further and more often than any predecessor. At each stop, almost without exception, she has spoken of the enormous, often neglected, potential of girls and women to create a saner and more harmonious world. She actually began this international mission in September 1995

---

[359] "The President's Speech in Cairo: A New Beginning," texts of presidential speeches, *White House* website.

at the Beijing's United Nations Women Conference. There she famously stated that "human rights are women's rights and women's rights are human rights." [360]

In March 2011, Secretary Clinton, certain of backing from President Obama, spelt out a powerful women-and-girls agenda. It was practically her marching orders for an enlightened complement to America's long-term national defense.

Among her arguments:

"... It's important to have women and girls at the forefront of American foreign policy. And there is so much evidence of this...a 2008 report commissioned by Goldman Sachs found that educating girls and women leads to higher wages, a greater likelihood of working outside the home and therefore having lower fertility, reduced maternal and child mortality, better health and education outcomes. And it's not only felt by the women themselves, but it improves opportunities for future generations."

Turning to women's role in lasting prosperity, Clinton added "... narrowing the gap in employment between men and women in emerging economies could raise incomes as much as 14 percent by 2020, and 20 percent by 2030... the World Bank has documented that women tend to invest a much higher part of their earnings in their families and communities than men do. They spread wealth..."

"On the other hand," went on Clinton, "when women are forced to the margins and denied economic and social advancement, their societies stagnate. In the landmark 2002 [U.N.] *Arab Human Development Report*, it was found that Arab women's political and economic participation was the lowest in the world .... And the 2005 report on the Arab world called women's empowerment a "prerequisite for an Arab renaissance, inseparably and causally linked to the fate of the Arab world."

... "The case has been made," she recalled. "It's made over and over again... where women do not have the opportunity to fulfill their ... potentials, it is far less likely that democracy and

---

[360] "Remarks to the U.N. 4th World Conference on Women Plenary Session," Hillary Rodham Clinton, September 5, 1995.

prosperity go hand-in-hand; it is far less likely that peace and security are present..."

"I am often asked," she concluded on the core defense theme, "why on earth do I believe that women and girls are a national security issue. Well, I believe it because I know that where girls and women are oppressed, where their rights are ignored or violated, we are likely to see societies that are not only unstable, but hostile to our own interests." [361]

Was Secretary Clinton just preaching to her feminist congregation? Hardly. She served for six years on the Senate Armed Services Committee, and for two years on the Senate Budget Committee – the latter also deeply engrossed in defense strategy and options. On both committees, she was known as a hard-probing, highly knowledgeable "strong defense" senator. She has better defense credentials than a flag-waving army of knee-jerk "strong defense" apologists.

Taken together, how do these three speeches by Gates, Obama and Clinton clarify America's strategic muddle? Its dilemma of choosing between long-term practical peace-building and short-term, elusive "victories?" The speeches all tie into the young Arabs' 2011 cries for focused (and high-payoff) investment in law-governed societies, fairness, democracy and human rights – rights that, again, automatically include women's rights. The speeches also summarize well the case for a resist-and-reconcile approach to Islam: rejecting the jihadists in a robust but more frugal way, and reconciling with ordinary Muslims.

Either specifically or by implication, all three speeches favor reconciliation with those proven architects of peace, prosperity and security – the girls and women who, as the oft-quoted Chinese proverb assures, "hold up half the sky."

Former Secretary of State Condoleezza Rice famously mocked peace-building as social work disguised as defense. "We don't need," she quipped as Bush advisor during the 2000 presidential election, "to have the 82nd Airborne escorting kids to kindergarten." Yet after ten years of heavy U.S. fighting in

---

361 *Dipnote*, "Secretary Clinton Delivers Remarks at Second Annual Women in the World Stories and Solutions," *U.S. Department of State Official Blog*, March 11, 2011.

Afghanistan, top American and international commander General David Petraeus could still only promise "fragile and reversible" results. [362]

Anchoring anti-terrorist Afghan gains with base-restricted American military and civilian trainers makes sense. So, until Afghanistan's own tribe-divided forces can take control, might certain other careful, limited U.S.-Afghan collaborations. But trillion-dollar wars keeping huge U.S. armies in Muslim lands demonstrably don't work. They create more terrorists than they eliminate.

Making kindergartens and schools work, and putting women to work to run them – along with their lives and families and villages – looks like a much surer bet. Both for today, and for long after tomorrow.

****

President Eisenhower's dire warning 50 years ago about the military-industrial complex's growing stranglehold on America has come true. It's not a distant threat; it's fulfilled. Many believe that the complex's grip on politics, foreign policy, the economy and general U.S. culture may be irreversible.

Controlling this extraordinary influence – with the budget crisis it has helped cause – is the work of a generation. Doing so will drag America through wrenching battles – largely ideological, but also budgetary and industrial. It will pit deeply entrenched myths and illusions about U.S. "exceptionalism" against an emerging sense of America's belonging more to the larger human family. In deepening that sense, an increasingly multicultural, multi-ethnic America can find a new and reconciling role.

Already, as we've seen, senior defense officials realize that sending great armies abroad inspires great fear and great resentment. America needs a fundamentally new foreign policy in the

---

362 "Troop exit to go ahead from 'fragile' Afghanistan," Thom Shanker and Elisabeth Bumiller, *New York Times*, March 16, 2001. Also Tom Shanker, "General Sees Joint Bases for Afghans After 2014," *New York Times*, March 15, 2011. Note: General. Petraeus will move to the CIA later in 2011.

Muslim world, one not almost exclusively defined by military-industrial and energy interests. It needs a policy that draws on its proclaimed, though often abandoned, ideals – the ideals that peaceful young Arab revolutionaries celebrated as they toppled autocrats.

The "Arab Spring" of 2011 – think Bahrain, Qatar and Saudi Arabia – also made the U.S. taste the bitter stew of ideals mixed with energy and Pentagon bases. It's hard for defense planners to be saints. Genuine conflicts between values and security muddy moral waters. Yet there are limits to what values an ethical nation can renounce without losing its soul – along with the oil, gas and bases. No simple solutions exist – though future warfare may strengthen more offshore defense options: notably cyberwarfare and naval power.

But post-Tahrir, the paths to long-term peace with the Muslim world open brighter vistas. The half-dozen Muslim nations we've witnessed pioneering democratic reform are also broadening access to education, freer markets and human rights. They are also the nations advancing fastest in women's rights – today's open secret to prosperity and peace.

The U.S. has many allies in the "war on terror." But it has no allies more effective, more persevering, and more fertile in spin-off benefits than Muslim women. As mothers of the next generation, they will decisively influence what the Muslim world's many turmoils will engender: still more angry jihadists seeking paradise in an afterlife? Or young men and women with achievable dreams for this world?

America, the world's great magnet-nation for dreamers, should holster a few guns, and think about this: How, respectfully, can it help young Muslims make their dreams come true? This book has tried to highlight a few things – primordially, sound education – that support healthy dreams: those normal aspirations that can make an existence a life. Things that can help ordinary people find happiness in a difficult, often terrifying, world. Things that can bring prosperity, stability and harmony to whole societies. Things to make peoples at ease enough with themselves to seek peace.

Saying this is not to advocate social work in the name of defense. One last time: It's to promote hard-nosed, genuine "national defense" through smarter, more affordable, far more workable means. Means that promote peace, not endless war. Means that allow America to return to its roots, to its highest values, to itself.

Further Reading

Mohammed Ayoob, *The Many Faces of Political Islam*, University of Michigan Press, 2008.

Andrew J. Bacevich, *The New American Militarism – How Americans Are Seduced By War*, Oxford University Press, 2005.

Andrew J. Bacevich, *Washington Rules – America's Path to Permanent War*, Metropolitan Books, 2010.

Carl Boggs and Tom Pollard, *The Hollywood War Machine – U.S. Militarism and Popular Culture*, Paradigm Publishers, 2007.

John R. Bradley, *Saudi Arabia Exposed – Inside a Kingdom in Crisis*, Palgrave MacMillan, 2005.

Susan A. Brewer, *Why America Fights – Patriotism and War Propaganda From the Philippines to Iraq*, Oxford University Press, 2009.

Rachel Bronson, *Thicker Than Oil – America's Uneasy Partnership With Saudi Arabia*, Oxford University Press, 2006.

Pratap Chatterjee, *Iraq, Inc. – A Profitable Occupation*, Seven Stories Press, 2004.

N.J. Dawood (translator), The Koran, Penguin Classics, 2006.

Anthony DiMaggio, *When Media Goes to War – Hegemonic Discourse, Public Opinion, and the Limits of Dissent*, Monthly Review Press, 2009.

Daniel Dor, *The Suppression of Guilt – The Israeli Media and the Reoccupation of the West Bank*, Pluto Press, 2005.

Richard Heinberg, *The Party's Over – Oil, War and the Fate of Industrial Societies*, Clairview Books, 2005.

Ghada Karmi, *In Search of Fatima – a Palestinian Story*, Verso, 2002.

Gilles Kepel, *Jihad – the Trail of Political Islam*, President and Fellows of Harvard College, 2002.

Gilles Kepel, *The War for Muslim Minds – Islam and the West*, Belknap Press of Harvard University Press, 2004.

Nicholas D. Kristof and Sheryl WuDunn, *Half The Sky – Turning Oppression Into Opportunity for Women Worldwide*, Vintage Books, 2010.

John J. Mearsheimer and Stephen M. Walt, *The Israel Lobby – and U.S. Foreign Policy*, Farrar, Straus and Giroux, 2007.

Greg Mortenson and David Oliver Relin, *Three Cups of Tea – One Man's Mission to Promote Peace One School at a Time*, Penguin Books, 2006.

Moorthy S. Muthuswamy, *Defeating Political Islam – the New Cold War*, Prometheus Books, 2009.

Sari Nusseibeh with Anthony David, *Once Upon a Country – A Palestinian Life*, Farrar, Straus and Giroux, 2007.

Erna Paris, *The Garden and the Gun – a Journey Inside Israel*, Lester and Orpen Dennys, 1988.

Erna Paris, *The End of Days: Tolerance, Tyranny and the Expulsion of the Jews from Spain*, Prometheus Books, 1995.

Jerrold M. Post, *The Mind of the Terrorist – The Psychology of Terrorism from the IRA to Al-Qaeda*, Palgrave MacMillan, 2007.

Amed Rashid, *Descent Into Chaos – Pakistan, Afghanistan and the Threat to Global Security*, Viking Penguin, 2008.

Olivier Roy, *Globalized Islam – the Search for a New Umma*, Columbia University Press, 2004.

Marc Sageman, *Leaderless Jihad – Terror Networks in the Twenty-first Century*, University of Pennsylvania Press, 2008.

Edward W. Said, *Reflections on Exile and Other Essays*, Harvard University Press, 2000.

Tom Segev, *One Palestine, Complete – Jews and Arabs Under the British Mandate*, Henry Holt and Company, 1999.

Indries Shah, *The Way of the Sufi*, Jonathan Cape, 1968.

Avi Shlaim, *The Iron Wall – Israel and the Arab World*, W.W. Norton, 2001.

Roger Stahl, *Militainment, Inc. – War, Media and Popular Culture*, Routledge, 2010.

Craig Unger, *House of Bush, House of Saud – The Secret Relationship Between the World's Two Most Powerful Dynasties*, Gibson Square, 2007.

Early Reviews of *Sitting on Bayonets*...

"Ever insightful, journalist-writer Keith Spicer has given us an urgently needed, fact-packed, cogently analyzed deconstruction of a world hell-bent on reflexively using military might instead of creative diplomacy to resolve conflicts and remove despots. It's also a damning portrait of media and journalists as cheerleaders."
– **John Owen**, Professor of International Journalism in London's City University, and Executive Producer for Programs, *Al Jazeera* English Channel, co-author of *International News Reporting: Frontlines and Deadlines*.

"Canadian-born Keith Spicer uses his experience as professor, journalist-cum-author and public servant in North America, together with 14 recent years in Paris, to give a uniquely balanced commentary on the crisis of relations between the West and the Arab world. Rejecting a 'clash of civilizations', he affirms their common hopes for education, democracy, scientific advancement - and peace. Sharply critical of American policies, he sets imaginative challenges: for Barack Obama over Palestine, for Hillary Clinton on women's education and (glory be!) for Saudi Arabia on funding free e-libraries of the world's classics for Arab youth. A fresh, witty and very worthwhile book"
– **Clyde Sanger**, former *Economist* correspondent for Canada, Adjunct Professor, University for Peace, author of *The Law of the Sea*.

"At a time when the ground under the entire Middle East is shifting and no one knows in which direction, Keith Spicer in *Sitting on Bayonets* delivers a brilliant and penetrating analysis of where the entire Middle East has come from and where it may be heading. With a meticulous history of the recent past, Sitting on Bayonets makes a compelling case that the days of maintaining stability through American troops on the ground, if ever wise, is now counter-productive and destructive to the region's, America's and the world's interests. Spicer makes a

strong argument that the best path to containing terrorism, providing responsive government and promoting the rights of women will come through negotiation, public diplomacy and the social media."
  – **Jeff Cole**, Director, Center for the Digital Future, Annenberg School, University of Southern California, Director of the World Internet Project.

"From his perch on the Left Bank in Paris , self-confessed incorrigible Canadian and expat public intellectual Keith Spicer convincingly identifies the failure of military means to defeat radical Islam. He argues instead for the rebirth of a lucid American idealism, one that would educate women rather than killing men. Spicer would replace a war on Jihadism with reconciliation with mainstream Islam as the only sane course to avoid the predicted conflict of civilizations."
  – **Michael Adams**, President, Environics Group, author, analyst

www.ingramcontent.com/pod-product-compliance
Lightning Source LLC
Chambersburg PA
CBHW060232290526
45789CB00001B/12